Amanita muscaria　　　　　　　　　　　　　　　JOHN M. ALLEGRO

THE SACRED MUSHROOM AND THE CROSS

THE SACRED MUSHROOM AND THE CROSS

A study of the nature and origins of Christianity
within the fertility cults of the ancient Near East
by

John M. Allegro

40th Anniversary Edition

Published 2009
Gnostic Media
Research & Publishing
www.gnosticmedia.com

Library of Congress Catalog Card Number 73-111140
ISBN 978-0-9825562-6-9 Hardcover
978-0-9825562-7-6 Softcover

First published by:
In the U.K. - Hodder and Stoughton, London, May 1970
In the U.S. - Doubleday & Company, Garden City, NY, August 1970

Preface

The Sacred Mushroom and the Cross was one of the most controversial books written in the twentieth century. Not since Darwin's *On the Origin of Species* had a book caused such outrage. John Marco Allegro was a respected Dead Sea Scrolls scholar and had just left his post as a lecturer at Manchester University. Only expert philologists were in a position to assess the material presented in the notes at the back of the book so Allegro's opponents, as I detailed in my book *The Holy Mushroom: Evidence of Mushrooms in Judeo-Christianity*, 2008, resorted to unfounded attacks in the press, and intentionally avoided dealing with the specific information and ideas that Allegro was presenting. Even R. Gordon Wasson, the assumed founder of the field of ethnomycology, chose to deride Allegro's attempts to relate the discipline to Christianity, in contradiction of his own previous position.[1] Allegro, hoping for serious scholarly discussion, chose not to respond to what he saw as scurrilous and irrelevant attacks, with the result that Wasson and other critics continued their campaign unabated, causing a great and unnecessary schism not only in biblical scholarship, but also in the field of ethnomycology and psychedelic studies in general over the ensuing decades.

But since the original publication of *The Sacred Mushroom and the Cross* in May 1970, other linguistic and non-linguistic evidence has come to light in support of many of Allegro's theories. This includes a paper by Russian linguist Vladimir Nikolaevic Toporov, *On the Semiotics of Mythological Conceptions about Mushrooms*, 1985, as well as hundreds of iconographic images, like the Plaincourault fresco, along with several primary texts that refute most of his opponents' attacks. In April 2008 Professor Carl A. P. Ruck of Boston University, who has come out

---

[1]   For a critical examination of this issue, which is important for understanding the arguments both for and against mushrooms in Judeo-Christianity, and the relations between Allegro and Wasson, see *SMC* Ch. IX, note 20, and my book *The Holy Mushroom: Evidence of Mushrooms in Judeo-Christianity*, 2008, by Jan Irvin, pgs. 8 - 77.

publicly in support of Allegro's work[2], presented me with a postcard of a 13th century fresco from a chapel in Montferrand du Perigord, France, that depicts Jesus as a mushroom. I published this fresco on the cover of my book *The Holy Mushroom* wherein I included the ancient primary texts, including a 16th century Christian text, The Epistle to the Renegade Bishops, that explicitly discusses "the holy mushroom". Additionally, in May 2005 Judith Anne Brown published *John Marco Allegro, The Maverick of the Dead Sea Scrolls*, which uses Allegro's private letters and archives to set the record straight on his reasoning and motivation. Other scholars have also come out in support of Allegro's work, including Professor John Rush in his 2008 book *Failed God*, and Wolfgang Bauer, Edzard Klapp and Alexandra Rosenbohm in their book *Der Fliegenpilz*, 1991/2000, and Jack Herer who was working to complete his book *The Most High* before suffering a heart attack in September 2009.

Now at last is emerging a much clearer picture of the use of psychedelic drugs and fertility rituals in religion, including Judeo-Christianity. Today it is clear that Allegro was not a man who'd lost his mind, but a man who was ahead of his time.

Before his death on his 65th birthday, February 17, 1988, Allegro published five more books that take forward the work presented here: *The End of a Road, The Chosen People, Lost Gods, The Dead Sea Scrolls and the Christian Myth*, and *Physician, Heal Thyself*. Although these books take a milder tone, they develop themes that stem from his original views set out in *The Sacred Mushroom and the Cross*.

In this edition of *The Sacred Mushroom and the Cross*, only minor corrections, including grammatical, have been made. Otherwise it is presented exactly as Allegro originally intended, except that the images of the Plaincourault fresco and *Amanita muscaria* are printed in black and white within the text, and the the Plaincourault fresco is also presented on the back cover in color. A foreword has been added by Judith Anne Brown, and an addendum by Professor Ruck.[3] The layout

---

2   Professor Ruck first went public with his support for Allegro in an interview at his home in Boston, MA in April 2008 with Jan Irvin. See Gnostic Media's podcast #01 available from www.gnosticmedia.com. See also the included addendum, Fungus Redivivus, by Carl A. P. Ruck.

3   To further discussion, we've included Professor Ruck's article Fungus Redivivus as an addendum because it focuses on academic issues relating to Allegro's work. I have drawn attention to my points of difference with Professor Ruck about Wasson in my book *The Holy Mushroom*, 2008, by Jan Irvin. I feel that further investigation of Wasson's motivations and background is necessary.

and design is by Aaron Welton, to whom we owe our thanks. Several earlier editions, including those in foreign languages, were printed without the extensive notes at the back of the book. In keeping with the way Allegro originally intended to present this work, a copy of these notes, with a few minor corrections, is provided in full for academic inquiry.

As someone who has personally dedicated more than 15 years to the study of the use of psychedelic drugs within Judeo-Christianity, I am more than grateful that the Allegro estate has encouraged me to return the pages of this lost treasure to the enquiring minds of the world. With this, I am honored to present you with this 40th anniversary edition of John Marco Allegro's *The Sacred Mushroom and the Cross.*

- Jan R. Irvin

Publisher, Gnostic Media Research & Publishing
Author of *The Holy Mushroom: Evidence of Mushrooms in Judeo-Christianity*
Co-author of *Astrotheology & Shamanism: Christianity's Pagan Roots*

Foreword

I see *The Sacred Mushroom and the Cross* as a challenge and a work in progress.

As John Allegro intended, it challenges conventional views of religion. It looks at how man has conceived of god, and sought to commune with god, from earliest times. God clearly comes with different faces for different purposes. But from the time of the first written records, people have seen the essence of divinity, its first and most fundamental purpose, as the bestowal of fertility, the bringing of life on earth.

This book shows the power and persistence of this idea, and of the fertility cults and rituals by which people tried to attain divine vision and know the mind of their god. Central to such cults, over thousands of years and across the continents, has been the use of entheogens (psychoactive substances derived from plants) to reach a higher consciousness, a sense of community with the gods. One of the chief sources was the sacred mushroom, *Amanita muscaria* – at once the symbol and embodiment of fertility, and the means to understand it.

Earlier scholars had already realised the significance of entheobotany in various religious practices, and of fertility motifs in myth and legend. John Allegro had the temerity to relate these themes to Christianity and Judaism. He found they represented a continuity of religious experience which must completely transform our interpretation of the Old and New Testaments.

The evidence for this continuity is in language – successive languages as they have evolved from the first written codes inscribed on plinths and tablets some six thousand years ago in ancient Sumer. The discovery of Sumerian as the ancestor of later Indo-European languages was the tool that enabled Allegro to perceive the transmission of religious ideas through successive cultures.

But his philological approach was in itself controversial, and following the argument is another challenge. His reasoning is set out in the end-notes, which are difficult to assess without prior knowledge of ancient languages. Some scholars denied there was any link at all between Sumerian and later Indo-European languages; most denied that enough was known about it to prove many of the etymologies he suggested. (However, none of these critics showed any signs of having looked at the end-notes before denouncing the book.) Indeed, Allegro admitted that many of his word links were conjectural; he put asterisks against all the combinations that seemed possible but hadn't yet been found on extant inscriptions, and there were too many asterisks. This is why I call the book a work in progress: where John Allegro pointed the way, today's linguists need to carry on testing his word derivations and researching the development of Sumerian links.

Where did Allegro's ideas come from? Since studying biblical languages at the University of Manchester he had realised that the conventional translations were far from fixed. He found that many Old Testament stories came directly from Babylonian traditions, and that passages whose cadence and imagery had grown venerable through use could actually mean something completely different. As with parables, and as illustrated in the commentaries found among the Dead Sea Scrolls, passages of scripture could hold layers of meaning that could appeal at different levels to different people and could enrich the text to exegetists who wished to explore its every significance. Allegro started with biblical names, titles and phrases, often those whose interpretation had long puzzled translators, and asked whether their etymology might throw light on their meaning.

The etymology suggested underlying religious ideas that went back to the fertility cults of ancient Sumer. So could the beliefs and practices of such cults, based on mushroom use and copulation, still be alive in first-century Judaea? Allegro thought they were, but secretly, and that cult members circulated them disguised within innocuous gospel stories.

There are undoubtedly difficulties with the thesis of *The Sacred Mushroom and the Cross*. For a start, many of the word derivations need further verification, and the secret-code idea seems improbably complicated. Religious ideas do change to suit the times, or are subsumed into new philosophies whose origin is then forgotten. Mushrooms themselves were not forgotten – they recur in a Christian context in medieval and renaissance art much more widely than Allegro realised at the time. Evidence from the art world might have gone a long way to convince his critics that his ideas were reasonable. But whatever the difficulties, the ideas that he uncovered and set out in this book challenge us to follow up his search for the truth about the development of religion.

Republishing *The Sacred Mushroom and the Cross* will, I hope, give scholars the opportunity to pursue John Allegro's research into the beginnings of language and thought, and to take a more objective approach to the study of religion than either the theologians or the linguists of the 1970s found possible.

- Judith Anne Brown

Author of *John Marco Allegro, the Maverick of the Dead Sea Scrolls*
pb. Wm. B. Eerdmans Publishing Co., Grand Rapids, 2005

Author's Note

This book is the first published statement of the fruits of some years' work of a largely philological nature. It presents a new appreciation of the relationship of the languages of the ancient world and the implication of this advance for our understanding of the Bible and of the origins of Christianity. It will be appreciated that such a statement has to be furnished with the technical data, even though much of it must be outside the scope of the general reader, for whom the book is primarily intended. In order to leave the text as unencumbered as possible, these notes have been gathered in a body at the end of the book, and the numbered references within the text may be safely ignored by the non-specialist.

Acknowledgements

Quotations from the Revised Standard Version of the Bible, copyrighted 1952 and 1956, are used by permission.

Quotations from the *Homeric Hymns,* Pliny's *Natural History,* and Josephus' *Jewish Wars and Antiquities* are used by permission of the Loeb Classical Library.

The frontispiece photograph is used by permission of Rex Lowden. The photograph facing page 74 is used by permission of Photographe Thuillier.

Contents

Illustrations

Images

Introduction

No one religion in the ancient Near East can be studied in isolation. All stem from man's first questioning about the origin of life and how to ensure his own survival. He has always been acutely conscious of his insufficiency. However much he progressed technically, making clothes and shelter, conserving food and water supplies, and so on, the forces of nature were always greater than he. The winds would blow away his shelter, the sun parch his crops, wild beasts prey on his animals: he was always on the defensive in a losing battle. Out of this sense of dependency and frustration, religion was born.

Somehow man had to establish communications with the source of the world's fertility, and thereafter maintain a right relationship with it. Over the course of time he built up a body of experiential knowledge of rituals that he or his representatives could perform, or words to recite, which were reckoned to have the greatest influence on this fertility deity. At first they were largely imitative. If rain in the desert lands was the source of life, then the moisture from heaven must be only a more abundant kind of spermatozoa. If the male organ ejaculated this precious fluid and made life in the woman, then above the skies the source of nature's semen must be a mighty penis, as the earth which bore its offspring was the womb. It followed therefore that to induce the heavenly phallus to complete its orgasm, man must stimulate it by sexual means, by singing, dancing, orgiastic displays and, above all, by the performance of the copulatory act itself.

However far man progressed in his control of the world about him there remained a large gap between what he wanted at any one time and what he could achieve on his own account. There was always some unscalable mountain, some branch of knowledge which remained unpenetrable, some disease with no known cure. It seemed to him that if he had managed painstakingly to grope his way to a knowledge and dexterity so far above the animals, then in some mysterious way his thinkers and artisans must have been tapping a source of wisdom no less real than the rain that fructified the ground. The heavenly penis, then, was not only the source of life-giving semen, it was the origin of knowledge. The seed of God was the Word of God.

The dream of man is to become God. Then he would be omnipotent; no longer fearful of the snows in winter or the sun in summer, or the drought that killed his cattle and made his children's bellies swell grotesquely. The penis in the skies would rise and spurt its vital juice when man commanded, and the earth below would open its vulva and gestate its young as man required. Above all, man would learn the secrets of the universe not piecemeal, painfully by trial and fatal error, but by a sudden, wonderful illumination from within.

But God is jealous of his power and his knowledge. He brooks no rivals in heavenly places. If, in his mercy, he will allow just a very few of his chosen mortals to share his divinity, it is but for a fleeting moment. Under very special circumstances he will permit men to rise to the throne of heaven and glimpse the beauty and the glory of omniscience and omnipotence. For those who are so privileged there has seemed no greater or more worthwhile experience. The colours are brighter, the sounds more penetrating, every sensation is magnified, every natural force exaggerated.

For such a glimpse of heaven men have died. In the pursuit of this goal great religions have been born, shone as a beacon to men struggling still in their unequal battle with nature, and then too have died, stifled by their own attempts to perpetuate, codify, and evangelize the mystic vision.

Our present concern is to show that Judaism and Christianity are such cultic expressions of this endless pursuit by man to discover instant power and knowledge. Granted the first proposition that the vital forces of nature are controlled by an extra-terrestrial intelligence, these religions are logical developments from the older, cruder fertility cults. With the advance of technical proficiency the aims of religious ritual became less to influence the weather and the crops than to attain wisdom and the knowledge of the future. The Word that seeped through the labia of the earth's womb became to the mystic of less importance than the Logos which he believed his religion enabled him to apprehend and enthuse him with divine omniscience. But the source was the same vital power of the universe and the cultic practice differed little.

To raise the crops the farmer copulated with his wife in the fields. To seek the drug that would send his soul winging to the seventh heaven and back, the initiates into the religious mysteries had their priestesses seduce the god and draw him into their grasp as a woman fascinates her partner's penis to erection.

For the way to God and the fleeting view of heaven was through plants more plentifully endued with the sperm of God than any other. These were the drug-herbs, the science of whose cultivation and use had been accumulated over centuries of observation and dangerous experiment. Those who had this secret wisdom of the plants were the chosen of their god; to them alone had he vouchsafed the privilege of access to the heavenly throne. And if he was jealous of his power, no less were those who served him in the cultic mysteries. Theirs was no gospel to be shouted from the rooftops: Paradise was for none but the favoured few. The incantations and rites by which they conjured forth their drug plants, and the details of the bodily and mental preparations undergone before they could ingest their god, were the secrets of the cult to which none but the initiate, bound by fearful oaths, had access.

Very rarely, and then only for urgent practical purposes, were those secrets ever committed to writing. Normally they would be passed from the priest to the initiate by word of mouth; dependent for their accurate transmission on the trained memories of men dedicated to the learning and recitation of their "scriptures". But if, for some drastic reason like the disruption of their cultic centres by war or persecution, it became necessary to write down the precious names of the herbs and the manner of their use and accompanying incantations, it would be in some esoteric form comprehensible only to those within their dispersed communities.

Such an occasion, we believe, was the Jewish Revolt of AD 66. Instigated probably by members of the cult, swayed by their drug-induced madness to believe God had called them to master the world in his name, they provoked the mighty power of Rome to swift and terrible action. Jerusalem was ravaged, her temple destroyed. Judaism was disrupted, and her people driven to seek refuge with communities already established around the Mediterranean coastlands. The mystery cults found themselves without their central fount of authority, with many of their priests killed in the abortive rebellion or driven into the desert. The secrets, if they were not to be lost for ever, had to be committed to writing, and yet, if found, the documents must give nothing away to betray those who still dared defy the Roman authorities and continue their religious practices.

The means of conveying the information were at hand, and had been for thousands of years. The folk-tales of the ancients had from the earliest times contained myths based upon the personification of plants and trees. They were invested with human faculties and qualities and their names and physical characteristics were applied to the heroes and heroines of the stories. Some of these were just tales spun for enter-tainment, others were political parables like Jotham's fable about the trees in the Old Testament, while others were means of remembering and transmitting therapeutic folk-lore. The names of the plants were spun out to make the basis of the stories whereby the creatures of fantasy were identified, dressed, and made to enact their parts. Here, then, was the literary device to spread occult knowledge to the faithful. To tell the story of a rabbi called Jesus, and invest him with the power and names of the magic drug. To have him live before the terrible events that had disrupted their lives, to preach a love between men, extending even to the hated Romans. Thus, reading such a tale, should it fall into Roman hands, even their mortal enemies might be deceived and not probe farther into the activities of the cells of the mystery cults within their territories.

The ruse failed. Christians, hated and despised, were hauled forth and slain in their thousands. The cult well nigh perished. What eventually took its place was a travesty of the real thing, a mockery of the power that could raise men to heaven and give them the glimpse of God for which they gladly died. The story of the rabbi crucified at the instiga-tion of the Jews became an historical peg upon which the new cult's authority was founded. What began as a hoax became a trap even to those who believed themselves to be the spiritual heirs of the mystery religion and took to themselves the name of "Christian". Above all they forgot, or purged from the cult and their memories, the one supreme secret on which their whole religious and ecstatic experience depended: the names and identity of the source of the drug, the key to heaven – the sacred mushroom.

The fungus recognized today as the *Amanita muscaria,* or Fly-Agaric, had been known from the beginning of history. Beneath the skin of its characteristic red and white-spotted cap, there is concealed a powerful hallucinatory poison. Its religious use among certain Siberian peoples and others has been the subject of study in recent years, and its exhilarating and depressive effects have been clinically examined. These include the stimulation of the perceptive faculties so that the subject sees objects much greater or much smaller than they really are; colours and sounds are much enhanced; and there is a general sense of power, both physical and mental, quite outside the normal range of human experience.

The mushroom has always been a thing of mystery. The ancients were puzzled by its manner of growth without seed, the speed with which it made its appearance after rain, and its as rapid disappearance. Born from a volva or "egg" it appears like a small penis, raising itself like the human organ sexually aroused, and when it spread wide its canopy the old botanists saw it as a phallus bearing the "burden" of a woman's groin. Every aspect of the mushroom's existence was fraught with sexual allusions, and in its phallic form the ancients saw a replica of the fertility god himself. It was the "son of God"; its drug was a purer form of the god's own spermatozoa than that discoverable in any other form of living matter. It was, in fact, God himself, manifest on earth. To the mystic it was the divinely given means of entering heaven; God had come down in the flesh to show the way to himself, by himself.

To pluck such a precious herb was attended at every point with peril. The time – before sunrise, the words to be uttered, the name of the guardian angel, were vital to the operation, but more was needed. Some form of substitution was necessary, to make atonement to the earth robbed of her offspring. Yet such was the divine nature of the Holy Plant, as it was called, only the god could make the necessary sacrifice. To redeem the Son, the Father had to supply even the "price of redemption". These are all phrases used of the sacred mushroom, as they are of the Jesus of Christian theology.

Our present study has much to do with names and titles. Only when we can discover the nomenclature of the sacred fungus within and without the cult, can we begin to understand its function and theology. The main factor that has made these new discoveries possible has been the realization that many of the most secret names of the mushroom go back to ancient Sumerian, the oldest written language known to us, witnessed by cuneiform texts dating from the fourth millennium BC. Furthermore, it now appears that this ancient tongue provides a bridge between the Indo-European languages (which include Greek, Latin, and our own tongue) and the Semitic group, which includes the languages of the Old Testament, Hebrew and Aramaic. For the first time, it becomes possible to decipher the names of gods, mythological characters, classical and biblical, and plant names. Thus their place in the cultic systems and their functions in the old fertility religions can be determined.

The great barriers that have hitherto seemed to divide the ancient world, classical and biblical, have at last been crossed, and at a more significant level than has previously been possible by merely comparing their respective mythologies. Stories and characters which seem quite different in the way they are presented in various locations and at widely separated points in history can now be shown often to have the same central theme. Even gods as different as Zeus and Yahweh embody the same fundamental conception of the fertility deity, for their names in origin are precisely the same. A common tongue overrides physical and racial boundaries. Even languages so apparently different as Greek and Hebrew, when they can be shown to derive from a common fount, point to a communality of culture at some early stage. Comparisons can therefore be made on a scientific, philological level which might have appeared unthinkable before now. Suddenly, almost overnight, the ancient world has shrunk. All roads in the Near East lead back to the Mesopotamian basin, to ancient Sumer. Similarly, the most important of the religions and mythologies of that area, and probably far beyond, are reaching back to the mushroom cult of Sumer and her successors.

In biblical studies, the old divisions between Old and New Testament areas of research, never very meaningful except to the Christian theologian, become even less valid. As far as the origins of Christianity are concerned, we must look not just to intertestamental literature, the Apocrypha and Pseudepigrapha, and the newly discovered writings from the Dead Sea, nor even merely to the Old Testament and other Semitic works, but we have to bring into consideration Sumerian religious and mythological texts and the classical writings of Asia Minor, Greece, and Rome. The Christian Easter is as firmly linked to the Bacchic Anthesteria as the Jewish Passover. Above all, it is the philologian who must be the spearhead of the new enquiry. It is primarily a study in words.

A written word is more than a symbol: it is an expression of an idea. To penetrate to its inner meaning is to look into the mind of the man who wrote it. Later generations may give different meanings to that symbol, extending its range of reference far beyond the original intention, but if we can trace the original significance then it should be possible to follow the trail by which it developed. In doing so, it is sometimes possible even to outline the progress of man's mental, technical or religious development.

The earliest writing was by means of pictures, crudely incised diagrams on stone and clay. However lacking such symbols may be in grammatical or syntactical refinement, they do convey, in an instant, the one feature which seemed to the ancient scribe the most significant aspect of the object or action he is trying to represent. "Love" he shows as a flaming torch in a womb, a "foreign country" as a hill (because he lived on a plain), and so on. As the art of writing developed further, we can begin to recognize the first statements of ideas which came later to have tremendous philosophical importance: "life", "god", "priest", "temple", "grace", "sin", and so on. To seek their later meanings in religious literature like the Bible we must first discover their basic meaning and follow their development through as far as extant writings will allow.

For example, as we may now understand, "sin" for Jew and Christian had to do with the emission to waste of human sperm, a blasphemy against the god who was identified with the precious liquid. If to discover this understanding of "sin" seems today of only limited academic interest, it is worth recalling that it is this same principle that lies at the root of modern Catholic strictures against the use of the "Pill".

As far as the main burden of our present enquiry is concerned, our new-found ability to penetrate to the beginnings of language means that we can set the later mystery cults, as those of Judaism, the Dionysiac religion and Christianity, into their much wider context, to discover the first principles from which they developed, probe the mysteries of their cultic names and invocations, and, in the case of Christianity at least, appreciate something of the opposition they encountered among governing authorities and the measures taken to transmit their secrets under cover of ancient mythologies in modern dress.

Our study, then, begins at the beginning, with an appreciation of religion in terms of a stimulation of the god to procreation and the provision of life. Armed with our new understanding of the language relationships of the ancient Near East, we can tackle the major problems involved in botanical nomenclature and discover those features of the more god-endued plants which attracted the attention of the old medicine men and prophets. The isolation of the names and epithets of the sacred mushroom opens the door into the secret chambers of the mystery cults which depended for their mystic hallucinatory experiences on the drugs found in the fungus. At long last identification of the main characters of many of the old classical and biblical mythologies is possible, since we can now decipher their names. Above all, those mushroom epithets and holy invocations that the Christian cryptographers wove into their stories of the man Jesus and his companions can now be recognized, and the main features of the Christian cult laid bare.

The isolation of the mushroom cult and the real, hidden meaning of the New Testament writings drives a wedge between the moral teachings of the Gospels and their quite amoral religious setting. The new discoveries must thus raise more acutely the question of the validity of Christian "ethics" for the present time. If the Jewish rabbi to whom they have hitherto been attributed turns out to have been no more substantial than the mushroom, the authority of his homilies must stand or fall on the assent they can command on their own merit.

What follows in this book is, as has been said, primarily a study in words. To a reader brought up to believe in the essential historicity of the Bible narratives some of the attitudes displayed in our approach to the texts may seem at first strange. We appear to be more interested with the words than with the events they seem to record; more concerned, say, in the meaning of Moses' name than his supposed role as Israel's first great political leader. Similarly, a century or so ago, it must have seemed strange to the average Bible student to understand the approach of a "modernist" of the day who was more interested in the ideas underlying the Creation story of Genesis and their sources, than to date, locate, and identify the real Garden of Eden, and to solve the problem of whence came Cain's wife. Then, it took a revolution in man's appreciation of his development from lower forms of life and a clearer understanding of the age of this planet to force the theologian to abandon the historicity of Genesis.

Now we face a new revolution in thought which must make us reconsider the validity of the New Testament story. The breakthrough here is not in the field of history but in philology. Our fresh doubts about the historicity of Jesus and his friends stem not from new discoveries about the land and people of Palestine of the first century, but about the nature and origin of the languages they spoke and the origins of their religious cults. What the student of Christian origins is primarily concerned with is: what manner of writing is this book we call the New Testament, and in particular just what are the narratives called the Gospels trying to convey? Is it history? This is certainly a possibility, but only one of many. The fact that for nearly two thousand years one religious body has pinned its faith upon not only the existence of the man Jesus, but even upon his spiritual nature and the historicity of certain unnatural events called miracles, is not really relevant to the enquiry. A hundred years ago this same body of opinion was equally adamant that the whole of the human race could trace its origin to two people living in the middle of Mesopotamia, and that the earth had come into existence in the year 4004 BC.

The enquirer has to begin with his only real source of knowledge , the written word. As far as Judaism and Christianity are concerned, this means the Bible. There is precious little else that can give us details about what the Israelite believed about his god and the world about him, or about the real nature of Christianity. The sparse references to one "Christus" or "Chrestus" in the works of contemporary non-Christian historians tell us nothing about the nature of the man, and only very dubiously, despite the claims often made for them, do they support his historicity. They simply bear witness to the fact, never in dispute, that the stories of the Gospels were in circulation soon after AD 70. If we want to know more about early Christianity we must look to our only real source, the written words of the New Testament. Thus, as we have said, the enquiry is primarily philological.

The New Testament is full of problems. They confront the critical enquirer on every side: chronological, topographical, historical, religious, and philological. It is not until the language problems have been resolved that the rest can be realistically appraised. When, in the last century, a mass of papyrological material became available from the ancient world and cast new light upon the nature of the Greek used in the New Testament, scholars felt that most of the major obstacles to a complete understanding of the texts would be removed. But, in fact, to the philologian the thorny questions remain firmly embedded in the stories, and they have nothing to do with the plot of the narratives, or the day-to-day details which add colour to the action. The most intransigent concern the foreign, presumed Aramaic transliterations in the text, coupled often with a "translation" which does not seem to offer a rendering of the original, like the nickname "Boanerges", supposed to mean "Sons of Thunder"; or the name "Barnabas", said to represent "Son of Consolation". Try as they will, the commentators cannot see how the "translations" fit the "names".

To the general reader, and particularly to the Christian seeking moral or spiritual enlightenment from the New Testament, such trivia have meant little. To many scholars, too, details like these are of less importance than the theological import of Jesus' teaching. It has been assumed that somewhere along the line of transmission some textual corruption occurred in the "names", or that the "translations" were added by later hands unfamiliar with the original language used by the Master and his companions.

As we can now appreciate, these aberrations of the proper names and their pseudo-translations are of crucial importance. They provide us with a clue to the nature of original Christianity. Concealed within are secret names for the sacred fungus, the sect's "Christ". The deliberately deceptive nature of their mistranslations put the lie to the whole of the "cover-story" of the man Jesus and his activities. Once the ruse is penetrated, then research can go ahead fast with fitting the Christian phenomenon more firmly into the cultic patterns of the ancient Near East. Many apparently quite unrelated facts about the ubiquitous mystery cults of the area and their related mythologies suddenly begin to come together into an intellectually satisfying whole.

In any study of the sources and development of a particular religion, ideas are the vital factor. History takes second place. Even time is relatively unimportant. This is not to underestimate the importance of political and sociological influences in the fashioning of a cult and its ideology; but the prime materials of the philosophy stem from a fundamental conception of the universe and the source of life. Certain highly imaginative or "inspired" men may appear from time to time in a people's history and affect the beliefs and manner of life of their contemporaries and successors. They adapt or develop what they find and give it a new impetus or direction. But the clay they are freshly modelling was there already and forms the main object of enquiry for the student of the cult's development.

We are, throughout this book, mainly interested in this "clay" and the very strange shapes it assumed in the mystery religions of which we may now recognize Christianity as an important example. Of course, history now and again forces itself on our attention. Did Abraham, Isaac, and Jacob ever exist as real people? Was there ever a sojourn in Egypt of the Chosen People, or a political leader called Moses? Was the theologically powerful conception of the Exodus ever historical fact? These and many other such questions are raised afresh by our studies, but it is our contention that they are not of prime importance. Far more urgent is the main import of the myths in which these names are found. If we are right in finding their real relevance in the age-old cult of the sacred mushroom, then the nature of the oldest Israelite religion has to be reassessed, and it matters comparatively little whether these characters are historical or not.

In the case of Christianity, the historical questions are perhaps more acute. If the New Testament story is not what it seems, then when and how did the Christian Church come to take it at its face value and make the worship of a single man Jesus, crucified and miraculously brought back to life, the central theme of its religious philosophy? The question is bound up with the nature of the "heresies" that the Church drove out into the desert. Unfortunately we just have not sufficient material to enable us to identify all these sects and know their secrets. The Church destroyed everything it considered heretical, and what we know of such movements derives largely from the refutations by the early Fathers of their beliefs. But at least we no longer have to squeeze such "aberrations" into a century or two after AD 30. "Christianity" under its various names had been thriving for centuries before that. As we may now appreciate, it was the more original cult that was driven underground by the combined efforts of the Roman, Jewish, and ecclesiastical authorities; it was the supreme "heresy" which came on, made terms with the secular powers, and became the Church of today.

We are, then, dealing with ideas rather than people. We cannot name the chief characters of our story. Doubtless there were real leaders exercising considerable power over their fellows, but in the mystery cults they were never named to the outsider. We cannot, like the Christian pietist, conjure for ourselves a picture of a young man working at his father's carpentry bench, taking little children in his arms, or talking earnestly with a Mary while her sister did the housework. In this respect, our study is not an easy one. There is no one simple answer to the problems of the New Testament discoverable to anyone just reshuffling the

Gospel narratives to produce yet another picture of the man Jesus. Ours is a study of words, and through them of ideas. At the end we have to test the validity of our conclusions not against comparative history, least of all against the beliefs of the Church, past or present, but against the overall pattern of religious thought as it can now be traced through the ancient Near East from the earliest times. The question we have to ask is, does Christianity as now revealed for the first time fit adequately into what went *before* the first century, not what came after in its name?

1

In the Beginning God Created . . .

Religion is part of growing up. The reasoning that taught man that he was cleverer than the animals made him also aware of his own deficiencies. He could catch and kill beasts stronger and fleeter than himself because he could plan ahead, seek out their paths, and construct booby-traps. Later that same foresight led him to the art of farming and conserving his food supplies against the seasonal dearths. In the lands of marginal rainfall he learnt eventually the technique of digging and lining cisterns, and civilization began. Nevertheless, vast areas of natural resources were outside man's control. If the animals did not breed there was no hunting. If the rain did not fall the furrowed earth remained barren. Clearly there was a power in the universe that was greater than man, a seemingly arbitrary control of Nature which could make a mockery of man's hunting and farming skills. His very existence depended upon maintaining a right relationship with that power; that is, on religion.

Interesting as it is to speculate on the precise forms prehistoric religious thought and ritual may have taken, we have in fact very little direct evidence. The cave drawings found in France, Spain, and Italy tell us little more than that some ten to twenty thousand years ago man was a hunter, and that he may have enacted some kind of sympathetic ritual of slaughter to aid him in the hunt. This practical use of the graphic arts is paralleled today by Australian aborigines who accompany their symbolic portraiture with ritual mime, dancing, and recitation of traditional epics. Doubtless primitive man of the Palaeolithic periods did much the same, but the oral part of his rituals, which alone could adequately explain the drawings, is lost for ever. The relics of his plastic arts, relief carving and clay modelling emphasize his interest in fecundity. The Gravettian culture, extending widely over South Russia and central Europe, and spreading to Italy, France, and Spain, abounds in examples of the so-called "mother goddess" figurines. These clay models of women with pendulous breasts, huge buttocks, and distended bellies have obvious sexual and reproductive allusions, as do their male counterparts.[1]

Doubtless all these had magical or religious purposes, but it is not until man has learnt the art of writing that he can communicate with a later age. Only then can we with any real assurance begin to read his mind and thoughts about God. Unfortunately, this only happened comparatively late in his development, in terms of evolutionary time barely a minute or two ago. By then he was by no means "primitive". The first known attempts at connected writing were crude affairs, registering no more than lists of objects and numbers. But their very existence points to an advanced stage of economic administration, which is amply supported by archaeology. The wonder is that man had been able to progress so far without writing, the one facility we should have thought essential for social progress. How, we are inclined to ask in our "jotting-pad" age, was it possible to administer a region, farm out temple lands, collect revenues, fight wars, and maintain communications over long distances without easy means of documentation? We are apt to forget that in those days they still had memories. The kind of superhuman results promised the modern subscriber to correspondence courses in memory-training must have been commonplace among intelligent people six thousand years ago. Even today it is not uncommon to find a Muslim who can recite the whole of the Qur'an (Koran), or a Jew who knows long sections of the Bible and Talmud by heart.

The first books, then, were the brain's memory cells; the first pen was the tongue. It was the ability of Homo sapiens to communicate with his fellows, to organize community life, and transmit hard-earned skills from father to son that raised man far above the animals. It was this same means of communication that brought him in touch with his god, to flatter, cajole, even threaten to obtain the means of life. Experience showed that, as in his human relationships, some words and actions were more effective than others, and there arose a body of uniform ritual and liturgy whose memorizing and enactment was the responsibility of the "holy men" of the community.

When, around 2500 BC, the first great religious poems and epics of the Near East came to be written down, they had behind them already a long history of oral transmission. The fundamental religious conceptions they express go back thousands of years. Yet there were still another fifteen hundred years to go before the earliest text of the Old Testament was composed. It is not, therefore, sufficient to look for the origins of Christianity only within the previous thousand years of Old Testament writing, nor to start the history of Judaism with a supposed dating of the patriarchs around 1750 BC. The origins of both cults go back into Near Eastern prehistory. The problem is how to relate specific details of these comparatively late religions with the earliest ideas about god.

Our way into the mind of ancient man can only be through his writings, and this is the province of philology, the science of words. We have to seek in the symbols by which he represented his spoken utterances clues to his thinking. The limitations of such study are obvious. The first is the insufficiency of the early writing to express abstract ideas. Even when the philologist has collected all the texts available, compiled his grammars and dictionaries, and is confident of his decipherment, there still remains the inadequacy of any written word, even of the most advanced languages, to express thought. Even direct speech can fail to convey our meaning, and has to be accompanied with gesture and facial expression. A sign imprinted on wet clay, or even the flourish of the pen on paper, can leave much uncommunicated to the reader, as every poet and lover knows.

Nevertheless, the written word is a symbol of thought; behind it lies an attitude of mind, an emotion, a reasoned hypothesis, to which the reader can to some extent penetrate. It is with words and their meanings that this book is largely concerned. The study of the relationship between words and the thoughts they express is called "etymology" since it seeks the "true" (Greek *etumos*) meaning of the word. The etymologist looks for the "root" of the word, that is the inner core which expresses its fundamental or "radical" concept.

For example, if we were to seek the root of a modern barbarism like "de-escalate", we should immediately remove the "de-" and the verbal appendage "-ate", slice off the initial "e-" as a recognizable prefix, and be left with "scal-" for further study. The Latin *scala* means "ladder" and we are clearly on the right track. But at this stage the etymologist will look out for possible vocalic changes occurring between dialects. One of the more common is between *l* and *n*, and we are not surprised to find that an early form of the root has *n* in place of *l*, so that Sanskrit, one of the earliest dialects of Indo-European, has a root *skan-* with the idea of "going up". Sibilants can interchange, also, such as *s* and *z*, and short vowels can drop out in speech between consonants, like *i* between *s* and *c*. In fact, we can break down our Indo-European root *scan-*, "ascend", still further into two Sumerian syllables: ZIG, "rise", and AN, "up".[1a]

Or again, should we wish to track down the root of our word "rule", meaning "control, guide, exercise influence over", etc., we should find that our etymological dictionaries will refer us through an adaptation of Old French back to the Latin *regulo,* "direct", connected with *regno,* "reign", *rex,* "king", and so on. The root here is plain *reg-* or the like, and its ultimate source we can now discover by taking our search back another three or four thousand years to the earliest known writing of all, that of ancient Sumer in the Mesopotamian basin. There we find a root RIG,[2] meaning "shepherd", and, by breaking the word down even further, we can discover the idea behind "shepherd", that of ensuring the fecundity of the flocks in his charge. This explains the very common concept that the king was a "shepherd" to his people, since his task was primarily that of looking after the well-being and enrichment of the land and its people.

Here etymology has done more than discover the root-meaning of a particular word: it has opened a window on prehistoric philosophic thought. The idea of the shepherd-king's role in the community did not begin with the invention of writing. The written word merely expresses a long-held conception. If, then, in our search for the origins of religious cults and mythologies, we can trace their ideas back to the earliest known written texts we can use etymological methods to probe even further into the minds that gave them literary form.

Having arrived back at the primitive meaning of a root, the philologist has then to work his way forward again, tracing the way in which writers at different times use that root to express related concepts. For, of course, the meanings of words change; the more often they are used the wider becomes their reference. Today, with faster and easier means of communication, it is becoming increasingly difficult to maintain control over the meanings of words, and this at a time when the need for understanding each other is most crucial. In antiquity, people and ideas did not move quite so fast. Travel was not easy; remote areas would stay remote over generations and their languages would preserve old words and linguistic forms long lost in places more open to foreign influence.

Religious terminology, which is the special interest of this work, is least susceptible to change. Even though day-to-day words must develop their meanings to accord with social conditions and the invention of new crafts, communication with the god required a precise unchanging liturgy whose accurate transmission was the first responsibility of the priesthood. In the study of ancient literatures the scholar has to bear in mind that the language of the hymns and epics may well differ considerably from the common tongue of the same period. One of the problems facing the student of Old Testament Hebrew is the probability that the classical tongue of the Bible does not accurately represent the spoken language of the ancient Israelites. Certainly the vocabulary of the Bible is far too limited in extent to tell us much about the workaday world of ancient Canaan. When it comes to analysing the linguistic and phonetic structure of biblical Hebrew in terms of actual speech, the conviction grows that what we have is not the spoken dialect of any one community living in a single place at one time, but a kind of mixed, artificial language, composed perhaps of a number of dialects and used specifically for religious purposes. The importance of a liturgical language from our immediate point of view is that it will have been essentially conservative. It is in such writing that we can expect to find words used in their most primitive sense.

If religious terminology in general tends to resist change, this is even more the case with proper names, particularly those of the gods and epic heroes. It now appears that in many cases these have survived unaltered over centuries, even millennia, of oral as well as written transmission. In this one category of words lies the greatest scope for present and future researches into the nature and meaning of the old mythologies. To be able to decipher the name of the god will tell us his prime function and thus the meaning of the prayers and rituals by which he was worshipped.

The difficulty in this study has always been that the names are often very much older than the literature in which they occur, and are indecipherable in that language. So often the commentator on some Greek myth, for example, has to confess that the hero's name is "pre-Hellenic", of uncertain origin and meaning. All that he can do in such cases is to gather together all the references he can find to that character and see if there is some common denominator in the stories or epithets which will give a clue on the meaning of his name. Anyone who has tried this procedure on his own account, or studied in detail the efforts of others, will know too well that the results are often at best tenuous, and the exercise, to say the least, frustrating. One problem is that the same god or hero is differently described in different places. Zeus merits distinctive epithets and worship in Athens and in Crete, for example. What you expect of your god depends on your physical and spiritual needs in the immediate situation, and the stories you make up about him will reflect the social and ethnic conditions of your own time and place. Clearly, the mythologist can best estimate these local and temporal factors in his material if he knows the god's original place in the order of nature, that is, if he knows the source and meaning of his name.

The dramatic step forward that is now possible in our researches into the origin of Near Eastern cults and mythologies arises from our ability to make these decipherments. We can now break down god-names like Zeus and Yahweh/Jehovah, and hero-names like Dionysus and Jesus, because it is possible to penetrate the linguistic barriers imposed by the different languages in which their respective literatures have reached us. We can reach back beyond the Greek of the classics and the New Testament and the Hebrew of the Old Testament to a linguistic source common to all.

Furthermore, as might be expected in such a limited geographical area as the Near East, we find that not only have the names a common derivation but many of the religious ideas variously expressed by the different cultures stem from the same basic ideas. The forms of worship, as far as we can reconstruct them from our limited literary and archaeological evidence, may appear quite unrelated, and the stories that circulated about the gods and heroes may reflect different social and ethnic backgrounds, but the underlying themes are turning out often to be the same. The worshippers of Dionysus headed their cultic processions with an erect penis, while those of Jesus symbolized their faith with a fish and a cross, but essentially all represent the common theme of fertility and the creative power of the god.

Even within the Bible, language has hitherto posed a major barrier to research into Christian origins. Jesus and his immediate followers are portrayed as Jews, living in Palestine and adopting Jewish customs and religious conventions. The religion propounded by the New Testament is at root a form of Judaism, but the language in which it is expressed is Greek, a non-Semitic tongue. Words and names like "Christ", "Holy Ghost", "Jesus", "Joseph", and "Mary" come through Hebrew channels but have Greek forms or translations in the New Testament. The words of Jesus are quoted freely and often given the weight of incontrovertible authority, but in fact nobody knows for certain what he said, since what we have are translations of a supposedly Aramaic original of which all trace has otherwise been lost.

A large part of Christian scholarship has been devoted to trying to reconstruct the Semitic expressions underlying New Testament phraseology, with varying degrees of success but little absolute certainty. In the forms in which we know them, Greek and Hebrew are very different in vocabulary and grammatical structure. They belong to different language families, the one Indo-European, like Latin and English, the other Semitic, like Aramaic and Arabic. Translation from one into the other can be at times extremely difficult, since they express not only distinctive linguistic attitudes but underlying philosophies. One impediment to mutual understanding between the Semitic and non-Semitic world today is that mere mechanical translation of, say, Arabic words into English cannot express adequately the intention of the speaker and dangerous misunderstandings can too often arise as a result.

What we have now discovered is that by going far enough back in time it is possible to find a linguistic bridge between these ethnic and cultural groups. However far apart their respective languages and philosophies may have become, they stem from a common, recoverable source, and it is there that any realistic study of Christian and Jewish origins must begin. The root of Christianity in this sense lies not in the Old Testament, but, like that of Judaism itself, in a pre-Semitic, pre-Hellenic culture that existed in Mesopotamia some two or three thousand years before the earliest Old Testament composition. The Christian doctrine of the fatherhood of God stems not from the paternal relationship of Yahweh to his chosen people but from the naturalistic philosophy that saw the divine creator as a heavenly penis impregnating mother earth. The idea of divine love came not from the Israelite prophet's revelation of the forgiving nature of his god, but from a very much earlier understanding of the essential need for balance and reciprocation in nature, moral as well as physical.

II

Sumer and the Beginnings of History

Civilization began in Sumer,[1] in the Land of the Two Rivers, Mesopotamia (figs. 1, 2). No one knows where the Sumerians came from, but about 4000 BC they were already developing a culture which was to affect the whole world for over five thousand years.

The rich agricultural land of the alluvial plains meant there was always sufficient food for man and beast; fowl and fish were in abundance and the Bible did well to find here its Garden of Eden. Amid such plenty nomadic man needed no more to move from place to place as he exhausted the land's resources. His was now an urban culture. He could build cities like ancient Eridu accommodating several thousands of people. His simple buildings became classic examples of monumental architecture rising high above the surrounding plains. Arts and crafts became the specialist industries of the few.

The overbrimming wealth of Sumer could attract raw materials and services from less favoured lands round about, and a class of traders arose to channel imports through their warehouses and to travel abroad seeking more. Labour was organized and rigorously controlled for efficient production, and in every city management of the economy, religion, and culture was in the hands of the king and the priesthood.

For the land was the god's, without whose procreative power all life would cease. The king was his bailiff, a lesser, temporarily earthbound god whose function was also to ensure the productivity of the community. The administrative centre of each district was the god's house, the temple, with its priestly officials whose control over the people was absolute. The temple was the seat of justice, land administration, scientific learning, and theological speculation, as well as the theatre of religious ritual. It was the community's university and main school, to which small boys would drag their unwilling steps each day to set the pattern of grammar school curricula for more than five millennia. It

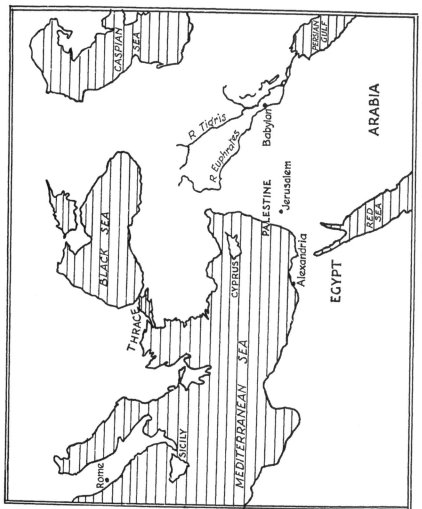

1 THE NEAR EAST

was in such temple colleges that their tutors built, over the next two thousand years, some of the richest and most extensive libraries of the ancient world.

From the ruins of ancient Nippur on the lower Euphrates, a hundred miles or so from modern Baghdad, have come several thousand literary texts. A large number were written in the most prolific period of Sumerian culture, from about 2000 to 1500 BC. They evince a wide range

2 SUMER AND ACCAD

of intellectual exploration in the fields of theology, botany, zoology, mineralogy, geography, mathematics, and philology, the results of centuries of creative thought.

Along with a continuing search for new knowledge went the systematic preservation of past results. The library of Nippur contained texts going back to around 2300 BC, as well as dictionaries, legal works, and myths reaching down nearly to the end of the second millennium.

Elsewhere, the library at Uruk held a range of literature stretching some 3,000 years, from the earliest times to a century or so before the

Christian era, when Sumerian was still being used as a special, esoteric language. For, although after 2360 BC Sumer had to share her hegemony of the region with her northern Semitic neighbours of Accad, and afterwards lost political control completely, she had set a seal upon the cultural life of the Near East and the world for all time.

Yet, a century ago no one had ever heard of the Sumerians. Archaeologists who were at all interested in Mesopotamia were looking for the remains of the Assyrians and Babylonians, referred to often in biblical and classical sources. About the middle of the nineteenth century Sir Henry Rawlinson and other scholars were examining clay tablets found in the ruins of ancient Nineveh. They were inscribed with wedge-shaped ("cuneiform") signs already familiar as the writing of Semitic-speaking Accadians (Assyro-Babylonians). To this family of languages belong Hebrew and Aramaic, sister dialects used in the Old Testament, and Arabic, the language of Muhammad's Qur'an and the modern Arab world. The initial decipherment of Accadian cuneiform had been made by Rawlinson in 1851, mainly on the basis of a trilingual inscription from Behistun in Persia. However, some of the tablets now being studied had, besides the familiar Semitic dialect, another quite unknown tongue, interspersed between the lines. The script was the same so that the phonetic values of each sign could be transcribed even though the string of resultant syllables made no immediate sense. There were also discovered amongst the tablets word-lists in which Accadian words were set alongside equivalents in this strange tongue.

Some scholars refused to believe it was a real language at all. They spoke of a "secret script" used by the priests to overawe the laity and preserve their rituals and incantations from the uninitiated. The name by which it was known in the texts, "the tongue of Sumer", was incomprehensible, and it was some years before the experts would take it seriously. However, when, later, monuments were discovered written only in this language and dating from a time before Semitic Accadian was being written in Mesopotamia, even the most sceptical had to admit that there must have existed in the area a pre-Semitic population from whom the Assyrians had borrowed the art of writing.

The cuneiform method of writing was well suited to the area. The alluvial soil of the plains provided an abundance of a particularly fine clay which could be moistened and shaped into a lozenge or pat in the palm of the hand. The earliest shape of "tablets" was roughly circular, smoothly rounded on top and flat underneath. It was the shape of the flat loaf of the East even today, or of the biblical "cake of figs" or circular disk of a spinning whorl. It was, in fact, the shape of the top of a mushroom, and it was from the fungus that it received its name.[2]

Later the primitive "bun" tablet was regularized into a rectangular slab some two or three inches long and one and a half or two inches wide, and capable of being held in the scribe's hand. The soft clay was firm enough to take and preserve the impression made by the squared end of his stylus, but not so tacky as to stick to the scribe's hand as he worked.

As the texts required to be recorded grew longer, the tablets were made larger so that they could no longer be held in the hand. This meant that when the bigger tablets were introduced the attitude of the scribe's hand to the clay as it lay now on the table underwent a change, and with it the orientation of the symbols, which turned ninety degrees.

The "jotting-pad" kind of tablet, recording some passing transaction or the like, was simply hardened by being baked in the sun. But this method gave too impermanent a result for more important legal or religious texts, and offered too much scope to the forger, who had simply to remoisten the clay, smear over the impression and write in a new word. Important documents were baked hard in an oven, and the method is used even today by archaeologists finding sun-baked tablets which could too easily suffer damage during handling.

When the Semites took over the Sumerian technique of writing, it had already developed stylized forms far removed from the first, crude pictorial signs we find on the earliest tablets. The oldest text we know is probably a tally list of some kind and dates from about 3500 BC.[3] It comes from Kish near ancient Babylon, and the signs at this stage are clearly recognizable representations of objects, like a head ♀, a leg ⌊, an erect penis ejaculating sperm ◻, and a hand ♈.

The signs had been made by drawing a pointed instrument through the clay like a pen. However, it was found that this method tended to push the clay into ridges before the stylus so that the signs became blurred and crossing over previous strokes obliterated them. So the scribes began simply pressing the end of the reed into the clay forming a series of separate wedge-shaped marks: ⟶, \, ⌈. Inevitably, the flowing line of the original drawings was lost, stylized into formal representations which became further and further removed from the subject. To take the above examples, we see the following sequence of development:

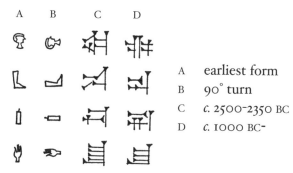

A earliest form
B 90° turn
C c. 2500–2350 BC
D c. 1000 BC-

The importance of such a primitive script for the etymologist is that he can illustrate the word with a picture, as a child is taught to read with bricks on which word and picture are printed side by side. Thus ♀ represents SAG, "head" (the Sumerian words are conventionally transcribed into capital letters, their Accadian equivalents into lower case type, italicized, in this instance, *rēshu*). Identification of the object with a human head here, of course, poses no problem, but there are instances where to have the accompanying picture is to gain a valuable insight into the Sumerian mind. For example, where one is trying to discover the significance of fire in fertility mythology, it is useful to know that to represent the idea of "love" the Sumerian scribe drew a simple container with a burning torch inside, ▯, to indicate the fermenting heat of gestation in the womb. Or again, as a sidelight upon social customs, the word for "male slave" was an erect, ejaculating penis superimposed with three triangular impressions used to express "hill-country" or "foreign land": ▯[4] and his feminine counterpart was the usual representation for "woman", the pubic triangle with the slit of the vulva, with a similar subscription: ▽.[5]

The word for "male slave", ERI,[6] leaves no doubt that his prime function was to procreate more slaves for his master, since a home-born slave was a better security risk than one dragged away from his native land as a spoil of war.

Unfortunately, this simple representative writing could not long survive the extension of the art to express more complex ideas than "laundry-lists". That same picture of the erect penis came also to be used, not unnaturally, to express "standing up straight",[7] or "length",[8] and so a number of verbs and nouns could ultimately be intended by the one picture. Furthermore, it could also represent the *sound* of the "penis" word, *ush*, and so could be used simply as a phonetic symbol where no reference to the meaning of the original was intended.

Our alphabet is also, of course, composed of symbols, which were originally pictures. The letter A, for instance, is derived from the picture of a bull's head, seen in its earliest form as ⚭, stylized in Phoenician as ⚇, and passing into early Greek as ⊳, and A, and so on into our western alphabet. Similarly, our letter B began as a picture of a house, or rather, the courtyard of a house, ⊡, which appears in Phoenician as ⅁, in Greek as ∂ and B. Our D was a door, hieroglyphic ⬒, from which it developed the characteristic triangular shape of Phoenician and Greek *delta*, ◁, and △. Our letter I came from a very much simplified version of a hieroglyphic hand, ⌒, through Phoenician ⊂, into Greek � and ⟩. And so on. But the idea of having symbols represent single sounds, consonants and vowels, was a major step forward and was not to be achieved for more than a thousand years after writing began in Sumer.

Just how great an advance this constituted can be appreciated by realizing that the cuneiform system required some three hundred different signs, and that each of these ideograms could represent a number of different sound-values. For instance, the sign for a road-junction, SILA or SEL, ⤞, also meant TAR, "make a decision, judge", or KUD, "cut", or KhASh, "break, grind up". All have this radical idea of "division" but its extension to similar motifs, physical and juridical, brings under the same ideogram a variety of different words. Similarly, the ideogram for "scrotum", simply a skin bag, 🜁, DUBUR, can also represent DUGGAN, "wallet",[9] KALAM, "kidney", and even GIRISh, "butterfly", presumably from its origins in a chrysalis.

When Accadian took over the cuneiform system, the Semitic scribes added to the lists of values attaching to each ideogram those relating to their own equivalents of the Sumerian words. For example, Sumerian SAG, "head", was translated by Accadian *rēshu*, so to the Sumerian values of the "head" ideogram, they added their own phonetic and etymological approximations, *sak, sag, saq, shak, shag, shaq, resh, res, rish, ris.* (Incidentally, it should be noted that Sumerian and Semitic had single consonants representing our *sh* sound, shown here as *sh* in Semitic and Sh in Sumerian.) Obviously learning to read and write would be very much easier if the student had only to memorize a couple of dozen signs representing individual sounds, consonants and vowels, and use these symbols to express the phonemes of which each sound-group or "word" was composed. He could then build up any word he wanted, like a Meccano model of standard-shaped pieces. Not surprisingly, until this radical step forward had been taken, proficiency in this highly complex cuneiform system was the privilege of a few, and, carrying with it power and prestige, tended to resist change and the wider dissemination of the craft.

Even when it did arrive, alphabetic writing was used to express only the "harder", consonantal sounds, whilst in reading the "softer" vowels had to be inserted according to the most likely meaning of the word in the context. This is still the case in many parts of the Semitic world, where vowelling words in Arabic newspaper printing, for example, is the exception rather than the rule. Indeed, full vowelling systems for most Semitic scripts were not introduced until the Christian era, and in the Bible considerable doubt can arise over the precise meaning of a passage because the text was only consonantally written and the context insufficiently clear to offer grounds for certain interpretation.

The advantage of the old, clumsy syllabic writing to the modern decipherer is that it shows the vowels as well as the consonants of the dead language. When one is trying to relate words from different language groups of widely varying dates, every scrap of information about their early pronunciation is of the utmost value. Because we have the vowels of Sumerian we can trace the developments of its vocabulary into related dialects with more certainty than would have been possible had the alphabet been invented and widely used a thousand years earlier.

The Sumerian language is put together like a house of bricks. First, there are certain word-bricks expressing basic ideas, like KUR, "conquer", BA, "give". On to these the writer adds other word-bricks, like TA or NE, modifying the verb in some way or adding a possessive suffix, like "my", "his" or "their", to a noun. These added particles do not concern us so much in this study, since the words we are interested in are built mainly of the basic word-bricks. What is of vital importance for our researches is, however, that unlike many other languages, including our own, Sumerian tends to keep these basic idea-words unchanged. English often expresses tense in a verb by altering the sound within the root, as "he gives", but, for the past tense, "he gave"; "I run", but "I ran", and so on. Sumerian will keep the same radical element, merely adding a particle word-brick to modify the verb or its relationship with other grammatical members of the sentence. Thus in our search for a Sumerian idea-word within Indo-European or Semitic names we can feel confident that, whatever phonetic changes it may have undergone through dialectal influences, the radical element we seek will originally have been a single, unchangeable word-brick. Once we can penetrate to that, we stand a good chance of deciphering the original meaning of the name.

Sometimes two or more radical elements can be combined to form a new word-brick like SILA, "road-junction",[10] abbreviated sometimes to SIL. Clearly this word is a combination of SI, "finger", and LA, "join together", the overall picture being that of Winston Churchill's "victory-V" sign. We should express that supposed original form of two separate but, as yet, uncombined elements as *SI-LA, with a preposited asterisk. This sign, here and elsewhere, indicates a verbal group whose constituent parts are known to have existed in Sumerian but whose grouping or combination in that precise form does not actually appear in literature so far recovered.

At this point it must be emphasized that although we now have thousands of tablets from which to reconstruct a great deal of the vocabulary of Sumerian, they represent only a fraction of the original literature. Doubtless there is much more to be found beneath Mesopotamian soil, for archaeology has already demonstrated the very high level of Sumerian civilization and extent of its accumulated learning. It is now possible to propose combinations of known root elements with a fair degree of assurance; nevertheless the asterisk will appear frequently in the following pages and serve to remind us that such reconstructions, however probable, must find adequate cross-checking through the cognate languages if they are to be anything but speculative. Furthermore, they are only possible when the phonetic rules governing consonant and vowel changes from one language into another have been established.

We know that Sumerian was spoken in more than one dialect. These are referred to in the texts but there is not yet sufficient material to reconstruct them completely, or to know for certain their geographical and literary boundaries. What is now apparent, however, is that some of the most important phonetic changes evinced by these dialects are observable in the forms of Sumerian words as they appear in Indo-European and Semitic. Perhaps in the future it may be possible to draw dialect boundaries which will show not only where the Sumerians originated but from what geographical points their language spread into the Indo-European and Semitic worlds. For the moment, to know the phonetic changes that may be expected in vocal transmission of Sumerian roots makes it possible to trace them in other language families.[10a]

For example, to our ears *m* and *g* could hardly be more different. In Sumerian, however, they are dialectally equivalent. The word AM, for instance, can appear as AG,[11] MAR as GAR,[12] and so on. The same variation can be seen in dialectal Greek, as in the word *magganon*, "hunting-net", which appears rarely as *gaggamon*,[13] and between Greek and Latin, as in *amnos*, "lamb", Latin *agnus*. Again, to us *g* is quite different from *b*, but they can fall together in Sumerian,[14] and also parallel one another in Indo-European dialects. For example, the Greek *balanos*, "acorn", is the Latin (and English) *glans*.[15]

Some phonetic correspondences are more easily understood since the sounds are, in any case, not far apart, like *b* and *p*, with their "soft" sounds *ph* and *f*. Latin *pater* is our "father". The sounds *m* and *n* are close enough to make their interchangeability easily comprehensible, as are the "liquid" letters *r* and *l*. But not so immediately obvious is a common variant in the Sumerian and Semitic worlds between *l* and *n*,[16] and *l* and *sh*, and this has particularly to be looked for when Sumerian origins are sought for names in Semitic format.[17]

Specialists will note for themselves phonetic correspondences affecting their own fields of linguistic interest, but another variant which may seem strange at first sight to the non-specialist reader is that between the Sumerian *Kh*, a somewhat throatish rasping sound akin to the *ch* in the Scottish "loch", and hard *g*. This interchange occurs within Sumerian[18] and also externally. For example, MAKh, "great", appears in Greek as *megas*, Latin *magnus*.[19] On the other hand, Sumerian *Kh* is found as its straightforward phonetic equivalent in the Greek *chei* (transliterated in these pages as *kh* for the sake of uniformity), in, for example, *khalbane*, a kind of gum, but as hard *g* in the Latin cognate *galbanum*.[20]

Vowels follow a fairly uniform and easily recognizable pattern. However, the sound *i* often disappears between consonants in the derived forms. For example the Sumerian BIL, "burn", appears in the Greek *phlegō* and Latin *flagro*, "burn" (the source of our "flame"), but the medial *i* has disappeared between the *b* and *l*. The full form of the Sumerian original was probably *BIL-AG.[21] The Greek, it will be noted, has depressed the *a* of the last element to *e*, although Latin pre-served the original sound. This "flattening" of the *a* sound is very common. Less expected is the frequent change of the Sumerian *u*, normally appearing in the cognates as *u* or *o*, to the Greek *ēta(η)*[22]

Among other vowel-changes which might be mentioned here are those combined vowels we call diphthongs. Some are predictable enough when they occur through the conjunction of *a* and *o*, for example, becoming long *ō*, or *e* and *i* becoming *ei*. But some diphthongs have arisen through the loss of an intervening consonant, particularly the letters *l*[23] and *r*.[24] An interesting example of this occurs in the title of Apollo, *Paian,* and the Greek plant-name *Paionia,* our Paeony. Both go back to an original *BAR-IA-U-NA, which reappears with only the *a* and *u* combined in the New Testament *Bariōnas,* "Bar-Jona", Peter's surname.[25]

Summarizing: in the language and culture of the world's most ancient civilization, Sumerian, it is now possible to find a bridge between the Indo-European and Semitic worlds. The first writing known is found on tablets from the Mesopotamian basin, dating some five thousand years ago, and consisting of crude pictures drawn with a stylus on to soft clay. Later the recognizable pictures became stylized into ideograms made up of nail- or wedge-shape impressions, so-called cuneiform signs, each representing syllables of consonants and vowels. These syllables made up "word-bricks", which resisted phonetic change within the language and could be joined together to make connected phrases and sentences. To such word-bricks we can now trace Indo-European and Semitic verbal roots, and so begin to decipher for the first time the names of gods, heroes, plants, and animals appearing in cultic mytho-logies. We can also now start penetrating to the root-meanings of many religious and secular terms whose original significance has been obscure.

III

The Names of the Gods

We are sometimes misled by the proliferation of gods and goddesses in popular mythology into believing that man started off his religious thinking with a vast pantheon of some hundreds of different gods; and that, however much his systematic theologians may have attempted to arrange them into some comprehensible order, it required a dramatic revelation from on high to convince him that there was really only one supreme moral deity.

This idea found great favour with the nineteenth-century theologians for whom the recently discovered laws of evolution seemed to offer a "scientific" explanation of divine revelation. The Old Testament, they suggested, showed how primitive animistic ideas, that is the deification of inanimate objects like stones and trees, gradually gave way to a more "spiritual" concept of one god, as man evolved towards a "higher" intelligence, and thus made it possible for the deity to communicate to mankind through his servants the prophets.

This singularly ill-conceived piece of biblical criticism had the advantage that its extension to the New Testament revelation by the Christian theologians showed that since Jesus stood later in time his revelation was necessarily more advanced than that of the Jewish prophets and, less explicitly, that the nineteenth-century theologians were rather better informed than either.

Unfortunately for these "evolutionary" thinkers the Old Testament will not bear the weight of their theory. Moses is portrayed as a mono-theist; the Church divided its Godhead into three. The Bible cannot be used to illustrate "primitive" religion. The philosophical and moral concepts displayed in its writings vary enormously, and there is no internal evidence for a steady "evolution" of ideas from a multiplicity of gods and moral barbarism to one, righteous and humane, heavenly father. The god who is annoyed because his servant Saul failed to carry out his bidding to wipe out every "man and woman, infant and suck-ling, ox and sheep, camel and ass" of the Amalekites (I Sam 15:3), is still pictured a thousand years later leaving his son to die in agony on a cross. On the other hand, the literature that contains the discourse of selfless love in I Corinthians 13 has already long before recounted a story which taught that lust without affection has a bitter fruit (II Sam 13:15).

If we are to make any enlightened guess at "primitive" man's ideas about god and the universe it would have to be on the reasonable assumption that they would be simple, and directly related to the world of his experience. He may have given the god numerous epithets describing his various functions and manifestations but there is no reason to doubt that the reality behind the names was envisaged as one all-powerful deity, a life-giver, supreme creator. The etymological examination of the chief god-names that is now possible supports this view, pointing to a common theme of life-giving fecundity. Thus the principal gods of the Greeks and Hebrews, Zeus and Yahweh (Jehovah), have names derived from Sumerian meaning "juice of fecundity", spermatozoa, "seed of life".[1] The phrase is composed of two syllables, IA (*ya*, dialectally *za*), "juice", literally "strong water", and U, perhaps the most important phoneme in the whole of Near Eastern religion. It is found in the texts represented by a number of different cuneiform signs, but at the root of them all is the idea of "fertility". Thus one U means "copulate" or "mount", and "create"; another "rainstorm" as source of the heavenly sperm; another "vegetation", as the offspring of the god; whilst another U is the name of the storm-god himself.[2] So, far from evincing a multiplicity of gods and conflicting theological notions, our earliest records lead us back to a single idea, even a single letter, "U". Behind Judaism and Christianity, and indeed all the Near Eastern fertility religions and their more sophisticated developments, there lies this single phoneme "U".

Quite simply, the reasoning of the early theologians seems to have been as follows: since rain makes the crops grow it must contain within it the seed of life. In human beings this is spermatozoa, ejected from the penis at orgasm. Therefore it followed that rain is simply heavenly semen, the all-powerful creator, God.

The most forceful spurting of this "seed" is accompanied by thunder and the shrieking wind.[3] This is the "voice" of God.[4] Somewhere above the sky a mighty penis[5] reaches an orgasm that shakes the heavens. The "lips" of the penis-tip, the glans, open, and the divine seed shoots forth and is borne by the wind to earth. As saliva can be seen mixed with breath during forceful human speech, so the "speaking"[6] of the divine penis is accompanied by a powerful blast of wind, the holy, creative spirit,[7] bearing the "spittle" of semen.[8]

This "spittle" is the visible "speech" of God; it is his "Son" in New Testament terms, the "Word" which "was with God, and was God, and was in the beginning with God; through whom all things were made, and without him was not anything made that was made. In him was life . . ." (John 1:1-4). In the words of the Psalmists: "By the word of the Lord the heavens were made, and all their host by the breath of his mouth" (Ps 33:6); or, "when you send forth your breath they are created, and the face of the earth is restored" (Ps 104:30).

This idea of the creative Word of God came to have a profound philosophical and religious importance and was, and still is, the subject of much metaphysical debate. But originally it was not an abstract notion; you could see the "Word of God", feel it as rain on your face, see it seeping into the furrows of mother earth, the "labia" of the womb of creation.[9] Within burns an eternal fire which every now and then demonstrates its presence dramatically, by bursting to the surface in a volcano, or by heating spring water to boiling point where the earth's crust is thinnest. It was this uterine heat which made generation possible, and which later theologians identified with the place and means of eternal punishment.[10]

Also beneath the earth's surface lay a great ocean whose waters, like those of the seas around and above the firmament (Gen 1:7) were the primeval reservoirs of the god's spermatozoa, the Word. They were therefore "seas of knowledge" as the Sumerians called them,[11] and could be tapped by seekers of truth, whether they looked "to the heavens or to the earth beneath" (Isa 51:6), that is, by means of astrology or necromancy, "divination from the dead". This notion that mortals could discover the secrets of the past, present, and future by somehow projecting themselves to the "seventh heaven" or down into the under-world gave rise to much mythology and some curious magical practices. Since common observation showed that dead and decaying matter melted back into the earth, it was thought that the imperishable part of man, his "soul" or spirit, the creative breath that gave him life in the womb, must either float off into the ether or return through the terrestrial vagina into the generative furnace. In either case he was more likely to have access to the fount of all wisdom than when his spirit was imprisoned in mortal flesh.

Since it was given to few men to be able to visit heaven or hell and return to tell what they had seen and heard, there arose the ideas of "messengers", or angels, those "workers of miracles" as their name in Greek and Hebrew means.[12] These demigods, or heroes, had access to both worlds and play an important part in ancient mythology. They could come from above in various guises or be conjured up from the ground, like the ghost of Samuel drawn to the surface by the witch of Endor for consultation by King Saul (I Sam 28). One important aspect of this idea of heavenly and subterranean founts of knowledge is that since plants and trees had their roots beneath the soil and derived their nourishment from the water above and beneath the earth, it was thought possible that some varieties of vegetation could give their mortal consumers access to this wisdom. Herein lies the philosophical justification for believing that hallucinatory drugs distilled from such plants imparted divine secrets, or "prophecies".

Such very special kinds of vegetation were, then, "angels" and to know their names was to have power over them. A large part of magical folk-lore was devoted to maintaining this vital knowledge of the names of the angels.[13] It was not sufficient simply to know what drug could be expected to have certain effects; it was important to be able to call upon its name at the very moment of plucking and eating it. Not only was its rape from the womb of mother earth thus safely accomplished, but its powers could be secured by the prophet for his "revelations" without incurring the heavy penalties so often suffered by those misusing the drug plants.

Just as these growths were more powerfully endowed with the god's semen than others, so men and animals differed in their possession of the vital force: some were more fierce and lustful and some were more wise. So-called "men of God" were particularly fortunate in this respect. They were in a very special sense his "sons", and had a particularly close relationship with the deity. He could speak through them; they caught his word, as it were, and spat it out to their less god-attuned fellow men. Priest and prophet believed that the spittle-laden breath that came from their mouth when they spoke as the god's messenger was not theirs, but the god's. Such words, once released, had a power and motivation of their own. They could not only foretell events; they brought them about. No wonder the beleaguered citizens of Jerusalem put Jeremiah and his gloomy prognostications into a miry cistern. Well might they say that in the face of the Babylonian armies he was "weakening the hands of the soldiers who are left in this city" (Jer 38:4). For the same reason the king cut Jeremiah's doom-laden scroll into small pieces and dropped them into the brazier (36:23). For the word was as potent in writing as when uttered in speech. In the Sinai myth, Yahweh himself writes the "Ten Words" or "Commandments" (Exod 31:18), and the tablets thus inscribed have thereafter to be kept in a box and venerated within the shrine as a divine manifestation (Deut 10:5).

God was the ultimate source of justice. By this was meant the ordering of society towards stability, maintaining a balance between opposing, otherwise disruptive forces. This might involve laying down certain regulations for conduct to which injured parties might appeal in the courts, but divinely given "law" was not simply a code of behaviour. It was another expression of natural equilibrium, that ordering of affairs that began when primeval chaos gave way to creation. "Law" was thus a gift of God. In Semitic the same words are used for "justice" and religious "alms-giving", and specifically in the Old Testament for "rain".[14] Thus the prophet Joel bids his listeners "rejoice in Yahweh, your God, for he has poured down for you a shower of rain" (Joel 2:23). The Hebrew "Law" (*Tōrah*) is, literally, the "outpouring"; the "lawgiver" or "teacher" is the "outpourer", properly of "semen, grace, favour".[15]

Kings and priests are "pourers of bounty", lawgivers and teachers, in their capacity as the god's earthly representatives. They were reckoned especially endowed with divine "grace", the word for which in both Hebrew and Greek refers to the flowing of seed. They were "shepherds" of their people, the idea behind which, as we saw above, had to do with promoting fecundity.[16] In that the king had within him the god's semen, he was held to be a strong man, representing his god on the field of battle, and no less virile in the harem. When this important faculty deserted him, he could be deposed. Hence King David, whose name means "lover" or "loved one",[17] when his manly prowess seemed to be failing, sought stimulation at the hands of a young and beautiful virgin, Abishag: "and she served the king, but he knew her not" (I Kgs 1:1-4).

The fertility aspect of divine and royal shepherding can be seen in another Sumerian word for "shepherd" which appears right across the ancient world in names and epithets. It is SIPA, literally "stretched horn", or "penis".[18] We may now recognize it in the biblical phrase Yahweh Sabaoth, from *SIPA-UD, "penis of the storm".[19] The Sumerian storm-god, Iskur, has a name with much the same meaning, "mighty penis".[20] Among the Semites he was known as Adad, "Mighty Father", with the same general idea of the great fecundator of the skies.[21] In the Old Testament, the name we know as Joseph means "Yahweh's penis", really just a shortened form of Yahweh Sabaoth.[22] Over in Asia Minor, this Old Testament divine title appears in classical times as an old cultic cry to the Phrygian deity Sabazios, euoi saboi. The name of the god itself is composed of the same Sumerian SIPA to which has been added the element ZI, "erect".[23] This is just one example of how we can now span the whole area of our study and bring together apparently quite disparate religious cults simply through being able to decipher the names and epithets of the respective gods.

Similar phallic designations are given, as we now see, to many Sumerian, Greek, and Semitic gods, tribal ancestors and heroes. Hercules, that great "club-bearer", was named after the grossness of his sex organ,[24] as was the Hebrew tribal ancestor Issachar.[25] Perhaps the best known of the old Canaanite fertility gods, Baal, derives his name from a Sumerian verb AL, "bore", which, combined with a preformative element BA, gave words for "drill" and "penis" and gave Latin and us our word "phallus".[26] In Semitic, baʿal, Baal, is not only the divine name but has also the general meaning of "lord, husband".[27] Hosea, the Old Testament prophet, makes a play on the general and cultic uses of the word when he has Yahweh say to Israel, "in that day you will call me 'my man' and you will no more call me 'my baal'; I shall banish the name of baals from your mouth . . ." (Hos 2:16 [Heb. 18]).

More than any other heavenly body, it was the sun which commanded most respect as the embodiment of god. It was the Creator, the fecundator of the earth.[28] The ancients saw the glowing orb as the tip of the divine penis, rising to white heat as it approached its zenith, then turning to a deep red, characteristic of the fully distended glans penis, as it plunged into the earthly vagina.[29] In the cultic centres this ritual was enacted imitatively by the entry of the priest into the god's house.

The temple was designed with a large measure of uniformity over the whole of the Near East[30], now recognizable as a microcosm of the womb. It was divided into three parts: the Porch,[31] representing the lower end of the vagina up to the hymen, or Veil;[32] the Hall,[33] or vagina itself; and the inner sanctum, or Holy of Holies, the uterus.[34] The priest,[35] dressed as a penis, anointed with various saps and resins as representing the divine semen,[36] enters through the doors of the Porch, the "labia" of the womb, past the Veil or "hymen" and so into the Hall.

On very special occasions,[37] the priestly phallus penetrated into the uterus where the god himself dwelt and wrought his creative works. Even today Christian ritual and architecture probably owes much to the ancient tradition, as the priest heads the processional through the body of the "womb", to reach its climax before the altar.[38]

The god was thought of as the "husband" of his land and people. This is a common figure in the Old Testament where Israel is featured as the "wife" of Yahweh,[39] usually thus spoken of in passages accusing her of infidelity and seeking other "lovers".[40] The Church is also described as the "bride" of Christ (Rev 21:2; 22:17). In both cases the god is the fructifying seed, the "Word" or Gospel, "good news", whose fruitfulness depends upon the receptivity of the "womb" of his people's minds and hearts.

The seed of God was supremely holy. Whether it appeared directly from heaven as rain, or as the sap or resin of plants and trees, or as spermal emission from the organs of animals or men, it was sacred and to waste it was a grievous sin. The processes and balance of nature demanded its effective use, since without it there could be no life or regeneration. The words for "curse" and "sin" have their roots in the idea of "seed running to waste".[41] This was the sin of Onan[42], who shirked his duty of giving his dead brother's wife more children by practising coitus interruptus, or, as the Bible says "spoiling it on the ground" (Gen 38:1-10). This was the sin, too, of Sodom[43], whose inhabitants preferred the attractions of two male visiting angels to Lot's daughters (Gen 19). That much-used religious word "sin", then, has basically the meaning of "making ineffective", "failing in one's object"; the direct opposite of "faith", which is, at root, "to make effective, or fruitful".[44] This very ancient regard for the sanctity of semen, which lies at the core of the fertility idea, is the ultimate cultic justification of the Roman Catholic strictures on birth control. The real objections to contraception have little to do with family morals or, indeed, with morality at all as the modern world understands the term; it is simply that wasting seed is a religious "sin"; it is a blasphemy against the "word of god", the "holy spirit".

In the same way, a barren woman was reckoned "accursed". Jeremiah vented his wrath upon his fellow-citizens who spurned his gloomy prognostications by wishing their "wives childless and widowed" (Jer 18:21). Most unhappy of women was she whose husband had divorced her for barrenness or died leaving her childless. The Hebrew word for "widow" meant originally "wasted-womb",[45] and similar derivations are to be found for the ancient words meaning "unlucky" or "the left side", being reckoned the unproductive side of the womb.[46]

In part derived from this idea of the sanctity of sperm and the importance of fertility is the crucial doctrine of the balance of nature. Upon this axiom rested the whole basis of moral and natural philosophy. God, as an act of grace,[47] gives the seed of life. Earth receives it and engenders food[48] for man and beast, who eat it and reproduce themselves after their own kind. At death they return to earth which, in turn, produces more vegetation to feed their offspring. So the cycle of nature continues season after season.

But man must soon have realized that this highly desirable state of affairs could continue only so long as new life followed death. Kill too many animals one year and there are insufficient to breed for the next. Reap too many harvests from the same field and you reduce it to a desert. In terms of human relationships, become too rich at the expense of your neighbours and eventually they will turn on you like starving wolves. Revenge blood with blood and your personal feud will become tribal war. Herein lies the root of the doctrine of loving one's neighbour; of the "soft answer that turneth away wrath".[49] Socially, as agriculturally, all life depends upon keeping the balance between giving and taking, and avoiding extremes.

Nevertheless, the cycle of nature had first to be set in motion by the creative act of the god, and thereafter the initiative remained with him. As the New Testament writer says: "By grace you have been saved through faith; and this was not from yourselves but as a gift from God"

(Eph 2:8). The Greek and Hebrew words for this kind of "saving" derive from a basic conception of "fulfilment", "restoration", "healing" or "life".[50] The same element in Sumerian ShUSh or ShU-A, appears in the name of Joshua/Jesus attached as an epithet to Yahweh.[51] This "salvation" in the Bible is the prerogative of the god, an act of unmerited love or grace. It followed, then, that man was continually in a state of indebtedness, or "sin", ever at the mercy of his divine creditor. When the god for some reason decided to withhold his seminal bounty, all life perished and there was nothing man could do about it.

The awareness of his insufficiency that makes the Psalmist cry plaintively: "What is man that thou rememberest him...?" (Ps 8:4 [Heb 5]) has had an important and largely deleterious effect on man's self-consciousness. On the one hand it urged upon him humility, and served as a brake to his self-aggrandizement over his fellows. The Roman general in his triumphal chariot had by him a slave continually to remind him, above the roars of popular acclaim, "Look back; remember you are but a man."[52] On the other hand, a basic insecurity tended to restrict man's natural curiosity and willingness to experiment dangerously, and has served his political and ecclesiastical masters rather better than his own spiritual and economic advancement.

Cultically, this state of indebtedness gave rise to the idea that man should make the god some token reimbursement, a sacrifice, a kind of atonement which might, in some small degree, restore the balance between benefactor and beneficiary. Since the first-born of men and beasts, and the first-reaped fruits of harvest, were considered to be more favourably endowed with the source of life than later progeny, and thus the more precious and strong, they were chosen for restoration to the deity.[53] The blood, containing the breath of life, the holy spirit,[54] taboo even now among Jews and Muslims, was first poured back into the earth's womb,[55] and the flesh then consumed by the element that had created it, fire. Alternatively, part at least of the flesh was eaten by the god's representatives, the priests.[56]

This idea of the atoning sacrifice had an important influence on later developments of the cult, particularly in Christianity and its immediate forerunners. Here attention was centred upon one particular piece of vegetation, deemed more powerfully endued with the god than any other, and whose "sacrifice" and consumption by the initiate was thought to restore the lost sense of balance, to heal the rift, and to make possible a mystical unity with the god.

Summarizing, then: we should not look for a multiplicity of gods in the ancient world, but rather many aspects of the one deity of fertility, the creative force that gives earth and its creatures life. The god was the seed, his name and functions finding verbal expression in the one Sumerian phoneme U; the whole fertility philosophy on which the various cults of the ancient Near East centred we may term simply a U-culture. The god expressed his seed from heaven as a mighty penis ejaculating sperm at orgasm. It entered the womb of mother earth through the labia, the furrows of the land, and formed a great reservoir of potency in the heart of the world. There gestation took place in the furnace of the terrestrial uterus. There, too, was thought to be the source of all knowledge, since the creative semen of the god was also the Word, acquisition of which by man gave him part of divine omniscience. It followed that those plants which were able to tap this power of knowledge to a greater degree than others, the sources of hallucinatory drugs, could impart to those who imbibed their juice "knowledge of the gods".

IV

Plants and Drugs

Vegetation was the fruit of god's union with earth. Like any other off-spring, some of the children were strong and vigorous, others weaklings. Some trees had wood that was hard and suitable for building houses and ships, others rotted quickly and proved treacherous. Some woods were springy and full of life, and gave the archer his bow. Others cracked easily and served only for kindling. Some fruits were soft and sweet, but others bitter and full of some strange power that could kill or cure.

Man's first experiments in the use of plants as drugs must have been extremely hazardous. Doubtless he watched first their effects on animals, as the shepherd Melampus is said to have discovered the purging properties of Hellebore by noting its effect on his goats.[1] Gradually experience, often painfully acquired, would have given the inhabitants of each locality a primitive pharmacopoeia for their use, and visitors from elsewhere would have introduced new plants and drugs.

Over the course of time a store of experiential knowledge would have accumulated and been made the subject of special study by a few of the elders, the "wise men".[2] Later the physicians were to become a privileged class of people, wielding tremendous power among their fellows, and ensuring a continuance of their position by maintaining strict secrecy over their craft.

Our first medical text is a Sumerian tablet from the end of the third millennium,[3] listing remedies made from milk, snake-skin, tortoiseshell, salt and saltpetre, and from plants and trees like cassia, myrtle, asafoetida, thyme, willow, pear, fir, fig and date. Later we find an abundance of medical tablets and botanical lists with their Sumerian and Accadian names for the trees and plants, their fruits, barks, saps and resins, and their preparation and uses in medicine. This kind of careful cataloguing of plant-life does not appear in the Western world until the fifth and fourth centuries BC, and particularly with Theophrastus (372-287 BC), a pupil of both Plato and Aristotle. His *Enquiry into Plants*[4] lists some 400 species with their forms, habits, habitats, fructification and cultivation, and their uses. Clearly he must have put the services of his two thousand or so students to good use since he quotes the results of first-hand enquiry in places which he could hardly have visited himself in one lifetime. He was also able to avail himself of the observations made into local botanical specimens by his contemporary Alexander the Great and his armies as they ranged widely over the Near and Far East.

Thereafter we have to wait until the first Christian century for a comparable systematic study of plants. Dioscorides, a contemporary of Claudius and Nero, has left us, in his *De Materia Medica*,[5] a conscious attempt to systematize rather than merely list the drugs he records. He separates his remedies into their respective vegetable, animal, and mineral sources. His descriptions are terse and acute, and largely free from "old wives' tales".

Happily, from our point of view, about the same time Pliny the Elder (AD 23-79) was writing a rather less "scientific" work, abounding in folk-lore as well as more sober gleanings from earlier botanists. His *Natural History*[6] is a mine of information, not so much for his descriptions of the plants and their identifications, many of which are quite unreliable anyway, as for the stories about them which had come down in popular mythology and folk-lore. He describes the superstitions that attended the plant's extraction from the ground, its preparation, and uses. He gives us stories about how their qualities were first observed by the ancients and why they were named as they were. Of course, factually his tales are often quite irrelevant, but very often there are elements which relate to a probable decipherment of the name and thus a positive link with another plant or drug listed quite separately. In our quest for the sources of ideas and mythologies, this kind of information is more important than detailed descriptions of the plants' physiology.

Old writings thought to contain secrets of the healing arts came to be highly prized. Josephus, in the first Christian century, says of the Jewish sect called the Essenes that they display "an extraordinary interest in the writings of the ancients, singling out in particular those which make for the welfare of the soul and body; with the help of these, and with a view to the treatment of diseases, they investigate medicinal roots and the properties of stones".[7] Such writings were often ascribed popularly to Solomon, credited in the Bible with knowledge of "trees, from the cedar that is in Lebanon, to the hyssop that grows out of the wall"' (I Kings 4:33 [Heb 5:13]). Later tradition ascribed to the king even greater powers, "knowledge of the art used against demons for the benefit and healing of men", as Josephus says elsewhere.[8] He adds that Solomon "composed incantations by which illnesses are relieved, and left behind exorcisms with which those possessed of demons drive them out, never to return".

Interestingly, the practice of this kind of Solomonic demonology was not dead in the first century. Josephus records actually seeing a cure effected by "this very great power", by one Eleazar, a fellow-country-man, and very possibly an Essene. "He put to the nose of the possessed man a ring which had under its seal one of the roots prescribed by Solomon. Then, as the man smelled it, he drew out the demon through his nostrils, and when the man at once fell down, he adjured the demon never to come back into him, speaking Solomon's name and reciting the incantations which he had composed."[9]

Identifying the drug-producing plants, then, was not the only factor in early pharmaceutical and medical practice. It was one thing to be able to recognize a drug plant, even to know its popular name; it was another to know how to extract and purify the active ingredient, and, above all, to know the right dosage. There were other complications. Some drugs were so powerful that they could only be safely administered on certain days, or after lengthy preparation of the body and mind. It was also well known that an over-powerful drug had to be countered with another having the opposite effect, as in the case of the purge Hellebore,[10] and some narcotics which had to be offset with stimulants. To know the correct dosages in these cases required an appreciation of the susceptibility of the patient to the drug's effects, perhaps the most difficult calculation of all. Much depended on the recipient's "fate" allotted him at his birth, the factor that determined his individuality, his physical stature, the colour of his eyes, and so on. Only the astrologer could tell this, so that the art of medicine was itself dependent for success on astrology and the considerable astronomical knowledge this presupposed.

Just such an astrological chart has come down to us from the Essene library recovered recently from the Dead Sea caves.[11] It is written in code, composed mainly by reversing the normal order of the letters, that is, reading from left to right instead of right to left in the usual fashion of Semitic scripts, and substituting Greek and other alphabets for some of the square-letter Hebrew writing found elsewhere in the Dead Sea Scrolls. The document is unfortunately only fragmentary, and has been put together from scores of tiny pieces found scattered on the floor of a cave. Nevertheless, the purport is clear. It is a chart of the physical and spiritual characteristics to be expected of people born in certain sections of the Zodiac. Thus, someone born under the sign Taurus would possess, among other features, long and thin thighs and toes. The spiritual make-up of the subjects was reckoned as so many parts of "light" and so many of "darkness", the total available for distribution being nine, presumably related to the months of gestation in the womb. The Taurus person would have a mere three parts of light to six of darkness.

More uncouth was the subject whose zodiacal assignment is missing from the text, but whose physical characteristics are marked with a certain coarseness, such as having thick fingers, hairy thighs, and short and stubby toes, and no less than eight parts derived from "the House or Pit of Darkness" and but one from "the House of Light". The best-favoured subject recorded in the extant text is a curly-bearded gentleman of medium height, with "eyes like black and glowing coals", well ordered teeth, and fine, tapering fingers, and the opposite apportionment of light and darkness to the last-mentioned bully.

The Dead Sea Scrolls, like the New Testament, make much of the antagonism between "Light" and "Darkness", and it is usually assumed that this everywhere is equivalent to "good" and "evil". Thus the so-called "Children of Light" are those who do good, and the "Children of Darkness" are those who want only harm their fellow-men. However, this distinction is not necessarily what we should call a moral one: the fruits of the "spirit of Truth", with which Light seems to be identified, begin with "healing", "peace in longevity", and "fruitfulness". The "ways of the spirit of Falsehood" are greed, wickedness, lies, haughtiness and pride, deceit, cruelty, bad temper, and so on,[12] what we should call, in general, faults of intemperance and arrogance, an imbalance of character. We might label such defects as "moral wrong" but in the eyes of the ancient philosophers, they were inherited predispositions occasioned largely by a man's fate allotted him at birth according to the stars. Medicine was as much a part of righting this imbalance of "moral" character as religion; the two were, in fact, inseparable. To administer the drugs correctly one had to know just what were the inherited traits of the patient's character, and for this enquiry, as our cryptic scroll from the Dead Sea shows, the physician looked to the stars.

The combined arts of medicine and astrology were known and practised by the Sumerians and their Mesopotamian successors, as we know from their cuneiform records as well as the repute they enjoyed in this respect in the ancient world. "Stand fast in your enchantments and your many sorceries, with which you have laboured from your youth", cries Isaiah to "the virgin daughter of Babylon"; "perhaps you may be able to succeed, perhaps you may inspire terror. You are wearied with your many counsels; let them stand forth and save you, those who divide the heavens, who gaze at the stars, who at the new moons predict what shall befall you" (Isa 47:12ff.).

Their cultural, if not ethnic successors were the Magi, the "wise men" of the Gospel birth story (Matt 2:1). They were the great drug-pedlars of the ancient world and are often cited by Pliny as sources of therapeutic folk-lore and of the less familiar names of plants and drugs. He treats them with contempt for the most part, but nevertheless quotes them at great length and says that the philosopher Pythagoras, first in his view to compose a book on the properties of plants, and his colleague Democritus, "visited the Magi of Persia, Arabia, Ethiopia, and Egypt, and so amazed were the ancients at these books that they positively asserted quite unbelievable statements".[13]

Dioscorides quotes them as sources of "special" names of plants under the title "prophets" (*prophētai*). This is particularly interesting because the old Sumerian word for "physician", A-ZU or I-ZU, literally, "water-, oil-expert" also stands for "prophet, seer". The name Essene, known otherwise only in its Greek, transliterated form, comes probably from the same root.[14]

Prognostication was always an important part of medicine. "It is most excellent for a physician to cultivate special insight (*pronoia*, knowing things about the patient without being told them)", writes a contributor to the *Hippocratic Collection* (after 300 BC). "Since he fore-knows and foretells the past, present, and future ... men would have confidence to entrust themselves to his care ... By an early forecast in each case he can tend aright those who have a chance to survive and by foreseeing who will die ... he will escape blame." However, there was much more to this pronoia than merely knowing who was likely to be in a position to pay your bill at the end of the treatment. The physician had to be able to communicate with the spirit world, to exercise influence over the gods and demons that controlled health and sickness. Each disease and each part of the body had its own demon. To know its name was to tap some of its power and use it on behalf of the patient. So Jesus enquires of the unclean spirit his name and is thus able to banish him into the unfortunate pigs (Mark 5:9).

The Greek word *daimōn* derives, through the Persian *dēw* (there is a strong linguistic affinity between m and w), from a probable Sumerian original *DA-IA-U-NA, meaning "having power over fertility". The demon thus had the power of affecting, for good or ill, birth and death and the various stages of health in between. The medicinal drug had similar powers, and the Hebrew word for "be sick", *dawah*, and its cognate noun in Arabic meaning "medicine", come from the same root. So the demon of health and sickness and the drug are radically one and the same.[15]

If it was vital for the doctor-prophet to know the names of the disease-demons he was trying to counteract, it was just as important to be able to call upon their opposite numbers, the powers of healing contained in the drugs. These were the angels whose names formed an important part of the Essenes' secret knowledge, to preserve which the initiate was put under "tremendous oaths".[16] The basic principle is the same when Josephus' friend Eleazar called upon the name of Solomon as he administered the prescribed root,[17] and Peter pronounces the name of Jesus Christ of Nazareth over the lame man (Acts 3:6), an incantation tried with apparently less success by "the seven sons of Sceva" (Acts 19:13f.).

Since all life derives from the divine seed, it follows that the most powerful healing drug would be the pure, unadulterated semen of the god. Some plants were thought to have sap or resin approximating to this, their "purity" or "sanctity" in this regard being measured by their power as drugs to kill or cure or intoxicate. In Sumerian the words for "live" and "intoxicate" are the same, TIN, and the "tree of life", GEShTIN, is the "vine". Similarly in the Greek *oinos* and the Hebrew yayin, "wine", there is probably a common Sumerian root *IA-U-NU, "semen-seed".[18]

The use of the name Jesus (Greek *iēsūs*) as an invocation for healing was appropriate enough. Its Hebrew original, *yehōshūa'*, Joshua, comes from Sumerian *IA-U-ShU-A (ShUSh), "semen, which saves, restores, heals". Hellenized Jews used for "Joshua" the Greek name *iasōn*, Jason, very properly, since iasōn, "healer", and the deponent verb *iaomai*, "heal", come from the same Sumerian source. In the New Testament taunt, "Physician, heal thyself" (Luke 4:23), we probably have a direct allusion to this meaning, as we certainly have in Jesus' title "Saviour", Greek *sōtēr*, the first element of which reflects the same Sumerian word *ShU*, "save", and so is rightly used in Greek for saving from disease, harm, peril, etc., and is a common epithet of Zeus and kings.

The fertility god Dionysus (Greek *Dionusos*), whose cult emblem was the erect phallus, was also a god of healing, and his name, when broken down to its original parts, IA-U-NU-ShUSh, is almost identical with that of Jesus, having NU, "seed", only in addition: "Semen, seed that saves", and is comparable with the Greek *Nosios*, "Healer", an epithet of Zeus.[19]

The fertility deity, then, appeared in all living beings, but in some more than others. Those plants especially endowed with power to heal or kill, the drug plants, became the subject of study among the witch-doctors, prophets, and priests of the ancient world and their experiential knowledge was passed on within their professional communities and zealously guarded. As well as the names and identities of the plants, they preserved those of the disease demons and the protective angels whose power was needed to secure and use the precious drugs. Furthermore, an essential part of "healing" or giving life was to know the patient's physiological and psychological make-up, and the degrees of the "spirits of light and darkness" that he had been granted by fate at his birth. These traits of character and bodily constitution could be determined by astrological means, so that the early doctors were also astrologers. He was also a prophet, a prognosticator. The arts of healing and religion were inseparable.

V

Plant Names and the Mysteries of the Fungus

It is in the secrecy surrounding the collection and transmission of the old medical prescriptions that we can see the beginnings of the mystery cults of the ancient Near East. If we are going to penetrate their secrets we have somehow to discover the names of their prime ingredients, the plants and drugs the prophets and doctors dispensed. We have now at least the advantage of knowing the most ancient language of the area and can in many cases begin to decipher the names of the plants and their attendant angels and demons. But it has to be recognized that of all branches of research into the life of the ancient world, identification of plant names is one of the most difficult.

The old botanists were as aware of the problem as the modern researcher. "An added difficulty in botany", wrote Pliny some nineteen hundred years ago, "is the variety of names given to the same plant in different districts".[1] The more "strange" the herb, the more noteworthy its characteristics, the greater the number of folk-names. Dioscorides, for instance, gives some two-score names to the Mandrake,[2] that famous aphrodisiac with which Leah purchased a night of connubial bliss with Jacob (Gen 30:14ff.), and whose narcotic properties could not suffice to give poor Othello "that sweet sleep which thou owedst yesterday".[3]

Until comparatively recently, botanists lacked adequate methods of classification, so that plants tended to be grouped together on the basis of what we nowadays would consider secondary characteristics. Thus speaking of the Ground-pine, Pliny records that "a third variety has the same smell and therefore the same name".[4] Even now, the inexactitude of local plant names is the despair of field botanists. Pliny felt as sorely frustrated: "The reason why more herbs are not familiar", he writes, "is because experience of them is confined to illiterate country-folk, who form the only class of people living among them. Moreover, when crowds of medical men are to be met everywhere, nobody wants to look for them. Many simples, also, lack names, though their properties are known . . . The most disgraceful reason for this scanty knowledge is that even those who possess it refuse to teach it, just as though they would themselves lose what they have imparted to others."[5]

We have now one great philological advantage over all previous researchers into the identification of plant-names. Despite the long gap in time between the Sumerian botanists and their Greek and Roman successors it now appears that many of the important names of plants remained virtually unchanged. During the course of thousands of years those titles became attached to different plants: hence the confusion in nomenclatures of which Pliny speaks. But if we can know what the name originally meant, what characteristic of the plant or its drug was foremost in the minds of its first chroniclers, we have a much better chance of discovering its original identity.

For example, we all know what the Paeony looks like: a beautiful herbaceous or shrubby perennial plant, bearing large double blooms in crimson, rose, blush, and similar colours, a joy to behold in our cottage gardens in May. Pliny says the name came from the physician god Apollo, whose chant of praise bears the same name, our "paean". But he goes on to say it "grows on shaded mountains, having a stem among the leaves about four inches high, which bears on its top four or five growths like almonds, in them being a large amount of seed, red and black. The plant also prevents the mocking delusions that the Fauns bring us in our sleep." Apparently, one has to be careful how you pick this precious herb. It is best done at night-time, "because the woodpecker of Mars, should he see the act, will attack the eyes in its defence".[6]

Well, of course, this is not our crimson Paeony. It is some magic plant, "the first to be discovered", as our Roman botanist tells us. For various reasons which will become apparent, we can now differentiate this very special "Paeony" from other plants to which the name was given, and identify it with the subject of our present study, the *Amanita muscaria*, the sacred mushroom. Doubtless, the flower Paeony gained the name originally because its flower was thought to resemble the colour of the red-topped fungus. It would not have been possible to deduce the relationship between the flower and the mushroom merely on the description given by Pliny: one had first to decipher the name "Paeony" and discover its original significance and point of common reference.

In this case, we can see its original in a Sumerian *BAR-IA-U-NA, "capsule of fecundity; womb", and connect it with a number of other mushroom names relating to the little "womb" or volva from which the stem of the fungus emerges.[7]

To take another example: Greek knows the plant Navelwort as *Kotulēdōn*, Latin *Cotyledon*. The word means any socket-shaped cavity, such as that of a hip-joint, or the inside of a cup, or the hollow of a hand. In botanical language the Greek word comes to mean the first or "seed leaves" of a plant, usually of simple form, but it can be applied to many plants having some part of them of a "cup" or "hollow" form. To discover some more particular reference of the name it is necessary to trace it back to its constituent elements. This we can now do for the first time, showing that its Sumerian source provided a phrase, *GU-TAL-U-DUN, meaning "ball-and-socket", or, particularly applied, "penis-and-vulva".[8] It is the sexual allusions of the name which, as we shall see, brought it into the range of fungus nomenclature. Furthermore, the specific reference in Greek of *Kotulēdōn* to "hip-joint" gave rise to a number of myths having to do with "mushroom" figures having their hips disjointed or being pierced in the hip or side of the body.[9]

For the decipherment of plant-names helps us not only to identify those characteristics which caused them to be applied to various species but also to discover the original sources and meanings of the tales which grew up around the plants and their drugs. It is becoming clear that many of the classical and biblical stories are based on pieces of vegetation, and in particular on the sacred mushroom. There is one overt piece of vegetation mythology in the Old Testament parable of Jotham in the book of Judges. In the story the trees of the forest ask representatives of each species to act as their king. The olive, fig, and vine are too busy giving of their fruits to men, and in desperation the trees ask the diminutive mushroom (as we may now most probably identify the plant),[10] who insists that in that case they must all take refuge under its canopy, that is, that they treat him as their protector, king indeed[11] (Judg 9:7-15).

This is a parable, rather like some of those in the New Testament, where the explanation is appended for the benefit of the listeners. Perhaps all plant mythology began in this way, each story having one point to make which was brought out by the narrator's explanation at the end. In course of time, the instructive element was lost and the parable told and retold without its exegetical commentary, in the end to circulate as just a good yarn. As antiquity came to lend certain of such stories a gravity perhaps not originally intended, they became accepted into a body of cultic teaching by religious authorities, who then set about providing their own explanations and homiletics and accorded the tales divine authority.

A vegetation myth could be adapted by a later writer, fully aware of its original significance, to serve as the medium for some new teaching. Such may be the case with the story of Jonah in the Old Testament, the prophet who was told to preach repentance to Nineveh. We are now able positively to identify this story as one of a mushroom group, since the famous plant which gave Jonah shade, which "came into being in a night and perished in a night", and was subject to the depredation of worms, was certainly a fungus.[12] Even the prophet's name Jonah reflects mushroom nomenclature,[13] and the quelling of the storm motif is found elsewhere in related mythology.[14] But the "moral" of the tale, in so far as we can understand it, seems to have no particular mushroom significance.

As we have said, the first step to discovering the nature of vegetation stories and the particular plant or tree that was originally involved is to decipher the proper names. However, in the case of plants regarded as especially powerful or "magic" like the mushroom, additional problems face the enquirer. The strange shapes and manner of growth of the fungus, along with its poisonous reputation, combined to evoke feelings of awe and dread in the minds of simple folk. Indeed, there must be few people even today who do not sense some half-fearful fascination at the sight of the mushroom, and shrink from taking it into their hands. Since certain of the species contain drugs with marked hallucinatory properties,[15] it is not surprising that the mushroom should have become the centre of a mystery cult in the Near East which persisted for thousands of years. There seems good evidence that from there it swept into India in the cult of the Soma some 3,500 years ago; it certainly flourished in Siberia until quite recent times, and is found even today in certain parts of South America.[16]

Partly because of the religious use of the sacred mushroom, and the fearful respect with which countryfolk have always treated it, its more original names became taboo and folk-names and epithets proliferated at their expense. It is as if, in our own language, the only name by which we knew the mushroom was the folk-name "toadstool", and that some researcher of the future was faced with the problem of deciding what species of plant life served as the habitual perch of large frogs. Thus the extraordinary situation has arisen that this most important mushroom cult, from which much of the mythology of the ancient Near East sprang, has been almost completely overlooked by the historians. In the Bible, for instance, where mushroom mythology plays a most important part, the word "mushroom" has been nowhere noted although one of its most ancient names, Hebrew *kotereth*, Accadian *katarru,* appears many times in its quite straightforward meaning of "mushroom-shaped capital of a pillar" (I Kgs 7:16, etc).[17]

Even among the Greek and Roman botanical works there are scarcely a dozen different words which have been recognized as relating specifically to the fungus, and the whole of extant Semitic literature can produce few more.[18] Mycology, as the study of fungi is called after the Greek *mukēs,* "mushroom", is a comparatively modern science.[19] Although the ancients knew that the mushroom's apparent seedlessness put it into a category of natural life all its own, they did not always differentiate it from other plants, so that its names have to be disentangled from those of quite unrelated species.

In seeking for mushroom folk-names and epithets, one of our main sources obviously will be its distinctive shape of a slender stem supporting an arched canopy, like a sunshade. This characteristic was made much of in mythology, like the Jotham and Jonah stories already referred to. Extended to gigantic proportions this figure is reflected in such imagery as huge men like Atlas holding up the canopy of heaven, or of mountains like Olympus serving the dual function of supporting the sky and providing a connecting link between the gods and earth.[20]

One of the ways we can now identify the Mandrake as the mushroom is that one of its Greek names, *Antimimon,* is traceable to a Sumerian original, meaning "heavenly shade", a reference to the canopy of the opened fungus. Incidentally, the same root, *GIG-AN-TI, gave the Greek *gigamtes,* and in English, "giants", in pursuance of the imagery of the "giant" holding aloft the arch of heaven.[21]

Above all, the mushroom provoked sexual imagery and terminology. The manner of its rapid growth from the volva, or "womb", the rapid erection of its stem like a sexually stirred penis, and its glans-like head, all stimulated phallic names. Of such is the Hebrew *kotereth,* just referred to, and, coming from the same Sumerian original, GU-TAR, "top of the head: penis", the most common Semitic name for the mush-room, *phutr* (Arabic), *pītrā'* (Aramaic), portrayed in the New Testa-ment myth as Peter.[22]

One of the names given the Paeony by Pliny is *Glycyside*. The name, which is meaningless in Latin or Greek, is but a jumbled form of an old Sumerian plant-name, UKUSh-TI-GIL-LA, meaning "bolt-gourd; mushroom".[23] The reference to the "bolt" is occasioned by the primi-tive key which consisted mainly of a rod surmounted by a knob,[24] with a right-angled bend at the other end.[25] It was pushed through the key-hole and simply lifted the latch on the other side. The phallic imagery of the "knobbed shaft" gave the "key" a sexual significance for the purposes of nomenclature which appears in many instances. The penis-mushroom was thus in mythological terms, the "key" of the earth, the way to the underworld, the "Peter", as it were, against which the gates of Hades would not prevail (Matt 16:18f.; Rev 1:18).

Decipherment of plant and drug names not only allows us to share the imagery their shapes provoked in the minds of the ancient botanists, but to learn of the demonic power they were supposed to wield. This is particularly important with regard to the Mandrake fungus. The Sumerian from which the Greek *Mandragoras* and our "Mandrake" came was *NAM-TAR-AGAR, "demon or fate-plant of the field". The consonants *m* and *n* have changed places and T has shifted to the closely related sound *d*.

This particular decipherment has the added interest of revealing the identity and source of another very famous name in drug folk-lore, the "Nectar" of the gods. The Sumerian M of NAM-TAR has made its common dialectal change to Indo-European *k* and thus produced the Greek *Nektar,* our Nectar, seen now to be none other than the sacred mushroom, food indeed of the gods.[26]

It followed, from the reasoning of the ancient philosophers, outlined earlier,[27] that if you knew the names of the demonic plants, like the sacred mushroom, you could control them to some extent. It might be possible to make them grow where and when you wanted, and, having found them, pronunciation of the name would enable the finder to take the herb from the ground with impunity. Furthermore, if, like the Man-drake, it had some special drug property which, taken without sufficient care and preparation might occasion bodily harm, it was necessary at certain points in the cultic ritual to speak the sacred name.[28]

There grew up, therefore, a body of cultic tradition primarily concerned with the accurate transmission of the special, occult names of the drug plants and their incantations. This was no more than an extension of the secret knowledge of the old witch-doctor or prophetic fraternities.[29] A combination of a highly sophisticated expertise in the nature and use of potent drugs with, at times, a pretence to political power, made such communities a menace to government and drew forth a vicious reaction from the authorities.

The whole point of a mystery cult was that few people knew its secret doctrines. So far as possible, the initiates did not commit their special knowledge to writing. Normally the secrets of the sect were transmitted orally, novices being required to learn direct from their mentors by heart, and placed under the most violent oaths never to disclose the details even under torture. When such special instruction was committed to writing, care would be taken that it should be read only by the members of the sect. This could be done by using a special code or cypher, as is the case with certain of the Dead Sea Scrolls.[30] However, discovery of such obviously coded material on a person would render him suspect to the authorities. Another way of passing information was to conceal the message, incantations or special names within a document ostensibly concerned with a quite different subject.

Plant mythology, known for thousands of years over the whole of the ancient world, provided the New Testament cryptographers with their "cover". Mushroom stories abounded in the Old Testament. The Christians believed, like their Essene brethren, that they were the true spiritual heirs to ancient Israel. So it was an obvious device to convey to the scattered cells of the cult reminders of their most sacred doctrines and incantatory names and expressions concealed within a story of a "second Moses", another Lawgiver, named after the patriarch's successor in office Joshua (Greek *Iēsous,* "Jesus"). Thus was born the Gospel myth of the New Testament. How far it succeeded in deceiving the authorities, Jewish and Roman, is doubtful. Certainly the Roman records speak with loathing of the Christians and they were hounded with extreme ferocity reserved for political troublemakers within the realm.[31] Those most deceived appear to have been the sect who took over the name of "Christian" and who formed the basis of the Church, the history of which forms no part of the present study. What is of far greater importance is that we may now break the code and discover the secret names of the Holy Plant, as it was called from the earliest times, and gain a deeper insight than ever before possible into the nature of the cult and its place in the ancient world.

In the following chapters we shall look in detail at the way this codification within the biblical stories was achieved. Foremost among the literary devices used was word-play or punning, already well-established as an important and widespread means of deriving hidden meanings from sacred texts.

VI

The Key of the Kingdom

In a passage dealing with the wisdom and apparent foolishness of Christian preaching, a New Testament writer includes these words:

> For Jews demand signs and Greeks seek wisdom, but we preach Christ crucified, a stumbling-block to Jews and folly to Gentiles . . . (I Cor 1:22f.).

In these words is an ingenious word-play or pun on two words for the sacred mushroom, the "Christ crucified", and it will serve as an example of this literary device and its extensive use in the New Testament.

The word "stumbling-block" (Greek *skandalon,* our "scandal") is properly used of a "trap" or "snare". It denotes a stick or bolt upon which bait is placed and which, if tripped by the prey, sets off the trap itself. So metaphorically it is used for any impediment which hinders or traps an unwitting person. The Greek word *skandalon,* we can now appreciate, originally meant "bolt" like its Aramaic equivalent *tiqlā',* and we saw earlier how the phallic mushroom was called a "bolt-plant" because the shape of the primitive key or bolt was in essence a short rod surmounted by a knob, and so likened to an erect penis.[1] Thus we may decipher the first part of the passage: "to the Jews" (that is, in the Jewish tongue, Aramaic), the "Christ crucified", the semen-anointed, erected mushroom,[2] is a *tiqlā',* "bolt-plant".

Another name of the mushroom is the Greek *Mōrios,*[3] and the word for "folly" is *mōria;* so the writer to Corinthians adds ". . . and folly (*mōria*) to the Gentiles" (that is, the Greeks), thereby completing the word-play and confirming the one against the other.

An amusing pun on the same Aramaic *tiqlā',* "bolt-mushroom" name, occurs in the story of Peter's encounter with the taxmen. "On their arrival in Capernaum", runs the story, "the collectors of the half-shekel tax went up to Peter and said, 'Does not your master pay the tax?'"

Peter assured them that he did, like any good Jew, since it was an obligatory levy for Temple funds. On receiving his report of the incident, Jesus reacted strongly. "'However', he concluded, 'so that we should not put a stumbling-block in their way (*skandalisōmen*), go to the sea and cast a hook, and take up the first fish that comes up, and when you open its mouth you will find a shekel'" (Matt 17:24ff.).

The word-play here is mainly on the various meanings of *tiqlā*', and its cognates: "mushroom", "shekel", and "tax".[4] The intriguing nonsense about the shekel in the fish's mouth has all the appearance of a piece of earthy folk-humour. The "knobbed-bolt" epithet of the mushroom, *tiqlā*', has strong phallic allusions, as we have seen. The fish's mouth also has a sexual connotation, being envisaged as the large lips of the woman's genitals. The "bearded" mullet in particular was credited with lustful tendencies and associated with the womb.[5] To have a "shekel (bolt) in the fish's mouth" was probably a euphemism for coitus.

Pliny has a curious little note which seems to support the idea that "shekels" and mushrooms were connected in folk-lore. He says that he knew "for a fact" that some years previously a Roman official in Spain had "happened, when biting a truffle (*tuber*), to have come upon a denarius inside it which bent his front teeth".[6] Pliny recounts this highly improbable "fact" to support his quite erroneous view that the mysterious fungus was a "lump of earthy substance balled together". Is it perhaps a Latinized version of a "shekel in the fish's mouth" name of the mushroom?

The Old Testament also contains a mushroom story based on the *tiqlā*', "bolt-fungus" – "shekel" word-play. It concerns the mysterious message written on King Belshazzar's dining-room wall. It will be recalled that the Babylonian monarch, in the days of Daniel the Jewish prophet, was about to sit down to what promised to be the Babylonian orgy of a lifetime. Scarcely had the drinks begun to flow and the party to warm up generally when a disembodied hand suddenly appeared before the astonished king and began writing the strange device: MENE, MENE, TEKEL, and PARSIN. (Dan 5:5-25). Much perturbed, he called for his magicians and other men of wisdom to explain the words to him; but all to no avail. Finally, in despair he called the hero Daniel, who treated the company to a long harangue on the evils of the Babylonian monarchy and Belshazzar and his forbears in particular.

He ended this enlightening discourse with his interpretation of the fateful words: "MENE, God has numbered the days of your kingdom and brought it to an end; TEKEL, you have been weighed in the balances and found wanting; PERES, your kingdom is divided and given to the Medes and Persians." In each of the mysterious words, Daniel found an Aramaic pun: MENE, on the root *m-n-y,* "number"; TEKEL, on the root *t-q-l,* "weigh" (cognate with the Hebrew *sheqel,* "weight, coin"); and PERES, a twofold word-play on the root *p-r-s,* "divide in two", and *Parsi,* "Persian", the Babylonians' hated enemies.

The introductory formula, MENE, MENE, is comparable in form and content with the invocation, Eloi, Eloi (E-LA-UIA) that preceded the secret mushroom name (see Ch. XVII). It refers probably to the Semitic god of fate, *Meni* (Isa 65:11; RSV "Fortune"), equivalent of the Sumerian NAM-TAR, "fate demon",[7] source of the mushroom designations Nectar and Mandrake. TEKEL is our "bolt-" fungus, and PARSIN is the Sumerian BAR-SIL, "womb", a reference to the mushroom volva. We meet PARSIN in the Greek form *Perseia,* as the magic herb that sprang from the ground after Perseus had dropped the chape of his scabbard (*mukēs,* also meaning "mushroom") whilst flying over the site of what was to become Mycenae (the "mushroom" city).[8] The combination TEKEL and PARSIN will then be of the "ball-and-socket", "penis-and-vulva" type of mushroom name.[9]

In his pseudo-translation of the awful message on the wall, Daniel refers TEKEL to the Semitic root of "shekel" just like the Gospel story about the tax-collectors. Apart from the pun involved, the particular interest of the tale for our present study is that the writer of Daniel has shown that the device used so often in the New Testament of following a genuine name for the sacred fungus with a false translation for the sake of the plot, was an established part of mushroom mythology long before the writer of Mark's gospel "explained" Boanerges as "Sons of Thunder".[10]

The "stumbling-block" figure occurs frequently in the New Testament, but of particular note is its application to the apostle Peter following Jesus' prophecy of his forthcoming suffering, "Peter took him and began to rebuke him, saying, 'God forbid, Lord! This shall never happen to you!' But he turned and said to Peter, 'Get behind me, Satan! You are a stumbling-block to me . . .'" (Matt 16:22f). Peter's name is an obvious play on the Semitic *pitrā',* "mushroom", and we have already seen that his patronymic, Bar-jonah, is really a fungus name cognate with Paeonia, the Holy Plant.[11] Now called a "stumbling-block", he is given the *tiqlā'*, "bolt-mushroom" name,[12] a theme which is repeated elsewhere in that over-emphasized and completely misunderstood passage about having the keys of the kingdom:

> And I tell you, you are Peter, and on this rock[13] I will build my church, and the gates of Hades shall not prevail against it. I will give you the keys of the kingdom of heaven . . . (Matt 16:18f).

The sacred fungus was the "bolt" or "key" that gave access to heaven and to hell, a double reference to its shape as a knobbed bolt for opening doors, and to its ability to open the way to new and exciting mystical experiences.[14]

Calling the apostle "Satan" is in line with his other title of Cephas. Both names are in fact plays on designations of the mushroom, elsewhere seen of that other "bulb" plant, the onion. Greek and Latin apply the name *sētanion, setania* to the onion, and Latin has *caepa, cepa* for that vegetable, cognate with the French *cèpe, ceps,* "mushroom".[15]

The well-known word-play in Matt 16:18: "you are Peter (Petros), and upon this rock *(petra)* I shall build my church . . . " can now be seen as of much greater relevance to the cult than a mere pun on Peter's title Cephas and the Aramaic word for "stone", *kēphā'*. The real point of the whole passage is the word-play on the names of the sacred fungus that "Peter" represented.

The commission of authority: "I will give you the keys of the kingdom of heaven, and whatever you bind on earth shall be bound in heaven, and whatever you loose on earth shall be loosed in heaven" (Matt 16:19), has its verbal basis in an important Sumerian mushroom name *MASh-BA(LA)G-ANTA-TAB-BA-RI,[16] read as "thou art the permitter (releaser) of the kingdom" by a play on three or four Aramaic words spun out of the Sumerian title.[17] It has, probably, like most other of the directives and homilies of the "cover" story, no real-life significance. Least of all would the passage have been taken by the cult members that one of their number should take upon himself the kind of spiritual authority indicated by the face reading of the text. The sole prerogative of "binding" and "loosing" lay with God. To the worshipper of the sacred fungus, the deity was present in the mushroom and offered his servants the "key" to a new and wonderful mystic experience. It was this "re-birth", as it was called, that cleared away the debts of the past and gave promise of a future free from the cultic "sin" that destroyed the initiate's free communion with God.

It was left to a later development of the cult, also calling themselves "Christians" and reading the words at their face value, to accord to their leader and his designates a divine authority for forgiving sins and pronouncing on moral matters which Judaism would have found abhorrent, even blasphemous.

If it seems strange to us that the writers of these stories should have used such a trivial literary device as punning so extensively, it should be remembered that they were heirs to a very long tradition of this kind of word-spinning. The Old Testament is full of it, particularly where proper names are concerned, and very many more instances almost certainly lie beneath the surface, where writers are playing with dialectal forms of the words which have become lost over the centuries. Furthermore, it is now becoming clear that many of the Old Testament traditions have reached us in a Semitic dialect which was not the one in which they were composed, so that the original word-play which they expressed has been lost.[18]

Again, what we call "the lowest kind of wit" was much more meaningful for the ancient writer. Words to him were not just vocalic utterances communicating ideas from one mind to another; they were expressions of real power in themselves. The word had an entity of its own; once released it could effect the desire of its creator. The god's or the prophet's word was a thing to be feared, and if maleficent, "turned back" as the Bible would say. Words which looked alike, we might think accidentally, were considered actually to be connected in some way. Therefore deriving some moral tale or religious instruction from a single word in the sacred text, even though it be interpreted in a way at complete variance to its context, and philologically quite insupportable, was quite legitimate to the ancient commentator on the Scriptures, as it often seems to be among modern preachers.

In the New Testament writings a further element is involved, however. Word-play here can be a purposeful disguise, a means whereby special, secret names of the Holy Plant could be conveyed to the initiate through his informed group-leader without their being revealed to the outsider.

In general, there are at least three levels of understanding involved in the New Testament writings. On the surface, there are the Greek words in their plain meaning. It is here that we have the story of Jesus and his adventures, the real-life backcloth against which they are set, and his homiletic teachings. How much reality there is at this level is a matter for further enquiry, but probably very little, apart from the social and historical background material.

Beneath the Greek there lies a Semitic level of understanding (not necessarily, or even probably, a Semitic form, that is, actual Semitic versions of the Greek texts). It is mainly in this level that the word-plays are made. For instance, in the "stumbling-block" cycle of stories just mentioned, the puns are on the various meanings of the Aramaic word underlying the Greek *skandalon,* that is *tiqlā',* "stumbling-block" – "shekel, tax" – "bolt-mushroom".

Under that again there lie the basic conceptions of the mushroom cult. Here is the real stuff of the mystery-fertility philosophy. For example, to find their parables of the Kingdom, the writers make comparisons with objects and activities which, at the surface level of understanding, are often really absurd, besides being self-contradictory about the manner and form of the Kingdom's coming. The passage that likens the Kingdom to a mustard seed, for example, and then speaks of birds nesting in the branches of the grown plant (Matt 13:31f., etc.), has driven the biblical naturalists to distraction looking for a mustard "tree" suitable as roosting places for the fowls of the air. They could have saved themselves the trouble since the reference, at the "lower" level, is simply a play on the Semitic *khardelā',* "mustard" and *ardīlā,* "mushroom".[19] Furthermore, the whole discussion about the Kingdom stems from a play on the secret mushroom word TAB-BA-RI, read as the Semitic root *d-b-r,* "guide, manage, control",[20] the real meaning of this mystic "Kingdom" into which the initiate into the mysteries hoped to pass.

For despite the trivial nature of the word-play by which it finds literary expression in the New Testament, the Kingdom of God was a very real experience in the minds of the Christians. It meant the complete domination of the mind and body of the celebrant by the god. He was "enthused" in the proper meaning of that word, "god-filled".[21] So in their respective times were the Maenads of Bacchus,[22] and, less violently perhaps, the Methodists of John Wesley. The manner and means of the "domination" were of the utmost importance to the initiate for he was entering upon an extremely dangerous experience. Even with all their knowledge of the identity and power of their drugs, these worshippers at the throne of the "Jesus Christ" fungus knew well that the "Kingdom" they sought might well be eternal as far as they were concerned. We should not, therefore, be tempted to underestimate either the intelligence of those participating in the cult, or their literary methods, in committing their vital secrets to written form. In view of the hostility understandably being shown them by the authorities of the time, Roman and Jewish, writing the New Testament at all was scarcely less dangerous than chewing the sacred mushroom.

It may be of interest here to list the more important secret names of the sacred mushroom on which much of the mythology and homiletics of the New Testament is based. The full forms given here are the Sumerian originals, found actually extant in the texts surviving, reconstructed from transliterations in other dialects, or composed from known values of the words on otherwise existing patterns: *LI-KUR-BA(LA)G-ANTA/AN-TI- TAB-BA-R/LI-TI; *LI-MASh-BALAG-ANTA; KUR-KUR; *MASh-TAB-BA-R/LI-TI; UKUSh-LI-LI-GI; *TAB-BA-RI-GI; and variants.[23]

In exactly what forms the Christians knew these words we cannot know; some will have been as Greek transcriptions, others in Semitic form. Now and again the names appear in vocabularies attached to other plants related in some way to the mushroom, and their original Sumerian form can be recognized. Of such are the Syriac and Arabic names for Hellebore, *khurbekānā'* and *kharbaq* respectively, traceable to Sumerian *KUR-BA(LA)G-ANTA, "cone of the erect phallus", that is, the mushroom top.

Sumerian KUR means a "mountain" or other conical shape.[24] So a doubled KUR will sometimes indicate a double-cone shaped or glans-headed plant. The mushroom with its split volva was so described, hence the derived Greek name Kirkaion among the Mandrake lists. Our word Crocus has the same Sumerian origin, referring to the phallic form of the flower stem and head. Another of our common vegetable names so derived is Chicory, a variant form of whose name in Greek is *Korkoron*. This last occurs also as a mushroom name, and Pliny's description of "Chicory" shows that whatever magic plant he is describing it is not the culinary root we know so well:

those who have anointed themselves with the juice of the whole plant, mixed with oil, become more popular and obtain their wishes more easily . . . so great are its health-giving properties that some call it Chreston . . .[25]

There has clearly been some confusion here in traditions regarding the plant with which we may reasonably identify the Kirkaion, Mandrake. The juice was to be "rubbed on" or "anointed" (*khristos*), and its properties were so beneficial that it was called Chreston (Greek *khrēstos*, "good, honest, health-bestowing", etc.).[26] One is reminded of the form of the name by which non-Christians spoke of the object of the sect's adoration, Chrestus. So Suetonius speaks of the emperor Claudius having to expel Jews from Rome because they were making a disturbance "at the instigation of Chrestus".[27] What Pliny is describing then is the "Jesus Christ" mushroom whose consumption brought on the first-century Christians the vilification and contempt of the Roman historians.

The Greek *Korkoron*, the "Christ" mushroom, appears also as an alternative name for Halicacabus,[28] another of the "bolt" designations of the fungus. Its name is related to the Semitic word for "star" envisaged as a penis in the sky, a miniature "sun". Our own word "star" comes via Greek from a Sumerian word for "knobbed bolt". Of Halicacabus, Pliny says:

> The root of Halicacabus is taken in drink by those who, to confirm superstitious notions, wish to play the inspired prophet, and to be seen publicly raving in unpretended madness.

He adds that the root is "so antipathetic to the nature of asps, that if it be brought near to the reptile it stupefies that very power of theirs to kill by stupefaction".[29]

Allusions like this to serpents and antidotes for their poisons or malign influences over the mind usually imply some special relationship between the plant and the reptile. Mushrooms and serpents are closely related in folk-lore, and in this case we are reminded of the Old Testament passage about Moses' brazen serpent, on which Jesus models himself,[30] that anyone "bitten by a snake might look on it and live" (Num. 21:9).

Of the other Sumerian elements that went to make up mushroom names, RI, or dialectal LI, also meant "cone"- or "bun"-shape, MASh (-TAB-BA), "twin", so LI-MASh meant "two cones" or "hemispheres", like, MASh-TAB-BA-R/LI. The word GI means "stem" so that LI-LI-GI could describe the mushroom as two halves of the volva separated by the erect stem.[31] Very common in the phallic nomenclature of the mushroom is the Sumerian BALAG, "crown of the penis; glans". Supplemented by ANTA, "raised", we shall meet the word in the name given to the Maenads, Bacchantes, and the Hebrew "weepers" for Tammuz.[32] In Sumerian, the orgiasts whose task it was to cause the erection of the male organ, and in the cult, the raising of the phallic mushroom, were called BALAG-NAR. By natural association of ideas this combined word came into Greek as the name for an axe-handle, *pelekunarion,* which was pushed through the central hole of the double-axe head, the *pelekus.*[33]

The extension of "erect penis" words to stakes, rods, cudgels, and the like is common in any language. Of the BALAG-derived words we might cite the Greek *phalagx,* Latin and our phalanx, meaning a "roller, log, or rank of soldiers".[34] Another onion name, referring to the "knobbed root" of the vegetable that provoked phallic allusions, was the Latin *pallacana,* precisely our Sumerian *BALAG-AN(TA).[35]

The ancient naturalists speak of a poisonous spider whose name *Phalaggion* stems from the same root. Its connections with the genital organ are clear from their descriptions of the effects of its bite:

> The eyes become bloodshot, a shivering settles upon his limbs, and straightway his skin and genitals grow taut, his penis projects, dripping with foul ooze . . .[36]

Among the antidotes for this fearsome poison is listed Asparagus, a well-known antaphrodisiac, and also named from the Sumerian BALAG, presumably on account of its straight stalk.[37]

Semitic made a number of roots from BALAG, "crown of the penis", and found therein words denoting a hemispherical or "bun" shape, as those for a young woman's firm breast, the similarly shaped whorl of a spindle, half a pomegranate skin, a human temple, and a cake of figs.[38] As in the title "Bacchante", the middle "L" of BALAG became assimilated to the following consonant in pronunciation, giving sounds like "bacc-" or (from the cognate BULUG) "bucc-". Latin thus gained its *bucca,* "cheek", and Hebrew one of its names for the mushroom, *paqqū'ah.*[39]

From the New Testament myth-maker's point of view, this double pronunciation greatly enlarged his scope for punning. He could use

BALAG in full for Semitic roots *like p-l-kh,* "make"[40] ("On this rock I will *build* (make) my church"), but could shorten it and run into the preceding MASh of the fungus name, finding roots like *sh-b-kh,* "bless, praise" ("*Blessed* art thou, Simon Bar-jonah. . ."),[41] and *sh-b-q,* "release, forgive" ("whatsoever you *release* on earth . . ."),[42] and so on.

Having seen something of how the New Testament writers use the old sacred names of the mushroom for their word-play, we have now to look again at the nature of the fungus itself. From the manner of its growth and its sexual resemblances come many of the "human" allusions in the stories that grew up round it. Its main parts, the "volva" and the "penis" stem, represented the essential distinguishing features of men and women, and in mythology they served as symbols for the male and female characters in the stories.

VII

The Man-child Born of a Virgin

Describing the growth of the mushroom (*boletos*), Pliny says: "the earth
... produces first a 'womb' (*vulva*) ... and afterwards (the mushroom)
itself inside the womb, like a yolk inside the egg; and the baby mushroom
is just as fond of eating its coat as is the chicken. The coat cracks when
(the mushroom) first forms; presently, as it gets bigger, the coat is
absorbed into the body of the footstalk (*pediculi*) ... at first it is flimsier
than froth, then it grows substantial like parchment, and then the mushroom ... is born."[1]

More prosaically, perhaps, the process is thus described by a modern
mycologist: "In the genus *Amanita* a membrane surrounds the young
fungus. In addition to this wrapper or volva there is another membrane,
stretching from the margin of the cap and joined to the stem, as in the
mushroom. Thus it is as if the 'button stage' were surrounded by an
outer skin. As the fungus develops this is torn apart. If its texture is
sufficiently tenacious to hold it together, it is left as a cup at the base of
the stem ... With growth the membrane covering the gills tears and
is left as a ring on the stem." Of the *Amanita phalloides*, the writer adds:
"Before the volva breaks the fungus looks somewhat like a pigeon's
egg half-buried, or like a small *phallus* 'egg'. It is common in glades in
woods and adjoining pastures after the first summer rains, and continues through early autumn."[2]

It was the fertilization of the "womb" that most puzzled the ancients,
and remained a mystery until the end of the last century. To Pliny the
fungus had to be reckoned as one of the "greatest of the marvels of
nature", since it "belonged to a class of things that spring up spontan-
eously and cannot be grown from seed".[3] It was surely "among the
most wonderful of all things" in that it could "spring up and live without a root".[4] Until the invention of the microscope the function of the
spore, produced by each fungus in its millions, could not be appreci-

ated. The mushroom has, indeed, no seed in the accepted sense, germinating and giving out a root and later a stem apex with or without seed leaves. The walls of each minute spore extrude to form thread-like tubes which branch further until all mass together to form the spongy flesh of the fungus. The result is neither animal nor vegetable, and the mystery of its proper classification persisted until relatively modern times. Thus a sixteenth-century naturalist wrote: "They are a sort of intermediate existence between plants and inanimate nature. In this respect fungi resemble zoophytes, which are intermediate between plants and animals."5

One explanation for the creation of the mushroom without apparent seed was that the "womb" had been fertilized by thunder, since it was commonly observed that the fungi appeared after thunderstorms. Thus one name given them was Ceraunion, from the Greek *keraunios*, "thunderbolt". Another was the Greek *hudnon*, probably derived from Sumerian *UD-NUN, "storm-seeded".6

It was thus uniquely begotten. The normal process of fructification had been by-passed. The seed had not fallen from some previous plant, to be nurtured by the earth until in turn it produced a root and stalk. The god had "spoken" and his creative "word" had been carried to earth by the storm-wind, angelic messenger of heaven, and been implanted directly into the volva. The baby that resulted from this divine union was thus the "Son of God", more truly representative of its heavenly father than any other form of plant or animal life. Here, in the tiny mushroom, was God manifest, the "Jesus" born of the Virgin, "the image of the invisible God, the first-born of all creation . . . in him all the fulness of God was pleased to dwell . . . " (Col 1:15ff.).

The phallic form of the mushroom matched precisely that of his father, whom the Sumerians called ISKUR, "Mighty Penis", the Semites Adad, or Hadad, "Big-father", the Greeks *Patēr-Zeus*, and the Romans Jupiter, "Father-god".7 To see the mushroom was to see the Father, as in Jesus the uncomprehending Philip was urged to look for God: "He who has seen me has seen the Father . . . Do you not believe that I am in the Father and the Father in me?" (John 14:9ff.). Even the demons recognized him as "the Holy One of God" (Mark 1:24), and it was as "the Holy Plant" that the sacred fungus came to be known throughout the ancient world.

The slimy juice of the mushroom which, in some phalloidic species, spills over the "glans" and down the stem, seemed to the ancients like the viscous exudation of the genital organs prior to coitus and the seminal discharge at orgasm. The Hebrew word for "smooth, slimy" derives from a Sumerian phrase meaning "semen running to waste",[8] and figures in a number of biblical allusions to the mushroom.[9] It was otherwise known as "spittle", and Job asks if there is any taste in the "spittle of the mushroom" (as we should now read the name of that plant) (Job 6:6).[10] To have "spittle in the mouth" was a euphemism in the Jewish Talmud for "semen in the vagina",[11] and the close relationship between the two fluids resulted in the very widespread belief that spittle had strong curative and prophylactic properties. Thus, as human semen was a cure for scorpion stings, according to Pliny,[12] spittle was a repellent to snakes and an antidote to snake venom.[13] Jesus is pictured making a clay poultice to lay over the eyes of the man born blind (John 9:6), mixing his spittle with dust, as Pliny reports that saliva used each morning as an eye ointment cured ophthalmia.[14]

Rain, the semen of the god, was spurted forth from the divine penis at his thunderous orgasm in the heavens, and was borne as "spittle" from the lips of the glans to earth on the storm wind.[15] It was a unique concentration of this powerful spermatozoa in the juice of the "Holy Plant" that the Magi believed would give anyone anointed with it amazing power. They could "obtain every wish, banish fevers, and cure all diseases without exception".[16] So the Christian, the "smeared or anointed one", received "knowledge of all things" by his "anointing from the Holy One" (I John 2:20). Thereafter he had need of no other teacher and remained for evermore endowed with all knowledge (v. 27). Whatever the full ingredients of the Christian unction may have been, they would certainly have included the aromatic gums and spices of the traditional Israelite anointing oil: myrrh, aromatic cane, cinnamon, and cassia, all representing the powerful semen of the god. Under certain enclosed conditions, a mixture of these substances rubbed on the skin could produce the kind of intoxicating belief in self-omniscience referred to in the New Testament. Furthermore, the atmosphere of the oracular chamber would be charged with reek of sacred incense consisting of "sweet spices, stacte, and onycha, and galbanum, sweet spices with pure frankincense . . ." (Exod 30:34), giving the kind of overpowering hypnotic effect referred to by an early Christian writer when he speaks of "the frenzy of a lying soothsayer" as a "mere intoxication produced by the reeking fumes of sacrifice".[17]

That these ingredients formed only part of the sacred incense formula is well known. Josephus says there were thirteen elements,[18] and the Talmud names eleven, plus salt, and a secret "herb" which was added to make the smoke rise in a vertical column before spreading outwards at the top.[19] With the characteristic shape of the mushroom in mind, we can hazard a fair guess now at this secret ingredient.

Knowledge and healing were two aspects of the same life-force. If to be rubbed with the "Holy Plant" was to receive divine knowledge, it was also to be cured of every sickness. James suggests that anyone of the Christian community who was sick should call the elders to anoint him with oil in the name of Jesus (Jas 5:14). The Twelve are sent out among their fellow-men casting out demons and anointing the sick with oil (Mark 6:13). Healing by unction persisted in the Church until the twelfth century,[20] and the anointing of the dying, the so-called "extreme unction" has persisted in the Roman Catholic Church to this day.[21] The principle behind this practice remains the same: the god's "seed-of-life", semen, found in spring or rain water, in the sap or resins of plants and trees, and above all in the slimy mucus of the mushroom, imparts life to the ailing or the dead.

Herein lies also the idea of embalming corpses with ointments and spices. They were not expected to halt decomposition, as Martha appreciated in the case of her four-day-dead brother Lazarus (John 11:39), although in Egypt additional measures were taken also to preserve even the flesh. The Hebrew of the story of Joseph's embalming for forty days uses the word "healers"[22] for the practitioners of the craft (Gen 50:2), and the word for "embalm" means also "to come fully to life, mature", as well as "make spicy".[23] The root goes back to Sumerian words for "spilling seed", and the conception seems to have been to impart life and rebirth to the dead person in the underworld. So the two Marys come to the grave to anoint the dead Jesus (Mark 16:1; Luke 23:56) as did Nicodemus, bringing myrrh and aloes for the purpose (John 19:39), and as Mary, Martha's sister, had earlier anointed his feet with nard, anticipating the event (John 12:3).

Things, as well as people, could be anointed with semen so that they became "holy", that is, separated to the god's service. The Semitic root *q-d-sh*, "holy", is, as its probable root meaning indicates, fundamentally a fertility word. It has to do specifically with the uterus,[24] the "holy of holies" of the female, and the inner sanctuary of the temple. So the cultic furniture was anointed (Exod 3:26, 40:10; Lev 8:11), and particularly the altar, that replica of the penis standing before the open portals of the temple. In the story of Jacob and his ladder dream, when he saw angels going up and down between earth and heaven, he took the stone on which he had laid his head in sleep and erected it as a pillar and "poured oil on the top of it" (Gen 28:10ff., cp. Gen 35:14).[25]

The anointing into holiness of kings and priests is again largely imitative in character. The prime duty of the king was to ensure the fertility of the land and well-being of his subjects. Many of the Greek and Semitic words for "lord" and "lordship" convey this idea when seen in their original form.[26] The priest's function was also to see that the god played his part in inseminating the land. The most common Hebrew word for "priest", *kōhēn*, familiar as a well-known Jewish surname, comes from a Sumerian title, GU-EN-NA, literally, "guardian of semen".[27] He had charge of the god's house, regarded as the uterus where he enacted his role of creator.[28] Pouring the god's semen over

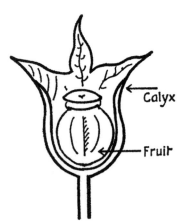

3 Section through the calyx and fruit of Henbane (after F. Howarth, in Josephus, *Jewish Antiquities* [Loeb, iv] p. 399)

the heads of these dignitaries was intended to represent them as "gods", replicas of the divine penis in heaven.[29]

The head-gear of the Jewish high priest, called simply a "turban" in the Old Testament (Exod 28:4, etc), was apparently intended to represent the glans penis. Josephus has an extended account of this piece

THE MAN-CHILD BORN OF A VIRGIN

of ceremonial attire.[30] He describes it by alluding to several different plants, all of them having a mushroom relevance. One, indeed, *Sideritis,* actually is a name of the Holy Plant.[31]

First, the priest dons a skull-cap (Greek *pilos,* Latin *pileus,* incidentally the botanist's name for the cap of the mushroom), as worn by the generality of the priesthood. Over this he puts a turban of violet embroidery, further encircled with a crown of gold. Sprouting from the top of this was a golden calyx, or seed-vessel. In order to satisfy the curiosity of his remarkably ill-informed readers, Josephus goes on to describe in great detail the nature and shape of the calyx, "for those unfamiliar with it", comparing it with that of Henbane, *Hyoscyamus niger* (fig. 3).

"Imagine", says our ingenious author, "a ball cut into two: the calyx at the stem presents the lower half of this, emerging from its base in a rounded form." He then enlarges on the graceful turn of the sides to the "rim" onto which the "hemispherical lid adheres closely". This calyx, he says, is enveloped in a husk or sheath which detaches itself of its own accord as the fruit begins to develop. This is not a very accurate account of the Henbane calyx and its ovary, but it well suits the volva of the Boletus mushroom as the embryo begins to expand. Josephus speaks further of the ragged edge of the lip of the calyx, "like thorns quite sharp at the end". This is presumably an allusion to the three-tiered golden crown surrounding the violet turban,[32] and in human terms to the edge of the circumcised foreskin. The Bible makes no mention of a golden crown, but it does speak of a "plate of gold" (*sīs*), affixed to the front of the priest's turban (Exod 28:36).[33] As Josephus was well aware, the word *sīs* is used in late Hebrew for the fringe of shreds of the prepuce remaining after an insufficient circumcision operation, a kind of "crown of thorns" around the bared glans.[34] In mushroom terms, this "fringe" will be the membrane that joins the margin of the *pileus* cap to the stem before its full development. When the skin breaks it remains as a ragged ring around the stem.

New Testament imagery has Jesus crowned with thorns and clothed with royal purple (John 19:2). The deep red cap of the sacred mushroom added to its phallic significance in the eyes of the ancients and provided them with words for that colour, as will be noted.

These "glans-crowned" officials, kings and priests were, then, the messiahs, or christs, said in the Old Testament to be "smeared with

Yahweh" (I Sam 26:11; Ps 2:2), "having the consecration or crown of God's unction upon them" (Lev 21:12). In that holy condition they were not allowed to leave the sanctuary precincts (Lev 21:12; cp. 10:7), unless by some ill chance and erotic dream they were to spoil their ritual purity by inadvertently mixing their own semen on their bodies with that of the god. In that case they were obliged to leave the sacred area of the Jerusalem temple by an underground passage leading to the profane area of the city.[35]

Both the Semitic and the Greek words for "christ", the "anointed, or smeared one", came from Sumerian terms for semen or resinous saps, MASh and ShEM. Used as descriptive titles in that language, they appear as a "MASh-man", exorcist, that is, the priest who drives away demons, and as a "ShEM-man" a compounder of perfumes, the equivalent of the Old Testament mixer of the holy anointing-oils.[36] Semitic furthermore combined both Sumerian words into a new root sh-m-sh, "serve" (tables, as a steward; the temple, as a priest; the heavenly throne, as an angel; the genitals, as a penis or a vulva). Thus the noun means a steward, priest, angel or prostitute.[37] An independently derived form very early on came to be used for the greatest "copulator" of all, the sun, Hebrew shemesh, whose fiery glans every evening plunged glowing into the open vulva of the earth, and in the morning "came forth like a bridegroom from his marriage chamber" (Ps 19:5).[38]

Another important word for a servitor of god in Greek was therapeutēs, the verb therapeuō implying both service to god and attendance on the body as physicians, in which sense we have derived our "therapy", "therapeutics", and the like. This root also has a sexual origin, as a "giver of life", and is connected with the Sumerian DARA, "beget", appearing as a name for the fertility and storm gods Ea and Adad.[39]

The word therapeutēs is of particular interest since it was the title of an ascetic, contemplative sect who have often been compared with the Essenes. They lived mainly in Egypt, at the turn of the era, but probably had a long history prior to that date. We know of them through the writings of the first-century Philo,[40] and Eusebius, the Church historian (third and fourth century).[41] The Therapeutae, as they are called, lived in mixed communities, cut off from their fellow-men, rejecting personal property, completely celibate, the women being mostly "aged virgins

. . . who have kept their chastity of their own free will in their ardent desire for learning". They all met together only on the sabbath, the women being separated from the men by a dividing partition in the assembly hall. But every seventh week after supper, both sexes mingled, singing and dancing until dawn, when they returned to their own quarters. Eusebius was so struck by the likeness of the Therapeutae to Christian monks of his own day that he thought they may have been Christians, and that the books referred to by Philo as "the writings of ancient men who were the founders of the sect" may have been the Gospels and Epistles through which they had become converted. The Church Fathers followed him on this and even Jerome reckoned the Jewish Philo as among the "Church historians".

We hear, too, of an unorthodox Christian sect called the Sampsaeans (Greek *Sampsēnoi),* whose name is certainly connected with the Semitic root *sh-m-sh* (and so has been hitherto thought to indicate "sun (shemesh)-worshippers").[42] Epiphanius, the fourth-century Christian writer, links these people with the Essenes but thought their Christianity was of a spurious kind, something between Judaism and the true faith.[43] Apparently in his time they dwelt in Transjordan, in Peraea, on the borders of ancient Moab, and by the eastern shores of the Dead Sea. Whatever their sectarian connections, their name, as we can now see, demonstrates a clear philological relationship with both the Essenes, "healers", "life-givers", the Therapeutae, and the Christians.

In the phallic mushroom, the "man-child" born of the "virgin" womb, we have the reality behind the Christ figure of the New Testament story. In a sense he is representative also of the initiates of the cult, "Christians", or "smeared with semen", as the name means. By imitating the mushroom, as well as by eating it and sucking its juice, or "blood", the Christian was taking unto himself the panoply of his god, as the priests in the sanctuary also anointed themselves with the god's spermatozoa found in the juices and resins of special plants and trees. As the priests "served" the god in the temple, the symbolic womb of divine creation, so the Christians and their cultic associates worshipped their god and mystically involved themselves in the creative process. In the language of the mystery cults they sought to be "born again", when, purged afresh of past sin, they could apprehend the god in a drug-induced ecstasy.

Fully to understand the part played by women in the mushroom cult it is necessary to appreciate their role in the creative process itself. The fungus represented a microcosm of the female part of the birth cycle. The "man-child" was born from a womb or volva and its gestation and parturition was as much a part of the female worshipper as the birth of a human baby required the active participation of the mother and the midwife. In the following chapters, then, we shall pay special attention to the woman and her special contribution to the process of conception and birth, her religious role as a cultic prostitute, and the part played by her ritual lamentation in the raising of the sacred mushroom.

VIII

Woman's Part in the Creative Process

Gestation of the foetus in the womb required three elements: the creative spirit, semen, and blood. The god provided the first, man the second, and woman the third. Of the human contributions, woman's was the most powerful and evoked most wonder among the ancients. They believed that it was menstrual blood that formed the embryo. Pliny describes the process thus: "(menses is) the material for human generation, as semen from the male acting like rennet collects this substance within it, which thereupon is inspired with life and endowed with body".[1]

Women who do not menstruate, records the same author, do not bear children, since the raw material of conception is not present in the womb. On the other hand, a woman who menstruates during pregnancy is likely to bring forth "a sickly or still-born offspring, or one full of bloody matter". The best time for conceiving was thought to be at the beginning or end of a menstrual period,[2] which is why in the story of David and Bathsheba in the Old Testament it is said specifically that the lovers had their illicit intercourse just after Bathsheba had menstruated (II Sam 11:4).

Galen, the second-century physician, has a rather more sophisticated theory of the generative process, but still sees semen and menstrual blood as its main factors. The semen, he thought, drew to itself just as much blood as it could deal with, using it as food with which to build the foetus.[3]

The Old Testament rules for the menstruant (Lev 15:19-25) emphasize the sacred nature of the blood. Whilst in that condition, everything the woman touches is reckoned "unclean" and this "uncleanness" can communicate itself to other people. A man having intercourse with her at this time renders himself liable to the same seven-day period of ritual disqualification as his wife. It has to be emphasized that this "uncleanness" has nothing to do with morals or hygiene. It is a religious state of taboo. A woman bearing a son is similarly "defiled" (having a daughter requires fourteen days separation), as is a man coming in contact with a dead body (Num 19:11). A priest is rendered "unclean" by touching a reptile or insect, or involuntarily discharging semen (Lev 22:4, 5).

Rachel used her real or pretended menstrual condition to prevent her sorely pressed father Laban from discovering his stolen property. When he finally caught up with his runaway daughter and son-in-law, Laban searched their tents seeking some household gods Rachel had taken. She put them under her camel saddle and begged to be excused from rising since the "manner of women was upon her" (Gen 31:34f). Even to have touched the saddle would have rendered Laban "unclean".

Menses could affect almost everything, by remote influence as well as direct contact. "Wild indeed", says Pliny, "are the stories told of the mysterious and awful power of the menstruous discharge . . ."[4] He relates a few of them and leaves us in no doubt about the fear and wonder that attended this monthly phenomenon in the eyes of the ancients. Of course, coming from the seat of creation, the womb, menstrual blood was credited with wonderful healing powers. It could cure gout, scrofula, parotid tumours, abscesses, erysipelas, boils, eye-fluxes, hydrophobia, and epilepsy, whilst quartan fever, according to one source, could be counteracted by sexual intercourse with a woman just beginning her period.

On the other hand, such a source of power was dangerous. Under the principle of like repelling like, which played an important part in ancient philosophy, menses was also considered to be an abortifacient. A smear of the blood could bring about a miscarriage, and even to step over a stain could bring about the same dire effect.[5] Similarly, it could abort fruit trees, dry up seed, blight crops, turn wine sour, as well as send dogs mad, rust metals, and dull mirrors. This last effect, incidentally, could be reversed by having the woman stare at the back of the mirror until the shine on the front was restored.[6]

The distinguishing feature of menstrual blood was its dark colour, contrasting with the brighter, oxygenated blood of the rest of the body. Thus dark red, purple, violet, and similar hues came to have a special significance, being so closely associated with fertility. Kings and magistrates wore purple garments, and the Latin *purpura* came to mean not only the robes themselves but the high dignity they conferred.[7]

Most prized of all was Tyrian purple, whose "highest glory", according to Pliny, "consists in the colour of congealed blood, blackish at first glance but gleaming when held up to the light; this is the origin of Homer's phrase, 'blood of purple hue'".[8] Further dyeing of a scarlet fabric with Tyrian purple produced the rich colour called in Greek *husginon,* the Sumerian origin of which shows that it meant properly "blue blood",[9] another popular mark of the aristocracy. The same origin can be found for "Hyacinth", in Greek mythology the name of the youth accidentally slain by his friend Apollo, and from whose spilt blood there grew the flower of that name.[10] Pliny offers a further connection between purple and menstrual blood when he says that the latter adversely affects this colour, another example of like repelling like.[11]

There is another reference to menstrual blood in the description Pliny gives of a fabulous dragon called the basilisk. It could apparently kill bushes with its breath, scorch grass, burst rocks,[12] and put other serpents to rout.[13] It was its blood, however, that was most in demand. According to the Magi, it brought a successful outcome to petitions made to gods and kings, cured diseases, and disarmed sorcery. This last claim was also made for menses, if daubed like Passover blood (Exod 12:7), on the subject's doorposts.[14]

The name basilisk actually means "womb-blood",[15] that is, menses. Pliny adds that some people call it "Saturn's blood", which looks like a reminiscence of the same verbal origin, since the name Saturn is partly composed of a Sumerian word ShA-TUR, "womb".[16]

One important characteristic of "Saturn's blood" was that it was of the colour and consistency of pitch.[17] The ancients saw a close relationship between this substance and menstrual blood, apparently believing that it was the earth's equivalent of human menses. Particularly noted in this connection were the lumps of bitumen that periodically rose to the surface of the Dead Sea, "in shape and size", according to Josephus, "like decapitated bulls". He goes on, "the labourers on the lake row up to these and, catching hold of the lumps, haul them into their boats. But when they have filled them it is no easy task to detach their cargo, which, owing to its tenacious and glutinous character, clings to the boat until it is loosened by the menstrual discharge of women."[18] This tradition is mentioned also by Tacitus,[19] referring to other ancient authorities among whom, we know, was one Poseidonius of the second to first century BC. So the relationship between pitch and menses was already well-established and can now be further supported linguistically.[20]

The connection of pitch with the womb would lead us to expect that it should be thought to have healing properties. As Josephus says, "it is useful not only for caulking ships, but also for the healing of the body, forming an ingredient in many medicines."[21] Dioscorides lists at some length the remedial characteristics of *asphaltos,* including that it is effective for "strangulations of the womb", and that, taken along with wine and castor oil, "it drives out menses".[22] The Judean bitumen is the best, according to the same authority, and he notes that "it shines like purple".

The inhabitants of Judea must have been well aware that the extraordinary rift valley of the Dead Sea was far lower than the surrounding country. In fact, as we know, the ground there is the lowest place on earth, some thirteen hundred feet below sea-level. It was small wonder, then, that the menstrual discharge of the womb of mother earth should be borne the comparatively short distance to the surface of the Dead Sea, and that it should have required the application of the menses of other wombs to loosen its sticky grip.

Perhaps the Dead Sea's proximity to the centre of the earth, and thus the seat of knowledge, played some part in the establishment along its western shores of the Essene settlement at Qumran, the home of the Dead Sea Scrolls. Certainly the blistering heat of the summer months, combined with the belief that there one stood closer than anywhere else to the eternal fires of Hades, had a large part in the formulation of the Sodom and Gomorrah myths, and their overthrow with fire and brimstone (Gen 19:24).

Further evidence of how close the ground here is to the fermenting heat of the earth's centre was recognized in the presence of hot springs on the east side of the Dead Sea, at a place called Callirrhoe. It was thence that the dying Herod was carried to try to find some relief from the pains that wracked his dropsical, gangrenous body.[23] As late as the last century, popular local belief held that the hot water was released from the lower regions by evil spirits, merely to stop it being available to assuage the pains of the damned in hell. Another legend said that King Solomon sent a servant to open the springs when he discovered how thin was the crust of the earth at this point. However, lest the threats of the subterranean devils deter his messenger, the wise monarch saw to it that he was stone deaf.[24]

Nearby stood Herod's great palace fortress Machaerus, and in its grounds, says Josephus, "grew a plant of Rue, of an amazing size; indeed in height and thickness no fig-tree surpassed it".[25] Rue was regarded as the prime abortifacient, as its various names now make clear.[26] Pliny said that it would open the womb, promote menstruation, bring away the after-birth and dead foetus; it was good for "womb-strangling" and for the genitals and anus, and at all costs should be avoided by pregnant women.[27]

Josephus' digression to speak of a particular Rue plant in a topographical account of the Machaerus fortress as it bore on a vital Roman campaign in Transjordan, is strange, to say the least. But we have already seen, when describing the high priest's head-gear, that the introduction by this author of plant physiology and folk-lore into an otherwise non-botanical discussion usually implies some hidden reference to a matter which he is reluctant to bring fully into the open.

Immediately following the description of the giant-sized Rue and its comparison with a fig, Josephus says that in a ravine to the north of the fortress town was to be found a magic plant called by the name of the ravine, Baaras. What he says about the plant tallies in some respects with traditional accounts of the Mandrake, which we have identified with the Holy Plant, the sacred fungus. One method of drawing it from the ground safely was to tie a dog to it, then call the animal to follow. The animal sprang to obey, pulling out the Mandrake, and promptly died, "a vicarious victim, as it were, for him who intended to remove the plant, since after this none need fear to handle it". The canine sacrifice was well worth the prize, since "it possesses one virtue for which it is valued; for the so-called demons – in other words, the spirits of wicked men which enter the living and kill them unless aid is forthcoming – are promptly expelled by this root, if merely applied to the patients".[28]

Of more immediate interest is the alternative method offered for capturing the root. "It eludes the grasp of persons who approach with the intention of plucking it, as it shrinks up and can only be made to stand still by pouring upon it a woman's urine and menses."[29] Thus the releasing agents for the Mandrake were the same as for the Dead Sea's bitumen. Furthermore, the Rue, which shared some of the medicinal and abortive characteristics of pitch, was highly regarded in antiquity as an antidote to poisons, particularly of serpents and fungi.[30] We may therefore suspect that in Josephus' mention of the hot spring of Machaerus, the giant Rue and the Mandrake in the same passage, he is quietly expressing a currently held belief that this particular location by the Dead Sea held a special relevance for the Holy Plant and its antidote. One or two other references support this idea, as we shall see.

The ancients recognized a homogeneity between mineral pitch and the resin of trees, particularly the pine, to which the name "pitch" more properly belongs. Thus Greek has the term *pissasphaltos,* that is, as Pliny remarks, "pitch combined with bitumen",[31] and this author states that bitumen is commonly adulterated with vegetable pitch.[32] Acacia was another tree whose resinous sap was compared with human menses. Pliny says that its "purple gum" had the best tonic and cooling properties and "checked excessive menstruation".[33] The Arabs are said to make amulets from the gum of the Acacia with the idea that it is the tree's menstrual blood, and that they may thereby avail themselves of its power.[34] The Acacia shared honours with the Cedar for providing wood for the furniture of the Jewish sanctuary, and was even used to construct the ark itself (Deut 10:3; Exod 25:5; etc).

Another property shared by bitumen and resin is their inflammability. Both are sources of fire, a necessary ingredient of generation. As we said earlier, the Sumerian ideogram for "love" consisted of a burning torch in a womb.[35] The dull-red tip of the penis was thought of as a fiery brand igniting the furnace of the uterus, as the sun each evening set alight the bituminous heart of the earth. As Job says, "As for the earth, out of it comes bread; but underneath it is turned up as by fire" (Job 28:5). So a pine-torch was carried in wedding processions, as the virgins of the New Testament parable of the Kingdom bore their lamps to meet the bridegroom (Matt 25). In the same way, torch-carrying formed part of the fertility rites of Bacchus.[36]

The same symbolism lies behind the seven-branched candlestick before the Holy of Holies in the Jewish temple (Exod 25:31ff.). The phallic nature of the lamps is illustrated by the terminology of its biblical description, beginning with the base as the "loins" out of which the "stalk" rises with its seven arms. On the top of each was "a cup shaped like an almond", consisting of a "rounded knob", or "capital",

and a "flower", or "bud". It is as difficult to envisage this ornamenta-
tion in literal terms as it is Josephus' description of the High Priest's
phallic head-gear. However, the reference to the "almond" is a clue to
the intended symbolism of the whole, since the name of the tree derives
from a Sumerian original meaning "stretched penis",[37] an allusion to
the tree's being the first to show its blossom.[38] The erection of the male
organ was its "awakening" and in Sumerian the idea was used to
express "sunrise".[39]

The lamps before the Holy of Holies in the Temple find expression
today in the lighted candles before the Virgin Mary in the Catholic
Church. The fertility significance of the practice is particularly clear in
the fire ritual of Holy Saturday, as the Church prepares for the rising of
the Christ on Easter Day. "New fire" is struck from a flint as a prelude
to the ceremonies, and coals lit from it outside the church. The fire is
blessed and brought into the church, eventually to light one candle in
which five grains of incense have been placed. Towards the climax of
the ritual, the biblical Creation story having been read, the part played
by the creative waters is rehearsed before the baptismal font. Prayer is
offered that God, "by a secret mixture of his divine power, may render
fruitful this water for the regeneration of men: to the end that those
who are sanctified in the immaculate womb of this divine font, and
born again new creatures, may come forth as heavenly offspring . . .
Therefore, may all unclean spirits by thy command, O Lord, depart
from hence: may all the malice of diabolical wiles be entirely
banished . . ."

Later the priest breathes three times upon the water in the form of a
cross, saying: "Do thou with thy mouth bless these pure waters . . . "
and dips the candle three times into the water "of the immaculate
womb", saying: "May the power of the Holy Ghost descend into all
the water of this font . . ." After breathing again three times on the
water, he goes on, "and make the whole substance of this water fruitful
for regeneration".

The classical example of the ever-burning fire before a virgin goddess
is the cult of Hestia-Vesta, the Greek and Roman representations of the
hearth-deity. The names and cults of the goddesses differ in some
respects but their origin is the same. The Greek Hestia's name is also
the common word for "fireplace" and "home", as well as for the
central fire of the universe. Euripides calls her "the Lady of Fire".[40]

Her domain was originally in the king's palace, but in the historical period it had become transferred to the town hall, the council-chamber of the magistrates, called in Greek *prutaneion*.[41]

Her mythology tells us that she spurned the hands of both Poseidon and Apollo: "she was unwilling, nay stubbornly refused; and touching the head of her father Zeus . . . that fair goddess swore a great oath that has in truth been fulfilled, that she would be a virgin all her days." As recompense for this great sacrifice, "Zeus the Father gave her high honour instead of marriage, and she has her place in the midst of the house, and has the richest portion. In all the temples of the gods she has a share of the honour, and among all mortal men she is chief of the goddesses".[42]

Not only was Hestia honoured in the council-chambers, but at every banquet wine was poured for her at the beginning and end of the meal.[43] For she was the first and the last of the children of Zeus, the beginning and end of the god's creation. Legend had it that the god swallowed each of his children at the moment of birth, but was ultimately forced to disgorge them. Hestia, being the first-born, was the last to be regurgitated, and so merited this title.[44]

This fancy is simply an attempt to put into mythical terms a central feature of the old fertility philosophy. It was believed that the first-born of the womb was the strongest of all the progeny because it was formed from menstrual blood at its most powerful. Next in excellence to the first-born of the young woman, stood the child of an older woman conceiving for the first time, just prior to menopause. The idea seems to have been that for some reason irregular menstrual discharge was more powerful than that which occurred at normal monthly intervals. So an adolescent girl's first period, like that of the older woman who had retained her virginity, was "spontaneous", and thus all-powerful. It is strong enough, says Pliny, "to make mares miscarry even at the sight of it over long distances".[45]

Menstruation was, naturally enough, connected with the moon, the "queen of stars" whose periodic waxing and waning controlled the blood of humans and sap of plants. As Pliny puts it: "the moon is rightly believed to be the star of the spirit . . . that saturates the earth and fills bodies by its approach and empties them by its departure . . . the blood even of humans increases and diminishes with its light, and leaves and herbage . . . are sensitive to it, the same force penetrating into all things".[46] Should menstrual discharge occur when the moon was not visible the blood was reckoned to have uncontrollable power: "if this female force should issue when the moon or the sun is in eclipse, it will cause irremediable harm; no less so when there is no moon. At such seasons sexual intercourse brings death and disease upon the man."[47]

In biblical mythology this idea of the potency of the first and last menses is expressed in stories of heroes born to aged, previously barren or virgin mothers, like Isaac (Gen 17), Samuel (I Sam 1), and Jesus. The New Testament describes the god-hero, like Hestia, as "the first and the last, the beginning and the end" (Rev 22:13), and "the first-born of all creation" (Col 1:15). Jesus is also "the first-born of many brethren" (Rom 8:28), since participation in the mystery of ingesting the Jesus-fungus was to avail oneself of the power of his primogeniture.

It will be appreciated that this sacred virginity, attributed somewhat incongruously to goddesses who spend most of their mythical lives leaping in and out of bed with gods and mortals, is not primarily or even essentially to do with having intact hymens. Their "virginity" lay in the power of their wombs to produce offspring whose excellence derived from menstrual blood perpetually at its most powerful.

The Roman version of the hearth-cult demonstrates certain features which are probably more primitive than the Greek. The central feature of the Vesta worship was the maintenance of an ever-burning sacred fire[48] by virgins, called Vestals. Originally representing the royal house, these maids, at first two, then four and later six in number,[49] were called "princesses" and given special privileges in accordance with their assumed rank. They dressed as brides, indicative of their virginity, and were between the ages of six and ten,[50] serving for five years,[51] that is, until the onset of puberty and marriageable age. In historical times this period of service was extended to thirty years, perhaps with the idea of bringing them into the second most powerful period of their reproductive lives. Marriage was permitted after their time of service but was unusual, being considered unlucky.[52]

The girls were released from parental control when they were admitted to the sacred office of Vestal, but thereafter came under the charge of the high-priest, the *pontifex maximus*. It was he who received them into the Order, taking each candidate by the hand and pronouncing a formula of admission over her. Her hair was then cut off and hung upon a certain tree.

Discipline was severe. If a Vestal neglected to maintain the sacred fire before the virgin goddess she was beaten. If she lost her virginity she was walled up in an underground tomb to die – or be rescued by the direct intervention of the goddess whom she had betrayed. Her duties involved bringing water from a sacred spring to use in the sanctuary, and the preparation of special foodstuffs. She also had the care of certain objects in the shrine. Since no one but the Vestals was allowed to enter the inner sanctum, little is known of the rituals and the holy objects of the shrine. As with most information about the mystery cults, accounts that have come down stem largely from guesswork.

At the time of the Roman New Year, our Eastertide, a ceremony of extinguishing and relighting the sacred fire was enacted. The Church strikes "new fire" from a flint; the Vestals used a fire-drill boring into a block of wood, an invention attributed to Hermes,[53] with whom the hearth-goddess was associated.

The shrine itself was a domed building, representing a potter's or refiner's furnace. Fire, in fertility philosophy, not only engendered new life, it purified the old. It is the Semitic word for a refiner's crucible that underlies the New Testament conception of "temptation", properly, "testing, trial".[54] So, for the theologians, the eternal fires of hell became the place of purging of the souls of the dead, and later Judaism and Christianity embodied this aspect of the fertility cult into their moral teaching.

The shape of the Vesta shrine had another significance for the mushroom cult, since it also represented the domed canopy of the expanded cap of the *Amanita muscaria*. Inside the shrine was preserved a thunderbolt cast down by Zeus, it was said, at the founding of the city of Troy.[55] To judge from the tradition that this votive object was a replica of the patron goddess Pallas Athena, whose name and epithet both mean "vulva",[56] and bearing in mind the traditional shape of the divine thunderbolt, a kind of dumb-bell or divided hemispheres, ⟨⊏⊐⟩,[57] it seems reasonable to assume that the Palladium, as this venerated relic was called, was in fact a representation of the sacred mushroom.

Fire and fertility are similarly connected in the person of the Greek goddess of childbirth, Eileithyia. She is depicted standing with one arm raised holding a pine-torch, the other outstretched with open palm, a gesture of prayer for an easy delivery.[58] She was the daughter of Zeus and Hera, "semen" and "womb",[59] and her name seems to be an amalgam of two elements which otherwise appear in Greek names for the Pine, *Elatē* and *Thuia*. Both in origin mean "fluid of generation", that is, "menses".[60] Confirmation of this comes from the botanist Theophrastus who says of the resinous extraction of Silver-fir (*Elatē*) that "it is what the prophets call 'the menses of Eileithyia', and for which they make atonement".[61] Thus, in Eileithyia we have a personification of menstrual blood, cedar resin, and creative fire.

The common Sumerian word for "Cedar" is ERIN, and this appears in another Greek word for "torch", *helenē,* or *helanē*. Here also is the source and meaning of the name of the Greek heroine and goddess, Helen.[62] As we saw earlier, she is portrayed in classical mythology as the daughter of Nemesis (or Leda) and Zeus, the result of her father's mating with her mother in the form of a swan. She was thus born from an egg, like her brothers Pollux and Castor. Nemesis, whose name has come down as the personification of divine retribution, is identical in meaning with the Sumerian original of Nectar, the "fate-decider", which otherwise appears as Mandrake, the sacred mushroom, or as the Semites called it, "the *egg* plant".[63]

A further link between Helen and Nectar appears in the drink Nectarion, wine spiced with a wonderful drug called Helenion, named after the good queen Helen. Legend has it that on one occasion when a supper party in the palace of Menelaus looked like being wrecked on the rocks of immoderate grief that followed the recounting of a particularly harrowing tale, Helen laced the company's wine with "a drug to quiet all pain and strife, and bring forgetfulness of every ill". Homer describes this pain-killer further: "Who so should drink this down, when it is mingled in the bowl, would not in the course of that day let a tear fall down over his cheeks, no, not though his mother and father should lie there dead, or though men before his face should slay with the sword his brother or dear son, and his own eyes beheld it."[64]

Pliny says that Helenion had its origins in the queen's "tears", adding, for good measure, that it was particularly popular in the island of Helene.[65] One supposes it was especially favoured among the ladies, for it was reputed "to preserve physical charm, and to keep unimpaired the fresh complexion of our women, whether of the face or of the rest of the body. Moreover, it is supposed that, by its use, they gain a kind of attractiveness and sex-appeal (*veneremque conciliari*)". It also killed mice.[66]

The "tears of Helen" will be the drops of resin that exude from the pine tree. Besides giving the fire of the processional torch (Greek *helenē*), and the intoxicant and beautifier Helenion, prime ingredient of Nectarion, this resin was thought to be the source of the sacred mushroom, the *Amanita muscaria*. As Pliny says, "the fungi. . . are all derived from the gum that exudes from trees."[67] It is to the gum of the pine that an Accadian incantation is directed: "O *kukru, kukru, kukru,* in the pure, holy mountains thou hast engendered 'little-ones' by a sacred prostitute, 'seeds-of-a-Pine' by a vestal . . .",[68] with the plea that whatever sorcery may thus have been begotten shall be dispersed. The "little-ones" and the parallel phrase "seeds-of-a-Pine" are clearly substitute-words for some magic vegetation too powerful even to be given their proper names. Their manner of "engendering" by sacred prostitutes and their resinous origin leave little doubt that it is the *Amanita muscaria* that is here involved, the "fate-deciding" Nectar.

The name by which the incantation addresses the pine-resin, *kukru,* is another link with the "swan" motif of the myth of Helen's birth. Both names go back to a Sumerian phrase meaning "pod": in the case of the Pine referring to that species which have kernels like small lice "pods", earning the name of "louse-tree"[68a]; and as regards the "swan", because like other fertility-birds, its name was connected with the "womb-pod".[69]

Helen's name, as we saw, means also "pine-torch", and an important source of names and attendant mythologies connected with the *Amanita muscaria* stems from its red canopy, studded with white flecks.[70] Furthermore, the cap has an extremely bitter, "fiery" taste, and a combination of both characteristics is partly responsible for the "burning coal" imagery of Isaiah: "Then flew one of the seraphim to me, having in his hand a burning coal which he had taken with tongs from the altar. And he touched my mouth . . ." (Isa 6:6, 7). Josephus describes the Baaras plant of Machaerus as "flame-coloured and towards evening emitting a brilliant light".[71] It is the same kind of conception that underlies the vision of the "son of man" standing in the midst of the seven golden lampstands, his face "like the sun shining in full strength" (Rev 1:12ff.), and of Moses whose face "shone because he had been talking with God" (Exod 34:29).

In later chapters we shall be looking in more detail at the allusions in names and colour to the striking deep red or purple cap of the

The Plaincourault fresco showing the *Amanita muscaria* as the tree of good and evil in the Garden of Eden, c.1291, Plaincourault chapel at Mérigny, Indre Dist., France.

Amanita muscaria. Even the white flecking caused by the fragments of the volva adhering to the surface was the subject of special epithets, not only on account of the peculiar colouring effect but because the "scabby" aspect reminded the myth-makers of skin diseases, particularly leprosy.

In this chapter we have seen how human gestation of the foetus in the womb was paralleled in the eyes of the ancients by the growth of the sacred fungus from the menses-like resins of certain trees, particularly the conifers. These were particularly powerful, personified in mythology by the goddess of childbirth, Eileithyia, and by Helen, sister of the mushroom pair, Castor and Pollux. The equivalent of such menstrual blood in human women could only be found in that of virgins, and females having their first child. Here, also, was another reason for seeing the product of the "virgin" vulva of the mushroom a very special growth endued with abnormal power.

If the sacred fungus was related by name and gestation to the female organs, the cult which centred on the *Amanita muscaria* depended in large measure on female participation. We have now to look at the role of the cultic prostitute in this and related religious practices.

IX

The Sacred Prostitute

In the incantation to the pine-resin quoted in the last chapter, the "little ones" were said to have been engendered by "a sacred prostitute". This cultic office was well known in the ancient world. It is usually assumed that the woman dedicated herself to the service of the god as a sexual partner in some imitative ritual designed to stimulate the generative faculties of the fertility deity. Doubtless in many of the cults she did perform such a function, copulating before the altar with the priests or other male worshippers at certain festivals. However, that this was not her only form of service, or even necessarily her prime function, is indicated by the vegetation reference of the *kukru* incantation.

In the Bible, the cultic title is used in one case when the woman plays the part of a common whore, where Tamar seduced her father-in-law at the road-side (Gen 38), but elsewhere the sacred prostitute plays her proper religious role, and is associated like her sister of the *kukru* incantation with hills and trees. Thus Hosea describes the apostate Israelites as harlots "sacrificing on the tops of mountains, making offerings upon the hills, under oak, poplar, and terebinth, because their shade is good" (Hos 4:13 [Heb. 14]).[1]

The Old Testament speaks also of male cult prostitutes, called otherwise "dogs". It is more likely that these persons were sodomites than that they served the female worshippers as counterparts to the feminine cult prostitutes. In which case the epithet "dog" is not necessarily a term of abuse, but merely descriptive of their manner of copulation.[2] It is perhaps significant that one of the Sumerian terms for "chanter-priest" is GALA, elsewhere meaning "womb", with a semantic equivalent, USh-KU, literally, "penis-anus". Their prime purpose may then have been as a means of providing or extracting semen for cultic purposes, particularly for the priest's anointing as a symbolic "phallus" before the god, a "christ".[3]

However that may be, it is the vegetative function of the female cult-prostitute that must engage our main attention. In the *kukru* incantation, she is credited with engendering the "little ones" from the tree's "menses", the resin. Bearing in mind the phallic form of the sacred mushroom, it is reasonable to assume that her task was to "seduce" the little "penis" from the ground by sexual wiles. Josephus tells us that to stop the Mandrake "shrinking away from the touch" and to make it "stand still" one was required to pour upon it the menses and urine of a woman.[4] Where the cult prostitute was herself present this was probably achieved directly, involving exposing her genitals to that part of the ground where the mushroom was thought to lie dormant.

Self-exposure of a menstruating woman for vegetative purposes is elsewhere recorded. Pliny says that, in order to utilize the harmful effect menses was believed to have upon "caterpillars, worms, beetles and other vermin", menstruants "walked around the cornfield naked", and the vermin fell to the ground. It was said that the discovery of the effects of menses in this respect was made initially in Cappadocia, "owing to a plague there of Spanish fly, so that women . . . walk through the middle of the fields with their clothes pulled up above the buttocks".[5]

There are indications that it was considered necessary to make some sort of booth or covering for the witch and the magic plant during the seduction. Hosea in the passage just quoted specifies that the sacred prostitutes practised their art under trees where "the shade is good". Ezekiel, in a most interesting passage describing the activities of female necromancers, speaks of some kind of full-length veil by which they "ensnared souls" (Ezek 13:18). The Holy Plant had to be uprooted under cover of darkness, "lest the act be seen by the woodpecker of Mars" (perhaps a folk-name for the red-topped *Amanita muscaria*),[6] or "the sun and moon".[7]

Among the Accadian magical texts is an instruction for the uprooting of the *tigilla*, the bolt- or phallus-plant, or mushroom. We have already met the Sumerian original of this name, UKUSh-TI-GIL-LA, a jumbled version of which gave the Greek name *Glukuside*, Glycyside, for the Holy Plant.[8]

> Go, my son [it reads], the *tigilla*, which springs up of its own accord in the desert - when the sun enters its dwelling, cover your head with a cloth,

and cover the *tigilla,* surrounding it with flour, and in the morning before sunrise root it out of its place, and take its root . . .[9]

The necessity for covering oneself and the magic plant during the process of taking it from the ground, reminds one of another of those apparently banal asides of Josephus when describing the mysterious Essenes. In the midst of an important passage about their manner of discipline, he turns aside to tell us exactly how they perform their natural functions:

> they dig a trench a foot deep with a mattock – such is the nature of the small axe which they present to the neophytes – and wrapping their mantle about them, that they may not offend the rays of the deity, they squat above it. They then replace the excavated soil in the trench. For this purpose they select the more desolate places. And although this discharge of the excrements is a natural function, they make it a rule to wash themselves after it, as if defiled.[10]

Everything here except the ritual purification is decreed in Jewish Law (Deut 23:12ff.), and is no more than commonsense camp hygiene. There seems no point at all in the astute author wasting space describing this normal practice unless he means to convey another of his titbits of secret information for those who want to look beneath the surface. The reference to the "rays of the deity" and the lustration might give substance to the idea.

The shading by veil or booth of the mushroom-seeker was accompanied by other means of magical protection. Reference is made to drawing circles round the plant and its plunderer with a sword, the metal itself being considered fraught with supernatural power.[11] Another form of protection was to sprinkle flour round the plant, as the seeker of the *tigilla* was instructed in the Accadian incantation. In this case the encirclement offered some measure of protection and the flour was a token of compensation to the earth for its rape, as Pliny says when Asclepios, another name for the sacred fungus, is taken: "it is a pious duty to fill in the hole with various cereals as an atonement to the earth".[12] It is the same principle at work when the seers offered atonement to the Pine on taking the precious resin called Eileithyia, the "menses".[13]

The fundamental principle of fertility philosophy was that of balance, as we have previously noted.[14] To take any of the fruits of the earth necessitated some measure of compensation or sacrifice to the god. To be effective this return payment should be at least qualitatively equivalent to the gift received, so that only the best of the harvest, the first-reaped of the corn and first-born of the animals, was suitable. In the case of an especially powerful plant like the sacred mushroom, an atoning substitution posed special problems. Since the fungus was the god himself made manifest on earth, no atoning sacrifice by mortals could suffice. The seeker could only bring along with him the Holy Plant itself or some symbol of it, and this is probably the explanation of a curious phrase in Josephus' description of the seizing of the Mandrake: "to touch it is fatal unless one succeeds in bringing along the thing itself, the root, hanging from one's hand".[15] The verb he uses, *epipherō,* elsewhere refers to the bringing of a dowry by a bride to her husband, or the supplying of his own rations by the soldier himself during a campaign. In other words, only the god can atone for himself, and herein lies the basis of the Christian doctrine of the Incarnation and Atonement, which we must examine afresh in its cultic context in a later chapter.

Ezekiel, in describing the necromantic ritual of the witches, says they fastened "magic bands" *(kesātōt)* on their wrists, and with them "trapped souls like birds" (Ezek 13:20). This rare word is related to the Sumerian KI-ShU, meaning some kind of magical imprisonment, but we have to look to Greek for its precise significance. In the form *kistē,* Latin *cista,* it appears as a container used in certain mystery rituals of the Dionysiac cult, supposedly for the carrying of secret implements. In fact, wherever the *cista* is graphically represented it is shown as a basket from which a snake is emerging. Thus on sarcophagi inscribed with Bacchic scenes, the *cista* is shown being kicked open by Pan and the snake raising itself from the half-opened lid.[16] The snake is an important feature of the Dionysiac cult and imagery. The Maenads of Euripides' *Bacchae* have serpents entwined in their hair and round their limbs, and the snake was the particular emblem of the Phrygian Sabazios (Sabadius) with whom Dionysus is identified.[17]

It is not difficult to see the reasoning behind the ancient connection between the serpent and the mushroom, which played such a large part in mushroom folk-lore and mythology. Both emerged from holes in the ground in a manner reminiscent of the erection of the sexually awakened penis, and both bore in their heads a fiery poison which the ancients believed could be transferred from one to the other. "If the hole of a serpent", writes Pliny, "has been near the mushroom, or should a serpent have breathed on it as it first opened, its kinship to poisons makes it capable of absorbing the venom. So it would not be well to eat mushrooms until the serpent has begun to hibernate."[18]

The prime example of the relation between the serpent and the mushroom is, of course, in the Garden of Eden story of the Old Testament. The cunning reptile prevails upon Eve and her husband to eat of the tree, whose fruit "made them as gods, knowing good and evil" (Gen 3:4). The whole Eden story is mushroom-based mythology, not least in the identity of the "tree" as the sacred fungus, as we shall see.[19] Even as late as the thirteenth century some recollection of the old tradition was known among Christians, to judge from a fresco painted on the wall of a ruined church in Plaincourault in France (pl. 2). There the *Amanita muscaria* is gloriously portrayed, entwined with a serpent, whilst Eve stands by holding her belly.[20]

The Bacchic *cista* and Ezekiel's witches' "magic bands" were, then, probably meant to represent the lower "cup" of the mushroom volva, the little "basket" from which the stalk of the fungus emerged, like a snake being charmed from its box. In this conception lies the origin of such stories as Moses, the "emergent serpent", as now we may understand his name to mean,[21] in his papyrus ark, and Dionysus and Jesus in their "mangers", in essence, "covered baskets".[22] As objects attached to the wrists of the sacred prostitutes at the mushroom-raising ceremony, these replicas of the matted volva, perhaps already divided to reveal the emergent mushroom stem, were probably intended to offer a kind of imitative encouragement to the dormant fungus to open and reveal itself.

The ability of a woman even by her physical presence to induce a man's sex organ to stir into life, apparently without any control on its owner's part, must have been a source of great wonder to the ancients. It was sorcery, and as such viewed with apprehension and distrust by men generally, not unmixed with religious awe. This was particularly the case with those mystic orders which made use of the sexual power of women for their secret rites. Of the Essenes Josephus says: "They do not, indeed, on principle, condemn wedlock and the propagation of the human race, but they wish to protect themselves against woman's wantonness, being persuaded that none of the sex keeps her plighted troth to one man."[23] Of that order of Essenes who did marry, he says: "They think that those who decline to marry cut off the chief function of life, the propagation of the race, and, what is more, that, were all to adopt the same view, the whole race would very quickly die out. They give their wives, however, three years' probation, and only marry them after they have, by three periods of purification, given proof of fecundity.[24] They have no intercourse with them during pregnancy, thus showing that their motive in marrying is not self-indulgence but the procreation of children."[25]

One is reminded of the Church's oft-reiterated edict that the purpose of marriage is the procreation of children. It comes as something of a shock to us in the Western world, after centuries of religiously inspired puritanism, to learn that the ancients attributed the greater inclinations towards sexual indulgence to women. It was said that the seer Teiresias was chosen by Zeus and Hera to decide on the question whether the male or the female derived most pleasure from sexual intercourse. He replied that "of the ten parts of coitus, a man enjoys one only; but a woman's senses enjoy all ten to the full".[26]

However that may be, there is no doubt that the sexual power of women was vital to the mystery cults, and accounts in large measure for their attractiveness to women from the earliest times. It also has much to do with the antagonism towards sexuality generally and the distrust of women displayed by the later Church, and the readiness with which supposed witches were hounded by Christians until quite recent times. The telepathic control over people's minds exercised by such females, known the world over as "the evil eye", came originally from this ability to arouse men's passions. The Latin *fascinus,* from which our "fascination" comes, as well as meaning "bewitching", was also the proper name of a deity whose emblem was the erect penis, and this indeed, as we can now appreciate, is the original source of this word and the Greek *baskanos,* "sorcerer".[27] It was believed that the malign influences of "fascination", which came to be extended to any form of mental dominance, could be averted by wearing on the person a model penis, rather as the Christian symbol of the Cross is currently displayed by those within and without the Church to ward off evil. The worship of Fascinus was entrusted to the Vestal Virgins,[28] a further indication of the sexual nature of their sacred fire.

A similar connection between sexual influence and sorcery appears in the derivation of our word "magic". Its immediate source is the Latin *magus,* representing the Old Persian *magush,* the title of a religious official whose power of mind and body earned him a reputation for sorcery. We have met the Magi earlier as one of the prime sources in the ancient writings for plant names and medicinal folk-lore. Their title may now be traced to a Sumerian phrase for "big-penis", and seen to be cognate with the Greek *pharmakos,* "enchanter, wizard", from which comes our "pharmacist".[29]

Women, then, had an important part to play in the mushroom cult. It made them at once respected and feared. Their power over men and particularly over the male organ seemed magical, and the technical term for this influence, "fascination", became extended to any form of mental dominance, usually of a malign character.

Details of the way in which the cultic prostitutes drew forth the phallic mushroom can only be deduced from names and scattered references in literature. But one term seems continually in evidence in describing their activities, "lamentation". Just what this implies in its religious sense is the subject of our next chapter.

X

Religious Lamentation

Religious lamentation is a curious phenomenon. This sympathetic identification of the worshipper with a suffering god seems to be a necessary part of most religions, particularly those in which women play an active role. To see Catholic women, particularly in the Mediterranean countries, wracked with real grief at Eastertide as they contemplate the Crucifix and the wounds of their Lord, can leave little doubt that they are suffering real mental anguish. Doubtless the female votaries of the goddess Ishtar, bemoaning the fate of her husband Tammuz, in whatever terms the myth was recounted throughout the ancient Near East, were as genuinely moved in their emotions as the tearful suppliant at the foot of the Cross.

There is apparently in human beings, and in women particularly, a capacity for sympathetic grief which demands dramatic expression, however artificially contrived the stimulant, however historically improbable the tragic events and persons they re-enact in their imaginations. Aristotle, some twenty-two centuries ago, defined tragedy as "the imitation of an action that is serious, and also, as having magnitude, complete in itself. . . with incidents arousing pity and terror, with which to accomplish its purgations of these emotions".[1]

The psychologist will doubtless trace this female capacity for altruistic suffering to her sexual constitution. The curse pronounced upon womankind in Eden that she must find her physical fulfilment in pain has the ring of profound psychological truth: "I will greatly multiply your pain in childbearing; in pain you shall bring forth children, yet your sexual desire shall be to your man even while he rules over you" (Gen 3:16).

Certainly, ritual lamentation has a sexual significance, as can now be demonstrated by its terminology. Whatever inward emotional satisfaction the practice of lamenting the dead god may have achieved, its objective intention was to bring him back to life. In the case of agricultural communities, the dead god is but a personification of the fertility of the soil, deemed to have perished during the hot summer months but capable of being revivified under the influence of the autumn and spring rains, the spermatozoa of the father-god in heaven. Thus the lamentation ceremonies were intended to rejuvenate the dormant penis of the fertility deity. The common Hebrew word for lamentation is *qīnah*, used for a particularly compulsive rhythm of three heavy beats followed by an "echo" of two more. The word comes from the Sumerian GI-NA, "erect", coalescing into one word GIN, with the same meaning. Followed by URA, "penis", it is found in Greek as *kinura* and in Hebrew as *kinnor*, "harp" or "lyre"; properly, then, the musical instrument which had the power of causing sexual stimulation in the man, and in the god.[2] The Hebrew *kinnōr* was the harlot's instrument, according to Isaiah (23:16), had the sound of the "rumbling of the bowels" (Isa 16:11), and was played by David to relieve the maniacal Saul (I Sam 16:16, etc).

If, in historical times, the vocal efforts of the *kinura* players could be considered melodious, ritual lamentation was not originally designed to appeal to the musical ear. One of the Sumerian titles for the lamentation priest was I-LU-BALAG-DI, the latter part of which, meaning "penis-stirrer", has a Semitic equivalent meaning "screech, roar, wail", and is found in Arabic as the title of the peacock, "The Screecher". This Semitic root is itself derived from a Sumerian phrase meaning "hurricane", so we may assume that part of the idea of ritual lamentation was to imitate the storm-wind howling to its crescendo, an indication that the fertility god in the heavens was approaching his mighty orgasm and ejaculation.[3]

Presumably screaming was reckoned to have some erotic effect, and psychologically there may be some connection here with the extraordinary noise produced by teenage fans of pop-singers. The use of such tactics by female seducers of the Mandrake has perhaps found recognition in the long-standing tradition that when the magic plant is dragged from the ground it gives a demoniacal shriek.[4]

The root of *kinura*, "lyre", and its cognates appears in Greek mythology as the name of the king of Cyprus, Cinyras. He is said to have founded the cult of Aphrodite in that island, and his name is given to the Cinyrades, priests of the Aphrodite-Astarte fertility cult in Paphos.

Cinyras is also reputed to have introduced sacred prostitution into Cyprus, and to have been a musician.[5]

The same idea of sexual stimulation appears in other musical terms, and in general where "praising" the god is involved. Indeed, our word "music", as one of the arts of the Greek Muses, has at heart the Sumerian phrase for "raising the heart", which elsewhere indicates sexual stimulation.[6] In the classical world, the god Dionysus shares honours with his adoptive brother Apollo as "leader of the Muses". Another of his epithets was *Dithurambos,* Dithyramb, the original meaning of which has long been a mystery. It comes to be used of a Dionysiac song which possessed some infectious quality that led his votaries to take it up as a ritual chant. Later it became the subject for competition at Dionysiac festivals, and with its formalization it lost any spontaneity it may have possessed originally. Surviving fragments of the dithyramb show nothing to suggest its original connection with this fertility deity and his attributes.

However, it is now clear from its Sumerian source that "dithyramb" fits philologically into the pattern of other cultic musical terms, meaning literally "chant for erection of the penis".[7] Incidentally, this serves to confirm the opinion of the second-century writer Athenaeus that the god and this epithet *Dithurambos* were connected with the phallic deity Priapus, from whose name comes our word "priapism" or "erection of the penis".[8] It also confirms the suggestion that the Greek *dithurambos* is of the same root as the Latin *triumpus,* our "triumph".[9] This term was properly used of the victory procession through the capital city which was accorded a victorious general on his return from war. The wooden replica of the phallus which adorned his chariot emphasized the essentially virile nature of the "triumph".[10]

The original significance of the Dithyramb is of some importance for the nature and origin of Dionysiac music, and, indeed, for the history of tragedy generally. At the beginning of the fifth century BC, tragedy formed part of the Great Dionysia, the spring festival of Dionysus Eleuthereus. Three poets competed, each contributing three tragedies and one satyric play. The latter was performed by choruses of fifty singers in a circle, dressed as satyrs, part human, part bestial, and bearing before them huge replicas of the erect penis, as they sang dithyrambs. The Greek word *tragoidia,* "tragedy", has been connected with *tragos,* "goat", either because the satyr chorus wore goat-skins, or because a goat was the prize offered the successful competitors. In fact, the "goat" reference of the word is secondary; its prime significance, as the Sumerian original now shows, was a "lament raised to stimulate fecundity".[11] Thus the original intention of the tragedy, the singing of ritual laments and dithyrambs, was erotic.

One name by which Dionysus was known throughout the ancient world was Bacchus. A fourth-century BC hymn in honour of Dionysus contains the invocation: "Come to us, King Dithyramb, Bacchus, god of the holy chant."[12] The name Bacchus, Greek *bak-khos,* Latin *bacchus* is a shortened form of the Sumerian *BALAG-USh, "erect penis", made by assimilating the middle *l* to the following consonant. The word BALAG is made up of two elements, BAL, "borer", and AGA, "crown", so the whole properly meant the tip of the penis, the glans, or, in other circumstances, the boring bit of a drill.[13]

The same loss of the *l* occurred in certain derivative forms. Thus, directly connected with erotic "lamentation", Hebrew developed a verbal root *b-k-h,* "weep, bewail", so that, for example, Ezekiel's Tammuz-lamenters are *mebakkōth,* a feminine participle of this verb. Latin, on the other hand, preserved the *l* and gave us our word "plague", properly a "stroke", from *plango,* "beat (the breast, head, in lamentation), weep, bewail".

In extant Sumerian texts BALAG, "penis" is used specifically for the erotic instrument itself, prefaced or followed with the word for the instrumentalist, NAR, "eroticist".[14] Her counterpart in Greek was the *pallakis,* Latin *pellex,* Hebrew *pilegesh,* where the word had come to mean, generally, "concubine", or simply, "young woman".[15]

The female votaries of the phallus god Bacchus were known as the Bacchantes, that is, those whose cult centred on the BALAG-AN-TA the "raised mushroom/penis".[16] They were characterized by extreme forms of religious excitement interspersed with periods of intense depression. At one moment whirling in a frenzied dance, tossing their heads, driving one another on with screaming and the wild clamour of musical instruments,[17] at another sunk into the deepest lethargy, and a silence so intense as to become proverbial.[18] The Bacchantes both possessed the god and were possessed by him; theirs was a religious enthusiasm in the proper sense of the term, that is, "god-filled".[19] Having eaten the Bacchus or Dionysus, they took on his power and character as the Christians "carried in their bodies the death of Jesus, so that the life of Jesus might be manifested in their bodies" (II Cor 4:10). As the Old Testament put it, by eating of the fruit of the tree of life, the initiates had become "like one of us", the gods (Gen 3:22).

Outsiders were forbidden on pain of death from attending the secret rites, as Pentheus found to his cost in the myth on which Euripides based his tragedy, *The Bacchae*. So traditional accounts of the details of the Dionysiac, like any other mysteries, are bound to be somewhat distorted, if not purely imaginary. This is particularly so in the all-important matter of the identity of the sacred meal through which the mystic union between god and worshipper was achieved. What we now know to have been the *Amanita muscaria* is traditionally referred to as "fawns" or "little children", supposed to have been pulled asunder and eaten raw while the blood was still warm. The fact is that one of the names of the mushroom was "fawn" or "gazelle", so called mainly from a similarity seen between the large, round, shining eyes of these animals (from which the name "gazelle" is derived), and the top of the mushroom.[20] The biblical Song of Songs, which we can now begin to understand as a dramatic ode to the sacred mushroom and its seeker, describes the Shulammite in such terms: "your two breasts are like two fawns, twins of a gazelle" (Song of Sol 4:5, 7:3 [Heb. 4]).[21] Another animal closely connected with the god and his votaries is the panther. In this case it is the colour and markings of the skin that is the subject of comparison, corresponding to the dusky-red and white or yellowish spots of the *Amanita muscaria,* and even more to the closely related *Amanita pantherina* whose name is similarly derived.[22]

The "little children" reputed to have been torn apart by the raving Bacchantes will be of the same category as those "slain among the wadies, under the cleft rocks" by Isaiah's "sons of witches", who sought for "smooth things" by pouring out to them drink and cereal offerings (Isa 57:5, 6). We have seen the use of this substitution-word previously in the Accadian incantation to the *kukru*-resin of the pine tree, whose "little ones", or "pine-cones", the cultic prostitutes had "engendered".[23]

The same kind of distortion of facts in relation to secret fertility cults can be seen actually in operation in the Old Testament traditions. Towards the end of the seventh century BC the young King Josiah tried to purge Jerusalem of the old fertility worship. Among his acts of desecration was the defilement of Topheth "which is in the valley of the sons of Hinnom, that no one might burn his son or his daughter as an offering to Molech" (II Kgs 23:10).

Jeremiah also speaks of this Molech cult when he says of the wayward people of Jerusalem: "They built the high places of Baal in the valley of the son of Hinnom, to offer up their sons and daughters to Molech . . ." (Jer 32:35).

The commentators have drawn horrifying pictures for us of wicked men pushing little Solly and Rachel on to the funeral pyre outside Jerusalem's south wall for the benefit of this pagan deity Molech. The clue to what was really intended, and indeed, what was probably written in the first editions of Kings and Jeremiah, is to be found in the corresponding passage in the Law. It appears in the context of regulations about sexual "perversions", mainly concerning the degrees of family relationship within which the man may not have intercourse: mother, mother-in-law, sister, granddaughter, and so on. It goes on:

> You shall not give your seed to devote it to Molech. You shall not commit sodomy. You shall not commit buggery, and neither shall any woman have sexual relations with a beast; it is perversion (Lev 18:21-23).

The English versions fall into the same trap as did the early redactors of II Kings and Jeremiah. The Leviticus prohibition does not say "you shall not devote your *children* to Molech", but, literally, "your *seed*", that is, your spermatozoa. The word "seed" can of course be extended to mean offspring, but the context shows that the burden of the law is that you should not pollute the god-given semen, after which Yahweh was named, by misusing it either in the anus of another male or genitals of an animal, or, in some way, by using it in the worship of Molech.

The name Molech is philologically related to that group of mucilaginous herbs called "Mallow", to the magic plant Moly, and the Greek *Mukēs*, "mushroom". The root of all lies in the idea of the erect penis, so we may reasonably infer that the practice here objected to involved the dedication in some way of human semen in a phallic rite probably connected with the sacred fungus.[24]

In the awful silence that fell over the Bacchanal periodically, made more profound doubtless by its contrast with the maniacal raving preceding it, we may have a clue to another of the curious features of Essenism reported by Josephus. "No clamour or disturbance ever pollutes their dwelling;" he says, "they speak in turn, each making way for his neighbour. To persons outside *the silence of those within appears like some awful mystery* . . ."[25] The explanation he offers, that the limitation of their rations to bare necessities imposed a restriction upon their efforts, hardly justifies his praise for their self-discipline, nor adequately accounts for the profound silence that seems to the outsider like an "awful mystery". Nearer the truth, probably, is the comment of one scholar on the "Bacchic silence": "Is it", he asks, "the exhaustion that follows upon over-exaltation, or is it the very zenith reached by the flight of the spirit when voices and sounds are hushed, and in rapt silence the soul feels closest to God? That this was a method for attaining the highest and deepest communion was known to the ancient theosophists, and this mysterious proverb suggests that it may have been known to the followers of the wild Thracian god."[26]

In fact, there was a more clinical reason for the Bacchic lethargy. The poisons contained in the cap of the *Amanita muscaria* promote periods of intense excitement, accompanied by delirium, hallucinations, and great animation, but these are followed by periods of deep depression. To quote one witness to *Amanita muscaria* intoxication: "The person intoxicated by Fly-Agaric (a popular name for the *Amanita muscaria*) sits quietly rocking from side to side, not even taking part in the conversation with his family. Suddenly his eyes dilate, he begins to gesticulate convulsively, converses with persons whom he imagines he sees, sings and dances. Then an interval of rest sets in again . . ."[27]

Nevertheless, the Bacchanalian characteristic of uninhibited excitement succeeded by calm, was not a mere accident of drug therapy. Eating the god made it possible to induce and to some extent control an experience which was fundamental to fertility philosophy. The repeated bouts of drug-stimulated excitement were in the nature of violent and unnaturally prolonged sexual orgasms, whether or not they resulted in erection and ejaculation on the part of the men or spasmodic vaginal contractions by the women. As coitus is usually followed by sleep and a mildly depressive state of mind, so every Bacchic frenzy was followed by a time of calm.

Emotionally, and perhaps spiritually, these periods of physical relaxation were as essential to the mystic experience of the Dionysus worshipper as to the acts of human love. They were equally as necessary to the fertility cycle of the natural world. As sleep follows coitus, and a fresh-scented peace succeeds the storm, so too the land lies fallow after the "birth" of harvest. The Jewish mythologists traced their obligatory rest-day, the Sabbath ("heart's easement"),[28] back to their god's resting from his creative labours when he made the world (Gen 2:2f). But the Hebrew agriculturalist recognized a regular sabbatical rhythm in nature requiring a sabbath year after every six, when the fields might rest fallow to recoup their strength and restore the essential balance (Lev 25:3f). After forty-nine years, the "heart's easement" applied to every side of human experience: familial, economic, as well as agricultural (Lev 25:8-17). Perhaps as the pace of life increases we shall one day have to insist on all human beings reappropriating this sabbatical year principle of the fertility philosophy and applying it like the Hebrew Jubilee to every aspect of our family, economic, and social lives.

The raising of the sacred fungus, then, necessitated the use of "cultic prostitutes" whose bodily excretions and sexual fascination were thought to engender the "little children". Compensation was required if the balance of nature were not to be impaired when the Holy Plant was lifted from the earth. But these atoning sacrifices required no less the grace of the god, so that acceptance of his supreme gift required further sacrifice on his part.

The ritualistic lamentation which marked ceremonies devoted to the raising of the sacred mushroom was erotic in character, as, apparently, was all music and drama in its original intent. The female votaries of the god Bacchus were the prime exponents of the fungus cult in the ancient world, and in their orgiastic excitement interspersed with periods of extreme lethargy we see reflected the rhythms of sexual and agricultural experience.

XI

The Mushroom "Egg" and Birds of Mythology

As the virgin goddess plays an important part in fertility cults throughout the ancient world, so the virgin volva of the sacred mushroom, her real-life counterpart in Nature, figures largely in fungus nomenclature and mythology. Yet the mushroom is in some respects a hermaphrodite, displaying characteristics of both sexes. With the stem at full stretch, as we have seen, the *Amanita muscaria* seemed to the ancients like an erect, fiery-topped penis.[1] But if the volva is sliced open before it splits of its own accord, there will be found inside a fully formed mushroom waiting to expand, like a foetus in a womb, or a chick in an egg (fig. 4). It is small wonder, then, that the mushroom was spoken of as a "womb" and many of its folk-designations and imagery come from this concept.

One such name we have already noticed in Paeony, the Holy Plant, and, in mythological terms, "Peter, Bar-jona". Using the same Sumerian element in the last part of that word, *IA-U-NA, "fertility; womb", and prefaced with the Sumerian word GIG, "shade, protection"', there came into Semitic the name *qīqāyōn,* "pod-plant", used for Jonah's mushroom sun-shade.[2] That same word in Hebrew represented also a plant of a quite different kind but which also had pod- or womb-like fruits containing the laxative with which nursery tummy-upsets have made us all too familiar: castor oil. Our English translators of the Jonah story have sometimes had the unfortunate prophet seeking shade from the sun under a castor oil tree.

Our word "uterus" comes ultimately from a Sumerian phrase *USh-TAR with the same meaning. A fuller form of "Bar-jona" combined *BAR-IA-U-NA with *USh-TAR to make the Greek name of the Holy Plant, *Peristereōn*[3], which became most important for mushroom mythology in the Greek-speaking world and particularly in the New Testament. The old botanists not unnaturally connected the name with the "dove", Greek *peristera,* thinking the Holy Plant must have been the natural habitat for these birds. In fact, the connection is much more direct. The bird's name in Greek, as its equivalent *yonah* in Semitic (Jonah's name is the same word), actually means "womb"; the reference to the bird is secondary.[4]

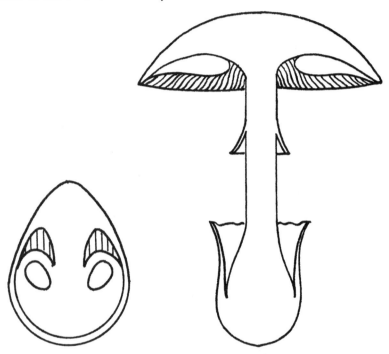

4 Diagrammatic section of (i) a volva before "birth" (ii) a mature mushroom

A number of birds are, like the dove, connected in ancient nomenclature and mythology with fertility and the womb, and thus with the mushroom. The dove is traditionally associated with peace, the word for which in both Greek and Semitic has an underlying significance of "fertility" and "fruitfulness".[5] In Hebrew the delightful word, *shālōm,* is used, like its Arabic equivalent, *salām,* as a traditional greeting, "Peace!" But it is more than not being at war with anything or anybody; it has, like the sound of the word itself, a sense of being replete, content, in the terms of the old fertility philosophy, in a state of balance with yourself and the world. Those people of the ancient Near East, who gave us our culture, would have viewed our concern with the Pill with incredulity. The barren womb was a plague from the god; a woman without a foetus in her belly was an insult to her sex and her man. In that house there could be no *shālōm,* no "peace".

The dove symbolized fruitfulness. As Nature is composed of opposites, and as the foetus is born of the white sperm of the male and the dark red blood of the female,[6] so the white dove has its counterpart in the black raven. Its name also can be traced back in Greek and Semitic to the womb idea,[7] and it too was traditionally associated with fertility. The Greeks invoked the raven at weddings, and there was a curious idea that, like the dove, the raven laid its eggs or mated through its beak.[8] Pliny poured scorn on the idea, and thought it was just a way of kissing. Nevertheless, he quotes the "old wives' tale" that pregnant women should avoid eating ravens' eggs lest they bear their children through their mouths. It was the same observation of the manner of courtship of these birds that led the Romans to call a man who indulged in labial kissing during sex-play a "crow".[9]

It was a raven that was sent out first from Noah's ark to survey the flooded world, and it was a dove sent out later that brought back evidence of new growth in its beak (Gen 8 :6ff.).

In the Old Testament account of the Creation, the spirit of God hovers like a bird above the primeval sea, wafting with its wing-beat the breath of God into the slime from which the world was made (Gen 1 :2). So Pliny speaks of "that famous breath (*spiritus*) that generates the universe by fluctuating to and fro as in a kind of womb".[10] It is much the same imagery that portrays the Holy Spirit fluttering down on the head of Jesus at his baptism (Matt 3:16), making him, too, a "Bar-jona", "Son of a Dove".

Another important example of the winged creature/fertility motif in the Old Testament is the idea of the cherubim. The modern popular image of the cherub as a rosy-cheeked and under-clad infant with diminutive wings owes more to late artistic conceptions of post-biblical Jewish angelology than the Old Testament. There the cherub is pictured as a strange hybrid creature, having two, four or six wings (counting Isaiah's "seraphim" as of the same order) and one, two or four heads, human and bestial. Yahweh rides upon a cherub, "swiftly upon the wings of the wind" (Ps 18:10 [Heb. 11] = II Sam 22:11), and is "the one enthroned upon the cherubim" (I Sam 4:4, etc). This last figure refers to the throne of Yahweh in the Holy of Holies of the Jerusalem temple where two cherubim stand on either side of an arched canopy[11] ("mercy-seat") over the ark of the testimony (Exod 25:17ff.). The outstretched wings of the cherubim form Yahweh's throne, and it is there that the god promises to meet Moses and his high priestly successors for oracular consultation.

The cherubim are here exercising a protective function as they do in the Garden of Eden (Gen 3:24), scene of the primeval creation. Similarly, Ezekiel speaks of them as the "screening cherubim of the anointing" in God's garden (28:13f). In classical mythology the counterpart of the biblical cherubim are the griffins who guard a source of treasure near a cave called "the Earth's Doorbolt", the entrance into the womb of mother Earth.[12] Like the cherub, the griffin is pictured bearing the god on its back, and drawing the chariot of the fertility goddess Aphrodite with her charioteer Eros.[13]

Ezekiel, and following him late Jewish mysticism, makes much of the cherubim and related chariot imagery. To the prophet, in some form of hallucinatory trance, they appear as grotesque apparitions in a storm, surrounded by flashes of lightning and roars of thunder (Ezek 1:4, 24). They move not only on outstretched wings but with whirling, eye-studded wheels, having in them the "spirit of life", and they bear the glory of Yahweh from the Temple porch (chs. 1, 10). Above their heads is a canopy and beneath it their wings are spread, two for flying and two to cover their bodies (Ezek 1:6, 23).

The mushroom imagery is here dramatically evident. The prophet sees the *Amanita muscaria,* its glowing red cap studded with the white flakes of the broken pellicle from the volva. In this skin lies the hallucinatory drug, one of whose properties is to enhance the perceptive faculties, making colours brighter and objects far larger or smaller than their real size.[14]

Philologically, also, the cherub-griffin is related to the fungus. The names in Indo-European and Semitic go back to another "pod-" or "womb-" word, *GUR-UB, similar in meaning to the source of the name of the well-known pod-plant, the Carob.[15] It was this Carob that supplied the horn- or uterus-shaped pods eaten by the Prodigal Son (Luke 15:16). Pliny described them as "not longer than a man's finger, occasionally curved like a sickle, with the thickness of a man's thumb".[16] The name had another reference in the ancient world, however. The Accadian botanists use the same Semitic word for Carob to describe the Sumerian "Seed-of-life" plant, the mushroom.[17]

The association between birds and the womb must have been in part due to the similarity seen between the chick in its pellicle of the egg and the foetus in the uterine membrane, just as Pliny drew a parallel between the baby mushroom in its "volva" and the chick in the egg. But for the idea of the outstretched wings of the womb-birds like the cherub-griffin, one should look to the fancied resemblance between the wings and the so-called "horns" of the uterus, the Fallopian tubes, which branch out from the top and terminate in the ovaries. A stylization of this kind appears in the Egyptian hieroglyph representing the bicornate uterus of the heifer, ꆱ.[18] It was this kind of imagery which brought together the name of the palm-tree, Phoenix, with the most famous of all the "womb-birds" of mythology. The relationship of the palm-tree, with its long stem surmounted by a canopy of leaves, and the mushroom, will be discussed later,[19] but the similarity between them both and the stylized uterus will be immediately evident.

The Phoenix bird was for centuries a favourite theme of mythology and philosophers, pagan and Christian.[20] It was believed to burn itself alive on its own nest at the end of an extremely long life, and from its body or ashes which had become fertilized there came forth another Phoenix. This offspring was, in some versions, created from the beginning a perfect replica of its parent, or, according to other reports, grew from a preliminary larval stage, like a grub.

The Phoenix-bird mythology is another piece of mushroom folklore.[21] As the foetus is generated in the furnace of the uterus, so the mushroom, that "evil ferment of the soil", as Nicander (second century BC) calls it,[22] is created, a "womb within a womb", as it were. Like the fabulous Phoenix, the mushroom is self-generated and regenerated, bursting forth from the volva, only to die as quickly and then apparently miraculously to reappear, a resurrection of its own self.

A great deal of the mythology of the ancient Near East hinges on the theme of the dying and rising god. It is usually, and correctly, seen as symbolism in story form of the processes of nature whereby in the heat of summer the earth's greenness disappears in death, to reappear the following spring in new birth. But, as we shall see, in the life cycle of the mushroom this natural cycle was quickened to a matter of days or even hours.[23] The fungus was a microcosm of the whole fertility process, the essence of god compressed into the womb and penis of the hermaphrodite mushroom.

It was long ago suggested that the Phoenix bird was the stork, ever the type and emblem of maternal and filial affection. The Latin name for this bird, *ciconia* is almost certainly derived from the Sumerian *GIG-IA-U-NA, "pod of fertility", the Hebrew *qīqāyōn* of Jonah's sunshade mushroom.[24] That it was the shape motif that earned for the bird this mushroom name, seems to be indicated by the use of *ciconia* in Latin for a "T"-shaped implement for measuring the depth of furrows in the field, as if this were the obvious characteristic of the bird as it stood on one leg, its body forming the "canopy".

The swan is another of the fertility birds. Possibly its long curved neck seemed to represent the vaginal passage, whilst its white body was the uterus and its outstretched wings were the Fallopian tubes. The Greek and Latin names for the bird, through which we received our "cygnet", are pod-names, derived from a Sumerian *GUG-NU,[25] "seed pod". In classical mythology, Zeus takes the form of a swan to mate with Leda, and from the union she was delivered of an egg from which came the heroine-goddess Helen and her twin brothers Castor and Pollux. The whole of this story is mushroom-inspired as we shall see, and the very common twin mythology of the ancient world comes directly out of the mushroom cult.

When the egg or volva of the mushroom splits into two, one half is left in the ground, the other forced upwards by the expanding stem or phallus, borne aloft as a canopy towards the sky. In those simplified terms, anyway, the old myth-makers saw the development of the fungus, and from that conception they formulated many stories and characters having to do with twin children, bearing names related to the "womb" and the "penis". When the offspring are combined into one person, like Adonis, Apollo, Dionysus, and so on, he is often pictured as a beautiful, rather effeminate youth, a favourite theme of the classical sculptors. On occasion, this person is a Hermaphrodite, a mixture of both sexes, the prime example of which was, as the name implies, the offspring of Hermes (Sumerian *ERUM-USh, "erect penis")[26] and Aphrodite (*A-BURU-DA-TI, "organ of fecundity", that is, the "womb").[27] In the following chapter we shall look at some "twin" stories derived from the "hermaphrodite"[28] mushroom, and at the symbolism it evoked.

XII

The Heavenly Twins

At first sight the portrayal of a fertility hero-deity like Apollo or Dionysus as a smooth-skinned, beardless stripling, almost girlish in features and deportment, seems to contradict their connections with sexuality and the fecundity of nature. Of a similar inconsistency are those "virgin" goddesses who seem to spend most of their time locked in copulatory embrace with husbands and lovers. Mercifully for our literary heritage, logic plays a very small part in religious mythology.

In the case of the "twin" stories, it seems equally strange that the children are usually featured as both of the same sex, usually boys or men. Whether they represent the male or female aspect of the mushroom, the "penis" or the "womb", can only be determined by reference to the original meanings of their names (a discriminatory problem with which we today are not entirely unfamiliar). This we can now do, thanks to our being able to trace the names back to their Sumerian origin. Thus the biblical brothers, Cain and Abel, represent the "womb" and the "penis" respectively. The first name comes from the Sumerian *GAR-EN, "seed-container",[1] and the second from BAL, "borer, phallus".[2] A fuller form of Abel's name, including the word TI, "organ", "instrument", produced the biblical proper name Tubal-Cain, the patron of metal-working, son of Zillah (Gen 4:22).[3]

These last references provide a good illustration of the way the Bible takes the fungus names of their heroes and heroines and provides the characters with their "parents" and "trades". Tubal-Cain's mother is Zillah, which, in the Aramaic-speaking community in which these stories must have originated, would have meant that he could be called "Bar-Zillah", "son of Zillah". The Semitic word for "iron" (properly "axe-head") is *barzelā'*, so naturally Tubal-Cain is a "metal-worker". The mushroom reference is to another meaning of *barzelā'*, "womb", actually the female "groin" (Sumerian *BAR-SIL(A), the "junction" of the body, where the legs meet the trunk, or, in the case of the "axe", where the haft is inserted in the V-shaped head). So two names for the fungus, the combined Tubal-Cain and *barzelā'* are spun out by the biblical myth-makers into a hero, his mother's name, and his trade.[4]

The ancient botanists give us an androgynous plant-name Eryngion (Greek *Eruggion)*, in which we can now recognize "Hermes" (ERUM) (the phallus) and "Cain" (the womb).[5] Pliny says of this plant:

> Marvellous is the characteristic reported of it, that its root grows into the likeness of one sex or the other. It is rarely so found, but should the male form come into the possession of men, they become lovable in the eyes of women. This, it is said, is how Phaon of Lesbos won the love of Sappho, there being much idle trifling on the subject not only among the Magi, but also among the Pythagoreans.[6]

Among its many reputed therapeutic properties, the Eryngion was said to correct "a deficiency or excess in menstruation, and all affections of the uterus".[7] It was also known as Hermaion, referring simply to the first element in its name, ERUM, "penis"; "Hermes". Another phallic name of the plant was Moly, properly the "knobbed-plant",[8] a common designation of the magic fungus in mythology.

Eryngion also appears among the names given the Aloe, otherwise called Amphibion, "double-life".[9] The prophet Tiresias was said to have been "amphibious" because he lived both as man and woman;[10] so perhaps our fashion designers have found themselves a new word in place of "unisex". Pliny says of the Aloe that its bulbous root resembles a Squill: "the root is single, as it were a stake sunk into the ground."[11] That is, the androgynous herb had a bulb (volva) and a phallic stem.

It may be that we should find in the double-sexed Eryngion, in whatever form the name appeared in Semitic, a name of the mushroom and the origin of one part of the Cain and Abel story. After Cain had slain his brother Abel, Yahweh condemns him to be a fugitive and wanderer on the earth (Gen 4:12). Cain complains bitterly that his punishment is more than he can bear. Being an outcast, without tribal protection, he will be at the mercy of all: "Whoever finds me will kill me." "Not so", replies Yahweh, "Every slayer-of-Cain (*horēg-Qayin*) will be subject to a seven-fold vengeance." The Hebrew phrase is strongly reminiscent of our bi-sexual plant name Eryngion (*ERUM-GAR-EN; Greek *Eruggion).*[12]

Incidentally, another phrase in that story is a similarly contrived play on the name of the mushroom, still in use today. After the murder, when Yahweh is looking for Abel, he demands of Cain, "Where is Abel, thy brother?" The miscreant replies rather petulantly with a question which has become a byword in discussions on the social responsibility of the individual: "Am I my brother's keeper (*shōmēr-ākhî*)?"

Even now in Persia the mushroom is known as *samārukh,* which is traceable to Sumerian *ShU-MAR-UGU/AGA, "crown of the womb-favourer", that is the "glans" or top of the fungus.[13]

The most famous of all twins in classical mythology are Castor and Pollux. They were born from an egg, the fruit of their mother's union with Zeus, who appeared to her in the form of a swan.[14] Their sister was Helen,[15] connected as we saw earlier, with the resin of the conifer, source of the *Amanita muscaria,* as was believed.[16] The mushroom affinities of the twins are therefore well established.

The two lads are known jointly as the "Dioscouroi", which the classical writers took to be a dual form of a Greek phrase *dioskouros,* "son of god". They therefore called the lads, "the sons of Zeus".[17] In actual fact, their name is not a plural form, or even Greek. It is a jumbled Sumerian title, *USh-GU-RI-UD, "erect phallus of the storm". The Greek rearrangement of the various verbal elements began with *ud-ush-gu-ri,* became *di-us-ku-roi,* and thus to *Dioskoroi* or, as it is otherwise written in the texts, *Dioskouroi.*[18]

We know their name in the rather more accurately transmitted form of USh-GU-RI-UD, "Iscariot", the name of Jesus' betrayer in the New Testament story.[19] Elsewhere, the writers and theologians read the name Dioscouroi in the manner of the classicists, by splitting a presumed singular into two, "son of God", as a title for their hero Jesus. Interestingly, the Sumerian original has come down into Persian as another name of the mushroom, *saqrātiyūn.*[20]

The name Castor is cognate with the Greek *gastēr,* "belly, womb" (our "gastric", etc)[21] and it is from the more general sense of "pod" that the name came to be applied to the plant from whose pods comes the medicament, castor-oil.[22] We have already noticed how this wider "pod" significance has led biblical commentators to wonder how Jonah found shade from the sun under the Castor-oil bush.[23] A similar mis-understanding underlies the widespread belief among the ancients that this valuable medicine could be obtained from the testicles of the beaver (Latin *castor*):

> The beavers of the Black Sea region [writes Pliny], practise self-amputa-tion (of the testicles) when beset by danger, as they know they are hunted for the sake of its secretion, the medical name for which is "beaver oil" (*castoreum*). Apart from this the beaver is an animal with a formidable bite, cutting down trees on the river banks as if with iron; if it gets hold of part of a man's body it does not relax its bite before the fractured bones are heard grinding together . . .[24]

So Nicander speaks of "the testicle that is fatal to the beaver".[25] The confusion here is between the "seed-bag" of the male, the testicle or "egg",[26] and the woman's uterus, "foetus-container". But the reference to cutting down trees, accurate enough of the riverside animal, may also contain an allusion to the fungus whose presence on broken and rotting wood must have seemed proof of the same destructive powers as were possessed by the beaver. One may also conjecture that the added note, about having once gripped "part of a man's body" it would not release its hold, has originated from a piece of earthy humour concerning the female organ.

Pollux was the strong man. His name is a somewhat jumbled form of the Sumerian phrase LU-GEShPU, "strong man", and so "guardian, jailor", from which also was derived the Greek *phulax,* of just that meaning.[27] In mythology Pollux is depicted as a "boxer, one good with his fists", the picture thus presented being that of the forearm and clenched fist, with the same phallic allusions as were implied in the Services' term for the penis, "short arm".[28] The development of the name Pollux and the Greek *phulax* from the Sumerian LU-GEShPU has a particular interest for us. The last syllable PU was detached and placed before the rest of the phrase, giving *pu-lu-gesh,* and thus brought into its derived forms (the longer Greek form of the twin's name, *Poludeukes,* comes from the same original to which a word DU, "adversary" has been added, in full *LU-GEShPU-DU).

It is this same GEShPU, "strong man", (the preformative LU simply indicates the meaning "man" for what follows) which forms the main part of the New Testament name for the brothers James and John,

"Boanerges".[29] The whole Sumerian phrase from which the Greek nickname comes was *GEShPU-AN-UR (read as *pu-an-ur-ges*) meaning "mighty man (holding up) the arch of heaven", a fanciful image of the stem supporting the canopy of the mushroom, seen in cosmographical terms. In a later chapter we shall deal in more detail with mushroom cosmography generally, based upon a view of the universe which saw heaven and earth as born from the volva of some vast primeval fungus.

The name "Boanerges" has given scholars a lot of trouble in the past.[30] For one thing it has been assumed to be Aramaic, a kind of semi-jocular nickname applied to the fiery-tempered brothers by Jesus in the colloquial Aramaic of Palestine of the first century, but which is incomprehensible in any known Aramaic dialect. The text adds the "explanation" of the name as "Sons of Thunder" (Mark 3:17).[31] Again, it has been assumed that the reference is to the brothers' suggestion that they call fire down upon the Samaritan village that would not receive the Master and his friends (Luke 9:54). The trouble has been that "Boanerges" does not, and in that form cannot mean "Sons of Thunder". For one thing the first part *"Boane-"* is not the Semitic *bnē-*, "sons of", even though it sounds something like it; for another, the remaining part, *-rges* does not mean "thunder".[32] All the same, the whole phrase has an air of authenticity which might deceive the cursory reader, and this was certainly its intention. Its real import was a secret name of the mushroom, found otherwise in "Pollux" and in other terms with the same meaning of an upholder of a heavenly canopy.

We have too readily assumed, in seeking an explanation for the strange incompatibility between "Boanerges" and its "translation", that the text was defective, or that later scribes being unfamiliar with Aramaic had miswritten the nickname. Now, thanks to our present discoveries, we are able to take a more appreciative view of the craft of the New Testament cryptographer. Neither he nor his copyists had made a mistake; we had, in taking the text at its face value. The name was not a jocular expression given by an Aramaic-speaking rabbi to two of his friends. It is not, as we now realize, Aramaic. The clue to its mushroom affinities has lain all along in the "translation" which, as such, is of course quite spurious. But "sons of thunder" *is* a well-known name for the fungus, found elsewhere in Semitic texts, and supported by the old Greek name *keraunion,* "thunder-fungus", after *keraunos,* "thunder".[33] The reference is to the belief that mushrooms were born of thunder, the voice of the god in the storm, since it was noticed that they appeared in the ground after rainstorms.

Later, we shall have to look again at this "Boanerges-Sons of Thunder" group, for it is a particularly clear example of a number of such instances in the text of the New Testament where a genuine mushroom name is followed by a spurious translation for the sake of the plot of the story. As here, the false renderings have usually some particular relevance for the sacred fungus, even though they do not interpret, as they affirm, the accompanying foreign word. What they do indicate very clearly is the unreal nature of the whole surface story of the Gospels and Acts. Put very simply, if the writer has gone to the trouble purposefully to conceal his secret name for the mushroom by giving it a misleading rendering, near enough in this case to deceive the cursory reader, then it follows that behind the story of Jesus and his companions there lies a secret layer of meaning which was not intended to be read or understood by the outsider. Since mushrooms nowhere appear in the surface story, and yet are clearly involved in the cryptic names, it must mean that the secret level of understanding is the significant one for the intended reader as for the cryptographer; what appears on the surface is unreal and never expected to be taken seriously by those within the cult. There is no escape from this dilemma: if our new understanding of "Boanerges" is correct, the historicity and validity of the New Testament story is in ruins. A subterfuge of this nature, bearing as it does on what we now see was a widespread and very ancient mushroom cult, can only mean that the "real" Christianity was heavily involved with it; in which case the story of Jesus was a hoax for the benefit of the Jewish and Roman authorities engaged in persecuting the cult. We shall give this matter more extended consideration later.[34]

To go back to Pollux: he represents the phallic side of the mushroom figure, the support to the upper half of his brother Castor's "womb". For when the mushroom canopy is fully spread, a new picture emerges, and one of particular importance for New Testament symbolism. This spread canopy was the upper half of the volva, so it was natural to envisage the stem as a human phallus supporting the open groin of the woman. In other terms, the shaft had been driven home into the axe-head, in this fashion: ↑.

This configuration of an upright supporting an apex or fork came to have a profound sexual significance. The upright was the strong arm or erect penis supporting the "burden" of the womb. The very word "burden", in Sumerian GUN, came down through Latin *cunnus* into our presently impolite designation of the female genitals, "cunt".[35] The "organ of burden", AR-GUN, appears dialectally in the name of Mount Hermon,[36] the Canaanite version of Olympus,[37] supporter of the heavenly arch.

Even trees having a broad comus like an enlarged mushroom were vested with sexual powers. The Plane tree[38] has had this significance from the beginning of recorded history. It was its shade that tempted the Sumerian goddess Inanna, wearied from her long travels, to sleep awhile. It stood in the garden of one Shukallituda, who found the lovely goddess sleeping and could not resist the temptation she offered. When she awoke to the discovery that she had not slept alone, she laid a terrible curse upon the land. The earth and wells were inundated with blood, like the land and river of Egypt when Pharaoh refused to let the Israelites leave (Exod 17.17ff.).

> The woman, because of her vulva, what harm she did! Inanna because of her womb, what she did do! All the wells of the land she filled with blood . . .[39]

Similarly, it was in the shade of the Plane tree that Zeus made love to Europa, after he had carried her to Crete from the mainland in the guise of a magnificent white bull.[40]

The Hebrew name for the Plane tree, *'armōn,* comes ultimately from the same Sumerian phrase AR-GUN as gave the name of the mountain Hermon.[41] Our own word "harmony", too, comes from the same source, for the word means properly "a joining together" the matching of the bearer and the burden. One who does this in carpentry is a "harmonizer".[42] He makes the hole and fits the joint; like Phereclus, the ship-builder, he is a *Harmonidēs,* "son of a carpenter".[43] So, too, is Jesus called in the New Testament (Matt 13:55; cp. Mark 6:3), for the mushroom was seen as both the "drill" and the effected "joint".

The ancient form of the drill was not unlike the mushroom in shape. In essentials it was a short rod surmounted by a bun-shaped whorl like a spindle for winding thread. At the lower end was the bit of iron or flint. We can see it so represented in the Egyptian hieroglyphs as 𓊨[44] and 𓆼.[45] The Sumerian ideogram for "carpenter" is 𓀀,[46] the notched whorl in this case being to take the string of the bow that gave the instrument its spin.

The male organ is the "borer" into the vagina, and the Latin *phallus* comes from the Sumerian BAL, "borer",[47] which also designates the weaver's spindle (ideogram ⚵[48]) and the mushroom. When the penis slides into the vagina, or the shaft into the axe-head,[49] "harmony" has been achieved, and the ancients saw the extended mushroom as representing that happy state.

Now that we can understand the sexual significance to the ancient mind of the inverted "V" formation, it is possible to appreciate why it was from Adam's rib that his partner was made:

> The man gave names to all cattle, and to the birds of the air, and to every beast of the field; but for the man there was not found a helper to suit him. So Yahweh God caused a deep sleep to fall upon the man, and while he slept he took one of his ribs and closed up the flesh in its place. And the rib that he had taken from the man he built up into a woman, and he brought her to the man . . . (Gen2:20f.).

The Hebrew name for "rib", *sela* is the Sumerian SILA, represented by the "V" shape,[50] and what the Old Testament writer clearly had in mind was a rib extending on both sides of the spinal column, giving the arched form associated with the open groin and the mushroom top. From this "rib" the god fashioned the significant part of the woman, supplying the canopy for the erect stem, and "harmony" for the hitherto deprived Adam.

The inverted "V" shape, the angular representation of the mushroom cap, was also the form of the old yoke that was laid across the shoulders of the servant or animal. Again, it is the Sumerian GUN, "burden", that is at the base of our word "yoke" (through the Latin *jugum*, Greek *zugon*).[51] In the extended mushroom ⋔ was seen an image of a neck bearing a yoke, and this idea came into the Twin mythology by portraying Castor as a "yoker" of horses, that is a horse-trainer.[52]

The "yoke" of a chariot was the cross-piece fastened to the central pole on either side of which the animals were fastened. At its very simplest, the traction end of the war chariot could be represented by a cross, †. The Greek word *harma*, "joining", like the Latin *jugum*, "yoke", could express "chariot", as could the Sumerian MAR, "axe-head; rainbow; and groin".[53] From this "forked burden" came the sexual allusions of chariots and chariotry noticed earlier.[54] To "drive a chariot" meant, then, to take an active role in the copulatory act. The sun is the great "charioteer" (Greek *harmelatēr)* of the heavens as it wheels across the sky and plunges into the vulva of mother earth at eventide. So Yahweh, the creator god, is seen riding upon the cherubim (Ps 18:11,[55] etc) and, among the lesser heroes, Jehu "drove furiously" (II Kgs 9:20).

The Greek word for "horse-driver" is *elatēr.* In derivation it is more related to the sexual affinities of the action than the equine, since it comes from the Sumerian E-LA-TUN, "strong water of the belly (womb)", that is, in its sexual application, "spermatozoa".[56] As *Elatērion* we find it as the Greek name of the Squirting Cucumber, *Ecballium elaterium,* whose phallic shape and periodic exudation of a mucilaginous juice gave it sexual allusions[57] which the modern Arab recognizes when he calls the plant, "donkey's cucumber".[58] In actual fact the intensely bitter juice of the Elaterium is anything but productive of fertility, being a violent purge and an abortifacient.[59] But like Hellebore, "strong water of defecation" as its Sumerian derivation shows the name to mean,[60] the Squirting Cucumber gathered to itself many names that belonged primarily to the *Amanita muscaria,* no less bitter and with similar gastronomic and intestinal effects.[61]

In mythology the horse- and cattle-driving theme appears frequently. The newly born Hermes leaps from his cradle and precociously drives away his half-brother Apollo's cattle.[62] Castor fights with his cousins over their driving away cattle and is killed in the battle.[63]

The yoke laid across the neck of a servant or an animal or the upright pole of a carriage, had another, more sinister application. It was also the *crux* ("cross")[64] or *furca* ("fork")[65] that the criminal carried on his shoulders to his place of execution, his wrists fastened to each end. At the gallows, at this stage simply the upright set in the ground, the Greek *stauros,*[66] the condemned man was hoisted up so that his legs were just clear of the ground and left there to die of exposure. To take some of the weight off the bonds at his wrists, the upright was sometimes provided with a horizontal peg to support the crutch, a kind of saddle (Latin *sedile*).[66a]

To "take up the yoke" or "cross" was thus synonymous with being crucified, and is a constant theme in the New Testament. It will also have been a euphemism for sexual copulation, the "yoke" being the "burden" of the woman's crutch borne gallantly by the erect penis. It is with this implication that the cross became the symbol of the phallic god Hermes. It consisted basically of an upright piece of wood with a cross-piece at the shoulders, and in its more sophisticated forms with an erect penis at an appropriate place on the shaft, indicating its phallic implications. Sometimes the top of the upright was carved with a two-faced representation of the god's head. The Hermes cross symbol was known throughout the classical world, and standing at crossroads was welcomed as a source of comfort and inspiration by the traveller.[67]

The similarity between this fertility symbol and the instrument of execution must have been obvious to all, even to the detail of the crutch-supporting *sedile* of the gallows finding its parallel in the replica phallus half-way up the Hermes upright. It is interesting that the eastern churches preserve this detail in their traditional form of the crucifix with the double cross-piece: ☦.

Castor and Pollux were also represented by crossed wooden beams in Sparta,[68] and the Greeks called the gibbet the "twin tree" (*xulon didumon*).[69] The Twins also carried a cross or star on their heads, surmounting a close-fitting felt cap, as we may see from coins on which the brothers are represented: ☆.[70] Presumably this characteristic headgear was intended to represent the half-egg (Castor) of the mushroom and the stalk and canopy of Pollux. In Christian iconography this symbol became the orb ♁, and the Sumerian ideogram for "fertility", ♁,[71] may possibly have been expressing the same motif.

The idea of crucifixion in mushroom mythology was already established before the New Testament myth-makers portrayed their mushroom hero Jesus dying by this method. The fungus itself was probably known as "The Little Cross",[72] and in the Old Testament the seven sons of Saul had been crucified as an expiatory sacrifice to Yahweh. The story runs that a three-year famine in the land drove David to seek from Yahweh an explanation for his disfavour. The god told him that there was a blood-guilt on Israel because David's predecessor Saul had executed the Gibeonites. These deaths had to be expiated before the fertility of the land could be restored. Thereupon David called the Gibeonites who demanded the atoning death by crucifixion of Saul's seven sons, one of whose names was Armoni, "the joiner, carpenter".[73]

After the deed, Armoni's mother Rizpah (Hebrew *r-z-p,* "join")[74] "took sackcloth and spread it for herself on the rock (of execution), from the beginning of the harvest until the rain fell upon them (the crucified) from heaven; and she did not allow the birds of the air to alight upon them by day, nor the beasts of the field by night" (II Sam 21:10).

Only after David had taken down the bodies and buried the remains, and those of Saul and Jonathan which had been similarly exposed, did "God allow himself to be entreated on the land's behalf" (v. 14).[75]

The verb used in this gruesome tale for "crucify" means properly "disjoint".[76] In the story of Jacob's wrestling match with the angel it expressed the dislocation of the hip-joint:

> When the man saw that he did not prevail against Jacob, he touched the hollow of his thigh; and Jacob's thigh was put out of joint as he wrestled with him . . . therefore to this day the Israelites do not eat the sinew of the hip which is upon the hollow of the thigh, because he touched the hollow of Jacob's thigh on the sinew of the hip (Gen 32:25, 32).

The "hip" motif is a recurrent theme in mushroom mythology. Adonis-Na'iman was killed, according to legend, by being run through the hip by a boar, sent, some say, by Artemis from jealousy. Dionysus, often connected with Adonis, was said to have been born from the hip of his father Zeus. His mother Semele, an earth-goddess, had been impregnated by the Father-god, but before her son could be born, she was struck by a thunderbolt. Her divine lover snatched the foetus from her womb and implanted it in his own hip, from which in due course the young Dionysus was born.[77]

Again, as Jesus hangs on the cross, a soldier runs him through the side with his spear (John 19:34). The resultant wound made a mark large enough for the doubting Thomas to put his fist in (John 20:25, 27). In all these references, the allusion is to the ball-and-socket picture presented by the hip-joint, by the head of the penis in the female vagina, or, as was fancifully imagined, by the stem in the cap of the mushroom,[78] and the separation of the one from the other by violent means.

As crucifixion was envisaged primarily as pulling apart of the limbs, so scourging also had a similar connotation. The victim was splayed on a frame to receive the lashes, like a starfish stretched out on the sand.[79] So in the Jesus story, he is scourged before being crucified. In this case, there is a word-play also involved, since his title, Christ, the "smeared, or anointed with semen", falls together in Aramaic with a verb meaning "to stretch out".[80]

The figure seems well suited to the mushroom, in the splitting of the volva from within, and the stretching of the stem and extension of the canopy. Some such terminology relating to the fungus probably accounts for the stories of the Bacchic Maenads pulling animals and children apart, limb from limb. Pictured in dramatic form, Euripides has Pentheus splayed upon a tree by Dionysus and then pulled down and torn apart by the Maenads in their drug-induced ecstasy.[81] In this version of the myth, Pentheus' mother takes an active part in the proceedings and returns from the frolic bearing her son's head proudly before her.[82] In the Old and New Testament versions, the chief victims' mothers lead the mourners.

To summarize: The division of the mushroom volva into two halves gave rise to a "twin" mythology. Since the two constituents of the fungus were envisaged as male and female, it is sometimes personified as a hermaphrodite, and its names like Tubal-Cain, and the Greek Eryngion, contain both male and female elements. Alternatively, the mushroom story presents two figures, usually male, like Castor and Pollux, Cain and Abel, and so on.

The most famous of all the mythological twins are Castor and Pollux, the "volva" and the "stem" of the fungus respectively. Their joint name, Dioscouroi, means "phallus of the storm", and appears in the New Testament as the name of Jesus' betrayer, Iscariot, and as the title of Jesus himself, "son of God".

The risen mushroom with canopy outstretched was seen by the ancients in the same sexual terms as the open groin of a woman penetrated by the male organ, or as an axe-head into which the shaft has been inserted. It was represented symbolically by the form of a cross, as a man or animal carrying a yoke, or as a criminal crucified. So the fungus was known as "the little cross" and its dismemberment as "crucifixion", giving in part that theme of the Christian myth.

The imagery that related the mushroom and the cross extended to "star" images, as we noticed in the case of the Dioscouroi's cap. In many respects the sacred fungus was a child of two worlds, heavenly and terrestrial, and, as the modern Arab calls the mushroom "star of the ground",[83] so in mythology there were always strong astral connections in its worship. Some of these we shall examine in the next chapter.

XIII

Star of the Morning

As Gemini, the Heavenly Twins, the Dioscouroi, were identified specifically with the morning and evening star. Similarly, Jesus proclaims himself to the visionary of the book of Revelation as "the bright and morning star" (Rev 22:16).[1] In part this is a word-play on one of the most important Greek names of the Holy Plant, *Peristereōn,* spelt out within the bilingual Christian communities as the Aramaic *Bar-,* "son of" and the Greek *astēr,* "star", and *heōs,* "of the morning".[2] The title "Son of the Star" had already a profound messianic significance within Judaism, deriving the idea from the promise in the Old Testament: "a star shall come forth out of Jacob, and a comet shall rise out of Israel" (Num 24:17). The leader of the Jewish rebels of the Second Revolt in the second century adopted the title as his own, continuing the Zealot tradition that the overthrow of the hated Romans by a star-born Jewish leader was a necessary preliminary to the dawn of the new era.[3]

The more precise relationship between the sacred mushroom and the "bright and morning star" is seen in the oracle of Isaiah, directed at the king of Babylon. He sees the enemy in terms of the fungus, whose life , so glorious in its heavenly conception and fulfilment, is yet so short-lived:

> How are you fallen from heaven, Shining One, Son of the Dawn! How are you cut down to the ground, you who laid the nations low! You said in your heart, "I will ascend to heaven; above the stars of God I will set my throne on high; I will sit on the mount of assembly in the far north; I will ascend above the heights of the clouds, I will make myself like the Most High." But you are brought down to Sheol, to the depths of the Pit . . . (Isa 14:12-15).

The application of the mushroom epithet to the Mesopotamian

monarch was possible through a similarity between the name of the city "Babylon" and that for the fungus, which came down into Greek as *Boubalion,* attached, like many fungus names, to the Squirting Cucumber, *Elaterion.*[4] The phallic connections in the case of that plant are obvious, as they are in the case of the mushroom, and the common name in fact derived from a Sumerian phrase, GU-BAR, "top of the head; glans penis".

An amusing instance of this same association of the Mesopotamian city-name and the mushroom, this time quite unintentional, is detectable in Pliny's description of a certain parasite which takes possession of a "Babylonian" thorn bush:

> We must not leave out a plant that at Babylon is grown on thorn-bushes, because it will not live anywhere else – just as mistletoe grows on trees, but the plant in question will only grow on what is called the "royal thorn". It is a remarkable fact that it buds on the same day as it has been planted – this is done just at the rising of the dogstar – and it very quickly takes possession of the whole tree. It is used in making spiced wine, and it is cultivated for that purpose. This thorn also grows on the Long Walls at Athens.[5]

It is this last phrase which, more than anything, identifies the "thorn" in question. The tradition must have come down to Pliny through Semitic sources which preserved an original name for the mushroom based upon the Sumerian *GU-TAL-U-DUN, "ball-and-socket; penis-and-vulva", already noticed. It will have been mistakenly understood as the Semitic phrase *kōtel-'Attūnā'*, "long wall of Athens", and hence Pliny's strange restriction of the growth of his parasite to this one spot.[6] It is by such intentional and unintentional puns on names that botanical references were confused and misapplied, and can in some cases now be restored.

The morning and evening star is, of course, Venus. To appreciate the relevance of this luminary to the sacred fungus we must try to understand its place in the astral system as anciently understood, and the fertilizing power that it was supposed to wield. Each morning, before the sun-god withdraws his penis from the earth's vaginal sheath, a rival to the heavenly father slips from the nuptial chamber and heralds the coming dawn. This star is second only to the sun and moon in brightness, and usurps some of their glory by lightening the eastern sky in the morning and holding back the veil of night until the moon rises. This star they called Venus, Juno, Isis or Aphrodite. Thus Pliny:

> Before the sun revolves, a very large star named Venus, which varies its course alternatively, and whose alternative names in themselves indicate its rivalry with the sun and moon – when in advance and rising before dawn it receives the name of Lucifer, and being another sun and bringing the dawn, whereas when it shines after sunset it is named Vesper, as prolonging the daylight, or as being deputy for the moon . . . Further it surpasses all the other stars in magnitude, and is so brilliant that alone among stars it casts a shadow by its rays. Consequently there is a great competition to give it a name, some having called it Juno, others Isis, others the Mother of the Gods.[7]

As we may now understand, their names for "star" show that the ancients pictured these luminaries as penes in the sky,[8] their light fancifully seen as the "glow" of the glans' fiery crown. At first sight it seems then strange that this most powerful of all stars should be given female names like Venus and Juno. The reference, however, is to its generative power. When this lesser penis of heaven slipped from the connubial bower before its master, it came dripping with the semen of the terrestrial womb. The sun, yawning and stretching its blazing path across the sky would burn away the fragrant drops that his forerunner scattered. Until then they would remain as dew on the earth, the most powerful conceptual fluid of Nature. Thus again Pliny:

> Its influence is the cause of the birth of all things upon the earth; at both of its risings it scatters a genital dew with which it not only fills the conceptive organs of the earth but also stimulates those of all animals.[9]

Even the sea creatures were affected by this seminal fluid from the sky. Pearls were "born" within the shell by the direct influence of dew; well might Aphrodite have been portrayed sailing ashore on the coast of Cyprus in such a "womb" of the sea bed. Again Pliny:

> The source and breeding-ground of pearls are shells not much differing from oyster-shells. These, we are told, when stimulated by the generative season of the year, gape open, as it were, and are filled with a dewy pregnancy, and consequently when heavy are delivered, and the offspring of the shells are pearls that correspond to the quality of the dew received:

if it was a pure inflow, their brilliance is conspicuous, but if it was turbid, the product also becomes dirty in colour. Also if the sky was lowering, they say, the pearl is pale in colour: for it is certain that it was conceived from the sky, and that pearls have more connexion with the sky than with the sea . . .[10]

If the dew could penetrate even to these "volvae" of the sea, its undiluted sprinkling on dry land could be expected to produce powerful drugs:

After the rising of each star, but particularly the principal stars, or of a rainbow, if rain does not follow but the dew is warmed by the rays of the sun . . . drugs (*medicamenta*) are produced, heavenly gifts for the eyes, ulcers, and internal organs. And if this substance is kept when the dog-star is rising, and if, as often happens, the rise of Venus or Jupiter or Mercury falls on the same day, its sweetness and potency for recalling mortals' ills from death is equal to that of the Nectar of the gods.[11]

So it was, when the Israelites awoke in the desert after an evening of idling their bellies with quail flesh, it was to discover that the "spermal emission" of the dew had left behind it Manna, the "bread" of heaven, which we may identify with the sacred fungus (Exod 16:13f.).[12]

We shall see later how mushroom worship was closely connected with necromancy, that is, the raising of the spirits of the dead for fortune-telling.[13] It is in this context that we should now read a passage in Isaiah:

"O dwellers in the dust, awake and sing for joy! For thy dew is a dew of light, and on the land of the shades (Rephaim) thou wilt let it fall" (Isa 26:19). The "Rephaim", as their name can now be seen to mean, were those "cast down from heaven",[14] the fallen angels of the sixth chapter of Genesis, and a common theme of Jewish mythology. As the morning dew brought forth the sacred mushroom, so, in the eyes of the prophet, would it give life to these denizens of the underworld. Pliny draws a further connection between dew and the Holy Plant when he says that even the demonic power of the Mandrake is increased when touched with morning dew.[15]

In a very special way, then, the sacred fungus was the offspring of the Morning Star, as Jesus proclaims himself to be to the mystic. It thus had the unique ability of forming a bridge between man and god, being not entirely divine nor yet merely mortal. It gave men the power to become for a little while like the gods, "knowing good and evil".[16] Like the mushroom itself, it allowed mortals to become "Dioscouroi", or as the Greeks understood that name of the sacred fungus, "sons of God". As the New Testament writer says of Jesus:

> To all who received him, who believed in his name, he gave power to become children of God; who were born, not of blood nor of the will of the flesh nor of the will of man, but of God. And the Word became flesh and dwelt among us, full of grace and truth; we have beheld his glory, glory as of the only Son from the Father . . . (John 1:12f).

The mysteries that the "Jesus"-fungus could impart were heavenly in origin, since it itself, as its Hebrew name implies, is "That-which-comes-from-heaven'".[17]

> Truly, truly, I say to you, we speak of what we know, and bear witness to what we have seen . . . No one has ascended into heaven but he who descended from heaven, the son of man (John 3 :11f.).

Because the mushroom's affinities were primarily celestial, it was thought able to control heavenly phenomena, the atmosphere, winds, and tempests. The Dioscouroi were seen in the atmospheric electrical discharges known as St Elmo's fire, and to our airmen in the war as "gremlins" that accompanied them on their missions. Thus again, Pliny:

> Stars also come into existence at sea and on land. I have seen a radiance of star-like appearance clinging to the javelins of soldiers on sentry duty at night in front of the rampart: and on a voyage stars alight on the yards and other parts of the ship, with a sound resembling a voice, hopping from perch to perch in the manner of birds. These when they come singly are disastrously heavy and wreck ships, and if they fall into the hold burn them up. If there are two of them they denote safety and portend a successful voyage; and their approach is said to put to flight the terrible star called Helena: for this reason they are called Castor and Pollux, and people pray to them as gods for aid at sea. They also shine round men's heads at evening time; this is a great portent. All these things admit of no certain explanation; they are hidden away in the grandeur of Nature.[18]

In their capacity as saviours of men in storms, the writer of the Homeric Hymns lauds the Dioscouroi thus:

> Bright-eyed Muses, tell of the Tyndaridae, the Sons of Zeus, glorious children of neat-ankled Leda; Castor, the tamer of horses, and blameless Polydeuces. When Leda had lain with the dark-clouded Son of Cronos, she bare them beneath the peak of the great hill Taygetus, – children who are deliverers of men on earth and swift-going ships when stormy gales rage over the ruthless sea. Then the mariners call upon the sons of great Zeus with vows of white lambs, going to the forepart of the prow. But the strong wind and the waves of the sea lay the ship under water, until suddenly these two are seen darting through the air on tawny wings. Forthwith they allay the blasts of the cruel winds and still the waves upon the surface of the white sea; fair signs are they and deliverance from toil. And when the mariners see them they are glad and have rest from their pain and labour.[19]

Well might Paul's "Alexandrian ship" out of Malta carry the sign of the Dioscouroi at its mast-head (Acts 28:11).

Part at least of the ancient belief that the Dioscouroi could avert storms lies in the idea that in nature like repels like. The antidote to any poison will be found in an object or drug most nearly resembling the baneful source. Since the Dioscouroi, Pollux and Castor, are basically mushroom demons and the source of the "Sons of Thunder" is the storm, it follows that the sacred fungus will have the power to repel the tempest. Similarly, since the *Amanita muscaria* is a denizen of the conifer forests, and receives its being on the mother's side, as it were, from the "menstrual blood" of the cedar,[20] this substance also can affect storms. Thus Pliny:

> They say that hail-storms and whirlwinds are driven away if menstrual fluid is exposed to the very flashes of lightning: that stormy weather is thus kept away, and that at sea exposure, even without (actual) menstruation, prevents storms.[21]

In the mushroom's supposed power over the weather lies the basis of the quelling of the storm mythology of the New Testament and of Jonah:

> But Yahweh hurled a great wind upon the sea, and there was a mighty tempest on the sea, so that the ship threatened to break up. Then the

mariners were afraid and each cried to his god; and they threw the cargo that was in the ship into the sea, to lighten it for them. But Jonah had gone down into the bowels of the ship and had lain down and was fast asleep. So the captain came and said to him, "What's the matter, sleeper? Get up and call on your god! Perhaps the god will give us a thought that we don't perish."

After casting lots to find out who was to blame among them for their plight and the god's wrath, the sailors discovered that Jonah was the culprit, since he was fleeing from the face of Yahweh.

Then they said to him, "What shall we do to you, that the sea may abate for us?" For the sea was becoming more and more tempestuous. He said to them, "Take me up and throw me into the sea; then the sea will quieten down for you."

This the sailors eventually did, praying at the same time to be freed from blood-guilt on Jonah's account, "and the sea ceased from its raging" (Jonah 1: 4-15).

Compare now the story of Jesus and his disciples on the Galilean sea:

On that day when evening had come, he said to them, "Let us go across to the other side." And leaving the crowd they took him with them, just as he was, in the boat. And other boats were with him. And a great storm of wind arose, and the waves beat into the boat, so that the boat was already filling. But he was in the stern, asleep on the cushion; and they woke him and said to him, "Teacher, do you not care if we perish?" And he awoke and rebuked the wind, and said to the sea, "Peace! Be still!" And the wind ceased, and there was a great calm. And he said to them, "Why are you afraid? Have you no faith?" And they were filled with awe, and said to one another, "Who then is this, that even wind and sea obey him?" (Mark 4:35-41).

In both stories the underlying factor is the supposed ability of the sacred fungus to quieten storms. However, as with other such myths as expounded in the Bible, there are several layers of literary construction. For example, behind the whole of the Jonah story there is probably a play on the name of the sacred fungus, latterly known in Greek as *Peristereōn,* but originally the Sumerian *BAR-USh-TAR-IAU-NA.[22] In whatever form it was known among the Semites, the name was capable of being teased out by the myth-makers into something like *bar-setārā' – yōnā'* "Jonah – son-of-hiding, concealment", on which that element of the Jonah story about his flight from Yahweh's presence would appear to have been used.

In the New Testament we can penetrate to the second layer of literary composition, where every word of the story can be examined for possible word-plays. Thus, for example, "silencing the storm" is a pun on the fungus name, *MASh-BA(LA)G . . ., which provided the myth-makers with the Semitic root *sh-b-kh*, "pacify",[23] and is so used of Yahweh in Psalm 65: "who does still (Hebrew *mashbīakh*) the roaring of the seas, the roaring of their waves . . ." (v. 7). The Sumerian name GI-LI-LI(LI-LI-GI), properly the "reed with two cones" describing the two halves of the volva separated by the stem of the mushroom, gave by word-play the Semitic root *g-l-l*, "waves", and the proper name Galilee.[24]

The sacred mushroom, then, was a being of two worlds, heavenly and terrestrial. Its affinities in the heavens lay with the stars, and in a special sense it was the child of Venus, the morning and evening star. The heavenly dew which this luminary was thought to disperse on the earth was considered of special power, and the appearance of the mushrooms on the ground at dawn seemed evidence of a special relationship between the star and the fungus.

The Heavenly Twins, the Gemini or Dioscouroi, were identified with the Morning Star, as is Jesus in the New Testament. These mushroom characters were similarly credited with power over storms, since the sacred fungus was itself a product of the storm-god in the tempest.

So far we have looked at those aspects of the mushroom which offered the mythologists material for descriptions and stories from its characteristic shape, and from its unique conception as a "child of God". We saw how its sexual form, male and female, gave rise to androgynous names and epithets, and how the conjunction of penis and vulva as fancifully seen in its most developed form offered comparison with the human copulatory act and similar sexual imagery in the axe-head and the cross. The significance of its heavenly origin appears in those stories about the mushroom which portray the heroes quelling storms and, theologically, in imparting to its worshippers a knowledge of heavenly things normally beyond the reach of mere mortals.

We may now take our quest further, and discover how other characteristics of the mushroom, and of the *Amanita muscaria* in particular, offered even wider scope to the myth-maker, classical and biblical. Its colour in particular seems to have made a deep impression on the ancient world, to judge from the way fungus names are used for red and purple dyes. Furthermore, the cap of the *Amanita muscaria* has a strange, white-flecked appearance deriving from the particles of the volva still adhering to the surface. This, as we shall see, gave a cycle of mushroom stories all its own.

XIV

Colour and Consistency

How, it may be asked, can one be sure that it was one particular member of the fungus species that was the subject of the sacred mushroom cult? Even the canopied Boletus type offers a wide range of specimens, and more than one kind of this variety has in its cap a hallucinatory drug.[1] The answer is that the sacred mushroom was characterized in name and mythology by its distinctive colouring, the deep red of the cap contrasting with the white stem, and with the white or yellowish "warts" standing out against the red, remnants of the broken volva from which it grew. In the following chapter we shall look at the names deriving from the colour and "scabby" form of the *Amanita muscaria,* and how its distinctive appearance contributed in no small measure to the awesome wonder with which its worshippers regarded the fungus, and the stories woven around it.

The Fleecy Cloak

The colour characteristics of the sacred mushroom provided folk-lore with a number of day-to-day allusions, among them being that the red top flecked with white particles seemed like a red woollen cloak or "fleece". The most famous of all classical myths derived from this characteristic is the story of the quest for the "Golden Fleece" by Jason and the Argonauts. By "golden" in this context we have to think of the red gold most common in the ancient world, rather than the purer, yellow metal of modern jewellery. The story runs as follows:

Phrixus and Helle, the two children of the Boetian king Athamas, were hated by their step-mother Ino. Their lives were threatened and Hermes gave them a fabulous ram on which they fled to safety. The ram had a fleece of gold and could fly as well as reason and speak. The two children climbed onto its back and flew off. Helle fell off as they crossed the sea named after her, Hellespont, "Helle's Sea" (Dardanelles), but Phrixus managed to remain aboard until they reached Colchis on the Black Sea. The unfortunate ram was then sacrificed, and its wonderful fleece offered to the king of that country, Aeetes, who hung it on a tree and set a dragon to guard it night and day.

Meanwhile at Iolchus in Thessaly, one Jason, attempting to win back part of his rightful heritage of the kingdom from his wicked uncle Pelias, was set the task of finding and bringing back the Golden Fleece. With the help of Hera and Athene he built a fifty-oared ship called the Argo, in which he had set a bough of the prophetic oak of Zeus at Dodona. Among his heroic crew were the Dioscouroi, setting the mushroom seal firmly upon the myth. After many adventures the Argonauts managed to lull the dragon and seize the Fleece and make good their escape, with the help of the king's daughter Medea, who went with them. She married Jason and they lived happily for ten years before the hero fell in love with another and abandoned Medea. She avenged herself by sending the new bride a costly robe which, immediately it was put on, consumed her with inextinguishable fire.[2]

The ram was a prime symbol of fecundity in the ancient world but this story illustrates another of its virtues: its hair was of great importance for weaving outer garments and tent-cloths. In Sumerian the same word DARA is used of the animal and for hair dyed red. When the latter significance was required a determinative SIG, "hair", could be put before the word. From the reversed combination DARA-SIG, the Greeks obtained their word for "hair" generally, *thrix,* through **tra-igs.*[3] Properly it meant "red hair" and it is probably with this sense that a similarly derived word *Thraikos* is used of the people of Thrace, the "Thracians", the "red-headed people".[4]

Dionysus was a Thracian god,[5] and his frantic Maenads were called Threiciae. But the reference here is probably not primarily to the homeland of the cult but to the "red-cloaked" *Amanita muscaria* that sent them berserk. This may have been what Josephus had in mind in a particular reference to the Jewish priest-king Alexander Jannaeus. Following an abortive revolt by his Jewish subjects against him, the king is said to have crucified eight hundred of his subjects in Jerusalem, about the year 83 BC. So, says Josephus, the people called him a "Thracian".[6] This may have been an allusion to a suspicion that he was an eater of the sacred mushroom himself, or to the popular imagery that linked the mushroom with the cross of crucifixion. It would seem from one of the names given by Dioscorides to the Mandrake that it was also called by the name "Thracian".[6a] It would be interesting to know if the people of Thrace, apart from their religious interest in the "red-haired" *Amanita muscaria*, were themselves "red-headed" as their name implies. Certainly they were famed for their viciousness on the field of battle, and it is interesting that the idea that associates red-headed people with quick tempers persists even to this day.[7]

In the Old Testament, the story of how the crafty, smooth-skinned Jacob managed to trick his red, rough-skinned brother Esau out of his birthright is another presentation of the "red-cloaked" mushroom theme in mythology:

> But Jacob said to Rebekah, his mother, "Behold my brother Esau is a hairy man, and I am a smooth[8] man. Perhaps my father will feel me, and I shall seem to be mocking him, and bring a curse upon myself and not a blessing." His mother said to him, "Upon me be your curse, my son; only obey my word, and go, fetch them (the kids) to me." So he went and took them and brought them to his mother; and his mother prepared savoury food, such as his father loved. Then Rebekah took the best garments of Esau her older son, which were with her in the house, and put them on Jacob her younger son; and the skins of the kids she put on his hands and upon the smooth part of his neck; and she gave the savoury food and the bread, which she had prepared, into the hand of her son Jacob.
>
> So he went in to his father, and said, "My father"; and he said, "Here I am; who are you, my son?" Jacob said to his father, "I am Esau your first-born . . . " Then Isaac said, "Come near, that I may feel you, my son, to know whether you are really my son Esau or not." So Jacob went near to Isaac his father, who felt him and said, "The voice is Jacob's voice, but the hands are the hands of Esau." And he did not recognize him, because his hands were hairy like his brother Esau's hands . . . (Gen 27:11-23).

Esau's name, as we may now recognize, is from the Sumerian *E-ShU-A, "raised canopy",[9] a fitting epithet for one who represented in mythical form the cap of the *Amanita muscaria*, as his brother Jacob (Sumerian *IA-A-GUB, "pillar") was the mushroom stem.[10] The "redness" of his skin is remarked upon in the story of the twins' birth:

> And Isaac prayed to Yahweh for his wife, because she was barren; and Yahweh granted his prayer, and Rebekah his wife conceived. The children

struggled within her and she said, "If it be thus why do I live?" So she went to enquire of Yahweh, and Yahweh said to her, "Two nations are in thy womb, and two peoples born of you shall be divided; the one shall be stronger than the other, the elder shall serve the younger." When her days to be delivered were fulfilled, behold there were twins in her womb. The first came forth all red, all his body like a hairy mantle;[11] so they called his name Esau (Gen 25:21-25).

So striking was the colour of the cap of the *Amanita muscaria* that it gave its name to red or purple dyes in the ancient world. Of such was the Greek *phoinix,* the "Phoenix", name of the palm tree, the bird, and the Levantine coast, as well as a famous purple dye. As we shall see, the Greek word was derived from a Sumerian phrase "mighty man holding up the sky", a fanciful descriptive epithet of the mushroom.[12] The Latin *tablion,* also, denoting the purple fringe of authority, derives from the Sumerian *TAB-BA-LI, literally "double-cone", or "cup", being the two halves of the split mushroom volva.[13] Of particular interest for our study is the Sumerian word GAN-NU, used of the red dye cochineal.[14] This, also, derives very probably from the red top of the *Amanita muscaria,* since GAN also means a cone or hemispherical shape, such as the lid of a bowl,[15] or a woman's breast. It is from this latter use in the fuller Sumerian phrase AGAN, "breast", that Greek obtained its name for the mushroom, *Amanita,* properly the "breast-shaped object", referring to the cap.[16]

From the Sumerian GAN-NU, denoting the red dye, came the Hebrew word *khānūn* for the red cap or daub put as a protection on the head of ewes in pasture.[17] Such a red cap well described the pileus of the *Amanita muscaria,* and it provided a most useful epithet for the sacred mushroom to the New Testament myth-makers. For *khānūn* looks exactly like another Semitic word meaning "be gracious", source of many personal names in the Old Testament, like *Khānān,* Hanan; *Khānūn,* Hanun; *Khannah,* Hannah; *Yo-khānān* ("Yahweh has been gracious"), John (Greek *Iōannēs),* and so on.[18] Thus, seeking Semitic personal names for their characters in the Gospel stories, the writers had in these "gracious" Old Testament names a rich store from which to choose. So we have an "Anna", and "Annas" and several "Johns". The colour reference of the latter name is particularly clear in the case of John, the brother of James, the Boanerges. The name James is, of course, the English representation of "Jacob" (Greek *Iakōbos,* Hebrew *Ya'aqōb),* whose brother in the Old Testament story is Esau, the "red-skinned" one, and the counterpart of the New Testament "John".

In the better known "John the Baptist", the colour reference is also prominent. The myth-makers have simply added to the name the Semitic epithet *Tabbal,* "the dipper" (baptizer), or "dyer",[19] derived ultimately from the same Sumerian *TAB-BA-R/LI, "mushroom", that gave Accadian its *tabarru,* "red dye", and Latin its *tablion,* "purple fringe", just mentioned. The name and title of "John the Baptist" in the New Testament story then, means no more than the "red-topped mushroom", but in giving him the added fungus name, *TAB-BA-LI, the story-tellers were able to assign him an important role in the story as the "baptizer" of Jesus and others. In the added descriptions and stories of this desert prophet in the Gospels further mushroom names and epithets were played upon.

Now John wore a garment of camel's hair . . . (Matt 3:4).

The prophet's description is modelled, of course, on that of Elijah, the Old Testament prophet who "wore a garment of hair-cloth" (II Kgs 1:8).[20] But the New Testament writer's addition that the hair came from a "camel" is an interesting illustration of the way he and his fellow exegetes adapt the ancient traditions to fit their purposes. The point of "camel" here is that the Hebrew name for the animal, *kirkārah,*[21] formed a useful word-play or pun on the Greek name for the Mandrake, *Kir-kaia.* In fact, we may now trace back both words to a common Sumerian root, KUR-KUR, a name of the Holy Plant. It means "two cones": applied to the mushroom it denoted the two halves of the volva, like TAB-BA-LI above, and to the camel, the double hump.

. . . and his food was locusts and wild honey (Matt 3:4).

The "locusts" part of the prophet's diet has given the biblical naturalists much trouble. There were, of course, edible locusts known in those times, but popular tradition fancied the Carob as the most likely reference of the text, and today the *Ceratonia Siliqua* is known as "St John's Bread".[22] Unfortunately, this Carob is not a desert plant, so discussion on the identity of the "locust" has continued unabated. In fact it now seems much more likely that the source of the reference is another word-play between the Semitic *gōbāy, gūbā'*, "edible locust", and *gab'a*, "mushroom". The similarity is not accidental: both come from a Sumerian root, GUG, "pod", the locust reference being to the larva of the insect, the mushroom's to the volva from which it develops.[23] Even the popular designation of the Carob as "St John's Bread" is not all that removed from the truth, since the Carob, as we have seen, shared at least in ancient Accadian the same name as the mushroom.[24]

No story in the New Testament has so gripped the imagination of authors, artists, opera librettists, and others than that of the death of John the Baptist at the instigation of a jealous woman:

> But when Herod heard of it he said, "John, whom I beheaded, has been raised." For Herod had sent and seized John, and bound him in prison for the sake of Herodias, his brother Philip's wife; because he had married her. For John said to Herod, "It is not lawful for you to have your brother's wife." And Herodias had a grudge against him, and wanted to kill him. But she could not, for Herod feared John, knowing that he was a righteous and holy man, and kept him safe. When he heard him he was much perplexed, and yet he heard him gladly. But an opportunity came when Herod on his birthday gave a banquet for his courtiers and officers and the leading men of Galilee. For when Herodias' daughter came in and danced, she pleased Herod and his guests. And the king said to the girl, "Ask me whatever you wish and I will grant it." And he vowed to her, "Whatever you ask me, I will give it, even half of my kingdom."
>
> And she went out and said to her mother, "What shall I ask?" And she said, "The head of John the baptizer". And she came in immediately with haste to the king, and asked, saying, "I want you to give me at once the head of John the Baptist on a platter." And the king was exceedingly sorry, but because of his oaths and his guests he did not want to break his word to her. And immediately the king sent a soldier of the guard and gave orders to bring his head. He went and beheaded him in the prison, and brought his head on a platter, and gave it to the girl; and the girl gave it to her mother . . . (Mark 6:16-28).

The whole story is woven from names of the sacred mushroom. The most obvious word-play is between the "Baptist's" name, *Tabbālā';* the "platter" (Latin *tabula,* borrowed as *tablā'* into Semitic); and the mushroom TAB-BA-LI.[25] But other, more subtle punning has provided most of the details, such as the "banquet for the men of Galilee",[26] the offer of gifts "unto half my kingdom",[27] the prophet being "bound in prison",[28] and so on. The "daughter of Herodias" or "the little heron" as the name means, is a piece of mushroom nomenclature, as is the use of the name "Herod" itself throughout the story.[29] Here, as elsewhere, real-life characters feature in the story, otherwise quite fictional, largely because their names lent themselves to easy punning on mushroom names or epithets.

Red and White

It is the deep red of the canopy of the *Amanita muscaria* that first attracts attention. But closer examination shows that the red background is flecked with white, the wart-like remains of the volva adhering to the cap.

The "flaky" nature of the white particles also contributed to mushroom nomenclature and folk-lore. In the Esau story, for example, it was not only the redness of his skin that marked him off from his smooth brother Jacob, but the roughness of its texture, an allusion to the "scabby" cap of the mushroom. In the vision of the *Amanita muscaria* that must now seem the most likely reference of the first chapter of the book of Revelation, the mystic, being "in the Spirit", as he says, saw this white flecking of the shining "sun"-like face of the mushroom as "white wool":

> I heard behind me a loud voice like a trumpet saying, "Write what you see in a book. . ." Then I turned to see the voice that was speaking to me, and on turning I saw seven golden lampstands, and in the midst of the lampstands one like a son of man, clothed with a long robe, and with a golden girdle round his breast; his head and his hair were white as white wool, white as snow; his eyes were like a flame of fire, his feet were like burnished bronze, refined as in a furnace, and his voice was like the sound of many waters; in his right hand he held seven stars, from his mouth issued a sharp two-edged sword, and his face was like the sun shining in full strength (Rev 1:10-16).

Such a distinctive and striking appearance as that presented by the cap of the *Amanita muscaria* gives us a great advantage in our search for old mushroom names. But it leads us into strange places and into comparisons with the most unlikely objects, animals, plants, and even gems which, apart from their colour characteristics, have little to do with the mushroom. This is largely why the mythology and symbolism of the sacred fungus has managed to keep its secrets for so long.

The Panther

In the Jewish Talmud, Jesus is sometimes referred to as *Bar Pandērā'* "Son of (the) Panther".[30] Most fanciful ideas were expressed about someone called "Panther" whose relations with the Blessed Virgin and paternity of the Babe were the subject of much rich speculation by the Jews of later times, to the annoyance of the Christians. But the epithet has remained a mystery and has survived even the zealous activities of the Christian censors largely because its relevance had been forgotten. We can now see that it is, in fact, a descriptive title of the sacred mushroom, the Semitic word being a transliteration of the Greek *panther,* our "panther". The reference is to the markings of the animal's coat, described by Pliny as "small spots like eyes on a light ground".[31] The ancient botanists must have used the name of the animal for the fungus, just as today the near-relative of the *Amanita muscaria, Amanita pantherina,* is so named among modern mycologists.[32]

References to the Christian "Jesus"-figure occur but sporadically in old Jewish traditions, for it is here that the Christian censors, who came to control most of the libraries of the civilized world, have understandably been most active. Where the name does occur, it is often attached to epithets or "incidents" whose significance has been lost. These now need a thorough re-examination, for the "Pandera" references show conclusively that the early Jews were well aware of the original mushroom nature of the Christian cult, even though, later, through persecution and the passage of time, this knowledge was lost or, at least, no longer expressed in literary form.

In the New Testament, a straight pun is made on the descriptive title of the fungus, when one of the "red-cap" figures, Annas, is said to have been the "father-in-law" (Greek *pentheros)* of Caiaphas (John 18:13). This piece of information is unsupportable from historical sources,[33] and probably quite untrue. It is merely one item in a grouping of mushroom epithets which include also the title of the high priest, Caiaphas, properly "Overseer", but used in the New Testament, along with Peter's surname, "Cephas", as a play on the mushroom word, Latin *cepa.*[34]

We are now able to trace the origin and thus basic meaning of the

Greek *panthēr*.[35] It comes from the Sumerian BAR, "skin", and the word we met before with the meaning "red-wool", DARA. Another use of DARA is with the significance of "spotted, variegated in colour" and so *BAR-DARA will have meant "spotted, variegated skin", and came dialectally into Greek as *panthēr*, as a descriptive title of the peculiarly marked animal.[36]

In Hebrew this same original phrase can now be recognized behind its word for the gum *Bedōlakh* (Latin *Bdellium*).[37] The Old Testament includes it among the sources of comparison when it describes the heaven-sent Manna of the wilderness (Num 11:7). The Manna, as we have already noted, is to be understood as the mushroom, and the reference to Bdellium is due to the appearance of that gum, containing, as Pliny says, "a number of white spots, like fingernails".[38]

The Opal, or Paiderōs, "the beloved"

The same derivation and appearance leads us into the realm of precious stones in our search for mushroom epithets. The stone Opal, Latin *Opalus,* is probably related through its distinctive colouring with the mushroom, whose name (Sumerian *U-BAL)[39] it bears. The Greeks called the stone, *Paiderōs,* and again we turn to Pliny for an early description of this gem:

> The defects of the opal are a colour tending towards that of the flower of the plant called Heliotrope, or of rock-crystal or hail, as well as the occurrence of salt-like specks or rough places or dots which distract the eye . . . the dominant colour of the Paederos is a mixture of sky-blue and purple . . . Those in which the brilliance is darkened by the colour of wine are superior to those in which it is diluted with a watery tint.[40]

The name *Paiderōs* is also given to a thorn, *Akanthos,* "with a reddish root and a head like a thyrsus (penis)",[41] and to a vegetable dye of a purple colour.[42] A point of special interest in the name is that Pliny assumes that it comes from the Greek *pais, paidos,* "boy, son", and *erōtis,* "beloved", and that it is related to the Greek *paiderastēs,* "boy-lover", usually in the bad sense of our "pederast".[43] He says the stone earned its name through being "exceptionally beautiful".[44]

The New Testament, apparently recognizing the specific mushroom application of the name, meaning "red and white spotted skin", plays upon this understanding of *Paiderōs* on a number of occasions. For example, when Jesus is being baptized by John in the Jordan, a voice from heaven calls out, "this is my son, the beloved" (Matt 3:17), precisely the *pais-erōtis* false etymology of *Paiderōs* displayed by Pliny in his description of the opal.

Similarly, taking "son" as meaning "disciple", the New Testament myth-makers offer us the cryptic epithet, so long the subject of speculation, "the disciple whom Jesus loved", that is, the "beloved-son", *pais-erōtis, Paiderōs*. A particularly interesting example of this epithet appears in the story of the Last Supper:

> When Jesus had thus spoken he was troubled in spirit and testified, saying, "Truly, truly, I say to you, one of you will betray me." The disciples looked at one another, uncertain of whom he spoke. One of his disciples, whom Jesus loved, was lying in Jesus' bosom; so Simon Peter beckoned to him and said, "Tell us who it is of whom he speaks." So lying thus, in Jesus' bosom, he said to him, "Lord, who is it?" Jesus answered, "It is he to whom I shall give this morsel when I have dipped it." So when he had dipped the morsel, he gave it to Judas, the son of Simon Iscariot (John 13:21-26).

Here again we have the "dipping" theme derived from a play on the mushroom name *TAB-BA-LI and the Semitic root *t-b-l*, "dip, dye". The words "the disciple whom Jesus loved", the *Paiderōs*, "red and white spotted skin", continue the colour allusions of the passage.

The "Scabby One" and Lapis Lazuli

The characteristic peeling, "scabby" aspect of the *Amanita muscaria* is also reflected in its nomenclature and mythology. The Arabs call the mushroom, "the scabby one",[45] and it is probably this feature of the sacred fungus to which Isaiah refers when he warns the "daughters of Zion"[46] engaged in witchcraft[47] that "the Lord will make your crowns scabby and denude your vulva (?)" (Isa 3:17). The prophet seems to be alluding to the "scabby one" they were adoring in their cult, and the reference is probably the same when he has Yahweh complain to Israel that he had planted her as a vine[48] and hoped to reap "justice" (*mishpat*), but had received for his pains only "fungi", scabs (*mispakh*), making a pun on the two words (Isa 5:7).

As the reader will appreciate, it is only now that we are beginning to understand the significance of the mushroom cult in the ancient world that the relevance of many such passages and allusions in the prophetic writings of the Old Testament can be understood. This is not a matter into which we can go deeply in this work, but clearly one necessity for any future study of the prophetic writings will be to try and sift out all such cultic references and perhaps discover how far the prophetic movement in Israel was averse to the fungus cult completely, and how far the Yahwists of, say, the eighth century BC, were merely making their stand against certain aspects of the old religion.

One thing is now quite certain: the situation was never the clear-cut opposition of Yahwism versus the old fertility cults that later Jewish and Christian theologians liked to suppose. Yahweh was himself a fertility god,[49] and the cult of the sacred mushroom against which Isaiah in certain passages like the ones above seems to be railing, was but an esoteric development of that fertility religion.

But to return to our "scabby" mushroom. As one might expect, the flaking of the surface of the *Amanita muscaria*, with its "wart"-like particles of white skin against the red of the cap, reminded the myth-makers of sufferers from leprosy and other skin diseases. So we should be prepared to find in biblical stories concerned with lepers allusions to the mushroom. In the Gospels people so afflicted are commonly mentioned, but one "ulcerous" character claims our special attention, mainly because of his name, Lazarus (Luke 16:19-31).

On the face of it, "Lazarus" is simply a form of the Old Testament name Eleazar.[50] But here, as so often with New Testament names, we have in an approximation to a biblical name an epithet of the mushroom. What the New Testament cryptographer had in mind here in his "Lazarus" was the word we know in English as "Lazuli", usually found in conjunction with "Lapis" ("stone") to describe a blue mineral containing flecks of gold, as Pliny describes it, adding that it can be "tinged with purple".[51]

Our name "Lazuli" comes from the Persian *Lazhurward,* and, as we can now trace it back, ultimately from a Sumerian phrase *AR-ZAL-DARA, "brightly shining variegated (stone)". The Persian form is simply a jumbled form of the Sumerian, and from it Semitic derived its *Lazrad* on which form the New Testament word-play with "Lazarus" was made.[52] To the writer of the Gospel the significance of the name lay in the speckled, purplish colour of the *Amanita muscaria,* to which, in his description of the unfortunate beggar, he added the "scabby, ulcerous" appearance given by the warty surface of the cap: "more-over, the dogs came and licked his sores" (v. 21).

Barnabas, "Son of Consolation"

The reference to Lapis Lazuli furthermore opens up to us a line of approach which helps us solve another intriguing problem of New Testament nomenclature. The proper Sumerian name of the mineral is ZA-GIN, "flecked stone". These words came into Semitic in a variety of forms; the consonants underwent various dialectal changes *en route,* and they became jumbled out of their original positions. However, it is usually possible to pick out the new forms now that the phonetic correspondences can be recognized. In Hebrew, for instance, the Z-G-N of the Sumerian became *s-p-r,* giving *sappir,* "Lapis Lazuli", and the same form is found in the Greek *sappheiros,* our "sapphire", usually attached to quite another stone.[53] From our more immediate point of view, a more interesting development was to produce the group *n-b-s.* Thus Accadian had *nabāsu,* "red dyed wool", and in Aramaic *nabūsa* is the name of a certain red woolly caterpillar that infects the Service tree, *Sorbus domestica.*[54] The motif of "red flecked with white" continues in the Greek and Latin names of the "giraffe", *nābūs,* which Pliny describes as "an animal with a neck like a horse, the feet and legs of an ox, a head like a camel, and is of a ruddy colour picked out with white spots",[55] which is a good description of the colouration of the *Amanita muscaria.* It is, as now we see, the same *n-b-s* verbal group that is the significant part of the name of the New Testament character, "Joseph, called Barnabas":

> Now the company of those who believed were of one heart and soul, and no one said that any of the things which he possessed was his own, but they had everything in common . . . There was not a needy person among them, for as many as were possessors of lands or houses sold them, and brought the proceeds of what was sold and laid it at the apostles' feet; and distribution was made to each as any had need. Thus Joseph who was surnamed by the apostles Barnabas (which means Son of Encourage-ment), a Levite, a native of Cyprus, sold a field which belonged to him, and brought the money and laid it at the apostles' feet (Acts 4:32-37).

The surname of this philanthropist has caused the commentators much trouble in the past,[56] for the New Testament cryptographer has given us another of his pseudo-translations, telling us that "Barnabas" means "Son of Encouragement". He implies thereby that the first part "Bar-" is the Aramaic "Son of-" and that the *nabas* at the end represents another Semitic word meaning "Encouragement". In point of fact, there is no extant root which offers that meaning and which looks like -*nabas*. The name is not, indeed, Aramaic at all: the first element is the Sumerian BAR, "skin", and the second is our "giraffe", "red-with-white-spots" word, the whole being yet another epithet of the *Amanita muscaria*.

The pseudo-translation, "Son of Encouragement", refers not to Barnabas, but comes from a word-play we have already met, between the roots *kh-n-n*, "gracious, encouragement", and *kh-n-n*, "red" (our "red-cap").[57] The writer points the way to decipherment himself when he says that Barnabas was "a native of Cyprus" (*Kuprios*). He and his readers were well aware that the Greek word for the red dye "Henna" is *kupros,* the Hebrew *kōpher,* Aramaic *kuphrā*.[58] The similarity which made the word-play here possible is not, as we can now appreciate, purely coincidental. Both go back to an original Sumerian GU-BAR, "top of the head; glans penis";[59] in the case of the offshore island, the reference is to the old fertility geography of the area which saw the island as the tip of a penis awaiting entry into the "groin" of the mainland. The dye "Henna", *kuphrā*, gave a colour which seemed to the ancients to resemble the suffused red of the glans penis.[60]

Even the philanthropist's first name, Joseph, had probably a similar reference in the myth-maker's mind. The name means, as we have seen, "Yahweh (semen)-penis", from Sumerian *IA-U-SIPA/SIB.[61] Cognate with this is the name of the precious stone we know as "Jasper", the Greek *iaspis,* Hebrew *yāshepheh,* all deriving from a Sumerian *IA-SIPA/SIB, "penis-stone", again referring to the colour of the glans.[62]

The point of the story itself, the sale of the field and donation of its value, is another allusion to the "Akeldama" theme of the Iscariot story. It will be remembered that the story-teller played it in that instance on the idea that the miscreant's blood-money was used to buy a "field" which, because of its associations, became known as the "Field of Blood" (Acts 1:19). As we shall see,[63] word-play there is between the Aramaic *demā',* "blood", and *dāmē,* "price, value", and between *'akal,* "food", and *khaqal,* "field". The real relevance of the name "Akeldama" was "food of compensation" or "atonement", being equivalent to other names of the Holy Plant which referred to it as God's atoning sacrifice made to the earth on man's behalf, the "price" of salvation. So, in the story of Barnabas' gift from the proceeds of the sale of his "field", the theme is the same, giving us a name of the sacred fungus, together with an allusion to its "Akeldama" title and cultic significance.

Joseph's "coat of many colours"

Our work enables us now to open up a major new line of approach to the patriarchal myths in the Old Testament, but on a smaller scale it also helps to solve a number of niggling points of Hebrew philology which, although not important in themselves, have served to remind us continually of our ignorance of so much early Semitic vocabulary. One such problem was the description of the tunic given to a more famous Joseph by his adoring father Jacob/Israel:

> Now Israel loved Joseph more than any other of his children, because he was the son of his old age; and he made him a "coat of many colours" (or, as our modern translations have it, "a long robe with sleeves") (Gen 37:3).

The older understanding of the nature of the tunic came from the early Greek translators who received a tradition that the rare Hebrew word *passīm* meant "many coloured, spotted".[64] More recent translators have favoured an alternative rendering which described not the colour of the garment but its shape and size. They have seen in *passīm* a word meaning "palms of the hands", so that, somewhat improbably, the description implied that the sleeves of the tunic reached to the "palms", hence their "long robe with sleeves". Happily, thanks to the prompting of the "Barnabas" decipherment we can make a fresh assessment of the rare Hebrew word, finding in it a root cognate with the latter part of Barnabas' name and meaning "red, spotted with white", or, as a related Aramaic word denotes, "freckled".[65] The Greek translators of Genesis are thus vindicated, and we traditionalists can cling on to our "coat of many colours" (AV, RV).

To conclude: it is hardly surprising that the worshippers of the sacred fungus found in its distinctive colouring and surface texture a rich source of material for descriptive epithets and folk-tales. Our modern fairy-tale writers are no less attracted by the red-topped toadstool that decorates the covers of so many children's books. The classic story of the Golden Fleece has come from the "woolly" nature of the mushroom cap as the ancients envisaged it, and old words for "dyeing red" have their original reference to the *Amanita muscaria*. In the New Testament, the myth-makers seized upon the similarity with the Semitic word for "red-cap" to name a number of their characters, including John the "Baptist". The Jews have managed to preserve a name for Jesus, the "Panther", or "Spotted-skin", which shows that at first, anyway, the real significance of the Christian myth and cult was not lost to their contemporaries.

Decipherment of the name of the "ulcerous" Lazarus, has led the way to appreciating for the first time the nature and meaning of the New Testament cryptographer's "Son of Encouragement", applied as a pseudo-translation to the colour epithet of the sacred fungus, "Barnabas".

One of the effects claimed for the hallucinatory drugs in the cap of the *Amanita muscaria* is that the subject sees objects and colours larger and brighter than life. Applied to the mushroom itself, the prime example of such drug-inspired vision is to be found at the beginning of the "Revelation to John", noticed on a number of occasions. But, as we can now appreciate, this enlarged view of the object of their adoration had long before given the ancients a major source for their cosmographies, accounts of the beginnings of the world. They saw the whole universe as a monster mushroom, the earth as the lower "cup" of the volva, the heaven stretched out above as a great pilleus, supported on a pillar of some sacred mountain. Out of this conception came stories of giants holding up the canopy of heaven, and another source of folk-names and mythology of the mushroom. Furthermore, we can now begin to understand names given to the environs of Jerusalem, and the relevance of the proximity of the Dead Sea to the fertility cults centred on that city. On a larger scale, it is possible to appreciate the derivation and significance of names of the areas bordering on the eastern Mediterranean, regarded as the "crutch" of the earth and thus the entrance to her womb.

In the beginning was the volva ...

XV

Mushroom Cosmography

The cult of the mushroom produced its own cosmography. The volva of some vast primeval fungus split asunder, the lower hemisphere containing the amniotic fluid of creation, the biblical "deep", and the upper being forced upwards to make the canopy of heaven. In the Accadian version of the myth it is the creator, phallic god Marduk, "womb-favourer", who splits the volva asunder. In this case, the volva is seen as the egg of a mighty serpent called Tiamat, the equivalent of the biblical *tehōm,* "subterranean deep", or, as its Sumerian origin implies, "womb." It is Tiamat's body which forms in its two parts heaven and earth.[1] Properly speaking, the "serpent" in the mushroom physiology is the stem that arises from the volva to bear aloft the upper half as its expanded head, or, in phallic terms, its glans penis. Cosmographically, the mushroom stem is represented by a great mountain whose top is lost in the clouds of heaven. This was the seat of the gods, the Olympus of the Greeks, *Sāphōn* ("north") of the Semites, both names having reference to their cosmic functions. Olympus can now be shown to mean "city of the support of heaven";[2] the Semitic *Sāphōn,* "north", means properly "the fulcrum".[3]

In Greek mythology, Atlas is a mighty giant standing in the west, holding aloft the heavens on outstretched arms. His name, as that of the mountain in North Africa that was identified with him, means "heavenly shade", Sumerian *ANDUL-AN.[4] We noticed previously how our own word "giant" comes from a similar Sumerian designation, found in Greek form as the name of the mushroom.[5]

In the Semitic world of Canaan, it was Mount Hermon, "organ of support",[6] which held up the sky. Farther south, Jerusalem, "city of the heavenly womb", as we may now interpret the name, was conceived as bearing up the "groin" of the sky as a phallus carries the splayed legs of a woman in coitus,[7] and the axe-shaft the head.[8] The other name by which the Holy City was known, "virgin daughter of Zion" had a similar connotation.[9]

The "Atlas"-type of a man with arms outstretched supporting the roof we met earlier in discussing the origin of the name Pollux, the stem of the mushroom supporting the canopy, the upper half of the "womb" of his brother Castor.[10] It was there seen that the derivation of "Pollux" from the Sumerian LU-GEShPU, "strong man", was paralleled in the formation of the New Testament name for the brothers James and John, the "Boanerges", so-called "Sons of Thunder". In the one case LU-GEShPU became *pu-lu-ges and thus "Pollux"; in the other, a phrase *GEShPU-AN-UR became *pu-an-ur-ges and thus "Boanerges". In mushroom terms, James (Jacob) is the "pillar" and John is the red-topped canopy.

A very similar vocalic jumbling from the Sumerian occurred in the case of another Greek mushroom word which extended into extra-ordinarily disparate fields of reference, phoinix, our Phoenix. As the designation of the palm-tree it signified fancifully a kind of overgrown mushroom, the fronded leaves representing the canopy; the tall trunk, the mushroom stem. The Greek word comes from Sumerian *GEShPU-IMI, with just the same meaning as *GEShPU-AN-UR, "strong man (holding up) the sky", the Boanerges. The development was as follows: *pu-imi-ges to *pu-ini-ges to the Greek phoinix.[11] It is the same mush-room connection that brought the Phoenix into the category of "womb-birds" mentioned earlier.[12] We noticed that the Phoenix was the centre of much speculation among classical and Christian writers about resur-rection from the dead.

Sumerian's common name for the palm-tree, GIShIMMAR, like the cognate Hebrew tamar, contains the element MAR, representing an inverted "V" shape. So it appears in words for the head of a double-axe or mattock, for a rainbow, and for a woman's crutch, or womb.[13] The Hebrew word and its cognates extend to forms like a signpost, a column of smoke spreading into a "mushroom-cloud" at the top. The "small palm-tree" forms a significant part of the Temple decorations (I Kgs 6:29).[14]

The close relationship in imagery between a mushroom and a palm-tree may help us to understand a curious reference in Pliny's descrip-tion of the Essenes by the Dead Sea. He says that having renounced all sexual pleasures in their ascetic existence, they contented themselves with the "company of palm-trees" (*socia palmarum*).[15] Even the female variety of the palm one would have thought was hardly adequate consolation for celibacy. It is more likely that our author had heard that the cult centred around the "Phoenix-fungus" or "-gourd" and he knew the name only as referring to the tree.

Perhaps the Greek *phoinix* is best known for its derived form *Phoinikia*, the home on the Levantine coast of those intrepid seamen of the ancient world, the Phoenicians. This geographical use of the name raises another interesting aspect of mushroom cosmography. Here the mushroom has to be imagined horizontally, lying on its side, so that the canopy forms the curving sweep of the Palestinian coastline. This, then, is the "crutch" of the earth, the "legs" being represented by the coast of Asia Minor in the north, and Egypt and North Africa to the south (fig. 1). For the Mesopotamian myth-maker, the sun's glowing orb plunged every evening into this "vulva" of the west.[16]

The conception of the land mass at the eastern end of the Mediterranean as the earth's vaginal entrance is reflected in the biblical name of the area, Canaan, Hebrew *Kena'an*, now to be recognized as from the Sumerian *KI-NA-AN (-NA), "nuptial couch of heaven".[17] Within the same general concept of fertility geography, the offshore island of Cyprus was reckoned as a "glans" poised for entry into the Canaanite womb, as is suggested not only by its name, Greek *Kupros*, from a Sumerian *GU-BAR-USh, "head of the erect penis",[18] but also the importance of the fertility cults of Cinyras, already noted, and of Aphrodite.[19]

In any population centre in the ancient Near East where a fertility religion was practised, the royal city and its cultic centre, the palace-temple, was the seat of the god's creative activity. It was thus the "uterus" to be sanctified and fertilized by his presence.[20] It is in such terms that the topography and nomenclature of Jerusalem/Zion has to be understood.

One story for the choice of the site for the Jewish Temple places it on "the threshing floor of Araunah" (II Sam 24:15ff.). David had made a census of the people, the necessary prerequisite to an efficient income-tax system. Yahweh (who had suggested it [v. 1]) punished this act of impiety by sending a pestilence upon Israel from which seventy thousand men died in three days. The avenging angel was just about to smite Jerusalem in a similar way when the god called a halt, and at that spot

David raised an altar to Yahweh and later his son Solomon built the Temple.[21]

Appropriately enough the place was a threshing floor, the Hebrew word for which means originally, as we see, "seed-container".[22] The name of the owner, Araunah, may be explained similarly from the Sumerian as "pounder of the womb", that is, the phallus that grinds up the ingredients in the uterine "mortar". So the site of the god's creative activity for the future was the "belly" of the city and, in the eyes of the local religionists at least, of the world. So today the centre of the earth, the "navel", is portrayed in the Church of the Holy Sepulchre in Jerusalem, as in classical times the worshippers of Apollo found it in the temple at Delphi.[23]

South of the Temple area lay the Jebusite stronghold of Zion proper, the *mons veneris*, as it were, of the city (fig. 5). On its south-western flank was the Pool of Siloam ("place of washing") where Jesus sent the blind man to wash off the clay poultice he had laid on his eyes (John

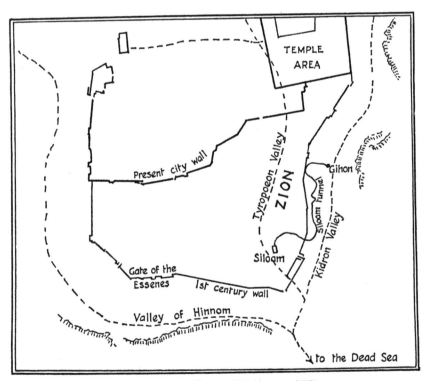

5 Zion, and the valleys of Kidron and Hinnom

9:7)[24] The water of the Pool came from an underground conduit cut in the time of Hezekiah from the spring of Gihon on the other side of the hill. It was considered of such sanctity that the Temple cultus demanded that only Siloam water should be used in its special rites.[25]

Beneath the *mons veneris* was the junction of the two valleys circumventing the city on three sides (fig. 5). From the west, and sweeping round the south, was the valley of the "son(s) of Hinnom", the site, as we saw earlier, of the Molech cult.[26] The name of the valley in Hebrew is simply an attempt to put into recognizable Semitic a phrase whose original Sumerian meant "penis-sheath", that is, "vagina" (*BAR-ERUM).[27] Below Zion, the valley combined with another, the Kidron, which cut the city sharply off on the east and separated it from the Mount of Olives. The resultant depression ran down through the desert to the south and east into the Dead Sea basin, the bowels of the earth (fig. 6).

This gorge was the original "valley of the shadow of death", as its Hebrew designation *salmaweth* is wrongly translated in Psalm 23:4, and elsewhere. The real meaning of the original Sumerian *SILA-MUD means rather the opposite, "way of birth", that is, "birth-canal".[28] Now the point of Molech having his "sperm-dedication" ceremonies here is clearly seen. So also can be appreciated the Psalmist's concern that his shepherd-god Yahweh should guide him by "rod and staff" through the valley, that he should fear no evil. As a baby's fragile body needs the firm but gentle hand of the midwife as it is pressed into life through the vagina, so the religious mystic needed to put his hand in his god's as he passed through the experience of re-birth.

The Arabs call the valley the Wady of Fire.[29] It is well-named. Not only does the summer sun raise the temperature within its gorges to almost unbearable heights, but at its lower end it debouches onto the Dead Sea, the nearest point on the world's surface to the generative furnaces of mother earth's womb. Later theologians associated this heat to which the soul returned for purging and rebirth with retributive punishment for sins committed, so "the valley of the sons of Hinnom", or Gehenna as it became known, was identified with hell-fire, which had little to do with the original fertility concept.[30]

Reverting once more to the "vertical" aspect of mushroom cosmography, we have a good example in the Old Testament myth of Jacob and his ladder (Gen 28:10ff.).

And Jacob came to a certain place, and stayed there that night, because the sun had set. Taking one of the stones of the place, he put it under his head and lay down in that place to sleep. And he dreamt there was a ladder set up on earth, and the top of it reached to heaven; and behold, the angels of God were ascending and descending on it! . . . Then Jacob awoke from his sleep, and said, "Surely Yahweh is in this place, and I did not know it." And he was afraid, and said, "How awesome is this place! This is none other than the house of God, and this is the gate of heaven."

Jacob's name means "pillar", properly "standing-stone" (Sumerian *IA-A-GUB).[31] His equivalent in the Twin mythology of the classical world is Pollux, the "mighty man supporting heaven". In the New Testament he is represented by James (Greek *Iakōb)*, one of the Boaner-ges brothers, and a "pillar" of the Church (Gal 2:9).

In mushroom terms, Jacob is the stem of the fungus, and his "red-skinned" brother Esau is the scarlet canopy of the *Amanita muscaria*. As the phallic stem of the mushroom, Jacob is the "anointed one" running

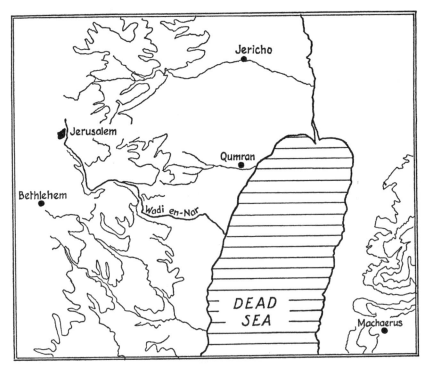

6 Jerusalem to the Dead Sea

with the precious "semen" of the god.[32] It is in the light of this aspect of mushroom physiology as seen by the ancients that the remainder of the Jacob's ladder story has to be understood.

> So Jacob rose early in the morning, and he took the stone which he had put under his head and set it up for a pillar and poured oil on top of it . . . (vv. 18ff.).

Another well-known Old Testament story illustrating the mushroom idea of a pillar reaching to the canopy of heaven is the myth of Moses and Mount Sinai. The name of the sacred mountain as we may now recognize means "brazier" (Sumerian ZA-NE) hence its description as "wrapped in smoke . . . like the smoke of a kiln" (Exod 19:18).[33] It is at the fiery head of this "brazier" that Moses meets Yahweh, and finds after the interview that his face is glowing so much that the people were afraid to approach him (Exod 34:29). Another important detail in the myth is the writing by the finger of God of the ten commandments on tablets of stone (Exod 24:12).[34] The origin of the "tablets" theme is the "bun"-shape of the primitive clay tablet, resembling the top of a mushroom. Indeed, it is from one of the names of the fungus, the Sumerian *TAB-BA-LI, "twin-cone", that, through Greek and Latin, we have received our word "tablet". The two slabs of stone in the story represent the two halves of the split mushroom volva.[35] The "ten commandments" or "ten words" as they are known in the Bible, in their number and in their content are but word-plays on Sumerian fungus names.[36] Later we shall look closer at these "Words" when we enquire more deeply into the moral content of the biblical writings.

To the mushroom cosmographer, then, the universe was a "gigantic" (literally) fungus. At the base was the cup-shaped volva containing the waters of creation. The central pillar, variously identified with sacred mountains, supported the heavenly canopy. In sexual terms, the phallic pillar supported the sky, as the groin of a monstrous woman. On a horizontal plane, the same overall picture presented the land mass of the eastern Mediterranean as the "crutch" and offshore islands as the tips of penes awaiting entry into the vagina of earth's womb. Inland, Jerusalem was the belly of the world, at least to the fertility cults centred in that city, and it was the beginning of the ever-deepening gorge of Gehenna which plunged down into the Dead Sea rift, the "bowels" of the earth.

Here, again, is a field for much further research. If names like Jeru-salem and Zion are primarily Sumerian and not Semitic, then we must seek a very early Sumerian influence in this area, which left later inhabitants not only designations of the city and valleys but a fertility cosmography in which Jerusalem played a central role. Other peoples elsewhere saw an equal importance in their own religious centres, as the Greeks revered Delphi, but whoever named Jerusalem, "city of the heavenly groin", understood this area to be the belly of the earth, and thus the main seat of the creator-god's activity. The idea that it was a Hebrew king called David that, around 1000 BC, instituted Yahweh worship here, in a previously "pagan" land (II Sam 6), must therefore be seriously questioned. Indeed, these present discoveries of the place of mushroom worship in the religion of ancient Israel, and the origin and nature of much Old Testament mythology, raise such doubts about the historicity of many aspects of the story of the Israelites. In the chapter that follows we shall see that even the account of the sojourn in Egypt must be radically re-examined. Whether it will ever be possible to draw a clear line of distinction between fact and fiction in the biblical records is very doubtful. The story of David, the hero-king, is a prime example of the dubiety which must now hang over the Old Testament as being in any sense a work of history, or based on history.

XVI

David, Egypt, and the Census

In the Old Testament, David, the "lover" or "beloved" as we may render his name,[1] is the counterpart of the Semitic and classical Adonis,
first among the fertility hero-gods of the ancient world. The name
Adonis is related to the Semitic common noun 'adōn, "lord". The root
meaning of both we may now trace to the same Sumerian ANDUL,
"heavenly shade", as gave the name Atlas to the mighty man of mythology who holds aloft the canopy of heaven.[2] The basic conception is
one of "protection" and thus "lordship" in that sense of shielding the
land and people from outward harm. The same picture is presented in
another of the god's names, Na'iman, traceable now to a Sumerian
*NA-IM-A-AN, "stretched across the sky".[3] Thus, within the mush-
room cult, both names, Adonis and Na'iman, can have a specific reference to the canopy of the fungus, viewed in the kind of cosmographical
terms we have just discussed. Later, we shall look again at the Adonis-
Na'iman figure in its particular application to the cultivation and use of
the sacred fungus.[4] For the moment, we may study more particularly
his Old Testament representative David, whose Adonis and fertility
connections are plainly set out in the oracle ascribed to his authorship:

> The oracle of David, son of Jesse; the oracle of the erect phallus (RSV
> "the man who was raised on high"), the semen-smeared (RSV "anointed")
> of the God of Jacob, the Na'im ("heavenly canopy", RSV; "sweet") of the
> stretched penis (RSV: "psalmist") of Israel (II Sam 23:1).

The "patronymic" epithet, "Son of Jesse", is really an attempt to
hebraize an original Sumerian *BAR-USh-SA, "erect penis", thus con-
forming to the other phallic names given the hero figure. The phrase
has some particular interest since in the form *Briseus* or *Brēseus* we may
now recognize it among the titles of the phallic Dionysus/Bacchus.[5] In
the description of David as the "Na'im of the stretched penis (*z-m-r*)

of Israel" there is a clear connection with a passage in Isaiah about the "Adonis plantations": "You plant the plants of Na'iman (Adonis), you sow the penis *(z-m-r)* of the field (?)" (Isa 17:10).[6]

The English versions usually render the word in the David oracle as "songs" since the root *z-m-r* means also "sing". But this is just another instance of the idea that singing was primarily a sexual activity whose function was to stimulate new life, demonstrably by causing an erection in the male organ. It is, thus, a cultic word, as singing, like lamentation, was part of the stimulatory worship of the fertility deity.[7]

It is in this cultic phallic sense that we find *z-m-r* used again in Ezekiel's vision of the abominable practices being carried on in Jerusalem during his absence. Having been shown the women bewailing Tammuz/Adonis at the entrance of the north gate of the Temple:

> . . . he brought me into the inner court of the house of Yahweh; and behold, at the door of the temple of Yahweh, between the porch and the altar, were about twenty-five men, with their backs to the temple of Yahweh, and their faces towards the East, worshipping the sun towards the East. Then he said to me, "Have you seen this, O son of man? . . . Lo, they stretch out the erect phallus before them" (RSV: "put the branch to their nose") (Ezek 8:17).[8]

The bearing of the phallus was a marked feature of the Dionysiac processionals,[9] but as we now know, it had more than a purely physiological significance. The penis was not only the sign of human generation but within the mushroom cult it symbolized the sacred fungus itself, the "phallus of God".

The root *z-m-r*, "stretch out", is but a jumbled form of another root *m-s-r* or *m-z-r* of the same meaning, derived, as we may now appreciate, from a Sumerian word SUR, "stretch out, measure a boundary".[10] Its use and word-play in cultic mythology has probably caused more misunderstanding in later generations about the history of the Jews than almost any other. We happen to know that one of the names of the mushroom was the "stretched gourd", for it has come down to us, transliterated in Greek from the old language of the North African Semites, as *Koussi Mezar*, and confused, as so often with names for the fungus, with the Squirting Cucumber.[11] The root *m-z-r/m-s-r* is also known in Semitic as the designation of the country of Egypt, "The Territory", or in the dual form, as normally in Hebrew, "The Two

Territories", that is, Upper and Lower Egypt. So modern botanists have understood the old Semitic name *Koussi Mezar* as "the Egyptian gourd". And what the moderns have done unwittingly, the old myth-makers did intentionally: the sacred fungus was known as "the Egyptian mushroom", and from that playful designation was born the myth of the Israelites' sojourn in that land.

The New Testament also took up the theme and has the Holy Family flee to Egypt to escape the highly improbable persecution by Herod "of all the male children in Bethlehem and in all that region who were two years old or under" (Matt 2:13ff.). It cites as justification of the exercise the text from Hosea:

> When Israel was a lad I loved him, and out of Egypt I called my son (Hos 11:1).

Israel as the god's first-born son in Egypt is the theme of the whole of the captivity and deliverance cycle of the Exodus. Thus Moses is com-manded to approach Pharaoh with these words:

> Thus says Yahweh, Israel is my first-born son, and I say to you, "Let my son go that he may serve me"; if you refuse to let him go, behold, I will slay your first-born son (Exod 4:23).

The carrying out of this threat to kill all the first-born of the land of Egypt forms the setting for the institution of the Passover. After the escape, Yahweh commands:

> Consecrate to me all the first-born; whatever is the first to open the womb among the people of Israel, both of man and beast, is mine (Exod 13:2).

Earlier on in this book we examined the philosophy of the fertility religions of the ancient world with regard to the special favour ascribed to the first-born, connected as it is with the power of the first menstrual blood of the virgin. Custom demanded that these specially endowed offspring should be returned to the god as a token towards restoring the balance of nature disturbed by their birth and human appropriation.[12]

This is the cultic background of the Exodus Passover tradition, but the story itself hinges on the play between the name of the fungus as *Mezar,* "erect, stretched", and *Masōr,* "Egypt", to set the place of the myth; and upon the common Semitic name of the mushroom, *Pitrā',* and the root *p-t-r* which gave "first-born", "release", and "unleavened bread". The Hebrew story-teller thus had in the mushroom name and epithet the main ingredients of his Exodus story.[13]

The New Testament writers were not slow to see the possibilities of this *Mezar* epithet of the fungus for their myth-making. The root *m-s-r* in its various forms provides a rich harvest of puns for story-telling, and the New Testament abounds in instances. Perhaps the best known is the epithet given to Judas Iscariot[14] that has characterized him and those named after him throughout the civilized world, "he who betrayed him".[15] The verb *m-s-r* means "hand over" as a betrayal, particularly to Gentiles, so Iscariot is the arch-*māsōr*, "betrayer" of all time.

Another word of different root but similar in sound is *mēsōr*, meaning "bonds, imprisonment". Playing on this word and the *Mezor* of the fungus, together with the *p-t-r* root, giving "Peter", the apostle, and *pattīrā'*, "unleavened bread", we have the story in Acts which begins:

> . . . and when he (Herod) saw that it pleased the Jews, he proceeded to arrest Peter also. This was during the days of the Unleavened Bread. And when he had seized him, he put him in prison . . . (Acts 12:3f.).

"Pleasing the Jews" stems from the Sumerian mushroom name MASh-TAB-BA-RI, read as "that which is pleasing to the Hebrews (Jews)", by a word-play with Aramaic.[16] The name Herod, meaning "heron" (Latin *ardeola*) serves throughout the New Testament as a useful play on the Semitic *'Ardila'*, "mushroom", as does the feminine form "Rhoda" who opened the door to Peter after his release from prison (Acts 12:13).[17]

Another form of "restriction" is the girdle or loin-cloth, and words for this in Semitic are similarly formed, as the Aramaic *mēsārā'*. Taking the old Punic name *Koussi Mezar* (properly **kisshu'ath*[18] *mesōrah*, or the like) as the pattern, the myth-makers formed the play "girdle-clothing" (*kesāyā'*)[19] that is, "waist-band, or loin-cloth". In the prophetic symbolism of the seer Agabus, plays on both "girdle" and "betrayal, handing over" are extracted from the mushroom name:

> . . . a prophet named Agabus[20] came down from Judea. And coming to us he took Paul's girdle and bound his own feet and hands, and said, "Thus says the Holy Spirit, 'So shall the Jews at Jerusalem bind the man who owns this belt and deliver him into the hands of the Gentiles . . .'" (Acts 21:10f.).

The patronymic by which David is known in the Oracle quoted above and elsewhere, "son of Jesse", is, as we have seen, also an old Sumerian name for the erect phallus, *BAR-USh-SA. The same word USh-SA appears again in the name of one of Jacob's sons, Issachar.[21] The story of his birth is a good example of word-play based on a well-known name. But here the play is on a fanciful Hebrew derivation of the name and is obvious: indeed, the writer spells it out for us in so many words:

> In the days of the wheat harvest, Reuben [another of Jacob's sons] went out and found mandrakes in the field, and brought them to his mother Leah. Then Rachel [Jacob's barren wife] said to Leah, "Give me, I pray thee, some of your son's mandrakes." But she said to her, "Is it a small matter that you should have taken away my husband? Would you take away my son's mandrakes also?" Rachel said, "He can sleep with you tonight for your son's mandrakes."
>
> When Jacob came from the field in the evening, Leah went out to meet him, and said, "You have to have intercourse with me, because I have hired (s-k-r) you with my son's mandrakes." So he slept with her that night. And God favoured Leah and she conceived and bore Jacob a fifth son. Leah said, "God has given me my hire (s-k-r) . . ." so she called his name Issachar (Gen 30:14-18).

The author of this little tale finds his theme in the fancied meaning of the name Issachar as 'ish, "man" and sakar, "he has hired", taking the name as if it were Hebrew. In the cycle of birth and naming stories contained in that and the previous chapter, the writer has tried to find in each of the names of Jacob's children some Hebrew root on which to make a punning reference to some aspect of his origin or character. Thus "Reuben" is understood as if it contained the roots r-'-h, "see", and '-n-h, "afflict" – "Yahweh has *looked* upon *my affliction*" ;[22] "Simeon", as if it contained the root sh-m-', "hear" – "Yahweh has *heard* that I am hated";[23] "Levi", as if it were of the root l-w-h, "join" – "this time my husband will *be joined* to me" ;[24] "Judah" as if it were of the root y-d-h, "praise" – "I will *praise* Yahweh",[25] and so on.

Even if the names were Semitic, let alone Hebrew, some of the supposed derivations would be philologically impossible. Happily, mythmakers were not academic pedants, or the world would be lacking some of its finest literature. Such stories do not necessarily indicate whether or not the people who composed them had lost the real meanings of the names by that time, for word-play among the ancients, as we have seen, was a legitimate means of religious exposition and source of cultic story-telling. For the purposes of the plot and its moral, it was quite in order to spin out the old patriarchal names in this far-fetched way if the end-product served the cause of pious homiletics.

However, there are passages in some of the older oracles of the Old Testament where it is clear that the writers were aware of the meanings of the ancient names. For example, of Issachar Deborah sings:

Why did you lie between the sheep-folds, listening to the piping of the flocks? (Judg 5:16).

Much the same phrase occurs of Issachar in the ancient oracle of Jacob on his sons:

Issachar is a . . . ass, lying between the sheepfolds; and he saw a resting-place that it was good, and the land that it was sweet (na'imah); and he put his shoulder to the burden, and it was for him a worker's labour (Gen 49:14f.).

Now, in such oracular snatches we have word-play of a very different order from those tales just quoted. And because they are dealing with the *real* meanings of the tribal names, as distinct from the fanciful plays on supposed Semitic roots, we have hitherto been at a loss to understand many of the references and allusions. Now at last we shall be able to start breaking them down, but it will be no easy task. Since they ceased to be understood from a comparatively early time, the chances are that many of the key words will have been changed during transmission. Happily oral traditions are not so susceptible to change as those which are passed on by the written word. Children will remember a poem or song by heart without necessarily understanding every word. We all have doubtless wondered in our youth why a "green hill" should *need* a "city wall" anyway. So for centuries the songs and oracles of the Old Testament will have come down exactly by word of mouth even though their dialects had ceased to be used, or the words had been carried out of their original territories.

Nevertheless there will come a time when the poems will find written form, and the scribes will puzzle over forms and words quite strange to them. They will guess at their meanings and here and there substitute more common words, or even add the colloquial "explanation" along-side the original. The modern researcher has to try and sort out the different literary strands. But if he himself has lost the key – in the case of the oldest Hebrew writings, the nature of the cult from which they came – there is little he can do but wait and hope that further archaeo-logical or philological discoveries may shed new light on the points of difficulty.

Unfortunately, when the writings become the central fount of authority for another religion, or a wayward development of the old, there is a temptation to make sense of the inherited scriptures at all points, and at any cost. In such cases basic principles of grammar and syntax, and a free admittance of lexicographical ignorance, too often give way before the need for pious exposition.

To return to Issachar, "crouching between the sheep-folds", Debor-ah's taunt rests upon a word-play on the Sumerian mushroom name, *LI-MASh-BA(LA)G-ANTA-TAB-BA-RI, read as "why are you resting (Semitic *sh-b-kh,* "be still, at peace") in the pasture?"[26] The next line of the Jacob Blessing: "and he saw a resting-place and it was good . . ." gives a more obvious play on the Adonis mushroom name Na'iman (Semitic *n-'-m,* "be sweet").[27] The last phrase: "it was for him a worker's labour" (Hebrew *mas-'ōbēd*) provides a good instance of a change made in the text at some stage when the original word became dialectally out of fashion.[28] The text probably first read *mas-palakh* and was intended as a play on MASh-BALAG of the mushroom name.[29] Both phrases meant the same "forced labour" and to judge from the number of times that this theme appears in the Old Testament myths, it served their authors as a favourite source of word-play.

The forced labour to which the Israelites were subject in their mythi-cal sojourn in Egypt was in this way derived from the name of the sacred fungus. David's successor on the throne, Solomon, for all his much-vaunted wisdom in offering to share a baby between its rival claimant mothers with a knife (I Kgs 3:16-28), showed less acumen in demanding forced labour from his subjects (I Kgs 12:4). Furthermore, the same phrase also had the implication of making a census of the people and thus administering a tax as well as a work-levy system. Not un-naturally this kind of administrative advance was not welcome. One account of David's eventual fall from grace was that he had designed such a census and was punished by his god for doing so (II Sam 24).

The MASh-BALAG-"census" theme of mushroom mythology gave the New Testament story-teller the dramatic means of bringing the pregnant Mary over a hundred miles of some of the roughest terrain in the world from Nazareth to Bethlehem to be delivered of the Christ child. It is the ungrateful pedant, or over-zealous religionist, who bothers overmuch about the likelihood that any Roman governor would have been so stark, raving mad as to require everyone in his territory to do a kind of "general post" to the place of their tribal origin for the purpose of being counted (Luke 2:3).

That particular author could, however, have saved subsequent less imaginative readers a great deal of worry and spilt ink if he had not seized upon a recollection of the name of one Syrian governor, Quirinius, to add colour to the tale. Unfortunately Quirinius did not become governor until AD 6, and King Herod, in whose time the birth of Jesus was supposed to have taken place, died a decade or so earlier.[30] Still, even the best myth-makers cannot have everything their own way. The point of Quirinius (Greek *Kūrenios*) is that his name made an excellent word-play with both *Grunon* and *Geraneion,* Greek names of the fungus.[31]

The mushroom allusions in the snatches of song about Issachar are not only verbal. The "resting-place" sheepfold had a special significance in fungus imagery. It consisted basically of two barriers set out like a funnel, or an open "V" shape, through which the sheep could be driven into their fold.[32] We have in this structure the stylized configuration of the mushroom cap, supported by the stem, "lying between the folds". In human physiological terms, Issachar, "mighty penis", lies between the opened legs of the woman, and seeing "a resting place that it was good, and the land that it was sweet, puts his shoulder to the burden . . ." To use another mushroom metaphor, Issachar stands ready to "take up the yoke", or to "bear his cross".[33]

The word-play used to produce this "resting-place of animals" from *LI-MASh-BA(LA)G-ANTA-TAB-BA-RI, served also the New Testament writers for their story about the "stable" at Bethlehem:

And while they were there, the time came for her to be delivered. And she gave birth to her first-born son and wrapped him in swaddling cloths, and laid him in a manger, because there was no place for them in the inn (Luke 2:7).

The authors spun out from that name of the sacred fungus "for him a resting-place in an animal's stall", as well as the more obvious play on *pitrā*, "mushroom", and *peter,* "first-born".[34] At a more basic level of mushroom mythology was the image of the fungus as a "manger" with a sheltering canopy held by the stalk above the "cradle" or "feeding trough" of the lower half of the volva. Possibly Euripides knows of a similar tradition to the Christian story when he has Pentheus order the unrecognized Dionysus to be carried off and "tied where the steeds are bound; let him lie in a manger, and stare into the darkness".[35]

Adonis, then, was the prime fertility hero-god of the ancient Semitic and classical worlds. We have seen how his names fit into the mushroom pattern, and it is also apparent that the Hebrew David figure is portrayed in the same phallic form. The Oracle ascribed to him paints him in these terms without any doubt, and his supposed patronymic, "Son of Jesse", is but an attempt to reproduce in Hebrew form a Sumerian name of the phallus and probably the mushroom. The tribal name Issachar has a similar derivation and again, in the oldest oracles referring to this character, its fungus nature is plainly evident.

It appears that in the Old and the New Testaments, one of the old Semitic names for the mushroom, extant in a Punic version from North Africa, was misunderstood as suggesting an Egyptian origin for the fungus, and a resultant mythology brought Israel and the Holy Family from that country.

The question must now be asked again, as indeed these studies must continually provoke the enquiry: how much, if any, of these biblical traditions is history? Despite the obvious allusions to an Adonis background for many of David's epithets in the oracles and in the stories recounted about him, was there ever a *real* King David whose court chronicles gave some historical framework at least for the tales? Was there, for that matter, any Exodus, any Moses, any Abraham? One difficulty in sorting out fact from fiction in folk-tales is that the characters are often made so human that the listener finds it quite easy to imagine them as real people, even identify himself with them. Where the same themes have been treated over centuries of story-telling, successive narrators have embroidered the tales and made the characters more and more believable until the point comes when even the most far-fetched adventures, the most unlikely exploits, amatory, warlike, or muscular, do not deter us from wondering whether behind it all there was not a real Adonis, a real Hercules, a real David . . .

Well, perhaps there was. What we are concerned with in this present work is not trying to sift fiction from reality, the man David from the "stretched penis of Israel", but to find out what we can from the names and epithets and from the various mythologies of the ancient world, to what extent and in what ways the sacred mushroom was worshipped, and how far its cult was responsible for the later mystery religions of the Near East and Christianity in particular. It would not be surprising if real kings and heroes received names from their parents or their admirers traceable to titles of the mushroom, if they were adherents of the cult of the Holy Plant. Their historicity is not proved or disproved thereby. Nevertheless, if all we know of a character in our sparse records of the ancient world reflects only mushroom mythology, like Jacob and Esau, for instance, or Cain and Abel, then there seems little point in arguing that they were ever real people. If there was a real Jacob, good; but then it has to be admitted we know very little about him.

A quite different situation obtains, however, with regard to the New Testament characters. Here, for reasons already stated and which by now should be apparent to the reader, we are dealing with a cryptic document. This is a different kind of mythology, based not on pious aggrandizement by later admirers, as has been so often assumed in the past, but a deliberate attempt to mislead the reader. There is every reason why there should *not* have been a real Jesus of Nazareth, at least not one connected with the sect of Christians, nor a real John the Baptist, Peter, John, James, and so on. To have named them, located their homes and families, would have brought disaster upon their associates in a cult which had earned the hatred of the authorities.

XVII

Death and Resurrection

We have earlier spoken of the treatment of death and resurrection in the fertility philosophy.[1] The ancients knew well that life and death are merely facets of the same creative process. To have crops in the Spring the land must die in the Autumn, and many of their myths deal with the "killing" of Nature after the harvest, and bringing it to life with the new agricultural year. This same experience of death and resurrection is no less at the heart of the more sophisticated forms of the fertility cult, the mystery religions of which Christianity is the best known example. It seemed to the mystics that it might be possible to enact within the mind and body a spiritual "death" and "resurrection" so that, however anchored the mortal frame might be to a terrestrial existence, the soul could be released as if at death and given the freedom they believed it had experienced before birth and would do so again at death. Thus Josephus says of the Essenes, "It is a fixed belief of theirs that the body is corruptible and its constituent matter impermanent, but that the soul is immortal and imperishable. Emanating from the finest ether, these souls become entangled, as it were, in the prison-house of the body, to which they are dragged down by a sort of natural spell; but when once they are released from the bonds of the flesh, then, as though liberated from a long servitude, they rejoice and are borne aloft . . ."[2]

The way to this release of the soul was by asceticism and particularly by fasting, but the same effects could be achieved and more quickly by the use of drugs, like those Josephus says the Essenes sought out "which make for the welfare of the soul and body".[3] Above all, the sacred fungus, the *Amanita muscaria,* gave them the delusion of a soul floating free over vast distances, separate from their bodies, as it still does to those foolish enough to seek out the experience. The Christians put the matter thus: "If the Christ is in you, although your bodies are dead through sin, your spirits are alive through righteousness. If the

Spirit of him who raised Jesus from the dead dwells in you, he who raised Christ Jesus from the dead will give life to your mortal bodies also through his Spirit which dwells in you" (Rom 8:10, 11).

Not only could the drug contained under the skin of the sacred fungus give to the initiate at will this illusion of spiritual resurrection, of victory over death, but in the conception and growth of the mushroom he could see a microcosm of the whole natural order. Before his eyes the cycle of life and death was enacted in a matter of hours. The *Amanita muscaria* was the medium of spiritual regeneration and at the same time in itself the supreme example of the recreative process in the world of Nature. No wonder the fungus attracted so much awesome wonder among the ancients, or that it inspired some of literature's greatest epics.

To the mystic, the little red-topped fungus must have seemed human in form and yet divine in its power to change men and give them an insight into the mysteries of the universe. It was in the world, but not of it. In the New Testament myth, the writers tried to express this idea of the duality of nature by portraying as its central character a man who appeared human enough on the surface but through whom there shone a god-like quality which manifested itself in miracle-working and a uniquely authoritative attitude to the Law. The extent to which they succeeded can be seen today in the mingled sympathy and awe with which Jesus is regarded in the Western world, even among people for whom the Christian religion offers no attractions.

The myth of the dying and rising god is variously treated within the mushroom cycle. One of the best-known stories is that of Persephone/Kore, her mother Demeter, and the wicked uncle Pluto.[4] The beautiful virgin who is the heroine of the tale presents in her double name the equivalent of the effeminate male Hermaphrodite. Her two names can now be seen as two aspects of the mushroom, Persephone being the volva (Sumerian *BAR-SIB-U-NI, "container or the penis of fecundity") and Kore the stem of "phallus" (Sumerian *GU-RI, as in the storm-god's name, *USh-GU-RI [ISKUR]).[5]

Put in other fungus folk-lore terms, Kore is the charmed and erect "serpent", thrusting open the egg of Persephone. It is with this sense that *SIB-U-NI comes into Hebrew, in the form *siph'ōnī*, "adder", which has a specific mushroom reference in a passage in Isaiah. The prophet warns that those who "split" the "eggs of the *siph'ōnī*, adder", will bring death upon themselves, and those who weave with "spiders' spindles" (*qōrē*, the spindle rod with its whorl) will never weave such a web as will cover their cultic malpractices (59:5f.). Doubtless both these expressions will have been common folk-names for the mushroom.

Persephone/Kore was passionately loved from afar by her uncle Pluto, god of the underworld. Although her father Zeus approved of the match, her mother Demeter (listed along with her daughter's names among those of the Holy Plant),[6] strongly objected to the arrangement, not least because the marital home would have been outside her influence. However, Pluto, with the connivance of his brother, arranged that a large and beautiful flower[7] should one day appear at the feet of his beloved as she walked in her Sicilian home. Unable to resist the blossom, the girl picked it, and immediately a yawning chasm appeared at her feet, revealing her suitor complete with chariot and horses to carry her off struggling to his subterranean palace.

Not unnaturally, her mother was upset by the turn of events and began a long and variously recounted search for her daughter. Unhappily, even when she discovered her whereabouts, it was to find that the hapless child had eaten some magic herb[8] that made it impossible for her to leave Hades for ever. An agreement was finally reached that she should remain in her husband's home for a third (or half) the year, and spend the rest of the time on earth with her mother.

It has seemed strange to scholars that Pluto, the god of the underworld, should elsewhere be reckoned as a god of fertility. It is true that much of our western classical and Semitic tradition has led us to think of Hades[9] as a place of dull lifelessness, or even of retributive torture of the damned. More original, as we have seen,[10] is the conception of the earth's bowels as the seat of creation where all life is conceived and after death recreated.[11] In the subterranean oven, the god's seminal fluid is processed into living matter, and the Word made flesh.

The name Pluto, Greek *Plouton,* is primarily a fertility word, now recognizable as coming from an original Sumerian *BURU-TUN, "deliverer of the womb", of which the element BURU, "deliver, release", is cognate with the Greek *bruō,* "teem with, be full, burst forth".[12] The same Sumerian word appears in such names as Apollo, Aphrodite (from which comes our "aphrodisiac"), and the plant name Abrotonon, "Southernwood", a sprig of which under the pillow, Pliny tells us, "is the most effective countercheck of all to magical potions given to produce sexual impotence".[13]

A story with a similar ending to that of Persephone's myth is found related of Castor and Pollux. Following Castor's death in battle at the hands of his cousins who had driven away some cattle, brother Pollux was cast into despair. At last, in answer to a prayer to Zeus that he too might die and leave this earth to rejoin his twin in Hades, Father Zeus agreed that he might spend one day with his peers the gods and the other in the earth with his brother. "Thus," says Homer, "these two the earth, the giver of life, covers, albeit alive, and even in the world below they have honour from Zeus. One day they live in turn, and one day they are dead; and they have honour like unto that of the gods."[14]

The death and resurrection story of Jesus follows the traditional pattern of fertility mythology, as has long been recognized. The hero is miraculously born, dies violently, returns to the underworld, and is then reawakened to new life. We may now go further and connect the details of the story more closely to the mushroom culture of which it is part. Indeed, the reference is plain within the text, where Jesus is made to relate his coming death by "being raised up" with the brazen serpent of Moses: "As Moses lifted up the serpent in the wilderness, so shall the son of man be lifted up, so that all who believe in him shall have everlasting life" (John 3:14). The reference is to the incident recorded in Numbers 21:9: "And Moses made a brazen serpent and put it on a sign-post so that if anyone was bitten by a snake he might look on the brazen serpent and live."[15]

Easter and its Dionysiac equivalent

Every springtime the Christian world celebrates its Easter festival when the Church focuses attention on the death and resurrection of Jesus. In the ceremony of the sacred fire and the dipping of "penis" candles into a "womb" font, previously noted,[16] tradition demonstrates clearly the sexual nature of the occasion. We are now able to draw some important parallels between the Christian festival and the Spring feast of the Dionysiac Anthesteria. On the twelfth of the month bearing that name (end of February to the beginning of March), there began a three-day festival of three parts, the Pithoigia, Choes, and Chutroi.[17] All too little is known from the records of the details of this great occasion; inevitably mystery rites were involved which were not for public viewing or recording. However, we are in a better position now to probe its secrets, not least because we can decipher its names.

In the first place, "Pithoigia" had nothing to do with "wine-jars" (*pithoi*).[18] Indeed, the Anthesteria was not primarily a vine festival at all, despite early traditions to that effect, and Bacchus/Dionysus was not really a wine god, for all the colourful imagery that the name has long evoked. The confusion arose mainly through the "vine-cluster" symbolism that formed such an important part of the Bacchic regalia.

The vine-cluster, like the ivy-cluster which also appears freely represented in Bacchic symbolism, evoked the shape of the conical end of the erect penis, the glans. The form is well illustrated in the earliest Sumerian ideogram for the vine, ⛨ .[19] The connection is explicit in the old names for the vine-cluster, like the Greek *botrus* and the Hebrew *'eshkōl*, both derived, as we now realize, from Sumerian phrases meaning "top of the erect penis".[20] So the Bacchic worshippers symbolized their god's phallic and mushroom connections by carrying with them a long rod, entwined with ivy and bearing at its end a vine- or ivy-cluster. This staff is called a Thyrsus, "womb-favourer; penis", as its Sumerian derivation now shows it to have originally meant. A modern Arabic version of the name is used for the mushroom.[21]

During the course of the Athenian festival of Skira, two male votaries of the goddess Athena, dressed as girls, carry vine-clusters between the temple of their goddess and that of Dionysus. The rare Greek word given to these objects, *oskhos,* we may now relate through its original Sumerian form to the Hebrew *'eshkōl,* "vine-cluster".[22] In the Song of Songs, the Shulammite's breasts are likened to such "vine-clusters", where the reference is certainly to the mushroom cap.[23]

The "vine-cluster" became, then, a useful synonym for the sacred mushroom, and is used with this allusion in a composite picture of the Tree of Life in the Garden of Eden given in the post-biblical book of Enoch. We noticed earlier how Josephus used this quaint literary device to portray in a roundabout way the phallic and mushroom significance of the High Priest's helmet.[24] A number of plants are brought together to illustrate various aspects of the actual object being cryptically described. Taken at their face value the resultant picture is absurd, but each of the plants so adduced contains some allusion, by shape, or simply by a pun on its name, which, to the initiated, conveys the intended meaning of the whole. In the case of the Tree of Life, whose fruit made Adam and Eve like gods, the apocryphal writing says it had "the height of a fir, leaves like a carob, and fruit like a vine-cluster".[25]

Each of the comparisons bears upon the sacred mushroom, the *Amanita muscaria.* The "fir" because it is a denizen of the conifer forests;[26] the "carob" because this "pod" name was given to both the mushroom and the food of pigs and "Prodigal Sons";[27] and the "vine-cluster" because the red cap of the fungus was so pictured, as we saw above.

The luckless sons of the prophets who found "death in the pot"[28] when Elisha came to dinner, picked their mushrooms[29] from a "vine of the field" (II Kgs 4:38-41). This phrase has all the appearance of a folk-name for the fungus, as "vine of the earth" has been preserved in Syriac as a name of the Mandrake.[30] The same expression is used in the book of Revelation for the harvest to which the angel with the sharp sickle is bidden:

> Put in your sickle, and gather the clusters of the vine of the earth, for its grapes are ripe (Rev 14:18).[31]

It is the same imagery of the "vine-mushroom" that described Jesus as "the true vine" (John 15:1, 5), and in Jewish-Christian literature as "the Vine of David".[32]

So whatever refreshment cheered the hearts of the Bacchic revellers we may be quite sure that it was not just wine, and the vine imagery of their regalia conveyed to the initiates a more potent means of intoxication than the juice of the grape alone. Very probably it was a dried and powdered form of the *Amanita muscaria* that they used to lace their drink, and it was with this fiery beverage that they washed down the mushroom tops they chewed.[33] In any case, many of the more important Dionysiac festivals took place in winter when vine culture had little to offer as an excuse for a wine-bibbing orgy.[34]

The second and third days of the Anthesteria were called *hoi Khoes* and *hoi Khutroi* respectively, which have been taken to mean, "the pitchers" and "the pots", and to have reference to some part of the wine-making ceremony. However, now that we need no longer see the mystic festival of Anthesteria as a mere vine-harvesting or wine-making jollification, we can find a much more meaningful significance in the names of its various parts. The second day's designation, *hoi Khoes,* read as a singular noun and article, is remarkably reminiscent of the *oskhos* ceremony just mentioned, where the objects carried are the "vine-clusters" of Dionysus.[35]

The name *Khutroi* given to the third day of the Anthesteria festival is cognate with the Semitic *kōtereth*, "mushroom". The Greek word *kuthros (kutros)*, "pot", with which the name has been hitherto identified, comes also from the same ultimate source (Sumerian GU-TAR, "top of the head; phallus"), but is probably secondary, referring to the mushroom or phallic shape of the container.[36]

Turning to the name of the feast itself, Anthesteria, we may now find its source in a Sumerian phrase meaning "raising of the penis" (*ANTA-AShTAR),[37] where "penis" will have its dual sense in the cult of the male organ and the phallic mushroom. That both aspects of the word were involved is indicated by the fact that the festival included a ritual marriage between the god Dionysus and the wife of the archon or chief magistrate.[38] It is said to have involved a solemnization and consummation[39] of this mystic union, but exactly what physically took place we cannot know. The part played by cultic prostitutes in the mushroom-raising ceremonies we have earlier discussed,[40] and something of the kind probably lay behind this holy marriage between the god and his mortal priestess. Recalling that exposure of the female genitals and application of menstrual blood was considered an essential part of releasing the fungus, it is worth noting that one at least of the days of the Anthesteria was marked as "taboo" (*miara*), properly "blood-stained".[41]

A further confirmation of this is the tradition that on the day of Choes the celebrants anointed their doors with pitch,[42] whose relationship with menstrual blood in the ancient philosophies has been previously noted.[43] One is reminded also of the prophylactic daubing of doorposts and lintels with the blood of the Passover lamb by the Israelites in Egypt (Exod 12:7,22).

The Invocation and the Lord's Prayer

The cultic cry of the Bacchantes was the "paean", *eleleu, eleleu*.[44] The elements of this invocation can now be traced back to the same Sumerian words that gave the Hebrews the name of their deity *Elohīm*, translated "God" in our Bibles. It was a combination of Sumerian E-LA, "strong water, juice", and IA-U/UIA, "juice of fecundity, spermatozoa", in other words, the common Semitic name for god, "El", combined with the tribal god name Yahweh ("Jehovah"). In the invocation the original E-LA is doubled, and it is precisely this form that came down in the Bible in the chant of praise "Halleluia!"[45]

The cry *eleleu, eleleu* was so marked a feature of the Bacchic rites that the Bacchantes became known as the Eleleides,[46] and the chant itself the "Paean", and associated with Apollo who had the same epithet, *Paian,* in Greek.[47] The word, as we saw earlier, is another name of the mushroom, the equivalent of the New Testament's "Bar-jona", Peter's surname.[48] Now we can understand a reference in the botanist Dioscorides' account of the plant he calls "Hellebore", but which we can identify with the mushroom: "when they dig it they stand praying to Apollo and Aesculapius".[49] The latter is also a name for the "Hellebore" and means simply "head of the erect penis, the glans", or in mushroom terms, the "cap". Clearly, at the point when the sacred fungus was removed from the ground, or perhaps when it was being induced to rise, the celebrants were required to chant the "paean" to the god of the mushroom, *"eleleu, eleleu".*

In the Easter story of the New Testament the same incantatory expression is found, put into the mouth of the Jesus figure, splayed as the mushroom on the cross:

> At the ninth hour Jesus cried with a loud voice, "Eloi, Eloi, lama sabachthani!" which means, "My God, my God, why hast thou forsaken me?" And some of the bystanders hearing it said, "Behold he is calling Elijah" (Mark 15:34f, etc).

The name "Elijah" is formed of the same elements as the divine name Elohim and the Bacchic cry *"eleleu",*[50] and was doubtless intended to serve as a clue to the preceding cryptograph. The words, "Eloi, Eloi, lama sabachthani", but dubiously mean "My God, my God, why hast thou forsaken me?" as every Semiticist knows.[51] The "translation" is another of the New Testament "false renderings" of special cultic names or invocations, culled this time from the well-known passage in Psalm 22:1. The Hebrew here is nowhere rendered by the words "Eloi, Eloi, lama sabachthani" which, on any count, are strange Aramaic. The allusion in the text to the Psalm is but a "cover": *lama sabachthani* is a clever approximation to the important Sumerian name of the sacred mushroom *LI-MASh-BA(LA)G-ANTA, source by word-play of so much of the New Testament myth.[52] This is the second, or "Aesculapius" part of the incantation Dioscorides says was pronounced by those cutting the "Hellebore". The whole secret invocatory phrase, of which classical tradition brought down only the first part, was a colloquial equivalent of an original Sumerian *E-LA-UIA, E-LA-UIA, LI-MASh-

BA(LA)G-ANTA. Thanks to the Gospel myth-makers and crypto-graphers we are now able to supply the part the observers of the Bacchic festivals did not, or were not allowed to hear.

Another incantatory formula which appears, unusually, on the surface of the New Testament records, and has thereby caused much speculation among the critics and theologians, is the passage in the epistle to the Ephesians:

> Awake, sleeper! Arise from the dead, and the Christ will give you light! (Eph5:14).

Calls to "sleepers" to "awaken" are common enough in the Gospel stories, particularly in those dealing with the Agony in the Garden before the Crucifixion (Matt 26:40ff., etc). The interest of this particular incantation is that it is formed from a clever combination of, and word-play on names of the sacred mushroom, and even in its final Greek form is openly related to the necromantic cult from which it is derived. Breaking its code leads us to other important names of the Holy Plant, and to a new understanding of the most famous of all incantations, the Lord's Prayer.

The cry "Awake, sleeper!" is a word-play on the Aramaic level of the Sumerian phrase *AN-BAR (AB-BA)-NA-IM-A-AN, "canopy of the sky stretched out above", a descriptive epithet of the mushroom. The last part, NA-IM-A-AN, contains the ancient name of the fertility god-hero Adonis, Na'iman.[53] A shortened form of the whole phrase gave Hebrew its tribal name "Ephraim", and, following a different dialectal and vocalic development, the patriarchal name, "Abraham", the "father" of Israel.[54]

It is the first element of the name, AN-BAR, found also run together as AB-BA, "father", which has particular interest for us in this study. It means literally, "heaven-stretch"; that is, it offers the picture of a sheltering canopy overhead, and so is used of the "father" or "protector" of a family, the Sumerian coming directly into Semitic as 'ab, 'abbā', with that meaning. When, for the NA-IM-A-AN ending of the mush-room name above, the alternative Sumerian ending TAB-BA-RI is added, we can at last solve another perplexing little problem concerned with invocations in the New Testament.

In three places the New Testament writers give us a phrase which is a combination of a foreign word, usually assumed to be Aramaic, and

an appended "translation": "Abba, father".[55] Now, it is perfectly true
that the Greek *ho patēr*, "father", accurately represents the Aramaic
'abbā', but one would have thought that this extremely common
Semitic word for "father" would have been well enough known even
in a Greek-speaking area of the first century not to have necessitated a
translation every time it appeared in a text. Since also in each case it
appears in the Epistles it is related to the Spirit of God witnessing in the
heart of the believer, and in the third instance it is put into the mouth of
Jesus in the Garden praying to God (Mark 14:36), there might be in any
case reason for regarding it as some incantatory expression of more than
ordinary significance.

> "When we cry "Abba, father!" it is the Spirit himself bearing witness with
> our spirit that we are children of God (Rom 8:16).

> And because you are sons, God has sent the Spirit of His Son into our hearts,
> crying, "Abba, father!" (Gal 4:6).

The cry, "Abba, *(ho) patēr*!" is simply a play on the Sumerian mushroom phrase *AB-BA-TAB-BA-RI, the *b/p* and *t* being transposed.[56]

Daily Bread

The invocation of the "Father" reminds us of the opening words of
the Lord's Prayer, repeated millions of times a day all over the Christian
world. In the mouth of Jesus, the opening words, "My (our) father who
art in heaven" is used frequently as a surrogate for God. The very full-
ness of the phrase has seemed curious where one might have expected a
simple "God" or "Father" or the like. The explanation lies in the mushroom title *AB-BA-TAB-BA-RI-GI, a rather fuller version of the one
cited above and underlying "Abba, father". The cryptographers have
teased out the Sumerian into an Aramaic *'abbā' debareqī'ā'*, "O my (our)
father who art in heaven !"[57]

Having now penetrated the disguise and laid bare the original
Sumerian and the Aramaic phrase made from it, we can now recognize
it as a phrase we have all known from our childhood story-books for a
long time: "abracadabra". Originally it had a far more serious intent,
and is first found in the writings of one Q. Serenus Sammonicus of the
second-third century AD, a physician of the sect we know as Gnostics.
This author left precise instructions for the use of this cabbalistic phrase,

which was believed to invoke beneficent spirits against disease and misfortune. The magic word had to be stitched in the form of a cross and worn as an amulet in the bosom for nine days, and finally thrown backwards before sunrise into a stream running eastwards.

The sect of Gnostics provides one of the major keys to unravelling the mystery of how the mushroom-worshipping Christians became the Church of later times. The Gnostics were groups of ascetics, scorning the lusts of the flesh entirely, and convinced that they possessed a secret and mysterious knowledge denied to lesser mortals, vouchsafed to them by revelation from God. They claimed to be connected to their Saviour-god and the earliest Christians by a secret tradition, and to possess certain mystic writings which only they could interpret. The ultimate object of their faith was an individual salvation, the assurance of a blessed destiny for each soul after death.

They possessed many such formulae as "abracadabra", and having pride of place above all their secret knowledge were the names of the demons. Only when each soul knew such names and could thus control their power, could repeat the holy formulae and display the right symbol, and were anointed (i.e. "christened") with a holy oil, could he find his way to the seventh heaven, the kingdom of light. Thus, a principal feature of Gnosticism was the transmission to one another in strictest secrecy doctrines about the being, nature, names, and symbols of the Seven Demons or Angels who would otherwise bar their way to achieving the ultimate goal.

The movement came into prominence in the second century AD and reached its greatest influence in the third quarter of that century, after which it began to wane and was replaced by the closely related and more powerful Manichean movement. However, many of its ideas survived in mystic circles at least into the fourth and fifth centuries.

What became "orthodox" Christianity waged a war with Gnosticism which it finally won, and the books of the "heresy" were systematically destroyed. Most of what we know about the sect comes from the writings of its ecclesiastical opponents, but of recent years some of their lost books of the later period have been found in the sands of Egypt marvellously preserved, among them the Gospel of Truth.[58] We may hope for more and earlier works, but again, we have to remind ourselves that valuable as these lost works would be, the really secret doctrines are unlikely to have been written down in "clear", and the best we can hope for is another cryptic writing like the New Testament. Nevertheless, one fruit of these present researches must be a re-examination of the Gnostic material that has survived for more decipherable "abracadabras".

"Our father who art in heaven", then, is a cryptic way of expressing the name of the Saviour-god, the sacred mushroom. Having broken the code to this extent, it is possible to tackle other outstanding problems in the text. For example, we ask for "daily bread" upon "this day". In point of fact, we have never had a textual justification for doing so, since no one has ever been able to offer a definitive translation for the very rare Greek word *epiousion* which the text uses to describe the "bread".[59] The rendering "daily" is probably the least likely possibility;[60] the marginal reading of RSV, "our bread for the morrow"[61] is little better. It is only when we recognize the Sumerian name for the sacred fungus out of which the whole "Prayer" has been spun by word-play that we can see just why the cryptographers chose this Greek epithet, and why the other main alternative reading "give us (the bread) that is needful"[62] is the correct one. It is an attempt to render the Semitic verb *s-p-q*, "give what is needful", derived from a word-play on *MASh-BA(LA)G-ANTA-TAB-BA-RI read as "that-which-is-needful-give-now-bread".[63]

Temptation and preparation for the mysteries

Few parts of the Lord's Prayer have given more trouble to the praying Christian and more scope for the exegete than the verse:

And lead us not into temptation, but deliver us from evil (Matt 6:13).

The Greek word for "temptation", *peirasmos,* came in for special attention at the time of the decipherment of the Dead Sea Scrolls. It was realized correctly by scholars that behind this New Testament phrase lay the Semitic word for a place for "testing" metals, that is, the refiner's crucible.[64] The Essenes in the Scrolls talk of the "time of testing that is coming" using the technical word.[65] So, here, in the Prayer, the word-jugglers have taken its Aramaic equivalent, *kūr bukhānā*, "crucible of testing", out of *LI-KUR-BA(LA)G-ANTA, the mushroom name. The resultant phrase is particularly interesting because it is almost exactly the Aramaic name of the fungus as it has come down in literature, *khūrbakhnā'* or *khūrbekhānā'* (Arabic *kharbaq*), attached, like so many mushroom words, to the plant Hellebore.[66]

Taking the sacred fungus, or, in New Testament parlance, "eating the body" of the Christ, must have been a very real *peirasmos*, "trial", of the body and spirit. It would have seemed no accident to the cultic celebrant that the name of the mushroom and the phrase for "fiery furnace of testing" appeared the same. The customary translation of this powerful concept as "temptation" is almost ridiculous, recalling youthful experiences in the jam-cupboard or behind the woodshed with the girl next door. Well might the writer of Corinthians issue this warning:

> Whoever, therefore, eats the bread or drinks the cup of the Lord unworthily will be guilty of profaning the body and blood of the Lord. Let a man examine himself, and so eat of the bread and drink of the cup. For anyone who eats and drinks without critically treating his body, eats and drinks a "crisis" upon himself. That is why many of you are weak and ill, and some have died . . . (I Cor 11:27-30).

Isaiah long before had expressed the same warning about the planting of the Adonis (Na'iman): "though you make them grow on the day you plant them, and make them blossom in the morning that you sow, yet the harvest will flee away, in a day of grief and incurable pain" (Isa 17:10f).

The *Amanita muscaria* is, after all, a poisonous fungus. Whilst not the most dangerous, its drugs have a serious effect on the nervous system, and taken regularly over a long period would in the end kill the addict. Among its drugs so far isolated are Muscarine, Atropine, and Bufotenin.[67] The first causes vomiting and diarrhoea, and stimulates the parasympathetic nervous system so that the partaker is capable of great feats of muscular exertion and endurance. The stories which came down of the fantastic strength exhibited by cultic heroes, however mythical the events described, have probably that element of real fact. So, too, the idea that the Maenads in their wild raving through the conifer forests were capable of tearing animals limb from limb, was not entirely devoid of truth.

Atropine first stimulates the nervous system and then paralyses it. It is this poison that is primarily responsible for the hallucinatory effects of the sacred fungus, but also for the muscular convulsions that must have seemed to the bystanders like the demons within, wrestling with the newly imbibed power of the god.

Bufotenin, a secretion otherwise found in the sweat glands of the African toad, lowers the pulse rate and temperature. As a result, the mushroom eater has the strange sensation of feeling his skin hot and cold simultaneously: hot in some places, cold in others. He finds himself hypersensitive to touch, light, and sound. The day following his "trip" he will find all smells seem foul and a bad taste persists in his mouth. He feels an urgent need to urinate but is unable to do so.

We are unfortunately denied reports of such clinical observations as these in ancient literature. The initiates of the mushroom cult explained such sensations in terms of demonology. They believed that the god whose flesh they were chewing, or whose blood they were drinking in their drugged wine, was actually within their bodies. It was to be expected that his coming and going would be attended with dreadful physical and mental experiences, and the body needed lengthy preparation for the "trial" by fire. The actual eating of the bitter, burning fungus top, drinking of the laced wine, and perhaps sniffing up of the powdered agaric-like snuff,[68] would be only at the end of days of religious and physical preparation. To obtain some idea of the nature of these preparations and the fearfulness with which they were approached, we may read what Pliny says about the Hellebore. We have earlier noted that many of the mushroom names have come down to us attached to this potent herb, and it is not improbable that what the first-century botanist tells us about the taking of Hellebore similarly reflects traditions which he has picked up concerning the use of the fungus:

The best white Hellebore is that which most quickly causes sneezing. It is, however, far more terrifying than the black sort, especially if one reads in our old authorities of the elaborate precautions taken, by those about to drink it, against shivering, choking, overpowering and unseasonable sleep, prolonged hiccough or sneezing, fluxes of the stomach, vomiting, too slow or too long, scanty or too excessive. In fact, they usually gave other things to promote vomiting, and drove out the Hellebore itself by medicine or enema, or often they used even bleeding.

Furthermore, even when the Hellebore proves successful (as a purge), the various colours of the vomits are terrifying to see, and after the vomits comes the worry of watching the stools, of superintending the bath, of attention to the whole body, all these troubles being preceded by the great terror caused by its reputation, for it is said that meat, if boiled with it, is consumed.

It was a fault of the ancient physicians that because of these fears they used to administer this Hellebore in smallish doses, since the larger the dose the quicker it is eliminated. Themison gave doses of not more than two drachmae; his successors actually increased the amount to four, because of the fine testimonial given to Hellebore by Herophilus, who compared it to a truly courageous general; having aroused all within, it itself marches out in the van . . .

Care must be taken, even with favourable treatment, not to administer Hellebore on a cloudy day; for to do so is followed by unbearable torture. Indeed, there is no doubt that summer is a better season to give it than winter. For seven days previously the body must be prepared by acid (or, sharp-tasting) foods and by abstinence from wine; on the fourth and third days before, an emetic must be taken, and on the preceding day there should be abstinence from dinner.

White Hellebore is given even in a sweet medium [the black variety was considered dangerous if its bitter taste was so disguised with a sweet accompaniment that more was taken than the body could tolerate], although most suitably in lentils or pottage. Recently the method has been discovered of splitting radishes, inserting Hellebore, and then pressing the radishes together again, so that the property of the purge penetrates them: the Hellebore is thus administered in a modified form.

Vomiting begins after four hours, and the whole business is over in seven. . . . Hellebore is never prescribed for old people or children, or for those who are soft and effeminate in body or mind, or for the thin or delicate. For women it is less suitable than for men, unsuitable too for the nervous or when the hypochondria are ulcerated or swollen, very bad when there is spitting of blood, pain in the side, or sore throat . . .

Mixed with pearl barley it kills rats and mice. The Gauls when hunting dip their arrows in Hellebore, and say that the meat, when the flesh around the wound has been cut away, tastes more tender. Flies too die if pounded white Hellebore and milk are sprinkled about.[69]

This last use of Hellebore provides an interesting link with *Amanita muscaria,* or Fly-Agaric, as it is popularly known.

Linnaeus gave the fungus the Latin name (*musca,* "fly") precisely because of the age-old practice of killing flies or bugs with it. First attested in medieval times, it is said still to be the practice on the Continent to break up the mushroom into milk to stupefy flies. In Poland and Czechoslovakia a sugar solution is made for that purpose, or sugar sprinkled on the cap.[70] Perhaps it is its use to kill vermin like bugs that is meant when Pliny reports of "black Hellebore" that "with it they fumigate and cleanse houses, sprinkling it on sheep, and adding a formal prayer".[71] So also says Theophrastus: "Men purify horses and sheep with it, at the same time chanting an incantation"[72] (presumably one of the special names of the drug). It is this same authority that states that "the white and the black Hellebores appear to have nothing in common except the name".[73]

One is reminded of the Philistine god Baal-zebub, "Lord of the Flies", whom Ahaziah sought to consult for a prognosis on his health after he had fallen through his bedroom window (II Kgs 1:2ff.). Similarly the Elean god Muiagros was invoked when a swarm of flies brought plague; the flies died as soon as the sacrifice had been made.[74] Similarly, sacrifice to the god Myiodes ("Fly-catcher") at the Olympic games resulted in the mass emigration of flies from the territory.[75] One has to remember that in those climes and amid the usual lack of sanitation, flies were more than merely a nuisance. When they "ruined" the land of Egypt as a result of the Pharaoh's intransigence (Exod 8:24), they were a manifestation of the plague-god himself, which is why the Sumerian pest-demon NAM-TAR, Greek Nectar or Mandrake, could kill the pests when all else failed. Thus, to sprinkle "Hellebore" round the house, as Dioscorides says, was thought to preserve it from evil spirits.[76]

Pliny thought it strange that Hellebore, "once regarded with horror, should afterwards become so popular that most scholars took it regularly to sharpen their brains for their studies".[77] It is, perhaps, to the increase in perceptive faculties that the drug of the *Amanita muscaria* is said to offer, that we should seek for an explanation for Pliny's curious statement that Hellebore should not be given on a "cloudy day; for to do so is followed by unbearable torture. Indeed there is no doubt that summer is a better season to give it than winter".

In the story of Lot's visitation by the angels at Sodom, the men of the place, disregarding the traditional laws of Eastern hospitality, threatened to break Lot's doors down unless he would release his visitors to their perverted attentions. Despite Lot's generous offer of his virgin daughters in their stead, the men of Sodom persisted in their efforts to reach the new arrivals, who eventually struck them with a mysterious blindness, "so that they wearied themselves groping for the door" (Gen 19:1-11). It is the same sudden blindness that Yahweh, at Elisha's behest, sends upon the Syrian forces besieging Dothan, and which permitted them to be led away into an ambush (II Kgs 6:18ff.).

The closest approximation to the unusual Hebrew word for this blindness is found in an Aramaic incantation against a demon who brings about the same condition, described by the Jewish commentators as "dazzling sunlight coming through cracks or breaks in the clouds, being worse than the uncovered sun".[78] This sounds like attacks of migraine, characterized by just such flashes of blinding light and pain behind the eyes. But the names point to meanings more connected with a purge or abortifacient than "blindness" and may reflect another name for the *Amanita muscaria*.[19]

The increased sensory perceptiveness which is said to be a characteristic of the fungus drug would mean that sudden flashes of light, as shafts of sunlight through clouds, would be highly uncomfortable, if not acutely painful.[80] Perhaps here we have the basis for those stories of the sudden blindness of Sodom and Dothan, and for the revelatory illumination that strikes Paul on the Damascus road (Acts 9:3). The mystic under the influence of the mushroom drug might well believe that the common metaphor that associates inspirational knowledge with light in the darkness had become a reality. The kind of myth as that in which "a sudden light from heaven flashed about Paul . . . and when his eyes were opened he could see nothing", would seem a natural expression in story form of this mystic experience.

An interesting facet of Pliny's account of the body's preparation for receiving Hellebore is the recurrence of the number seven. For seven days previously the belly must be given a special diet of sharp-tasting foods, with an emetic on the fourth and third days and abstinence from dinner on the eve of administering the drug. Then, vomiting will begin after four hours, "and the whole business is over in seven". Elsewhere he says that the life of the mushroom is not more than seven days.[81]

Of course, the number seven had a very special potency for ancient philosophers, and particularly, as we saw, for the Gnostics. The whole of creation was divided into seven. The Bible allots seven days for the Creation cycle;[82] there were seven lamps on the candlestick in the Temple, representing, so tradition had it, the seven planets.[83] The Greeks believed that the whole body was renewed every seven years, and that certain of the seven-year cycles were of special importance, as the age of fourteen when a boy reaches puberty; at twenty-one he attains full sexual maturity; at forty-two a woman reaches her "grand climacteric", the menopause; at sixty-three men suffer a transitory sexual enfeeblement. The Bible allows mankind but "threescore years and ten" on normal reckoning.[84]

Nevertheless, the number seven seems particularly connected with the mushroom and the preparatory stages of treatment required by its use as a drug. In Revelation, the mystic speaks of "seven churches of Asia" which he then proceeds very cryptically to describe (Rev 1:11ff.). The geographical place-name "Asia" is almost certainly a play on the Semitic word for healing, '-s-y, giving 'asya', "physician",[85] still the most likely Semitic source for the sectarian name, "Essenes".[86]

With these "seven churches of healing" we may compare two references in the Essene scrolls from the Dead Sea that have recently come to light. In one, the sect is called "the seven divisions of the penitents of Israel".[87] The other, unfortunately broken, quotes two biblical passages:

> the promises of Yahweh are promises that are pure − silver refined in a furnace . . . purified seven times (Ps 12:6 [Heb. 7]).

> . . . the stone I have set before Joshua, upon a single stone with seven facets, its inscription is engraved, says Yahweh . . . (Zech 3:9).

The broken commentary following these quotations begins, "And I shall heal . . ."[88] It appears, therefore, that here, as in the New Testament reference, there is a conception of a seven-fold purification, or "healing". The figure of the "refining furnace" in the Psalms quotation is just that of the "temptation" motif of the Scrolls and the New Testament, based as we have seen, verbally and clinically, on the sacred mushroom. In the preparation of body and mind necessary before the participant in the mysteries reaches the climax of the fungus-eating ritual, there must, then, have been seven stages of inward purification.

The seven degrees of initiation of the widespread religion of Mithras, the Persian sun-god, may serve as an illustration, even if the connection goes no deeper. Since Mithraism was also a mystery religion we know all too little about its doctrines and secrets. But the seven stages of initiation have been left marked in the pattern of the mosaic floors of their meeting-places, and there would appear, from the design, to have been a major break between the first three and the last four stages.[89] One is reminded of Pliny's account of the preparation for Hellebore: an emetic has to be taken on the fourth and third days before, as if it were thought that the body at that stage had reached some particular point of crisis.

In Mithraism, the seven stages are linked with the seven "planets", Mercury, Venus, Mars, Jupiter, Saturn, with the sun and moon. In the New Testament, too, the "seven churches" are consciously identified with the "seven stars":

> As for the mystery of the seven stars which you saw in my right hand, and the seven golden lampstands [says the visionary mushroom, holder of the keys of Death and the underworld], the seven stars are the angels of the seven churches, and the seven lampstands are the seven churches (Rev 1 :20).

Substitution and Atonement

Christian theology has Jesus as the great atoning sacrifice made by God for mankind. The "Son of God", the image or replica of the divine Father, is sent to earth and sacrificed as an atonement to heal the rift that has opened between God and the world:

> All this is from God, who through Christ reconciled himself to us and gave us the service of reconciliation (exchange) (II Cor 5:18).

We saw, in an earlier chapter, how the state of imbalance or "sin" brought about when crops were plundered from mother earth, and more especially when the Holy Plant was snatched from her womb, had to be reconciled with compensatory offerings. Only the god himself could satisfactorily atone for this "sacrilege".[90] We noted that the sacred prostitute had to bring to the task of "fascinating" the phallic mushroom "a replica of the thing itself, hanging from her hand", as Josephus says.[91]

A liturgist, around 1400 BC in ancient Syria, cried to Baal to send down a compensatory offering for the release of the Mandrake. He calls

it, in the Ugaritic consonantal script, '-r-b-d-d, which, thanks to
Sumerian, we can now decipher as "Furrow-appeaser" (*URU-BAD-
BAD), and recognize it in the Greek name of the Holy Plant, *Orobadion.*
The ancient hymn, then, is asking the fertility god to send down the
Mandrake's "equivalent" to compensate the ground for its depriva-
tion.[92]

In the name of the first day of the Anthesteria ceremony, Pithoigia,
we may now recognize the same religious activity: compensatory
offering as an atonement for the Holy Plant. The Sumerian from which
we may now trace the derivation of the Greek word was the phrase
GI-DU, "table of offerings", and IGI, "face", that is, "offerings of the
presence", the precise equivalent of the Hebrew "bread of the presence,
or face", the so-called "Shewbread" which was placed before Yahweh
in the Temple (Exod 25:30).[93] These "loaves" are simply a further
instance of the atoning gifts spoken of by the ancient botanists as
"cakes", or "loaves", or "honey-combs" to fill the hole vacated in the
ground by the Holy Plant, and more precisely described by Josephus as
the Mandrakes "equivalent" necessary for a safe removal of that plant
by the Dead Sea. All refer to the mushroom itself by allusion to the
characteristic "bun"-shape of the all-important cap containing the drug.
When dried and skewered for preservation these fungus "lozenges"
were represented by the dehydrated ("massoth") loaves of the "unleavened bread" of the Israelites' Passover food, probably related
linguistically if not materially with the *mazōnes* of the Dionysiac
"cake" feasts.[94]

The New Testament relates the expiatory crucifixion of Jesus with
the sacrifice of the Passover Lamb of Exodus 12:21: "for Christ, our
paschal lamb, has been sacrificed" (I Cor 5:7). The story in the Old
Testament which is advanced to explain the origin of this offering of
the spring lamb rests in part upon a pun. The name of the animal
pesakh[95] is fancifully related to the verb *pāsakh*, "pass over",[96] and made
to refer to a myth in which the plague demon was induced to avoid the
houses of the Israelites when he smote the first-born of Egypt, man and
beast. In order to procure this mercy, the people had to sacrifice a lamb
for each family and sprinkle its blood on the doorposts and lintels of the
houses where it was eaten (Exod 12).

The name of the festival derives in fact from another Semitic root
p-s-kh, "appease, quieten".[97] It signifies that peace which comes after

the agony of parturition, when pain is forgotten and the newly born child or animal rests at its mother's side. Cultically, the Pesakh festival, "Passover", combined gratitude to the fertility deity for the new birth, and a ritualistic attempt to atone for the rape of the womb by a sacrifice of the first-fruits.

In the Bacchic Anthesteria and in the Christian Easter this "Passover" principle was enshrined in cultus and mythology. The Christians saw their Christ, the "anointed" and the "stretched, drawn forth" (the double-play on the root *m-sh-kh*)[98] as the divinely sent substitute offering for the rape of the fungus harvest. He is "raised up" as the "little-cross",[99] sacrificed, returns to the earth whence he came, and then resurrected to new life. He is a microcosm of the natural order. He sets the pattern and provides the means whereby celebrants of the mysteries may be "crucified with the Christ" and enter into a mystic experience of a purged and reborn soul, brought afresh from the creative womb of the earth:

> "Truly, truly, I say to you", says Jesus to Nicodemus, "unless one is born anew, he cannot see the kingdom of God." Nicodemus said to him, "How can a man be born when he is old? Can he enter a second time into his mother's womb and be born?" Jesus answered, "Truly, truly, I say to you, unless one is born of water and the Spirit, he cannot enter the kingdom of God." (John 3:3ff.)

Into the story of the betrayal and crucifixion of Jesus, the New Testament cryptographers wove another of their special, "compensatory" names for the sacred fungus. It lies in the incident after the crucifixion when Judas, overcome by remorse for his "betrayal" buys, or has bought on his behalf, a piece of land which is called "the Field of Blood", supposed to represent an Aramaic popular place-name "Akeldama". The story runs as follows:

> When Judas, his betrayer, saw that he was condemned, he repented and brought back the thirty pieces of silver to the chief priests and the elders, saying, "I have sinned in betraying innocent blood." They said, "What is that to us? See to it yourself." And throwing down the pieces of silver in the temple, he departed; and he went and hanged himself. But the chief priests, taking the pieces of silver, said, "It is not lawful to put them into the Treasury, since they are blood money." So they took counsel, and

bought with them the potter's field, to bury strangers in. Therefore that field has been called the Field of Blood, to this day (Matt 27:3-8).

A slightly different version of the story adds more enlivening details and ascribes the purchase of the field to Judas himself:

> Now this man bought a field with the reward of his wickedness; and bending over, he burst open in the middle and all his inwards fell out. And it became known to all the inhabitants of Jerusalem, so that field was called in their tongue, Akeldama, that is, Field of Blood (Acts 1:18f.).

Details of the story like the "thirty shekels" and the buying of a field by right of redemption are, of course, borrowed by the story-teller from passages in the Old Testament (Zech 11:12-13; Jer 32:6-15). Further graphic features like poor Iscariot's losing the contents of his belly owe much to the somewhat earthy, not to say lavatorial humour of the writer, since the sacred fungus, whose name the arch-betrayer bore, was a powerful purge.[100] Far more significant, indeed the point of the whole unlikely tale (why should the temple police need guiding to a spot a few hundred yards away from the city walls and have pointed out to them the person they had been watching for days?) is the title of the "field", Akeldama. We are here given another of the cryptographer's pseudo-translations, reading the word as if it were the Aramaic *khaqal demā'*, "field of blood", whereas what it really represented was the Aramaic *'akal dāmē'*, "food of price, or compensation".[101] One can follow the story-teller's line of thought in weaving his tale around the "price" idea, featuring it as the blood-money received by the betrayer Judas, and relating it to the strange passage in Zechariah about the wages paid to "the shepherd of the flock doomed to slaughter". But we can also see now for the first time how such a name as "food of compensation" fits precisely into the pattern of such epithets for the Holy Plant as *Orobadion*, "furrow appeaser", and the "bread of the presence" of the Jewish temple and the Bacchic Anthesteria.

Raising the dead

In raising the sacred fungus, the participants of the Anthesteria festival were calling up the dead. It is expressly stated by the ancient writers that the Anthesteria was devoted to tending the souls of the departed, and that during the festival the dead were supposed to rise to the upper world.[102] The cult of the sacred mushroom, then, was a manifestation of necromancy, "divination by the dead".

This extraordinary practice, attested all over the ancient world, lives on in various kinds of spiritualism. The root of the idea is that, since the souls left their bodies and returned to the bowels of the earth, they are in closer touch with the "waters of knowledge", as the subterranean abyss was called.[103] It follows that if one can draw them back in some way they can impart information about the future that is hidden from beings still imprisoned by their flesh. In the Old Testament we have the story of Saul in desperation for some guidance on future events, Yahweh having deserted his normal oracular devices, consulting a witch who lived at En-Dor (I Sam 28:7-14). At first suspicious of his intentions, since Saul in a burst of pious enthusiasm had earlier banished spiritualist mediums of her kind, the witch was eventually prevailed upon to disturb Samuel at his rest. "What do you see?" asks Saul. "I see God (*'Elōhīm*) coming out of the ground", she replies. "What does he look like?" questions her client. "Like an 'erection' [so the ancient versions][104] wearing a robe". Whereupon Saul recognized the dead Samuel's ghost, although for all the comfort that was forthcoming from that somewhat petulant source, he might have saved himself the trouble of his visit.

This connection between the sacred fungus and the omniscient souls of the dead leads to its names being often connected with demons of death. Thus the Sumerian NAM-TAR, which came into Greek as *Nektar,* our nectar, is used generally for "plague demon", and the Old Testament Lilith, the so-called "night-hag" which Isaiah threatens will haunt a desolate Edom (34:14) is probably an original mushroom word.[105]

In the New Testament rare reference is made to a festival called the Agape, so-called Love Feast (Jude v.12; II Pet 2:13(?)). The Syriac translators, at any rate, thought the practice had to do with the comforting of the dead,[106] and this certainly accords well with the meaning of *agapaō,* "love". This Greek word, so favoured by the New Testament writers, is used by the tragedians for affection for the dead, and specifically in the Bible for the relationship between man and God.[107] It is properly used in the Greek version of the Old Testament to translate a Hebrew word for "seduce, allure".[108] Its Sumerian original AG-AG means "love", and also "stretch, measure", semantically the equal of the Semitic *m-sh-kh,* "draw out". A cognate verb in Greek is *ago,* "lead; bring up, draw out, etc" used in such words as *nekragōgos,* "leading forth the dead", *psukhagōgeō,* "conjure up souls from the nether world", and so on.

The Agape seems to have involved a common meal of some kind, although New Testament references are too cryptic to tell us much, and post-biblical accounts of the Agape, as of most other aspects of the real nature of Christianity and its rites, too unreliable. If, as one suspects, the Agape is in fact another name for the fungus itself, then the feast will have included the eating of the mushroom's flesh and drinking of its juice, in other words, it will have been identical with the "Lord's Supper", the eating of the raised or "crucified" Christ:

> I have been crucified with (erected with) Christ; I live, yet it is no longer I, but Christ lives in me (Gal 2:20).

Thereafter the celebrant possesses the mystic "knowledge of God", so earnestly desired by the followers of the mysteries:

> I bow my knees before the Father . . . that he may grant you to be strengthened with might through his Spirit in the inner man, and that Christ may dwell in your hearts through faith; that you . . . may have power to comprehend with all the saints what is the breadth and length and height and depth, and to know the love of Christ which surpasses knowledge, that you may be filled with all the fulness of God (Eph 3:14-19).

Isaiah also looked for the manifestation of the spirits of the dead. He identified them with the "giants" of old, the Rephaim whose gift of knowledge to mankind had proved a not unmixed blessing:

> Thy dead shall live, their bodies shall rise.
>> O dwellers in the dust, awake and sing for joy!
> For thy dew is a dew of light,
>> and on the land of the Shades (Rephaim) thou wilt let it fall
>> (Isa 26:19).

We noticed this passage previously when discussing the mushroom as the "Morning Star", germinated by the dew that fell from Venus before the dawn.[109] It was pointed out there that the Rephaim were those "cast down from heaven", identified with the fallen angels of

Genesis and Jewish mythology. According to the Bible, these "sons of God" were seduced by the beauty of mortal women and begot a race of supermen (Gen 6:1ff.). Later Jewish tradition has it that their seduction was at least partly their own fault since they had taught the girls the art of cosmetics, and so had begun the awful progress of mankind to degeneracy and sexual abandon. More important, "they taught them charms and enchantments, the cutting of roots, and made them acquainted with plants . . . " (Enoch 7 :1ff.).

To raise these dormant spirits of the dead was the way to enlightenment. However, the noises produced by those through whom the spirits spoke were not necessarily intelligible. Isaiah speaks of such necromancers or ventriloquists ("belly-speakers") scornfully as "chirping and muttering" when they seek by oracle their god through "the dead, on behalf of the living" (8:19). In the New Testament it is called "speaking with tongues". Thus the faithful are encouraged to "pursue love (*agapē*), be zealous for spiritual gifts, especially that you might prophesy. For one speaking in a tongue speaks not to man but to God; for no one understands him, but he utters mysteries in the Spirit . . . He who prophesies is greater than he who speaks in tongues, unless someone interprets, so that the church may be edified . . . If even lifeless instruments, such as the flute or harp, do not give distinct notes, how will anyone know what is played? So with yourselves; if you in a tongue utter speech that is not intelligible, how will anyone know what is said? For you will be speaking into the air . . . Therefore, he who speaks in a tongue should pray for the power to interpret . . . tongues are a sign not for believers but for unbelievers, while prophecy is not for unbelievers but for believers. If, therefore, the whole church assembles and all speak in tongues, and outsiders or unbelievers enter, will they not say you are mad? . . ." (I Cor 14:1-23); which was perhaps better than accusing them, like the apostles at Pentecost of being "filled with new wine" (Acts 2:13).

Looking back over the discussion of this chapter, we can see how the worship of the mushroom encompassed every aspect of the processes of nature. When modern religious practice seems at times removed from reality, a Saturday or Sunday relaxation, even entertainment, rather than a concerted effort to influence the deity or be influenced by him, it is worth reminding ourselves that for the ancients it was a life-or-death matter. If the god did not respond to their pleas for rain or sunshine, they, their children, and their crops and animals died.

When, before their eyes, the greenness of the ground vanished under the wilting heat of the summer sun, the dwellers of Near Eastern lands then, as now, viewed the future apprehensively. Everything depended on the god's bounty in the Autumn and the following Spring. The enemy, in their mythological terms, had killed the fertility hero; would the New Year see his resurrection?

In the little mushroom, men could see a prime example of the transience of nature's gifts: in the morning it appeared, and by nightfall the worms had consumed it. The god himself had been among them; they sought him and apprehended him, but his manifestation was a temporary thing. For one fleeting moment he fulfilled his promise that those who received him could become the "children of God".

The worshipper could not approach the god empty-handed. He must bring with him a gift, itself god-given, as an atonement to the earth. Only thus, and by calling simultaneously upon the god by name, could he withstand the demonic power of the fungus. For to eat the god was to die with him; in the short hours of the initiate's complete communion with the deity he had "died" to the world. It was then that he was at most fearful risk, and the days of careful preparation for the ultimate mystery were given their most crucial testing. This was the time of "trial" or "temptation" through which every participant in the cult passed.

To raise the sacred fungus was to raise the spirits of the dead, and thus to communicate with the source of subterranean knowledge. This we may now identify with the Bacchic Anthesteria and possibly the Church's Agape feast, the "drawing up" of the phallic mushroom. Very much earlier than the documentary recording of either of these cultic practices is the raising of the fungus in the so-called "gardens of Adonis". For long this mystic practice has remained obscure in its details, although there has been little doubt that it had to do with the lamenting and raising of the dead god, and thus presumed to be connected with an agricultural cult. For the first time we can decipher the names involved and are thus able to draw together a number of other references to the mushroom religion and those who partook in its rites.

XVIII

The Garden of Adonis, Eden and Delight; Zealots and Muslims

The most explicit reference to the lamenting for the fertility deity in the Old Testament is found in the account of the prophet Ezekiel's vision of the Temple. In a psychedelic trance he fancied himself being carried hundreds of miles from Mesopotamia to Jerusalem:

> Then he brought me to the entrance of the north gate of the house of Yahweh; and behold, there sat women bewailing Tammuz. Then he said to me, "Have you seen this, O son of man? You will see still greater abominations than these" (Ezek 8:14f.).

Jerome translates Tammuz here as Adonis,[1] quite properly, since the Mesopotamian hero-deity was but another representation of the Semitic and Greek Adonis, known and worshipped, particularly by women, all over the ancient Near East. Jerome also records that in Bethlehem of his time (fourth–fifth century) there was still a grove connected with Adonis.[2] It was the practice in the so-called "gardens of Adonis" for women to gather round pots in which certain seedlings had been shallowly planted and to try and urge their germination by various means, including loud lamentation for the dead god. The heat of the sun and the method of planting and fertilization seem to have had a seemingly magical effect, but under the circumstances of their propagation the shoots soon withered away. Whatever the plants were that the women later chose for their agricultural ritual,[3] a kind of sympathetic magic to promote the growth of the crops, the origin of the cult is clearly seen in the search for the sacred mushroom in the "holy mountains" of the north.

The transient nature of the "gardens of Adonis" is exemplified in the rapid growth and as speedy disappearance of the mushroom. Jonah's "sunshade" fungus was eaten by worms the day after it appeared: "it came into being in a night and perished in a night" (Jonah 3:10). A modern observer of the *Amanita muscaria* detected its first appearance at 8 a.m. and by 4 p.m. the same day the fungus was fully grown and beginning to rot.[4] The Phalloidic species, like the Stink-horn, *Phallus impudicus,* rises some three inches in half an hour, and the whole erection is complete in one and a half hours.[5]

Isaiah comments on the same feature of the "Adonis plant" when he speaks of the cultic practice thus:

> For you have forgotten the God of your salvation, and have not remembered the Rock of your refuge; therefore, though you plant the plantings of Na'iman (RSV: "pleasant plants"), and sow the sacred mushroom (RSV: "set out ships of an alien god"), though you make them grow on the day that you plant them, and make them blossom in the morning that you sow; yet the harvest will flee away in a day of grief and incurable pain (Isa 17:10f.).[6]

The names Adonis and Na'iman given to the god, known in Mesopotamia as Tammuz ("Son of Life"),[7] have much the same meaning as we saw earlier. Adonis comes probably from a Sumerian phrase *ANDUL-AN, "heavenly shade", so that the use of the name in the Bible as a divine epithet and ordinary noun meaning simply "lord", implies the "protective, overshadowing" function of lordship.[8] Similarly, Na'iman derives from Sumerian *NA-IM-A-AN, "stretched across the heavens",[9] so that both Adonis and Na'iman can have a particular botanical reference to the cap of the mushroom.

This new tracing of the names of Adonis/Na'iman to their source enables us to discover the origin of the phrase "gardens of Adonis", as used by the ancient writers. It also points to the origin of the "Garden of Eden" story and its mushroom connections. We can even look on much further in time and for the first time uncover the source and nature of the name and associations of those warlike patriots of the Jewish world, the first-century "Zealots", as they were called.

First, the "garden" motif that is so prevalent in the mushroom culture and mythology. It derives from a misunderstanding (or fanciful interpretation) of a Sumerian word, GAN. This has two general meanings: first, an "enclosed area", a "field", or a "garden", and it is with this significance that it came on down into the Semitic world as *gan*. Second,

GAN meant the "canopy" top of the mushroom, or anything of similar rounded shape.[10] Prefaced to NA-IM-A-AN, "stretched across the heavens", it would have the latter connotation, "arched canopy, stretched across the heavens", a description of the cap of the mushroom, writ large, as it were. However, brought down as a name of the sacred fungus into Semitic, as *gan*-Na'iman, it would have been read as "garden of Na'iman, Adonis". In other words, what the botanists understood as a "grove" or "garden" dedicated to the god, was, in fact, just a name of the mushroom itself.

Mushroom names came to be used to express generally the idea of "good living, luxuriousness". In Semitic, Na'iman developed a root meaning "be sweet, pleasant, delightful".[11] Thus the phrase "*gan*-Na'iman" came to be understood not only as "the garden of Adonis/Na'iman" but also as "the garden of delight". Hebrew's equivalent noun for this kind of luxuriating is *'ēden*, and so was born the name of the homeland of our first parents, the "Garden of Eden".[12] In the Muslim Scriptures, the Qur'an, Paradise is given the more original form, "*gan*-Na'iman", in Arabic *gannati-nna'īmi*.[13]

In short, the biblical Garden of Eden, the Qur'anic "gardens of delight", the "Tammuz" whom the women bewailed at the Temple gate, and the Na'iman plants that Isaiah said would flee away in grief are all probably to be identified with the sacred mushroom.

The Zealots

We may now look to the "Zealots" who caused such upheaval and disaster in Jewish history. The Sumerian word just referred to, GAN, as well as meaning the cap of the red-topped mushroom, came also to signify the colour "red" and to be used of the red dye cochineal.[14] Among Semitic words derived from this root was one, *qanna'*, "be red in the face", implying a pent-up emotion like jealousy, zeal, eager rivalry, and the like.[15] It is thus used of God, as jealous of his honour, and of men as "zealous", or, as we might say, displaying a hot-headed emotion, letting their hearts rule their heads. Josephus speaks of the Maccabean rebels of the second pre-Christian century as "zealous for their country's laws and the worship of God".[16] In this he speaks with obvious approval. But he uses the same adjective as a proper name or title of another group of rebels of the first century AD who formed the hard core of the Jewish rebellion against Rome, which was to destroy the Temple and drive the Jewish people of Palestine to swell the ranks of the Dispersion. Josephus has little love for these "Zealots" (Greek *Zēlōtai*): "for so these miscreants called themselves, as though they were zealous in the cause of virtue and not for vice in its basest and most extravagant form".[17] This may not have been entirely fair, but certainly their actions brought death to thousands of innocent people. Believing themselves possessed of some special power and knowledge, the Zealots provoked a revolt throughout Palestine which brought down on Jews everywhere the might of Rome.

The Romans were ever tolerant of other people's religions or superstitions but they could under no circumstances allow political disaffection to take hold within the empire, on however specious a religious pretext. This was particularly the case with Palestine, which always was and still is the world's storm-centre of political and religious emotions. When the Zealot revolt began in Caesarea in AD 66, the Romans moved quickly and ruthlessly against the rebels, driving them south and finally besieging them in Jerusalem. In AD 70, the Temple itself was destroyed, and three years later the last rebel stronghold at Masada by the Dead Sea was reduced.

In the details of this bloody and quite unnecessary war, Josephus, although he grew to hate the Zealots, on whose side he had once fought, cannot refrain from expressing a grudging admiration for their almost inhuman disregard for their personal safety, and for the way in which they would willingly expose themselves and their families to certain death rather than submit to the enemies of their god. He tells us in the most moving terms of the events that led, in May, AD 73, to the final collapse of the revolt and the death of the last survivors. Nearly a thousand men, women and children, facing almost certain annihilation at the hands of the Romans besieging Masada, decided to commit suicide rather than fall into the power of the enemy. They chose ten men from the rest by ballot. These cut the throats of their comrades and their families, and, having chosen one of their number, submitted their own throats to his knife. When the gruesome deeds were done, and amidst the smoking remains of their last stores and the blood of his fellow Jews, this last Zealot plunged his sword into his own heart.[18]

Recent archaeological excavations at the great fortress site have added some measure of confirmation to the story,[19] embroidered though it certainly is by the Jewish historian's sense of drama. The long speech that he puts into the mouth of the Zealot leader in Masada, one Eleazar, must certainly be fictitious, not least in that he is made to blame his fellow sectarians for the misery the revolt had brought upon the Jews:

> For it was not of their own accord that those flames which were driving against the enemy turned back upon the wall constructed by us; no, all this betokens wrath at the many wrongs which we dared to inflict upon our countrymen . . .[20]

There is one section of the speech, however, which if it is not a verbatim report of what Eleazar actually said, may be assumed to be a summary of Zealot ideas about the nature of the soul and its loose association with the body:

> For from of old, from the first dawn of intelligence, we have been continually taught by those precepts, ancestral and divine – confirmed by the deeds and noble spirit of our forefathers – that life, not death, is man's misfortune. For it is death which gives liberty to the soul and permits it to depart to its own pure abode, there to be free from all calamity. But so long as it is imprisoned in a mortal body and tainted with all its miseries, it is, in sober truth, dead, for association with what is mortal ill befits that which is divine.
>
> True, the soul possesses great capacity, even while incarcerated in the body; for it makes the latter its organ of perception, invisibly swaying it and directing it onward in its actions beyond the range of mortal nature. But it is not until, freed from the weight that drags it down to earth and clings about it, the soul is restored to its proper sphere, that it enjoys a blessed energy and a power untrammelled on every side, remaining, like God himself, invisible to human eyes . . .
> Let sleep furnish you with a most convincing proof of what I say – sleep, in which the soul, undistracted by the body, while enjoying perfect independence the most delightful repose, holds converse with God by right of kinship, ranges the universe and foretells many things that are to come . . .[21]

One is reminded of what the historian had said about the Essenes in similar vein:

> For it is a fixed belief of theirs that the body is corruptible and its constituent matter impermanent, but that the soul is immortal and imperishable. Emanating from the finest ether, these souls become entangled, as it were,

in the prison-house of the body, to which they are dragged down by a sort of natural spell; but when once they are released from the bonds of flesh, then, as though liberated from a long servitude, they rejoice and are borne aloft . . .[22]

This belief that the soul could roam at will, once the body was asleep, lies at the base of drug philosophy of the ancient world. Its corollary is that information gained whilst in that condition is necessarily more accurate than what can be reasoned by the brain under normal conditions. It was this confidence in their own prophecies of the future, and their inalienable right to determine other people's lives, that made such religious fanatics a menace to themselves and their fellow-men. Given the idea that they had been vouchsafed by the god a source of knowledge unshared by other mortals, and were thus raised above the rest of the world as a master-race, this self-delusion could and did become a major political hazard. The kingdom of God became the kingdom of this world.

We may wonder, therefore, whether we should not see behind the complimentary title "Zealots", Hebrew *Qanna'īm*,[23] another word of exactly similar form corresponding to the Arabic *gannati-nna'īmi*, "gardens of delight", deriving as we have seen from the Sumerian mushroom title, *GAN-NA-IM-A-AN. If this is so, it places the first-century Zealots in the same category of mushroom-worshippers and users of the powerful drug obtained therefrom as the frantic Maenads and the Christians, similarly the object of persecution by upholders of law and order. That the Sumerian form just cited did in fact come into Hebrew at a very early stage is indicated by the name given in the Bible to the oldest inhabitants of the country around Hebron and Philistia, the *'Anāqīm*, in all probability a jumbled form of the Sumerian *GAN-NA-IM-A-AN.[24] These "great and tall people" (Deut 9:2) were identified with "giants" (*gigantes*) by the early Greek translators.[25] We saw earlier how that word derived from a Sumerian original meaning "sky-shade", implying a mighty man holding up the canopy of heaven, and how from the original form came the Greek *Antimimon,* as one of the names of the Mandrake.[26] It is, furthermore, to the same root that we may probably trace one of the Greek titles of the mushroom-twins, the Dioscouroi, *Anakes.*[27]

Other indications also point to the identification of the "Zealots" with the sacred fungus. They were otherwise known as the Sicarii, or Assassins. At least, it is generally assumed that where Josephus speaks of these "bandits", as he calls them, he is talking of the Zealots or ruffians associated with them. The passage is worth quoting in full since it indicates the kind of religious fanaticism which Josephus blames for the Jewish troubles of the first century:

> But while the country was being cleared of these pests, a new species of bandits was springing up in Jerusalem, the so-called Sicarii, who committed murders in broad daylight in the heart of the city. The festivals were their special seasons, when they would mingle with the crowd, carrying concealed under their clothing short daggers with which they stabbed their enemies. Then when they fell, the murderers joined in the cries of indignation and, through this plausible behaviour, were never discovered. The first to be assassinated by them was Jonathan, the High Priest; after his death there were numerous daily murders. The panic created was more alarming than the calamity itself; everyone as on a battlefield hourly expecting death. Men kept watch at a distance on their enemies and would not even trust their friends when they approached. Yet, even while their suspicions were aroused and they were on their guard, they fell; so swift were the conspirators and so crafty in eluding detection.
>
> Besides these there arose another body of villains, with purer hands but more impious intentions, who no less than the assassins ruined the peace of the city. Deceivers and impostors, under the pretence of divine inspiration fostering revolutionary changes, they persuaded the multitude to act like madmen, and led them out into the desert under the belief that God would there give them tokens of deliverance . . .
>
> A still worse blow was dealt at the Jews by the Egyptian false prophet. A charlatan, who had gained for himself the reputation of a prophet, this man appeared in the country, collected a following of about thirty thousand dupes, and led them by a circuitous route from the desert to the mount called the Mount of Olives . . .[28]

The name Sicarii is usually assumed to be a reference to the short sickle blade (Latin *sica*) carried by the assassins under their cloaks. Elsewhere, Josephus says that "they employed daggers, in size resembling the scimitars of the Persians, but curved and more like the weapons called by the Romans *sicae*".[28a] We may now reasonably suppose that the real allusion is to the sacred mushroom, the *saqrāṭiyūn* of the modern

Persian, the "Iscariot" of the New Testament story, the "Dioskouroi" of the classicists.[29] Certainly the *s-k-r* root and its variants came into Indo-European as in Semitic with the meaning of "curved", like the sickle-blade weapon, but its root as now we see lay in the Sumerian *USh-GU-RI, "knobbed bolt; phallus", which gave the name to the fungus. It was the curved top of the mushroom canopy that gave that connotation to the root.[30]

It would seem then that the "Zealots" and the "Sicarii" are one and the same, and that the common reference to both names is the sacred mushroom that gave them their dangerous hallucinations and much of their motive force. These Jewish fanatics were not the only drug-maddened lunatics to disrupt society with their inflated notions of self-importance and belief in a divinely ordained mission to change the world order. As we shall see in the next section, Islam, too, has had its "Zealots", prompted very probably by the same drug.

The "gardens of delight", the Muslims and their "Zealots"

In the Muslim Scriptures, Paradise is a wholly delightful place. Thus speaks the Qur'an on the subject:

> Lo, the pious are in a secure position, among Gardens and springs, wearing silk and brocade, facing each other. So it is! and we have paired them with wide-eyed houris; calling therein for every kind of fruit, in security . . . (Sur 44:51-55).

> Lo, the pious are in Gardens and delight *(na'im)*, enjoying what their Lord has bestowed upon them, and their Lord has protected them from the punishment of Hot Place. "Eat and drink with relish, for what ye have been doing." Reclining upon couches ranged in rows, and we have paired them with wide-eyed houris . . . (Sur 52:17-20).

> Those who go before . . . are in the Gardens of Delight (gannati-nna'imi), a company from former generations, and a few from later. Upon be-jeweled (?) couches they recline facing each other, while around circle boys of perpetual youth, with goblets and jugs, and a cup of flowing (wine), from which they suffer neither headache nor intoxication, and with fruit of their own choice, and bird's flesh of what they desire, and wide-eyed houris like treasured pearls – a reward for what they have been doing (Sur 56:10-23).

Wherever Muhammad found his (earthly) inspiration for the picture of heaven he paints in the Qur'an, it must have been within a community which still knew the name of the sacred fungus "*gan*-Na'iman" and associated it with the "tree of life" of Paradise, the "Garden of Sex" as the name probably meant originally.[31] Indeed, one of the many puzzles about the Qur'an and the Arabian prophet is where he found his Judaeo-Christian ideas.[32] That he was in touch with Jewish and Christian communities throughout his life and work is, of course, well known. But some of his versions of Bible stories, of the Old and the New Testament, are so strange and so interesting in themselves, that scholars have long been puzzled to know how many of them came to be in such aberrant forms, and under what circumstances the Prophet could have heard or misconstrued them. Even more interesting is the special vocabulary that he uses in the Qur'an. He employs words which are often not Arabic and are certainly derived from Christian Aramaic sources,[33] but sometimes with a peculiar connotation unexampled elsewhere. One or two very special phrases, like the "gardens of delight" above, seem to stem directly from the mushroom cult, and remembering that by his time (seventh century AD) the Church had managed to purge itself of its "heresies", driving these communities out into the deserts, one may reasonably wonder if some of the Christian communities with whom Muhammad fraternized may not have been more truly representative of the older and truer "Christianity" than the Byzantine Church that had taken their place. Here also, there is a promising field for further research.

For example, one intriguing problem about the Prophet's revelations of Paradise is the source of his ideas about the "wide-eyed houris" who were so warmly to entertain the heroes of Islam. Indeed, the precise significance of the epithet he applies to them of "wide-eyed" has been a matter for debate.[34] Literally the Arabic words mean "white of eye" signifying that the white of the eye has been accentuated, setting off the darkness of the pupil. As we know, this can be achieved cosmetically by painting the lids with a dark pigment. A woman so adorned is called in Aramaic *mestabātha'*, of the root *s-b-t*, "set right".[35] (Our word "cosmetics" comes from the Greek *cosmos,* properly "that which is in order", so the "universe". Cosmetics are, then, literally, what put a girl "right", at least in theory.)

It appears that Muhammad, in his description of the fair inhabitants of Paradise, is heir to a very old piece of word-play between the Aramaic *mestabāthā'*, "adorned woman", and the Sumerian mushroom name *MASh-TAB-BA-RI-TI.³⁶ We see it again in the story of Jezebel in an incident which is otherwise connected with mushroom nomenclature.

> When Jehu came to Jezreel, Jezebel heard of it; and she painted her eyes, and adorned her head, and looked out of the window. And as Jehu entered the gate, she said, "Is it peace, you Zimri, murderer of your master?" (II Kgs 9:30-31).

In "murderer of your master" it is not difficult to see a word-play on the plant-name Cotyledon, which we already noticed as derived from the Sumerian *GU-TAL-U-DUN, "ball-and-socket; penis-and-vulva", and thus to be related to the sexual characteristics of mushroom imagery.³⁷ Jezebel has become the prime exponent of the seductive art through her biblical portrayal, and similarly the "wide-eyed houris" of Muhammad's Paradise are the "adorned ones", the Semitic reading of *MASh-TAB-BA-RI-TI, the sacred fungus. We may therefore deduce that wherever the Prophet found his religious vocabulary relating to heaven, they were identifying by word-play the "*gan*-Na'iman", "Adonis-garden" or "garden of delight", with the *mesta-bāthā'*, "adorned one", and Muhammad not unreasonably took it that these ladies were the inhabitants of the heavenly gardens.

The New Testament has the same word-play in a passage whose fresh elucidation leads on to discovering more about Muhammad and his "Muslims". In the first epistle of Peter there is a long homily on the necessity for women to be submissive to their husbands. It reads:

> Likewise, you wives, be submissive to your husbands, so that some, though they do not obey the word, may be won without a word by the behaviour of their wives, when they see your reverent and chaste behaviour. Let not yours be the outward adorning with braiding of hair, decoration of gold, and wearing of robes; but let it be the hidden person of the heart with the imperishable jewel of a gentle and quiet spirit, which in God's sight is very precious. So once the holy women who hoped in God used to adorn themselves and were submissive to their husbands, as Sarah obeyed Abraham, calling him lord. And you are now her children if you do right and let nothing terrify you (I Pet 3:1-7).

The whole passage has probably been woven together from the

same name of the sacred mushroom, *MASh-TAB-BA-RI-TI from which the astute author derived Aramaic expressions for "be willing",[38] "be adorned", and "hope".[39] Of the overall tenor of the passage and its matrimonial relevance, either in the first century or in the twentieth, we need not dwell. We shall have occasion later to discuss the validity of the ethics and homiletic teachings of the Bible in the light of our new understanding of the cryptic nature of so much of the text. What is of more importance for the moment is the word-play between the Aramaic *mestebīthā'*, "submissive", and the mushroom name *MASh-TAB-BA-RI-TI, and its possible source for Muhammad's teaching. For the Prophet called his followers "The Submissive Ones", Muslims, literally, "those who have handed themselves over, are submissive",[40] and this complete submissiveness is an important characteristic of the religion, amounting in Western eyes often to a quite unacceptable fatalism. To the women of the East, this doctrine of submission has brought tragic results, symbolized by the veil which even now after some thirteen centuries is being cast aside only with the greatest difficulty. When, to the utter astonishment and disgust of the wives of his first Medinan followers, the Prophet insisted on their submission to their menfolk, tradition has it that the innovation met with some resistance. For among the desert-dwelling folk at least the women mixed freely with the men before the coming of Islam.[41] Muhammad's faithful disciple Omar is said to have bitterly complained that the men of his tribe used to dominate their women but "when we came among the 'Helpers' (the Ansār of Medina), they proved to be a people whose women dominated them, and our wives have come to copy the habits of the women of the Ansār".[41a] How far pre-Islamic Arabia was a matriarchal society is in dispute; perhaps the movement towards a patriarchal system was already in progress by the seventh century.[41b] Nevertheless, not all the women of the Faith accepted the veil so easily. The niece of 'A'isha, the Prophet's favourite wife, asserted her independence and persisted in going unveiled before all men despite her husband's protests.[41c]

In fact, the Qur'an is not at all clear in those texts[41d] which have been understood as making the veil obligatory, and it seems more than likely that the extremes to which the seclusion of women was taken in Islam owed more to the interpretation of later Persian theologians than the Qur'an itself.[41e] Nevertheless, the principle of "submission" was basic to the new Faith, and we may well wonder now whether this doctrine derived from the kind of Petrine homiletics we have just noticed, coming ultimately from word-play upon the name of the sacred fungus. Thus, anyway, the Qur'an speaks on the rightful attitude of women:

> The men are overseers over the women by reason of what Allah has bestowed in bounty upon one more than the other, and of the property which they have contributed (the marriage-price). Upright women are therefore submissive, guarding what is hidden in return for Allah's guarding them. Those on whose part ye fear refractoriness, admonish, avoid in bed, and beat. If they then obey you, seek no (further) way against them ... (Sur 4:38).

The Assassins

The demand made by Islam upon its adherents for "self-surrender" and submission to the will of Allah was carried to its greatest extremes in the fanatical sect known as the Assassins. Theologically they were of the Shī'ite branch of Islam, but their external policies were marked, like the Jewish Zealots, by utter ruthlessness in removing from their path any person who disagreed with their ideas. This they achieved by raising within their group a band of young fanatics called the *Fidā'īs*, the "devoted ones".[42] They were known more generally as "Assassins" because their complete subservience to the will of their religious masters, without regard for personal danger, was the result of their taking a drug known as *khashīsh*, our "Hashish".[43]

The sect was formed as a secret society around 1090 when they won control, by stratagem, of the mountain fortress of Alamut in Persia. In the eleventh and twelfth centuries they and their successors spread terror throughout Persia and Syria, and were finally only put down after some 12,000 of them had been massacred. For some time small bodies of Assassins lingered on in the mountains of Syria, and some think the cult is not entirely dead even now.

The herb which gave them their name, *khashīsh*, "Hashish", means in Arabic no more than "dried herbage". If used of a particular drug it properly requires some qualification, like "Red Hashish", meaning Belladonna, Deadly Nightshade.[44] The word Hashish alone has become attached to one particular form, *Cannabis sativa*, or Hemp, and the enervating drug made from its resin. But it is difficult to believe that the "pot"-smokers of today, the weary dotards who wander listlessly round our cities and universities, are the spiritual successors of those drug-crazed enthusiasts who, regardless of their safety, stormed castles and stole as assassins into the strongholds of their enemies. If their "Hashish" correctly interprets Cannabis then the latter must represent some more potent drug.

The Greek word *Kannabis* may now be traced to the Sumerian element GAN, "mushroom top", followed by the word which we saw earlier was part of the name of the New Testament Barnabas, and meant "red, speckled with white",[45] denoting, in other words, the colour of the *Amanita muscaria*. As well as the transfer of its name to the less powerful "Hashish", it underwent a jumbling of its form to produce the Greek *Panakēs*,[46] a mysterious plant also called Asclepion (elsewhere used of the mushroom), which required atonement to the earth of various cereals when pulled up.[47] It seems, therefore probable that the original Cannabis was the sacred fungus, and that the drug which stimulated the medieval Assassins to self-immolation was the same that brought the Zealots to their awful end on Masada a millenium earlier. Indeed, we may now seriously consider the possibility that the Assassin movement was but a resurgence of a cultic practice that was part of Islam from the beginning, and had its real origin thousands of years before that. It seems to be a pattern of religious movements based on the sacred fungus that long periods of relative calm and stagnation are interspersed with flashes of violent extremism which die away again after persecution, only to re-emerge in much later generations. In this, history is reflecting the action of the drug itself on its partakers. After hectic bouts of uncontrolled activity, the fungus-eater will collapse in a stupor from which only a resurgence of the stimulatory poison in his brain will arouse him.

Israelitism was based upon the cult of the sacred fungus, as its tribal names and mythologies now show. The extremes of some of its adherents bred their own internal and external opposition, and after the disastrous rebellions against the Assyrians and Babylonians of the eighth and sixth centuries BC, a period of reaction set in, and the past was forcibly expunged from Judaism under the reform movements of the sixth–fifth centuries. The mushroom cult went underground to reappear with even more disastrous results in the first and second centuries AD when the Zealots and their successors again challenged the might of Rome.

Christianity purged itself after the holocaust and drove its drug-takers into the desert as "heretics", and eventually so conformed to the will of the State that in the fourth century it became an integral part of the ruling establishment. By then its priests were raising wafers and sweet wine at the altar and trying to convince their followers that the host had miraculously become the flesh and juice of the god.

XIX

The Bible as a Book of Morals

Our new understanding of the relationship of the Indo-European and Semitic languages has opened up fresh fields of exploration. We are at the beginning of what could be the most fruitful and exciting period in the study of our own culture and its origins since objective, scientific research began. Now that we can decipher the old god and hero names and lay bare the fundamental conceptions of the ancient philosophies and nature-religions, we can better appreciate the import and motifs of their mythologies.

As far as the Bible is concerned, our new appreciation of the origins of Yahwism within the fertility philosophy and not, as has been commonly supposed, in opposition to it, means that we must start again in assessing the part played by the prophets in the cult's development. The old chronological framework on which so much of our understanding of religious "progress" has in the past been based is in ruins. The road from Abraham in Ur of the Chaldees through the patriarchs and Moses to the prophets and Jesus of Nazareth has vanished. Development there certainly was: the crude fertility imagery which saw a mighty penis in the sky ejaculating spermatozoa every time it rained had become by the first century, and indeed long before, a more sophisticated mystery religion. The remote phallic deity in the heavens could now be apprehended by the believer in possession of the secrets of the drug plants and fungi.

For the first time we can begin to understand the precise reference of some of the prophetic utterances about contemporary Yahwism. We have noticed a few instances, particularly in the book of Isaiah, where fresh light has been thrown on the place of the cultic prostitute in the local religious practices, and the nature of the "gardens" that she tended. In such places the prophet seems utterly opposed to the mushroom cult. On the other hand, where, for example, Ezekiel decries the cultic abominations of the Jerusalem temple, the phallic processionals and the women bewailing Tammuz, the very nature of the vision that transports him from Mesopotamia to Jerusalem and the apparitions of whirling, eye-studded wheels, are very reminiscent of the reported psychedelic effects of the drugs of the *Amanita muscaria*. Furthermore, the worship of the sacred fungus, as we can now appreciate, was an essential part of the oldest Hebrew heritage. Many of the patriarchal legends and names are based on mushroom imagery and nomenclature.

As we saw, mushroom worship, by its own extreme nature, its fanaticism and bouts of uncontrolled frenzy, bred its own opposition among normal people. More balanced religionists condemned these aspects of the cult, and the Old Testament records successive attempts by kings and prophets to purge its "abominations" from the land. But they were too deeply rooted to be wholly successful. Even the most intensive and successful of the purges, carried through with ruthless intensity during the Nehemiah-Ezra reforms after the Exile, simply drove the mushroom cult underground, whence it re-emerged in later centuries far more dangerously in the politically orientated movements, Zealotism and Christianity.

We must abandon then any over-simplification of the religious picture presented by the Old Testament: it is not the story of one people's revolt against the heinous fertility worship of the land to which their desert god had led them. Despite the dramatic episode of Elijah on Mount Carmel, the theme is not Yahweh versus Baal. Yahweh *was* Baal, as he was Zeus and Jupiter. The names, as we have seen, sound a common note of sexual import. In any case, the old idea that the religion of Yahwism centred upon a glorification of the desert "purity" as against the orgiastic fertility practices of the sown land had never quite as much textual support as some of its propounders liked to think.[1]

If we need radically to reassess the Old Testament traditions in the light of the new discoveries, the New Testament situation is far more bleak as far as the Christian is concerned. We must be in no doubt of the effect that importing a new, mushroom element into the New Testament picture must have on our understanding of the origin and nature of Christianity. It needed only the decipherment of one of the strange, non-Greek phrases in such terms to upset the whole previous picture of the beginning and growth of the Church. If, for instance, "Boanerges" is correctly to be explained as a name of the sacred fungus, and the impossible "translation" appended in the text, "Sons of Thunder", is equally relevant to the mushroom, then the validity of the whole New Testament story is immediately undermined. For the pseudo-translation demonstrates an intention of deceit, and since mushrooms appear nowhere in the "surface" tale of Jesus, it follows that the secret reference to the cult must be the true relevance of the whole. If the writers have gone to the trouble of concealing by ingenious literary devices, here, and as we have seen, in many cases elsewhere, secret names of the mushroom, not only must its worship have been central to the religion, but the exigencies of the time must have demanded they should be transmitted among the initiates and their successors in a way that would not bring their enemies down upon them. It therefore follows that the "surface" details of the story, names, places, and possibly doctrinal teachings must be equally as false as the pseudo-renderings of the secret names.

One immediate result of the cracking of the already very fragile skin of the New Testament story is that all those doubts about its details which have so exercised scholars over the years are brought sharply back into focus. There always have been extreme difficulties in understanding the story of Jesus. There are in the New Testament picture many kinds of problems posed on historical, geographical, topographical, social, and religious grounds, which have never been resolved. But to the Christian scholar they have always seemed of less relevance than the apparently incontrovertible fact of the existence of one, semi-divine man who set the whole Christian movement in motion, and without whose existence the inauguration of the Church would seem inexplicable. But if it now transpires that Christianity was only a latter-day manifestation of a religious movement that had been in existence for thousands of years, and in that particular mystery-cult form for centuries before the turn of the era, then the necessity for a founder-figure fades away, and the problems that have for so long beset the exegete become far more urgent. The improbable nature of the tale, quite apart from the "miracle" stories, the extraordinarily liberal attitude of the central figure towards the Jewish "quislings" of the time, his friendly disposition towards the most hated enemies of his people, his equivocation about paying taxes to the Roman government, the howling of Jewish citizens for the blood of one of their own people at the hands of the occupying power, features of the Gospel story which have never rung true, now can be understood for what they have always been: parts of a deliberate attempt to mislead the authorities into whose hands it was known the New Testament documents would fall. The New Testament was a "hoax", but nevertheless a deadly serious and extremely dangerous attempt to transmit to the scattered faithful secrets which the Christians dare not permit to fall into unauthorized hands but to whose preservation they were irrevocably committed by sacred oaths.

Let it be repeated: if even one only of the mushroom references of the cryptic phrases of the New Testament text were correct, then a new element has to be reckoned with in the nature and origin of the Christian religion. This new element, furthermore, is the key that fits the phenomenon of Christianity firmly into the surrounding mystery cult pattern of the Near East; but it does so at the cost of the validity of the surface story which knows nothing ostensibly of mushroom cults and which offers for its sacred cultic titles and invocations deliberately false "translations". This is not, then, the record of an evangelistic crusade, an open-armed invitation to all men to join a new society of the redeemed, whose sacred meal is no more than a service of remembrance. It is not the manifesto of an organization whose revolutionary tendencies go no further than the exercise of a group communism of property, but whose teaching urges women to submit at all times to their husbands, and slaves to their masters, being "obedient with fear and trembling". It was not for this pacificism that the Romans dragged forth the celebrants of the Christian mysteries and butchered them.

But if the stories of Jesus are no more historically real than those of Adam and Eve, Jacob and Esau, and even of Moses, what of the moral teachings of the Bible? Whilst it is true that, freed of the pious inhibitions we so often brought to the Scriptures, we can now more readily appreciate the literary qualities and humour of the legends, we have also to acknowledge that Jews and Christians have not gone to their Bibles for entertainment, or to be enlivened by its merry tales. Generations of believers have sought in these Hebrew, Aramaic, and Greek works the very Word of God. They have believed that here were enshrined laws for all mankind through which alone moral stability could be achieved, and defiance of which would mean ruin and punishment, if not in this life, in the next. The very dubiety of much of the text has seemed to many added reason for believing in its divine inspiration. The question has now to be asked, supposing for the moment that there ever was any foundation for the belief that the Bible was a guide-book to moral living, how far can our new appreciation of the origins and nature of Judaism and Christianity continue to give its teachings universal authority?

This, perhaps, is the most crucial issue raised by the present discoveries. It is not just that Jesus, and probably Moses, disappear from history; this loss might still be borne with equanimity, at least by those uncommitted to the religions they represent, if the teachings attributed to them could still be held as valid. There are many people who are not Jews, and whose "Christianity" stops short of participation in the ritual, but who fervently maintain the authority of the Ten Commandments and the Sermon on the Mount. They would argue, without necessarily having studied either passage very closely, that they embody a store of practical experience and moral idealism that will serve mankind for a long time yet, no matter what happens to the religions of Moses and Jesus.

This is not the place to answer these questions; but it would seem a useful exercise to end our study by setting out afresh for consideration some examples of this moral teaching of the Old and New Testaments, examining their immediate literary sources and keeping these larger issues in mind.

We might begin with the Ten Commandments, or "Ten Words" as they are called. We earlier saw how the myth of their revelation to Moses on Mount Sinai was formulated.[2] The idea of two "tablets" derived from the two halves of the mushroom volva, their round loaf-shape form being that of the very early clay tablets. From the Sumerian name TAB-BA-R/LI(-R/LI) came, indeed, our word "tablet" via the Greek and Latin *tabula*. The number of the commandments, or "words", comes from a play upon the same Sumerian name, in the fuller form MASh-TAB-BA-RI, read as "five words", that is, "five" on each tablet. Here they are:

"I am Yahweh your God who brought you out from the land of Egypt, from the house of bondage.

"You shall have no other gods before me.

"You shall not make yourself a graven image, or any likeness that is in heaven above, or in earth beneath, or in the water that is under the earth. You shall not bow down to them or serve them; for I, Yahweh your God, am a jealous god, punishing the wrong-doing of fathers upon sons, to the third and fourth generation of those who hate me, but show-ing kindness to intimates, to those who love me and keep my command-ments.

"You shall not swear by Yahweh your God insincerely; for Yahweh will not clear him who swears by his name insincerely.

"Take due note of the Sabbath, to set it apart. Six days you shall work and carry out all your tasks, but the seventh day is a Sabbath to Yahweh your God. You shall carry out none of your tasks, you, or your son, or your daughter, or your manservant, or your maidservant, or your beast, or the stranger who lodges in your house. For in six days Yahweh your God made the heavens and the earth, the sea, and everything in them, and he rested on the seventh day. So he blessed the Sabbath day and set it apart.

"Honour your father and your mother; in that way you will pro-long your life on the land Yahweh your God gives you.

"You shall not murder.

"You shall not commit adultery.

"You shall not steal.

"You shall not testify falsely against your neighbour.

"You shall not long for your neighbour's house; you shall not long for your neighbour's wife, or his manservant, or his maidservant, or his ox, or his ass, or anything your neighbour has."

As a code of laws these "Ten Words" leave much to be desired. The first four, perhaps five, seem to be purely religious and cultic; from the point of view of social relationships only the last five seem relevant, and the last is a matter of attitude rather than directly anti-social action. More serious, the stark commands of the code receive no qualification. In the desert community in which they are generally supposed to have had their primary relevance, "do not murder" and "do not steal" would be incomprehensible, since the Bedouin raid was a way of life and a necessary means of livelihood. Even taken out of this dubiously historical setting, whilst as a general rule of conduct these five com-mands are obviously good sense, they offer no guide about infringements of the laws, treatment of culprits and the all-important matter of making good damage done to other people.

Of course, in such aphorisms we should not expect to find the legal niceties stated in all detail: it is a statement of principles rather than legislation. But five or six principles are little enough on which to base a practical guide for the complexities of day-to-day living, of whatever age.

As a matter of comparison, we might cite a few examples of a real law-code from Mesopotamia around 1700 BC:

"If a citizen has accused another and charged him with murder, but does not substantiate the charge, the accuser shall be executed.

"If a citizen has stolen an ox, or a sheep, or an ass, or a pig, or a boat that is the property of the temple or of the crown, he shall make a thirty-fold restitution; but if it is the property of a vassal, he shall make a ten-fold restitution; if the thief is destitute, he shall die.

"If a citizen gives another for safe custody silver, gold, or anything at all, he must show witnesses everything that he has deposited. He must provide contracts and (only then) hand over the goods for safe custody.

"If he hands over into custody without witnesses or contracts and the custodian subsequently denies the transaction, then no claim is valid in such a case.

"If a citizen has handed over anything of his whatsoever for safe custody, and the place where it was lodged is broken into or reached with a ladder, and both his property and that of the houseowner is lost, the householder, who has been negligent, shall make restitution for what was deposited with him and was lost, and shall compensate the owner. Furthermore, the householder must search for the lost property and recover it from the thief.

"If a citizen's wife is caught having sexual intercourse with another male, they shall both be tied up and thrown into the water; if the wife's husband forgives her, then the king may reprieve his servant.

"If a citizen rapes another's wife, yet a virgin, and they catch him, that man shall be executed; the wife shall go free.
"If a citizen's wife is accused (of infidelity) by her husband, but she has not been caught in coitus with another male, she must take an oath (of innocence) on the god's name and return home.

"If a citizen's wife is accused of a relationship with another man, but she has not been caught in coitus with him, for her husband's sake she must throw herself in the river.

"If a citizen has taken a wife and she suffers from intermittent fever, and if he plans to take another wife, he may do so, but he must not forsake the sick wife. She shall dwell in a house that he shall provide and he must support her for life.

"If a son strikes his father, his hand shall be cut off.

"If a citizen destroys the eye of another of equal social status, his eye shall be forfeit.

"If he breaks the bone of another citizen, his bone shall be broken.

"If he destroys the eye or breaks the bone of a vassal, he shall compensate him one mina of silver."

(from the Stele of Hammurabi, c. 1792-1750 BC)

It is not the intention, in quoting from these examples of biblical and Mesopotamian laws, to make a comparison in their respective standards of morality. Canons of justice vary with the social stratification of communities. One law for the rich and another for the poor is an immense step forward from the stage where the have-nots could expect no justice at all. In the Hammurabi Code we have a systematic attempt to put the kind of overall principles crisply stated in the half-dozen or so relevant "Words" of Moses into some practical legislation. It is all very well saying "do not kill", but what happens when someone does shed another's blood and incurs blood-guilt? How does a community avoid family feuds which might trail on for generations? "Do not steal" is a fine sentiment; but there are more ways of stealing than entering somebody else's stockyard and roping one of his steers. A more subtle method is to wait until he entrusts you with his livestock before going on a journey and then swear he left only nine animals with you and not ten.

The "Ten Commandments", then, always have had to be enlarged upon, limited or extended, to make them relevant for any age, and it is in this adaptation of the principles they enshrine that subjectivity can most operate. If, in certain circumstances, the divine Author of the "Words" will allow you to flout the sixth, who is to decide whether the recipient of your bullet or napalm is a German, Russian, or Viet Cong; an American, Arab, or Jew? Or under what circumstances may you murder for judicial purposes? Yet it is not so much the insufficiency of the Mosaic Code that must now engage our attention as the authority biblical injunctions can any longer command.

A close examination of the Ten Words of the Bible show that they are probably derived from word-play on the two prime Sumerian fungus names: MASh-TAB-BA-R/LI(-R/LI) and *LI-MASh-BA(LA)G -ANTA-TAB-BA-R/LI(-R/LI), preceded by the invocatory *E-LA-UIA (-E-LA-UIA).

The preamble "I am Yahweh your God who brought you forth from the land of Egypt, from the house of bondage", is fundamentally based upon the name of the fungus as "the 'Egyptian' mushroom", properly, as we have seen, "the stretched or erect one".[3] The self-identification, "I am Yahweh your God" merely states in normal Hebrew the Sumerian original of those divine names, *E-LA-UIA, "juice of fecundity; sperm"; Hebrew 'Elōhīm, and Yahweh (Yāhō).[4] The play on *MASh-BALAG-ANTA and the Semitic phrase for "forced levy" (mas-palakh, -pulkhān) we noted in connection with Issachar.[5] The last part of the name, TAB-BA-RI gave the play on the root d-b-r, "lead out".[6]

"You shall have no other gods before me" comes from a play on the repeated invocatory *E-LA-UIA, E-LA-UIA, as if it read "there is no god save Elohim".[7] What makes this phrase especially interesting is that it is almost exactly the rallying cry of the Muslim, the witness that he makes on his "self-surrender" and takes the Faith: "There is no god save Allah."

Also using the invocatory *E-LA-UIA, repeated, the compilers of the Commandments produced the verbal basis of the third "Word": "You shall not swear by Yahweh your God insincerely." Here they have apparently taken E-LA-UIA for a play on the Semitic root '-l-h, "swear", used by Hosea when he says of Israel's backsliders: "they utter words – oaths of insincerity" (Hos 10:4).[8] For the remainder: "for Yahweh will not clear him who swears by his name insincerely", play is made on the name *MASh-BA(LA)G-ANTA as if it read "remission of sin".

Similar word-play underlies the extension to the Law on swearing put into the mouth of Jesus:

> Again, you have heard that it was said to the men of old, "You shall not swear falsely, but shall perform to the Lord what you have sworn." But I say unto you, Do not swear at all . . . Let what you say be simply "yes, yes; no, no"; anything more than this comes from evil (Matt 5:33-37).

The original reading here was probably, "yes – no; yes – no"; for this in Aramaic would sound remarkably similar to the invocatory mushroom name, *E-LA-UIA, *E-LA-UIA.[9] The added statement, "anything more than this comes from evil", confirms this, for that phrase is a play on the last part of the name, *MASh-BA(LA)G-ANTA, read as "what is surplus (to this is) evil".[10]

The whole of the Sabbath legislation of the fourth commandment is verbally based on the same title of the sacred fungus. From it the "law-makers" derived a Semitic root meaning "be still" and "to praise, hold in respect", and words for "working" and "creation".[11]

Similarly, "honour your father and your mother" is a rendering of the injunction spun from the fungus name: "give praise to those who created you".[12] The somewhat amoral reason for doing so, "that you may live longer on the land Yahweh your God gives you", is verbally inspired in part by the same Semitic word "honour", which can also mean "increase, make a profit".[13]

The New Testament writers develop the theme in their "fulfilment" of the Law in the mouth of Jesus:

> If a man says to his father or his mother, What you might have profited by me is Corban (that is a Gift) – then you no longer permit him to do anything for his father or mother . . . (Mark 7:11).

"Corban" is the technical term for gifts dedicated to God. In the story of Judas Iscariot's blood money, the priests refuse to put the thirty pieces of silver into the "Corban", the temple treasury, because it is tainted with guilt (Matt 27:6). The "interpretation" offered in Mark, "Gift", is hardly a satisfactory rendering of "Corban" and even writing the word with a capital letter does not convey its real import. As elsewhere, we have here a pseudo-translation, offering a clue to the underlying word-play. As far as the "gift" is concerned, the mushroom name *MASh-BA(LA)G . . . has given the myth-makers the root s-p-q, "give what is needful".[14] The technical term is a play on *LI-KUR-BA(LA)G-ANTA, read as "for Corban" (compare the mushroom name in its Semitic form *khurbekhānā*).[15]

"Honouring" one's parents, and "profiting" from the son, derive from a play on the same Semitic root sh-b-kh, "praise, honour; give increase, profit".

"You shall not commit adultery."

It is the New Testament elaboration on this theme which helps to identify the source of the word-play and the means of arriving at this terse command, expressed in a single Hebrew verb. At base is the mushroom name *LI-KUR-BALAG-ANTA, taken as "using a woman for adultery".[16] On this theme the New Testament expounds in words which perhaps have provoked more mental anguish and self-destruction than any other in the Christian writings:

> You have heard it said, "You shall not commit adultery." But I say to you that everyone who looks at a woman lustfully has already committed adultery with her in his heart . . . (Matt 5:27).

To this passage should be added:

> And the Pharisees came up and in order to test him, asked, "Is it lawful for a man to divorce his wife?"[17] He answered them, "What did Moses command you?" They said, "Moses allowed a man to write a certificate of divorce, and to put her away." But Jesus said to them, "For your hardness of heart he wrote you this commandment. But from the beginning of creation, 'God made them male and female.' For this reason a man shall leave his father and his mother and be joined to his wife, and the two shall become one flesh." So they are no longer two but one flesh. What therefore God has joined together, let not man put asunder."[18]
>
> And in the house the disciples asked him about this matter. And he said to them, "Whoever divorces his wife and marries another, commits adultery against her; and if she divorces her husband and marries another, she commits adultery" (Mark 10:2-12).

The extension of "adultery" to the mind reflects the age-old appreciation that in any moral situation the intention might be more important than the deed. Its statement and application here, however, come from adding TAB-BA-RI to the mushroom name quoted above, and thus reading, "an adulterous association with a woman (is) that which is in the mind".[19]

The second passage quotes the statements in Genesis from the Creation story about the joining of the sexes in marriage because "Woman had been taken out of Man" (Gen 2:23f). This in itself is a word-play on the mushroom name *LI-MASh-BA(LA)G-ANTA-TAB-BA-RI-TI, from which the authors extracted "leaves those who begot him", and "joined to his wife". Using the same mushroom name, the New Testament writers go further, producing an Aramaic phrase meaning, "from the source of creation".[20] The whole "divorce" theme comes by word-play on the name, since the technical word for "sending away a wife" is in Semitic *sh-b-q* which they saw in *MASh-BA(LA)G . . . The same root means "leave" (as here, "parents", or "home"). A very similar root, s-p-q, means "join together", and. so we have the "joining" of the husband and wife. From the central element in the name, -BAL-AG-, the authors extracted the Semitic root p-l-g, "divide", and the phrase about not putting the married couple "asunder".

The really crucial injunction for generations of Christians and others in the Western world is the addition attributed in the story to Jesus as a result of further enquiry from his followers:

> Whoever divorces his wife and marries another, commits adultery against her . . .

This comes from the two related names of the mushroom, *MASh-BA(LA)G-ANTA and *LI-KUR-BALAG-ANTA, spelt out into Aramaic phrases as "he who divorces (his) wife" and "for adultery takes the woman (wife)".[21]

It might be questioned if, in the social circumstances of the Near East in the first century, or indeed even now, this rule against divorce was either practicable or desirable. The basis of social life and morality in these lands has always been the continuance of the family. A man's sons are his Prudential life policy. If, when he is too old to work, or illness or other disaster overtakes him, he has no family to care for him, the man dies. If a woman can bear him no children, however good she may be at the cooking-pot or cows, she is failing in her prime mission in life. She has to go; or, at least, a more fertile substitute has to be found. If the man is rich enough he may be able to keep both women; but if not, the infertile woman must go back to her family. To forbid divorce in such circumstances makes nonsense of the whole basis for the moral and social stability of the ancient world.

Perhaps most clearly, indeed poignantly, this injunction about divorce and its Old Testament counterpart focuses our attention on the larger issues raised by these new discoveries. Were such "moral" teachings ever meant to be taken seriously? Certainly, there is nothing in the literary devices of word-play and biblical allusions which necessarily argues against it. A writer can express great thoughts and emotions by means of puns on important words or as supposed "fulfil-ments" of ancient laws, even if this method must tend to restrict his style and choice of words. The ideas of the New Testament teaching might still be valid despite the strangeness of the mushroom cult which gave them birth.

The emphasis placed in the New Testament teachings about "love" and non-retaliation, could, within a small closed society, be practicable. The accounts given by the historians of such in-groups as the Essenes and Therapeutae give that impression of brotherly love and self-control. Even the extraordinary attitude to women and sex and the practice of celibacy which Josephus reports of the Essenes and which became the ideal of the Church, might just be feasible in a desert community of ascetics. Less credible, perhaps, are those mixed settlements of the Therapeutae who kept the sexes strictly apart for most of the time but came together in holy concourse, with singing and dancing, every seven weeks.[22]

Nevertheless, what we learn of the Christians from the Romans who had to live with them, or at least had to try and keep the peace in a racially and religiously fragmented Empire, does little to convince us that the New Testament homiletic teachings were taken seriously by those most immediately concerned. The Roman historian Tacitus, to whom the Christian authorities have looked for the clearest "evidence" of the historicity of Jesus, can hardly find words base enough to use of the sect. "Nero", he says, speaking of the great fire of Rome of July, 64, "fastened the guilt and inflicted the most exquisite tortures on a class hated for their abominations,[23] called Christians by the populace. Christus, from whom the name had its origin, suffered the extreme penalty during the reign of Tiberius at the hands of one of our pro-curators, Pontius Pilatus,[24] and a deadly superstition,[25] thus checked for the moment, broke out not only in Judea, the first source of the evil, but also in the City (Rome), where all things hideous and shameful from every part of the world meet and become popular. Accordingly, an arrest was first made of all who confessed; then, upon their informa-tion, an immense multitude was convicted, not so much of the crime of arson, as of hatred of the whole human race."

Mockery of every sort was added to their deaths. Covered with the skins of beasts, they were torn by dogs and perished, or nailed to crosses, or were doomed to the flames. These served to illuminate the night when daylight failed. Nero had thrown open his gardens for the spectacle, and was exhibiting a show in the circus, while he mingled with the people in the dress of a charioteer or drove about in a chariot. Hence, even for criminals who deserved extreme and exemplary punishment, there arose a feeling of compassion; for it was not, as it seemed, for the public good, but to glut one man's cruelty, that they were being destroyed.[26]

How much substance there was in the charge that the Christians had set fire to the city,[27] we shall never know. It might well be that their fanatics had translated their visions of a fiery end to the world order into practical reality:

> But the day of the Lord will come like a thief, and then the heavens will pass away with a loud noise, and the elements will be dissolved with fire, and the earth and the works that are upon it will be burned up. Since all these things are thus to be dissolved, what sort of persons ought you to be in lives of holiness and godliness, waiting for and urging on the coming of the day of God, because of which the heavens will be kindled and dissolved, and the elements will melt in fire! (II Pet 3:10f.).

The political allusions in the book of Revelation have long been recognized, and "Babylon" identified with Rome:

> So shall her plagues come in a single day, pestilence and mourning and famine, and she shall be burned with fire; for mighty is the Lord God who judges her. And the kings of the earth who committed fornication and were wanton with her, will weep and wail over her when they see the smoke of her burning; they will stand far off, in fear of her torment, and say, "Alas! Alas! thou great city, thou mighty city, Babylon! In one hour has thy judgement come" (Rev 18:8-10).

> Hallelujah! Salvation and glory and power belong to our God, for his judgements are true and just; he has judged the great harlot who corrupted the earth with her fornication, and he has avenged on her the blood of his servants.
> Once more they cried, "Hallelujah! The smoke from her goes up for ever and ever" (Rev 19:1-3).

Powerful sentiments, indeed, but hardly likely to endear the Christians to their fellow-men, nor are they exactly expressions of love and universal brotherhood. Well might they be accused of "hatred of the human race" (odium humani generis).[28] In any case, Tacitus, who must have known the Christians at first hand and regarded them as entirely despicable, seems to have considered their arraignment on an anti-social charge as fully justified.

Suetonius, to whom reference has also been commonly made to support the historicity of the Gospels, says that, around the year 49, "the Jews constantly made disturbances at the instigation of Chrestus" and were expelled from Rome.[29] Whether, even at that early stage, the authorities were being led to believe that the Chrestus, or Christus, was a man and not the source of the "disturbing" drug,[30] we cannot tell from this passage. It is not impossible, although the Gospels can hardly have been in circulation around the communities before 70. The passing reference does at least witness to the fractious nature of the sect, and to the hostile attitude of Jews in the city on whom this kind of religious fanaticism, claiming for itself a Jewish origin, would inevitably react to their detriment. The Jewish leaders faced the same desperate situation in Palestine itself twenty years later when the Zealot madmen brought the might of Rome down on their nation because of similarly inspired excesses.

Elsewhere Suetonius speaks of Christians as "a class of men given to a new and wicked superstition",[31] and there seem to have been reports circulating that they practised infanticide, cannibalism, and incest.[32] One is reminded of the same things said about the Bacchantes, very probably for the same reason. Outside the societies of initiates, garbled reports about the sacred "Christ"-food, "crucified" and eaten in a common meal, would almost inevitably lead to the idea that the "Christians" were eating human flesh. Indeed, the Catholic worshipper is so assured even today that through the miracle of transubstantiation, he is actually eating Christ's flesh, and drinking his blood.

If, then, there seems little in the picture drawn for us of first-century Christians by contemporary pagan historians that is in any way attractive, how far were the writers of the New Testament homilies serious in their advocacy of love towards all men, and turning the other cheek? Was it valid, if at all, only for members of the closed communities, as the Essenes were told to love one another but detest the outsider?[33]

Perhaps even more fundamentally, now that we no longer need to view the Bible through the mists of piety, does it really matter in the twentieth century whether the adherents of this strange Judaeo-Christian drug cult thought their community ethics valid for the world at large, or not? If some aspects of the "Christian" ethic still seem worthwhile today, does it add to their authority that they were promulgated two thousand years ago by worshippers of the *Amanita muscaria*?

Notes

SIGNS

↑ see above
↓ see below
~ word-play upon
> develops to
< developed from
∥ parallel to

ABBREVIATIONS

AASOR	*Annual of the American Schools of Oriental Research*
Acc	Accadian
Aeol	Aeolic dialect
AIW	C. Bartholomae *Altiranisches Wörterbuch*, Strassbourg, 1904
AJArch	*American Journal of Archaeology*
Akk. Fremdw.	H. Zimmern *Akkadische Fremdwörter als beweis für Babylonischen Kultureinfluss*, Leipzig, 1917
APOT	*The Apocrypha and Pseudepigrapha of the Old Testament*, ed. R. H. Charles, 2 vols. Oxford, 1913
Arab	Arabic
Aram	Aramaic
Att	Attic dialect
AV	Authorised Version of the Holy Bible, 1611
BAram	Biblical Aramaic
BCH	*Bulletin de Correspondance Hellénique*, 1877–
Bez	C. Bezold *Babylonisch-Assyrisches Glossar*, Heidelberg, 1926
BH	Biblical Hebrew
CAD	*The Assyrian Dictionary* of the Oriental Institute of the University of Chicago, 1956–
CGS	L. T. Farnell *The Cults of the Greek States*, 5 vols. Oxford, 1896–1909

CGSL	W. Wright, *Lectures on the Comparative Grammar of Semitic Languages,* 1890
CIL	*Córpus Inscriptionum Latinarum,* Berlin, 1863–
CT	*Cuneiform Texts from Babylonian Tablets in the British Museum,* 1896–
DAB	R. Campbell Thompson *A Dictionary of Assyrian Botany,* London, 1949
Dalman *Gramm.*	G. Dalman *Grammatik des jüdisch-palästinischen Aramäisch,* 2nd ed. 1905
Dalman *Words*	G. Dalman *The Words of Jesus,* Engl. ed. of *Die Worte Jesu,* Leipzig, 1898, tr. D. M. Kay, Edinburgh, 1902
Danby *Mish*	H. Danby, *The Mishnah,* Oxford, 1938
DJD	*Discoveries in the Judaean Desert of Jordan,* ed. R. De Vaux O.P., Oxford, 1955–
Dor	Doric dialect
Dsc (Ps-Dsc)	Dioscurides *De Materia Medica* ed. M. Wellmann, 3 vols., Berlin, 1906–14
DSL	*Šumerisches Lexikon* ed. P. A. Deimel, Teile I–III, Rome, 1925–34
EB	*Encyclopaedia Biblica,* 4 vols., London, 1899–1903
Egyp	Egyptian
Enc. Brit.	*Encyclopaedia Britannica*
Ep	Epice, in the Epic dialect
For. Vocab.	A. Jeffery *The Foreign Vocabulary of the Qur'ān,* Baroda, 1938
Galen *NF*	Galen *On the Natural Faculties*
Gard. *EG*³	A. Gardiner *Egyptian Grammar,* 3rd ed. Oxford, 1957
GRD *SW*²	G. R. Driver *Semitic Writing* (Schweich Lecture of the British Academy 1944) rev. ed., London, 1954
HDB	*A Dictionary of the Bible,* ed. J. Hastings, 5 vols., Edinburgh, 1900–04
Heb	Hebrew
Hes *Th*	Hesiod *Theogony*
WD	Hesiod *Works and Days*
HGM	H. J. Rose *A Handbook of Greek Mythology,* 6th ed. London, 1958
Hsch	Hesychius
IG	*Inscriptiones Graecae*

Il	Homer's *Iliad*
Ion	Ionic dialect
JBL	*Journal of Biblical Literature*
JHS	*Journal of Hellenic Studies*
Jos *War*	Josephus *The Jewish War*
Jos *Ant*	Josephus *Jewish Antiquities*
JQR	*Jewish Quarterly Review*
JSS	*Journal of Semitic Studies*
Kautzsch *Gramm*	E. Kautzsch *Grammatik des Biblisch-Aramäischen*, Leipzig, 1884
K-B	L. Koehler and W. Baumgartner *Lexicon in Veteris Testamenti Libros*, Leiden, 1958
Lab *Man*	R. Labat *Manuel d'Épigraphie Akkadienne*, Paris, 1948
Lane *Lex*	E. W. Lane, *An Arabic-English Lexicon*, 8 vols., London, 1863–77
L & S	H. G. Liddell & R. Scott, *A Greek-English Lexicon*, 9th ed., ed. Jones & McKenzie, Oxford, 1940
Lightfoot *Coloss*	J. B. Lightfoot *Saint Paul's Epistles to the Colossians and to Philemon*, London, 1912
Lith	Lithuanian
Löw *Pfl*	I. Löw *Die Flora der Juden*, 4 vols., Wien & Leipzig, 1928–34
l.w.	loan-word
M	Mishnah
MAOG	*Mitteilungen der Altorientalischen Gesellschaft*, 1925–
Maqlû	Gerhard Meier *Die assyrische Beschwörungssammlung Maqlû* (*Archiv f. Orientforschung*, ed. E. F. Weidner, Beiheft 2), Berlin, 1937.
NH	late, post-biblical Hebrew
NHB	H. B. Tristram *The Natural History of the Bible*, 6th ed., London, 1880
Nic *Th*	Nicander *Theriaca*
Nic *Alex*	Nicander *Alexipharmaca*
Nic Fr	Nicander *Poetic Fragments*
NTS	*New Testament Studies*
Od	Homer's *Odyssey*
Pers	Persian
Pesh	Peshitta, Syriac version of the Bible
Pl *NH*	Pliny the Elder *Historia Naturalis*

Post *FP*[2]   G. E. Post *Flora of Syria, Palestine and Sinai* 2nd ed., 2
                  vols., Beirut, 1932–33
P-S   R. Payne Smith *Thesaurus Syriacus*, 2 vols., Oxford, 1879,
                  1901
Ps-Dsc   see Dsc
Rev. de Qum.   *Revue de Qumran*
REJ   *Revue des Études Juives*
RHPR   *Revue de l' Histoire et Philosophie de la Religion*
Roscher's *Lexikon Ausführliches Lexikon der griechischen und römischen Mytho-
                  logie* . . . ed. W. H. Roscher, Leipzig, 1884–1937
RSV   Revised Standard Version of the Holy Bible, 1952
RV   Revised Version of the Holy Bible, 1881–85, 1901
Skt   Sanskrit
Sum   Sumerian
Syr   Syriac
Targ   Targum(im)
Thphr   Theophrastus *Enquiry into Plants*
Ugar   Ugaritic
UM   C. H. Gordon *Ugaritic Manual*, 3 vols., Rome, 1955
ZA   *Zeitschrift f. Assyriologie*
ZAW   *Zeitschrift f. die alttestamentliche Wissenschaft*
ZDMG   *Zeitschrift der deutschen Morgenländischen Gesellschaft*
ZTK   *Zeitschrift f. Theologie und Kirche*

CHAPTER I

In the Beginning God Created . . .

1. See L. Passemard *Les statuettes féminines dites Vénus stéatopyges*, Nîmes, 1938,
   pp. 121ff.; originating from the valley of the River Don ? cp. E. A. Golom-
   shtok, *L'Anthropologie* XLIII (1933) pp. 334ff.; S. N. Zamiatnine *Paleolit.
   S.S.S.R.*, Moscow, 1935, pp. 26ff.; in general cp. E. O. James *Prehistoric
   Religion*, London, 1957, pp. 145ff.

1a. Sum ZIG (<ZI-GA>ZI(G)—(GA), *tebû* 'rise') + AN *elû*, 'be high'.

2. Sum RIG₇ *rê'û* (רעה), also *šarâku* 'give', RI-GA *leqû* (לקח) 'seize' $\underline{?}$ RI-A
   'fecundate' as in A-RI-A *rehû* 'procreate', NÍ-RI-A *kimtu* 'family'; cp. SIPA,

SÍB (rê'û) "stretch-penis" (↓III p. 24 n. 19), ? <SI qarnu 'horn' + PA âru 'branch' (שלח = ואר), kappu 'wing' (cp. PA-TE-SI = ENSI iššakku 'governor'; [botanically: > Πασιθέη = Παιωνία and Γλυκυσίδη (Ps-Dsc III 140) UKÚŠ-TI-GIL-LA tigillu ("bolt-gourd") ↓ VI pp. 49ff.] Cp. Cyrus, the Persian king, Pers kûraš, BH כּוֹרֶשׁ, Kῦρος (as "shepherd" Isa. 44:20) ? <*UŠ-KUR₄ (?<*GÚ-RI "erect-head") ᵈISKUR = ⁱˡ Adad, the storm deity (↓III p. 24 n. 20) = "mighty penis".

CHAPTER II

Sumer and the Beginnings of History

1. Acc Šumer (Sum KI-EN/IN-KI) ?<ŠÚ-MAR "favourer of the womb" (↓ III n. 50) = "penis"; cp. ᵈŠÚ = ⁱˡ Marduk (?<*MAR-DÙG id. BH קַרְדֹּם 'axe-haft' (↓ XII n. 4), Ugar qrdm (↓ XVII n. 92); > νάρθηξ 'Ferula' (as "phallic")) = שׁוּמָּר, ܩܣܡܐ, شمار, Acc šemrânu 'Fennel' (Sum ˢᵉᵐ BAL palukku <*BAL-UGU (>BULUG) ↓ III n. 26), cp. Arab شِمْرَاخ 'cluster of grapes, mountain summit' (for 'grape-cluster' = glans penis, ↓ XVII n. 20), Pers سماروخ samārūḫ '(phallic) mushroom'; ζωμαρῖτις, a Magian name for Hellebore, Ps-Dsc IV 162; cp. soma, the magic plant of the Rig Veda = Amanita muscaria? ↓ V n. 16.

The Sumerians, then, were the "men of Marduk": cp. κάρδακες Lat cardaces, 'Persian soldiers, mercenaries' ("from Persian κάρδα = τὸ ἀνδρῶδες καὶ πολεμικόν"' Strabo, Geographus 15.3.18), Aram קַרְדּוּ (Targ = BH ארט Gen 8:4), קרדויין, ܨܪܕܘܣ, ܨܪܕܘܢܐ, ܩܣܪܕܘܢܐ, Lat Gordueni, Gordyaei, Gordaei, the "Kurds" of Armenia (Arab كُرْدَى) Pl NH VI 118, 129 (mountains), all ?<*MAR-DU₁₀ (= DÙG). Perhaps also related philologically, if not ethnically, are the BH שֹׁמְרֹנִי, "Samaritans".

Botanically, with *MAR-DÙG, Sem qrdm "womb-favourer, phallus", Acc qarâdu "strong", cp. Κάρδαμον Cardamon and Καρδαμίνη Mint, as aphrodisiacs (cp. Sum ᵘBÚRU-DA urnû 'mint' and 'Αφροδίτη (*<Á-BÚRU-DA-TI "organ of fertility, giver of abundance" ↓ XI n. 27.

BH and cogn. שׁמר 'watch' <*ŠÚ-MAR as צפה ?<SIPA "stretched-penis", cp. שׁקד 'awaken early' <UŠ-GÍD "stretched penis" ↓ VIII n. 37.

2. For the shape, see GRD SW² pp. 8ff. BH לוּחַ <LI-U₅/'U-UM (li'u 'tablet')

> (*li-ug>) λόγος 'account, reckoning; law; word', etc. Cp. Lat *tabella*, ταβέλλα, 'writing tablet, letter, contract' = *tabula* 'list, censor's lists; 12 tablets of the Law; testament' <*TAB-BA-L/RI "two-cones, or -hemispheres" (for LI = 'cone' cp. ᵍⁱˢ LI 'pine tree'; ᵘᶻᵘLI-DUR 'navel'; LI-LI-EZ (= LILIZ) 'drum'; and as in Acc *Maštabbariru* = Sum ᵘ KUR-KUR "two-cones, hills, humps" = mushroom ("Hellebore"), i.e. *MAŠ-TAB-BA-RI-RI (-LI-LI) ↓ VI n. 16. Sum*TAB-BA-RI> דבר 'word' and, from the 'bun-' shape, > פַּטִּירָא 'unleavened bread' ↓ XVII n. 63.

3. GRD *SW²* pp. 4f., pl. 1, 2.

4. I.e. GÌŠ/UŠ + KUR *šadû*, 'mountain', *mâtu* 'land', also *kašâdu* 'capture'; cp. Lab *Man* ✳ 50.

5. GEMÉ *amtu*; Lab *Man* ✳ 558.

6. ÈR, ÈRI, ERUM *ardu*, ? <E₄-RI-A = A-RI-A *reḫû* 'procreate'.

7. Acc *išâru* = BH ישר; Sum UŠ-SA *emêdu* (= BH עמד), as in BH יששכר 'Issachar' ↓ XVI p. 145.

8. UŠ *šiddu* 'length', *redû* 'pursue'.

9. <DÙG-GAN ("semen-container"?), *tukkanu*, cp. Lab *Man* ✳ 400.

10. SÌLA (= SILA) *sûqu* 'road, path'; SÌL-MUD 'groin; womb' (= "birth canal" ↓XV p. 137); cp. SÌLA *naglabu* 'razor' and ᵘᶻᵘ BAR-SÌL *naglabu* 'groin' (the 'shaved' place). Sum SILA < SI 'horn' + LÁ = LAL "attach, stretch, place together": id. ⌐ Lab *Man* ✳ 481. Cp. ψιλός 'bare, stripped' ? < BAR-SÌL.

10a. The most consistent attempt to discover links between Sum and Indo-European was that of C. Autran (*Babylonica* VIII (1924) pp. 195–217; *Sumérien et Indo-Européen*, Paris, 1925). Had he concentrated more on nominal correspondences and less on morphology and syntax he might have had more success. His introductory words still ring true: "Malheureusement, la collaboration indo-européo-sumérienne n'a constitué, jusq'ici, qu'un accident anormal et de caractère toujours plus au moins précaire et momentané" (p. iv).

11. ÁG *râmu* 'love', as in ÁG-ÁG (*râmu*, and *madâdu* 'measure') ἀγαπάω 'love, attract, allure, incite" ↓ XVII n. 107.

12. GAR *šakânu* 'place' = MAR; GÍR = MIR; between Sum and Acc ŠE-MUŠ₅ *šegušu* 'a cereal'.

13. μάγγανον V = γάγγαμον (Hsch); μάγγονον (as βάλανος II. 4. 'bolt-pin')
?<GAG-GÀR (-BA) *sikkat karri* 'knobbed sword pommel' (*kakkâbu*, כּוֹכָב
'star' ↓VI n. 28); for μάγγανον 'means of bewitching, enchanting', ↓ V n. 24;
VI p. 51. κινυρός 'wailing' = μινυρός 'whining' <*GIN-URA "erect the
penis" in ritual lamentation, ↓ X n. 2. For an example in BH of a dialectal
variant, cp. אגדה Am. 9:6 'vault of heaven, band' and עמוד 'pillar', both
< Á-MUD/MUD-Á *uppi aḫi* 'shoulder blade'; MUD *uppu* 'strap, bridle'.

14. E.g. I-BÍ = IGI; GAN-NU *kankannu* 'lid' (= κάνειον) ≟ BAN 'arch' ↓ XIV
n. 15, URUDU-NÍG-KALAG-GA 'kind of tympanon' = -BALAG-GA,
through phonetic assimilation.

15. βάλανος "acorn, glans penis", etc. < *BAL-AN "top of a drill, phallus" (↓III
n. 26), cp. βόσκω 'feed' L & S cite √ *guō*, Lith *guotas* 'herd', βλήχων Penny-
royal = Ion Γλήχων. For Greek γ + σ (ξ) = Sum B + S, cp. ἀξίνη 'axe'
<AB-SÍN "vagina" (for relationship ↓ XII n. 4); for Greek π = Sum G,
cp. ἀγαπάω < ÁG-ÁG, ↑ n. 11.

16. Within Sum, TIN = TÌL (*balâṭu* 'live'); DÙN = TÚL *šuplu* 'depth'; ŠUDUN
= ŠUDUL *nîru* 'yoke'. Cp. AN *elû* 'high' < ÌL *našû* 'lift'. Sum L = Sem *n*:
Acc *andunânu* 'substitute' (Sum SAG-ÍL-LA) < AN-DÙL 'protection'.

17. Cp. BH שְׁאוֹל 'Sheol'? <*ÈŠ-ÚŠ "house of the dead"; שָׁאוּל 'Saul'? <UŠ-SA
'erect penis' (cp. Issachar, ↑ n. 7) ? > *SA-UŠ > *ša'ûl*. Sum MUŠ 'serpent'
(?<*GÚ-UŠ "erect head, glans penis") and MUŠ₄ = MÙL 'rodent'; GUL
(also <*GÚ-UŠ) in ZA-GUL *sâmtu* 'Chalcedony' (i.e. colour of the glans),
cp. BH גָּלְיָת 'Goliath' ?<*GUL-IA₄ (=ZA)-TI, "the red-topped organ,
phallus" (note the כּוֹבַע נְחֹשֶׁת on his head (I Sam. 17:5): כובע 'helmet'
?<GÚ-BA(R) 'top of the head'; נחשת 'bronze' <*NA(=ZA, IA₄)-ḪUŠ
"red-stone" i.e. copper ore; cp. GUŠKIN 'gold' where GUŠ <*GÚ-UŠ>
ḪUŠ 'be fiery red; angry' (cp. קִנֵּא 'zealous' = Arab قَنَأ 'be red' < GAN-NU
'cochenille' ↓ XVIII p. 179; cp. VI n. 42; XIV n. 14) and -KIN ?<GI-NA>
GIN 'erect'; cp. ᵍⁱˢKÍN Acc *kiškanû* 'chestnut'. Cp. also SAG-GÚL 'bolt' and
BH NH Aram גֻּלְגֹּלֶת 'skull'.

18. E.g. GÙB *kamâru* 'press down' and ḪÚB-ŠÚ *š/suḫar šêpi* 'ball of foot', ḪUB-
ḪUB 'spread out'; GUŠ = ḪUŠ ↑ n. 17; GÚM *kaṣâṣu* 'cut up small' and
GUM *ḫašâlu* 'pound' = ḪUM *ḫamâšu* 'grind' (cp. חֹמֶשׁ 'belly'). ?<*ŠU-
ḪUM (i.e. root + verbal preform.). SÚG *nazâzu* 'stand', cp. SUḪUŠ
(SUḪ-UŠ), SUḪ₆ '*išdu* 'base'. For GAN-NU *tabarru* 'cochenille' > NH
חַנּוּן 'red-cap', ↓ XVIII p. 178 and prev. note.

19. MAḪ 'be great': Skt *mahat, mahâ* and μέγας, μακρός, etc. Cp. BH מֶגֶד 'excellence' < MAḪ-DI *tisqaru* 'preeminent', note prop. name מַגְדִיאֵל, chief of Edom Gen. 36:43 etc. For Sum Ḫ = ⵎ = Arab غ (transl. *Γ*), cp. עֲמֹרָה (*Γομορρα*) 'Gomorrah' ? <*GUM-ÚR-RA "rub genitals" i.e. masturbate; cp. סְדֹם 'Sodom' <*SÌ-DÙG "destroy semen" ↓III p. 25. Cp. BH פֶּלַח 'mill-stone, slice of pomegranate, spinning whorl', etc. < BALAG, BULUG 'phallus' <*BAL-AGA/UGU ↓III n. 26; within BH cp. מרח and מרק 'rub'.

20. ⁽ᵍⁱˢ⁾ ŠEM-ḪAL = χαλβάνη, galbanum: ḪAL-ḪAL-LA = *garâru* 'run' = χαλ-(i.e. ḪAL ? >*gar*-). Cp. χρῖσμα <ŠEM-ḪAL/ḪAL-ŠEM, i.e. "running resin, semen". ↓ III n. 36. Acc *baluḫḫu* 'galbanum' and by metath. *ḫaluppu* 'willow' (Sum ᵍⁱˢ ḪA-LU-UB transl.).

21. φλέγω, φλεγέθω, φλόξ, Lat *flagro* ?<*BIL-ÁG "fire-maker". Cp. GIBIL *qilutu* 'brazier' ?<*GI-BAL "borer-reed", i.e. fire-drill, by assimilation to GIBIL, and divided out into the divine name ᵈBIL-GI = ⁱˡGibil the fire god. Cp. Hermes, inventor of fire: "he chose a stout laurel branch and trimmed it with a knife . . . held firmly in his hand, and the hot smoke rose up" (Hom. Hymns IV 108ff.). Cp. PIRIG *nûru* 'light', by metath. ? With *BIL-AG cp. BH prop. name בִּלְעָם 'Balaam', בְּנוֹ בְעוֹר.

22. E.g. κύημα 'foetus' ?<*GÚ(=GUN *biltu* 'burden' ↓ XII p. 103 n. 35) + UMU 'mother'. In this last word the initial U represented by Gk η is the result of attraction to the following M, itself probably representing an original U(*w*), i.e. ?<*Á — U₅ (— A) "possessor of fecundity" ?>BH proper name חַוָּה 'Eve'. Cp. also Sum AMA *ummu* 'mother'. For similar assimilation of Sum A to U in the presence of M, cp. MAŠ > MUŠ in ᵐᵘˡ NU-MUŠ-DA (glossed *namaššu ša* ⁱˡAdad), the constellation, for *NU-MAŠ-DA (MÁŠ-DÀ 'small cattle').

23. γαῖα 'earth' <GAL(L)A 'womb'; abbrev. γῆ = גִּיא ('fertile valley'); γαιάδας (= δῆμος) ?<*GAL(L)A-DÀ.

24. Cp. BH prop. name קַיִן 'Cain' (↓XII n. 1) ?<*GAR-ÈN "container of seed" (= womb) > GARIN 'pond' and AGARIN 'mother'; actively, as a "placer of seed", ENGAR > *ikkaru* (אגר 'hire') 'peasant, cultivator'. Cp. also βαίτυλος Lat *baetulos* 'a meteoric stone' (Pl *NH* XXXVII 135: a kind of *ceraunia* (cp. *cerauniae* 'mushrooms' ↓ XII n. 33) resembling axe-heads (i.e. vulvae, ↓ XII n. 4)), < BAR-TÙN/TÙN-BAR > παρθένος 'virgin' = BH בְּתוּלָה.

Cp. also παιδέρως, epithet of Hermes (↓ XIV pp. 126f.) ?<*BAR-DARA "red, variegated skin".

25. Παιωνία 'Paeony' <*BÁR-IÀ-U₅-NÁ "sac of fecundity" i.e. womb, > βαριωνᾶ Matt 16:17: as mushroom volva ↓ V nn. 12, 13: cp. Περιστέρεων 'Holy Plant' (Dsc IV 60) <*BÁR-UŠ-TAR-IÀ-U₅-NÁ = BH קִיקָיוֹן (↓ V n. 12); cp. *Paeanis* also called *Gaeanis*, a stone said "to become pregnant and give birth to another stone, and so thought to relieve labour pains" (Pl *NH* XXXVII 180). Cp. also Πληϊόνη, mother of the Pleiades, represented as 'doves' (BH יוֹנָה <*-IÀU₅-NÁ↓V n. 13). Cp. ῾Υπερίων 'Hyperion' the sun-god, ?<*U₅-BÁR-IÀ-U₅-NÁ, "fecundator of the womb" (↓ III p. 24, n. 29), and Παιάν (Ep Παιήων, Att Ion Παιών, Aeol Πάων) 'physician of the gods' (↓ XVII p. 158 n. 48) = Apollo (↓ XI n. 27).

Note also the combination *a+a>ai* as in BH אַיָּל 'stag' ?<*Á-A-RI-A "strong fecundator" (= DÀRA-BAR *aialu*), as Acc *naialu* 'roe-buck' (= DÀRA-MAŠ-DÀ) ?<*NÁ-A-RI-A. BH keeps the vowels separated by a guttural: נער(ה) 'lad, girl' but are assimilated into a unisyllable in Sum NAR 'singing-girl, eroticist'.

CHAPTER III

The Names of the Gods

1. *IÀ-U₅ as in UIA the goddess *Ištar* <*ÙŠ-TAR 'womb'. Thus BH יהו, יהוה 'Yahweh' <*IÀ-U₅ (-A) > *Jovis*, Ζεύς, διός, Skt *dyaús* ('sky' as source of semen); IÀ 'juice, semen' > *ze, di, de*; cp. Sum ZÁ = IA₄ 'stone' as in ζυγόν = Lat *jugum*, Skt *yuga* 'yoke' ?<*IA₄-UGÙN "stone of child-birth" i.e. birth-stool as 'forked' (↓XII n. 51), and διάκονος 'servant' ?<*IA₄-GUN 'bearing stone' as in BH צָפוֹן 'North', fulcrum of the heavenly arch, <*ZÁ/IA₄-GUN (↓ XV n. 3). Cp. BH יְהוֹשׁוּעַ 'Joshua' (Gk Ἰησοῦς) <*IÀ-U₅ + ŠÚ(Š) *gamâlu* 'be favourable, preserve'; *emûqu* 'strength': i.e. "life-giving semen"; > ζωός 'alive', ζωσώ 'impregnate', ζῷον 'living being' etc. Cp. also related σωτήρ 'saviour' ?<*ŠÚ-TÙN "giver of life to the womb" (cp. ᵈŠÚ 'Marduk' ↑ II n. 1) = θύρσος 'thursus' the Bacchic wand, i.e. phallus (<*TÙN-ŠÚŠ (↓ XVII n. 21)); and ᾿Ιασώ *Iaso* 'goddess of healing' and ᾿ιάομαι, ἴασις 'healing' <*IÀ-U₅. Cp. also Διόνυσος 'Dionysus' <*IÀ-U₅-NU-ŠÚŠ "seed of semen of life-giving, healing", and epithet Νόσιος

'Healer'. With Skt *dyau-* 'sky' as source of semen/rain, $<$*IÀ-U5, cp. Sum
IM, MÉR, Acc *šamû* 'rain' and also 'heaven, (BH שמים), and Sum UD, U4 =
Acc *ûmu* 'day' and *umšu* 'thunderstorm'. Lat *Jupiter, Jovis-pater* = Ζεὺς πατήρ
(cp. *Eupator*, Mithridates VI) $<$*IÀ-U5 + πατήρ $<$GÚ-TAR 'top of the head;
penis'. Cp. *Juno, Venus* $<$*IÀ-U5-NU "semen-pod" i.e. womb (cp. NU-
GIG, NU-MAŠ 'prostitute') and ζώνη 'woman's girdle; the waist (prop.
'womb, belly')'.

  BH אֱלֹהִים 'God', a false plural form from אֱלֹהִי $<$E4-LA6 (=ILLU)
"strong-water"; juice, resin, semen ($>$ אֵל, *illu*, etc.) + UIA (*IÀ-U5)
"fecundity" (= יהוה); i.e. אלהי(ם) is simply a combination of both semen-
god names: cp. ἐλελεῦ the cultic cry at the ὀσχοφόρια and 'Ελωΐ ἐλωΐ of Mk
15:34 ↓ XVII p. 157. With BH אֱלִיָּהוּ 'Elijah' (?$<$*E4-LA6-IÀ-U5) cp. 'Ελεία,
a title of Artemis at Cos (E. Schwyzer, *Dialectorum Graecorum Exempla
epigraphica potiora*, Leipzig, 1923, 251 B 5.) and 'Ελιεύς, a title of Zeus at
Thebes (Hsch).

2. Sum U5 *rakâbu* 'mount, serve'; *rikibtu* 'seminal discharge'; *banû* 'create';
   U4 (UD) *ûmu* 'day'; *umšu* 'thunderstorm'; Ú *šammu* 'herb' (and determin.);
   ᵈU ⁱˡAdad (?$<$AD-AD, cp. AD-DA *abu* 'father').

3. Cf. Sum U4 *umšu* 'thunderstorm' and U4 (UG4) *labbu* '(roaring) lion'
   (= UG̃ *labbu* and *aggu* 'furious'); UG *uggu* 'anger' and *ûmu* 'storm demon'.
   Sem √*srḫ* 'roar, scream, lament' ? $<$ZI 'raise' + RI-ḪA 'tempest' ($>$ רוּחַ,
   רֵיחַ 'wind').

4. BH קוֹלֹת Exod 9:23 etc. of God, as thunder.

5. Sum ᵈISKUR (= ⁱˡAdad) ?$<$*UŠ-GÚ-RI ($>$KUR4) ↓ XII n. 18 for the
   Dioscouroi, and ↓ p. 24 for BH צבאות $<$*SIPA-UD "stretched-penis of the
   storm".

6. Sum GÌŠ-DUG4-GA ("penis-speak") *reḫû* 'fecundate'; cp. "Ορτυξ-υγος
   Hsch γόρτυξ (Γόρτυξ) 'Quail' (the 'spittle' bird ↓ VII n. 13) ?$<$*BUR5-DUG4-
   GÌŠ. For the idea of the sperm as the 'word' bringing 'good news', cp. κηρύσσω
   'announce', κῆρυξ 'messenger' ?$<$GURUŠ ($<$*UŠ-GÚ-RI ↑ n. 5) 'hero'
   (prop. phallus (↓ nn. 18, 67), and BH בשר, בשורה, Arab بُشْر ?$<$*BA-ŠUR
   (= *ṣarâru* 'spurt, let flow'; *zanânu* 'rain').

7. Lat *anima* 'vital principle, breath of life; living being' ?$<$*AN-IM-A =
   IM-A-AN ("rain-wind-of-heaven") *zunnu* 'rain'; = ψυχή ?$<$*BA-SÌ-UḪ
   (BA + SÌ *nadû* 'eject' + UḪ 'spittle'; also $>$ Acc *sapâḫu* (= Sum BA) 'dis-

perse', BH סָפִיחַ 'scattered seed from harvest giving second growth'; cp. ἀφρός ?<*Á-BIR-UŠ₁₂ "scatter (sapâḫu)-spittle"; ἀ. αἵματος = σπέρμα (L & S 294ᵃ); Lat spiritus ?<*UŠ₁₂-BIR-TI "scatter-spittle".

8. Nidd. 16ᵇ עד שהרוק בתוך הפה euph. = 'while semen is in the vagina' ↓ VII p. 56.

9. Sum AB-SÍN abšinnu 'furrow' i.e. "window" of the womb; cp. ŠEN šennu 'container' and ŠEN-TAB-BA 'double-axe'; cp. ἀξίνη ↓XII nn. 2, 4.

10. ↓ XV p. 137.

11. Sum ZU-AB = AB-ZU apsû 'ocean' = ENGUR, ᵈENGUR (= ⁱˡ Engur, Ea) <*GUR₇-ÈN "seed-container" > BH גֹּרֶן 'threshing floor', cp. Sum GÚ-EN-NA 'depository'; Cp. the 'Sea' of the Jewish Temple (I Kgs 7:23–26), cp. Benzinger, Hebräische Archäologie³, 1927, p. 329; W. F. Albright Archaeology and Religion of Israel⁴, 1956, p. 148f.; also see A. Jeremias, Das Alte Testament im Lichte des alten Orients³, 1916, p. 488 and n. 1. BH יָם 'sea' ?<*IÀ-AMA "mother's juice" i.e. foetal waters.

   Cp. the classical Ὠκεανός Oceanus ?<*A-U₅ "semen" + KI-A (kibru 'border') + AN-NA, "seminal waters of the borders of the heavens": son of Uranus and Gaia (Hes Th 133, etc.), god of the primeval water and source of smaller waters (Il 21.195ff., Hes Th 368); conceived as a great river encompassing the earth's disc and returning to itself (Il 18.399, Od 20.65); the Outward Sea, opp. to the Inward Sea, the Mediterranean.

12. ἄγγελος and BH מַלְאָךְ ?<*GAL-AG "great-worker"; cp. Talm. Num.R. s. 10: "according to each miracle that he performs through us (angels) he names us" (ref. to Judg 13:18); cp. Enoch XX, etc.

13. Of the Essenes, cp. Jos War II 142; cp. the angelology of Zoroastrianism in this regard: Lightfoot Coloss. p. 385, and see Enoch VI 7f.

14. BH צֶדֶק 'bounty' ‖ עשר הון Pr 8:18; cp. Sum ZI(D) kênu 'sure, faithful' <ZI-DA as in Á-ZI-DA imnu 'right'; cp. NÍG-ZID kettu 'justice'; cp. ןכ‎, زكى 'justify' and زكاة 'legal alms' and زكّى 'make a plant grow'. Note: δίκη <DI-KU₅ dînu 'judgement'.

15. Cp. Hos 10:12 עד יבוא ויורה צדק לכם; √ירה ?<ÚR reḫû 'fecundate' ?<*U₅-RI-A as A-RI-A reḫû; cp. URÚ/ÙRU abubu 'flood', and ÚRU erêšu 'cultivate'.

16. ↑I n. 2; ↓ nn. 18, 19.

17. דָּוִד, √ דוד 'love' ?<DÙ-DÙ *epêšu* 'make', *banû* 'create' cp. TU *alâdu* 'beget', ᵈTU-TU = ⁱˡ*Marduk* ↑ II n. 1; ↓ XVI p. 141, n. 1.

18. ↓ I. n. 2; SIPA, SÍB.

19. *SIPA-UD (*umšu* 'storm'); for SIPA > צבא as 'progeny' cp. BH צפיעה ‖ צאצאים Isa 22:24; and צבי 'gazelle' as a product of fecundity = Sum MAŠ (-DÀ) *ṣabîtu*, and cp. BH צבה Num. 5:27 of the 'swelling' of the adulteress' belly.

20. ↑ n. 5.

21. ⁱˡ*Adad* ?<AD-AD; AD *abu* 'father', cp. ᵍⁱˢ ÁD *giṣṣu, eṭittu* 'thorn' (pricker, phallus ?) = Ú-GÍR = ATTU = BH אָטָד (↓ V n. 10); cp. κέντρον 'goad' < Sum KIN-TUR as in ⁱˡKIN-TUR *epitatu* 'nettle' = ⁱˡLAM-MA (where LAM = 'coitus', as in NITLÁM 'spouse', etc. and as in probable origin of λαγνεία 'coitus'); cp. Arab نخس 'prick, goad' also 'insert haft into axe-head' (XII n. 4) and BH נחשתן 'a processional phallus'? Ezek 16:36.

22. יוֹסֵף <*IÀ-U₅ + SIPA/SÍB.

23. Cp. Σαβάζιος, Σαβάδιον <SIPA-ZI as in ᵐᵘˡ SIPA-ZI-AN-NA "erect penis of heaven" = ᵏᵃᵏᵏᵃᵇᵘŠ*itadâlu* ("vast one") 'Orion'; Sabazios a solar power, acc. to Macrobius (I. 18, 11: "in Thracia eundem haberi solem atque Liberum accipimus"), called Dionysus by the Thracians: καὶ Σαβοὺς τοὺς ἱεροὺς αὐτῶν Schol. Aristophanes *Vespae* 9; see CGS v pp. 94ff.; For εὐοῖ σαβοῖ (= BH יהוה צבאות), see Demosthenes 18.260; CGS v p. 125.

24. Ἡρακλέης ?<*URA-GAL-UŠ "large, erect penis" cp. GURUŠ 'hero' ↑ n. 6, <*GÚ-RI> KUR₄ and GUR₄ *kabru* 'thick' Pers *kûraš* etc. 'Cyrus' ↑ I n. 2; > κύριος 'lord'. Cp. ἥρως 'hero' ?<*URA-UŠ "erect penis", and cp. the plant Polygonon, Πολύγονον ἄρρεν = Ἡρακλεία Lat *Seminalis* called by the Magi γόνος ἥρωός (Ps-Dsc IV 4).

25. ↓ XVI p. 145.

26. BH בַּעַל <*BA-AL> BAL *ḥerû* 'dig' (cp. AL in ᵍⁱˢAL(-LA) *allu* 'pickaxe, mattock' as a digger, and as a sower in AL-DÙ 'seed-grain', and in ᵍⁱˢNUMUN-GISAL (ᵍⁱˢ AL) 'seed-plough': cp. Ugar 67:II: 10, etc. *aliyn b'l* ‖ *aliyn qrdm*, where *qrdm* = 'axe-haft; penis' (↑ II n. 1). Cp. also Sum ALLA-*nu* a pseudo-id. *allânu* 'suppository' (= βάλανος, *glans*), ᵍⁱˢAL-LA-AN *allânu* 'oak' (BH אַלּוֹן).

   ᵍⁱˢ BAL *pilakku* 'spindle' (shaped as a drill ↓ XII p. 104), ᶻᵃBAL *pilakku* 'thunderbolt' (= *ceraunia* Pl *NH* XXXVII 134; as mushroom Pl *NH* XIX

36 ≟ *NÁ-BAL> BH נָבָל prop. name I Sam 25:25 etc., > √ נבל 'foolish', i.e. "soft-pate": ↓ VI p. 44f. n. 3 for μώριος 'mushroom' and μωρία 'folly', and cp. μαλάχη, μολόχη, 'Mallow', ↓ X n. 24); ˢᵉᵐBAL palukku 'Ferula' (= νάρθηξ ↑ II n. 1) <*BAL-UGU/AGA "drill-crown" i.e. the 'bit' or 'glans penis' > BALAG 'penis', cp. BALAG-NAR 'eroticist'; Sum BAL as 'boring' insect: UḪ-TI-BAL (= UḪ-GIŠ-ÙR-RA "roof-beam worm") = AN-TI-BAL bulṭittu, balṭitu 'woodworm'; cp. βωλίτης Lat Boletus <*ᵘBAL-TI/TI-BAL; cp. Ballote = Porrum nigrum, 'Black Leek' (Dsc III 103 Pl NH XXVII 54); NH Aram בָּלוּט 'acorn, oak'. *ᵘBAL 'mushroom' ?>BH עֹפֶל 'mound; haemorrhoid' (for mushroom connections in I Sam 5:5, see R. Graves, 'What Food the Centaurs Ate' in Steps, 1958, p. 335, suggesting that the votive haemorrhoids of the Philistines were "golden mushrooms"; cp. Pl NH XXII 98 for reputed value of hog fungi for clearing "fleshy growths of the anus"); BH אָבֵל, prop. name 'Abel' (the 'stem' of the cap, 'Cain' ↓ XII n. 2); ὀβελός 'spit, skewer, nail' (cp. Lat subula 'small weapon, awl', like פלשׁ, ܦܠܚ, Acc palâšu 'bore, break through', ?<*ŠU-BAL (ŠU emph.) dist. fr. ŠU-BAL šupêlu 'change') ; as a 'spindle-plant' cp. Διὸς ἡλακάτη = Περιστερεὼν ὕπτιος 'Holy Plant' (Ps-Dsc IV 60); as a 'mound' (as עפל), cp. βούνιον = Περιστερεὼν ὀρθός (Ps-Dsc IV 59); as a semi-precious stone (from colouring) > Opalus 'Opal' (↓ XIV p. 126 n. 39); as 'navel': ὀμφαλός 'navel, knob, boss', etc. ?<*UG(U)-BAL "crown of drill" i.e. as a whorl ? cp. Sum ᵘᶻᵘ LI-DUR abunnatu 'navel', where LI = 'hemisphere, cone' (↑ II n. 2); Acc abunnatu ?<AGÀN 'female breast' (*Á-GAN ↓ XIV p. 121 n. 16) >BH אַגָּן 'bowl, basin' Arab جِنَّةٌ أُ 'ball of cheek', etc.; BH שׁוֹר (Ezek 16:4; Ct 7:3 ‖ בטנך (LXX ὀμφαλός σου) < SUR 'spindle' (prop. 'whorl': id. �}), cp. MUG 'thread' (prop. 'spindle': id. ⟶Þ), ˡᵘ MUG 'artisan' (i.e. driller ? cp. NAGAR, Acc nagâru, Aram נַגָּרָא, etc., prop. turner ? <NA₄ 'stone' + GUR 'turn' ↓ XII n. 43), ˢᵉᵐ MUG pallukku 'Ferula' (<*BAL-UGU); Sum MUG ?<MULU, MÚL 'star' (cp. ἀστήρ <AŠTAR 'bolt' ↓ V n. 18) ?<MÙ 'grind' + LI 'knob' i.e. pestle, + UGU 'crown' giving *MUL-UGU abbrev. to MUG and ?>μύκης 'mushroom, any knobbed body, penis', etc. For the abbreviation, cp. Sum BULUG >Lat bucca 'cheek' (BH פלח 'mill stone, pomegranate skin, human temple' (↓ VI n. 38), but abbrev. to פֶּקַעֲה 'mushroom' < BALAG-GA/BULUG-GA ↓ V n. 18; Acc bukannu 'pestle' ?<*BULUG-AN-NA "raised penis".

For BALAG and der. = phallus (φαλλός <*BAL-UŠ 'erect borer') ↓ X p. 86; as > πληγή, Lat plaga ↓ X p. 86, and for MUG = glans penis, cp. ἀμυγδάλη 'almond' ↓ VIII n. 37.

27. Cp. Sum UMUN *bêlu* and UMUN *reḫû* 'beget'; κύριος 'lord' <*GÚ-RI-UŠ 'erect penis' > KUR₄ 'be dominant' ↑ n. 24; Sum NUN (?<NU₅-NU₅ "seeder") *rabû* 'prince'; Lat *magister, magester* 'master, chief, superintendent, etc. ?<MAḪ 'great' + AŠTAR 'penis; bolt' (<*UŠ-TAR), i.e. "big-penis"; Lat *dux* 'leader' ?<ŠUDÚG *pašišu* 'anointed' (= משיח) ?<DÙG 'penis; favour' + ŠÚ 'pour out' ↓ n. 36; VII n. 26.

28. ↓ VII p. 60.

29. See Ps 19:5f. לְשֶׁמֶשׁ שָׂם־אֹהֶל בָּהֶם: וְהוּא כְּחָתָן יֹצֵא פֵחֻפָּתוֹ LXX: καὶ αὐτὸς ὡς νυμφίος ἐκπορευόμενος ἐκ παστοῦ αὐτοῦ. Cp. Ὑπερίων 'Hyperion' ?<*U₅-BÁR-IÀ-U₅-NÁ 'fecundator of the womb' ↑ II n. 25.With παστός = παστάς II 'bridal chamber, bed'; παστάς I 'porch, colonnade' ?<*PEŠ(₄)-TU "womb-entrance", cp. BH אֵילָם (= אוּלָם) 'porch' ?<*É-LAM "house of meeting, copulation" (↓ n. 31); cp. ἠλέκτωρ '(shining) sun' ?<*É-LAM-TUR₅ "enterer of the porch (place of copulation)". Cp. Sum ᵈUTU (= ⁱˡŠamaš) ?<*U₅-TU "fecundator"; ↓ XV p. 135 n. 16.

30. See K. Möhlenbrink *Der Tempel Salomos*, 1932; C. Watzinger *Denkmaler Palästinas* I, 1933, pp. 88–95; G. E. Wright *The Biblical Archaeologist* iv. 2 (May 1941); W. F. Albright *Archaeology and Religion of Israel*[4], 1956, pp. 142ff. For the cosmic significance of the parts of the Temple, see Jos *Ant* III 180f.

31. אֵילָם n. 29; cp. אתוק (Kt; Qre אַתִּיק) Ezek 41:15, 16 ?<*É-DÙG "house of the penis," i.e. vagina (cp. Sum É-UŠ-GÍD-DA ("house of the stretched penis") 'granary'); BH מִפְתָּן 'threshold' ?<*GIB-TUR₅ "barrer of the entrance"; BH סַף 'threshold, sill', Aram סִפָּא etc. Acc *sippu* 'corner stone' (= Sum ZAG-DU₈) < ZAG *idu, aḫu* 'side'; *miṣru* 'frontier', etc., ?<*ZÁ-AGA/UGU "crown-stone", thus, probably, the key-stone of the arch and thus representing the entrance generally and the dividing mark or barrier between inside and outside. For ZAG in its proper "crown-stone" sense, extended to the head, glans penis, etc., cp. Sum SAG 'head' (= ZAG ?); Sum ᶻᵃNA-ZAG-ḪI-LI(-ŠAR) *elît urṣi* 'pestle', properly, "stone of the erect penis", cp. ZAG-ḪI-LI Acc *siḫlu* 'cress' (aphrodisiac, being a 'hot' plant) – ḪI-LI (LI = ÈN 'seed'), "run away seed, sperm" = Acc *kuzbu* 'lust' – and Ú-ZUG (? <*ZA-UGU, and U by assimil. from I 'raise') > Acc *usukku* 'prostitute' ("penis-raiser": cp. AN-ZÍB *id*); similarly derived BH שׂ/צחק, 'sport' (esp. Gen 26:8 of Isaac and Rebekah; cp. שׂמח 'rejoice' ?<*ZÁ-MAḪ (= Acc *aban rāmi* 'love stone' i.e. a talisman for inducing sexual desire),

cp. prop. name יִצְחָק יִשְׂחָק, 'Isaac' ? <*I-ZAG "raised penis" = mushroom top, as 'Jacob' is the stem, <*IA₄-Á-GUB "standing-stone" ↓ XV p. 138; cp. Isa 5:7 (Song of the Vineyard) ויקו למשפח והנה משפח לצדקה והנה צעקה (for משפח and the "scabby" epithet of the fungus, ↓ XIV pp. 124f.) and with צעקה (? צחקה) cp. Arab صاعقة 'thunderbolt' and Κεραύνιον 'mushroom', Thphr I vi 5. Cp. Sum ZAG-MÍN (= GIN 'erect') 'praise' (as sexually stimulating, ↓ X pp. 84f.). For further 'raised-head, phallus' epithets in names, cp. 'Goliath' (?<*GUL-IA₄-TI ↑ II n. 17) where GUL<*GÚ-UŠ "erect head") and Dionysiac title Ἴαχος (*IA₄-GUŠ) = Ζαγρεύς (<*ZAG-RI-UŠ "erect head" i.e. glans penis): CGS v p. 129. (Ἴαχος = BH יָקוּשׁ, 'stumbling-block' i.e. knobbed bolt, ↓ VI pp. 44ff.). Cp. also Σαβάζιος (<*SIPA-ZI(-UŠ) "erect phallus"), ↑ I n. 2; and ↑ n. 23.

For ZAG/SAG "head, beginning", cp. ZAG-MU(G) (↑ n. 26) zagmukku, rêš šatti 'New Year', and cp. BH and cogn. ראש, 'head, beginning' ?<*RÁ-UŠ "erect-penis".

For ZAG as "boundary mark" (Acc miṣru), cp. BULUG pulukku 'frontier' (properly "penis" ↑ n. 26), kudurru (<*KI-DUR; cp. KI-SUR(-RA) kisurru 'frontier', properly, "circumscribed place", ↓ XVI n. 11). Thus, ZAG gives words associated with the idea of 'sanctuary': Sum AZAG 'taboo' (*Á-ZAG "something restricted, circumscribed"; cp. Á-ZÀG asakku 'demon'); É-AZAG bît asakki 'sanctuary', and with similar meanings: ZAG, ZAG-DINGIR = UZUG, ZAG-GAN, É-ZAG-GAR-RA, Acc ašertu (BH˙ & cogn. אשׁור 'step' <*Á-SUR); with UZUG cp. SUG(-KU) parakku ('sanctuary) = فِرَك, BH פָּרֹכֶת 'curtain (of Temple) <BARAG, BÁR(A) > BH פרק 'separate'. From ZAG also Lat sanctus, sanctum 'holy place, sanctuary'; and UZUG > σηκός Dor σακός, 'pen, fold', II 'sacred enclosure'; and from Sum BARA-SIG₅ (Acc barasigû) 'chapel', properly "enclosure of favour", by transp. σαβαρίχις, σαβαρίχη 'female genitals' and cp. φράξις, φάρξις 'fencing, barricade' ?<BARA-SIG₅ + determ. GIŠ.

For ZAG as "restricted place" in smaller dimensions, cp. BH שַׂק 'sack' Gen. 4:27 (LXX μάρσιππος <*MAR-SIPA "penis-sheath" i.e. vagina; cp. Sum AL-KAD₍₅₎ ("tied") 'sack' = Acc azamillu, ?<*AZAG-ILLU "semen-container" i.e. womb, vagina, or testicle, scrotum, cp. DUGGAN 'wallet' = testicle ↑ II p. 14 n. 9. Also from ZAG, BH & cogn. גַּ 'grape-skin' Num 6:4 (+ חַרְצַנִּים ?<ḤAR 'husk, pod' + ZANGA (<ZAG-GA) ṣaḫâtu 'squeeze out'; cp. Sum ᵘᶻᵘ SUḪ-BAR-SÌL "lips of the groin, womb" i.e. vulva, = Acc ḫarḫazinnu, ?<*ḤAR-ḤAR-ZANGA); cp. BH אִזֵּק 'fetter' (Jer 40:1 'manacles') = Aram עִזְקָא 'fetter' also 'ring, anus' <*Á-ZAG. Cp. Sum

ZANGA as "threshold" of the mouth, 'toothgum', Acc *kanzuzu* <*GAN-ZU-ZU); as meaning *ṣaḥâtu* 'press out, express'; BH יצק 'pour out (oil in anointing)' ?<*IÀ- ZAG "express-juice, oil, etc." ‖ צוק; Hiph צוק = Arab ضاق 'be narrow, compressed'. > SANGA *šangu* 'priest' (id. = LAG *lâšu* 'knead') and SANGÁ *mullilu* 'purification priest' = ÍL-MÁ-SIG₇-SIG₇; cp. GA-MÁ-SIG₇-MAḪ *sangamaḫḫu* 'high priest', where GA = *šizbu* 'milk', cp. *šuzbu* = Sum ŠUZBU, SUSBU, *ramku* 'purification priest' (id. = SUḪ 'extract'), ?<* SUḪ-ZÍB "extract (semen from) penis". ↓ IX p. 76. Cp. GA-ZUM *mašâdu* 'squeeze' and ZUM *šassuru* 'womb' (<ŠÀ-SUR, 'vulva; larva') and *ḫâlu* 'exude sweat' (cp. *ḫîlu* 'sweat, resin, semen', etc. <E₄-LA₆ = ILLU ↑ n. 1); cp. BH & cog. כּוֹמֶר 'idol-priest', ?<*KU-MAR "anus-womb", i.e. sodomite, cp. Sum UŠ-KU "penis-anus" = GALA ('womb'), *kalû* 'priest'.

  Cp. νάρθηξ 'Ferula' (<*MAR-DÙG, "womb-favourer," i.e. penis, ↑ II n. 1); casket for unguents; forecourt of a church; cp. βακχεῖον = τελεστήριον 'place of Bacchic initiation' = νάρθηξ (Hsch); cp. νυμφών 'bridal chamber' (Matt 9:15), II 'temple of Dionysus, Demeter, Persephone'.

32. BH פרכת, ↑ n. 31.

33. BH הֵיכָל<É-GAL, *êkallu*.

34. ναός 'temple, innermost shrine', ?<*U₅-NÁ "womb", cp. Ù-NÁ *na'âlu* 'sleep, have coitus'. See M Nidd 2:5: "The sages spoke in a parable about a woman: (there is in her) a Chamber (חדר), Ante-Chamber (פרוזדור) and Upper Chamber (עליה)—blood in the חדר is unclean; if it is formed in the פרוזדור its condition of doubt is deemed unclean, since it is presumed to be from the fount (מקור)."

35. BH כֹּהֵן <ˡᵘGÚ-EN-NA "man of the depository of seed" (↓ VII p. 58) = Acc *šandabakku*, ?<*ŠEN-DA-BALAG "womb-penis"; cp. BH גֹּרֶן, 'threshing floor, granary' <*GUR₇-ÈN-NA = GÚ-EN-NA *qadûtu* 'depot'; É-UŠ-GÍD-DA (↑ n. 31) "house of the stretched penis" = Acc *araḫḫu* 'granary', ?<*Á-RAG-GA "womb"; cp. Sum AGRIG *abaraqqu* 'steward (of temple, palace)'; Sum & Acc ?<ANBAR (>AB-BA 'father, protector' ↓ XVII n. 54) + ÁG *râmu* 'love' i.e. protector of the womb; cp. NH Aram שַׁמָּשׁ 'server, attendant, angel'; penis; fem. 'prostitute' ?<ŠEM-MAŠ (↓ VII, p. 60, n. 37) "semen"; cp. ˢᵉᵐ ᵈMAŠ *nikiptu* 'styrax' and similarly of resins as 'semen': ERI₄-AN-NA ("semen of heaven") *maštakal* (<*MAŠ-DA-A-KAL "fecundity-juice") = A-RI-A-NAM-LÚ-ULÙˡᵘ

"semen-of-mankind"; cp. AŠ *pašâšu* 'anoint' with ú AŠ *edu* 'Assa', ú AŠ-PI-PI *aštabelu* 'Assa Foetida'; ᵈ AŠ = *il Aššur*.

36. ↓ VII pp. 58f.; BH מָשִׁיחַ ?<*MAŠ-IÀ, ↑ n. 35: = ŠUDÚG (↑ n. 27) *pašišu* 'anointed' <BA-ŠÉŠ (*pašâšu*); cp. Ì(-BA)-ŠÉŠ, *piššatu* 'unction'; ŠÉŠ ?<ŠE₈-ŠE₈> ŠÈŠ, ŠEŠ₄ *bakû* 'weep', *pašâšu* 'rub, anoint'; AŠ *pašâšu* and ú AŠ 'resin' ↑ n. 35; *AŠ-IÀ ?> Aram חַסְיָא 'holy', cp. Sum MAŠ *ellu* 'pure', ˡú MAŠ-MAŠ *mašmašu* 'exorcist' (= ˡú ŠEM-MÚ *âšipu*; cp. ˡú ŠEM *muraqqu* 'perfumier'). For χρῖσμα <ŠEM-ḪAL, "running semen, resin" ↑ II n. 20; cp. χυλός 'juice' <ḪAL; cp. ŠEM, ŠEM₄ *ḫalḫallatu* 'lamentation-drum' cp. ISÍŠ/ÉR-ŠÈM-MA *ḫalḫallatu* 'lamentation'.

37. Probably annually as in the Jewish Day of Atonement: Lev 16: 12–16, cp. Heb 9: 25.

38. ↓ VIII p. 69, for a clear fertility reference in the Easter Saturday ritual.

39. Cp. Isa 62:4ff.; Jer 2:2.

40. Cp. Jer 2:32ff.; Hos 2, 3, etc.

41. ÁŠ, ÁŠ-BAL ("pour out seed") *arâru* 'curse' (also *ṣibûtu* 'desire'); ú ÁŠ-DUG₄-GA *arâru* 'opium poppy' (cp. GÌŠ-DUG₄-GA "penis-speak" i.e. eject sperm (Acc *reḫû* 'fecundate'); for AŠ "semen" ↑ n. 36. For √ ארר 'curse'; <A-RI-A *ḫarâbu* 'go to waste' > ÁR *karmu* 'wasteland' > ἀρά 'curse' and ʾApá the goddess of destruction, revenge; cp. ἐρῆμος 'desert', ?<ÁR.

For √ קלל 'curse': < GIL *ḫalâqu* 'destroy'; cp. GUL *abâtu* 'perish'; for *ḫalâqu* 'destroy' ḪA-LAM, ↓ VII n. 8. Cp. BH חֵטְא, ?<*ḪE-ÈN>*ḪEN = ḪI-LI *kuzbu* lust ("ejection of seed") + DA (cp. ŠE-BI-DA *ḫîṭu* 'sin'); for ḪEN cp. ḪENBÚR (= ŠE-DÙ-A "seed-create"), = Acc *abaḫšinnu* (?<*AB-ḪA-ŠEN/SÍN i.e. AB-SÍN 'furrow, ear of corn' + ḪA = plural) 'shoot, sprout'; cp. BH חִטָּה 'wheat' (Aram חנטין, חטתא Arab حِنْطَة) ?<*ḪEN-DA/DÙ; cp. Sum god-name ḪENDUR (= *il Išum* = ᵈ ALAD, *il šêdu* 'protecting genius') ?<ḪEN-DÚR "establisher of ejected seed".

Cp. BH √ חנט 'spice, embalm' (NH 'bud, blossom'; Arab حنط 'become mature'; cp. Sum GIŠIMMAR-U₄-ḪI-IN *uḫênu* 'as yet unripened dates' (for sun-ripening), ?<*ḪEN-DA i.e. giving the dead the 'seed of life' ↓ VII p. 57, n. 23.

Cp. BH & cogn. √ חנן 'be gracious', חֵן 'grace', < ḪEN.

42. אֹמֶן, ?<*U₅-NÁ-NÁ "the fecundator: ejector of seed" >BH אוֹן 'vigour, wealth' ↓ VII n. 8; cp. ὄναρ 'dream'.

43. סְדֹם, ?<* SÌ sapânu 'cast down, destroy' + DÙG dumqu 'favour, sperm'; cp. עמרה 'Gomorrah', ?<*GUM-ÚR-RA "masturbate" ? ↑ II n. 19.

44. √ אמן 'faithful, sure, dependable' <*Á-GIN 'upright' (<GI-NA = Acc kânu, BH etc. כּוּן, בֵּן 'upright, honest'): cogn. with BH יָמִין Acc imnu 'right' = Sum Á-ZI-DA (>ZID kênu 'faithful, sure') > BH חָסִיד 'faithful', חֶסֶד 'covenant fidelity, love'; also = Sum UIA 'fecundity' (= god-name Ištar, ↑ III n. 1) and 'right' - as the more effective, fruitful part of the womb? Cp. Pl NH VII 37: "movement in the womb is more frequent in the case of males, and males are usually carried on the right side, females on the left." XI 210: "pregnant cows carry in the right cavity of the womb;" ↓ n. 46.

45. BH & cogn. √ עקר 'barren', ?<AGARGARÁ 'foetus' ('spawn'); 'defecation' <G/MAR "womb, container" (> Ἀγαρικόν, Agaricum, 'Agaric; fungus' the purge); cp. "Satan" (BH שָׂטָן, Arab شَيْطَان, Σατανᾶς = ὁ διάβολος 'the adversary' = "the aborter": ?<*ŠÈ-TÙN "abort-womb", and in excretory sense, cp. related BH פַּרְשְׁדֹנָה Judg 3:22, ?<*BAR-ŠÈ-TÙN; cp. Sum ŠÈ-BAR-RA ṣanâḫu 'have diarrhoea' (dist. fr. Setanium 'onion' = "seed-container" (vulva-plant), ?<ŠE-TÙN ↓ VI n. 15).

     Cp. Aram אַרְמְלָא, وأَرمَلة' (BH אַלְמָנָה, Acc almattu) 'widow', ?<*ÁR-GALA "wasted-womb" (↓ VIII n. 26, on Rue).

46. BH and cogn. שְׂמֹאל 'left', ?<SIG enêšu 'feeble' + ÙŠ 'foetus'; cp. σκαιός 'left', ?<SI-GAR 'bolted, barred' (BH & cogn. סגר, סכר); cp. Lat sinistrum 'left,' ?<*SIG-ÙŠ-TAR "feeble-womb"; ἀριστερός 'left', ?<*ÁR-ÙŠ-TAR "wasted, desolate womb"; opp. dextera, dextra, δεξιός, ?<*DÍM-ÙŠ-TAR "creative-womb" ↑ n. 44. Cp. Sum 𒐖𒌋𒌋𒌋 (= Acc šumêlu 'left') ≟ MIN + BÀ "the other half", a euphemism?

47. ↑ n. 41.

48. Cp. Galen NF I vi 1: κατα βληθέντος δὴ τοῦ σπέρματος εἰς τὴν μήτραν ἢ εἰς τὴν γῆν, οὐδὲν γὰρ διαφέρει . . .

49. Lev. 19:18; Prov 15:1.

50. σώζω = √ ישע & cogn. <ŠÚ-ŠÚ> ŠÚŠ gamâlu 'be favourable, preserve' (BH √ גמל 'deal fully, requite; ripen (fruit)'); ↑ n. 1; ↑ II n. 1.

51. יֵשׁוּעַ, יְהוֹשׁוּעַ, Ἰησοῦς, <*IÀ-U₅-ŠÚ-A; prev. n. and refs. and ↓ IV p. 35.

52. "respice post te, hominem te memento" (Juvenal X 41).

53. See W. R. Smith *Religion of the Semites*³, 1927, pp. 458ff.

54. Gen 9:4; cp. Pl *NH* XI 181 for blood as *vitae causam et originem*—when shed, it draws the breath (*spiritum*) with it (XI 221).

55. Lev 9:9.

56. Lev 10:14.

CHAPTER IV

Plants and Drugs

1. Thphr IX x 4; Dsc IV 162; Pl *NH* XXV 47.

2. Sum A-ZU, Ì-ZU ("water/oil-expert"), *asû* (Aram אסיא) 'physician' cp. Arab حكيم 'wise man, doctor'.

3. See S. N. Kramer, in *Illustrated London News* Feb 26, 1955, pp. 370ff.; *History Begins at Sumer*, N.Y. 1956, London 1958, pp. 100–4, 327–28.

4. περὶ φυτῶν ἱστορία, edd. J. G. Schneider (and Linck), Leipzig, i–iv, 1818; v, 1821; Kurt Sprengel, Halle, 1822; Fr. Wimmer, Breslau, 1842; in Loeb, A. Hort, 2 vols., 1916.

5. *De Materia Medica* (Περὶ ὕλης ἰατρικῆς) i–v; ed. M. Wellmann, 3 vols., Berlin, 1907–14.

6. *Naturalis Historia*, edd. D. Detlefsen, Berlin, 1866; L. von Jan (Teubner), re-ed. K. Mayhoff, 2 vols., 1905, 1909; in Loeb, H. Rackham & ors., 10 vols., 1938–62.

7. *War* II 136.

8. *Ant* VIII 45ff.

9. *Ant* VIII 46f.

10. Sesamoides was added "for safety": Dsc IV 159, cp. Pl *NH* XXII 133; XXV 52.

11. See Allegro *JSS* ix (1964) pp. 291–94, *DJD V*, 1968, 4Q 186 (pl. XXXI) pp. 88–91.

12. 1QS iv 7-8; 9-11: *The Dead Sea Scrolls from St Mark's Monastery*, ed. M. Burrows, ii 2, New Haven, 1951.

13. *NH* XXV 13.

14. Sum A-ZU, Ì-ZU, *asû* 'doctor', *bârû* 'seer' ≟ 'Εσσαῖος, 'Εσσηνός, etc., ↓ XVII n. 86.

15. δαίμων (LXX for BH שֵׁד, אֱלִיל) 'divine power, deity', etc, ?<*DA-IÀ-U₅-NÁ "having power over fertility" > Zend *daēwa*, Pers دیو pl. دیوان *dēwân* 'demons'; ݂ذُمِ 'evil spirit, devil'; cp. BH דַּוָּי 'faint', Arab √ دوی, دَوَاء 'medicine', ?<*DA-UIA, and, transposed *IÀ-U₅-DA >BH prop. name יְהוּדָה 'Judah' (and יָד 'hand' = ἰῶτα; prop. "phallus" ↓ XVI n. 25).

16. Jos *War* II 142.

17. Jos *War* VIII 45f.

18. BH יַיִן ?<*oiyan = οἶνος, vinum, ?<*UIA-NU; cp. Διόνυσος (?<*IÀ-U₅-NU-ŠÚŠ ↑ III n. 1) = οἶνος, Orphica *Fragmenta* 216 (ed. O. Kern, Berlin, 1922). Cp. Sum ú NAM-TÌL-LA ("life-plant, drug") 'Opium poppy'.

19. ↑ III nn. 50, 51.

CHAPTER V

Plant Names and the Mysteries of the Fungus

1. *NH* XXV 29.

2. IV 75.

3. III iii 331.

4. *NH* XXIV 29.

5. *NH* XXV 16.

6. *NH* XXV 29.

7. ↑ II n. 25.

8. κοτυληδών 'cup-shaped hollow or cavity' (hip-joint, etc.); *Cotyledon Umbilicus* Dsc IV 91, 92; Pl *NH* XXV 159, etc. ?<*GÚ-TAL-Ù-DUN "head-and-socket", cp. alternative name of the plant σκυτάλιον (Dsc IV 91) and cp.

σκυταλή 'cudgel' ?<*SI-GÚ-TAL "knobbed-horn"; cp. σκυταλίας ('cudgel-shaped') = σίκυος 'gourd' (Thphr VII iv 6) <*SI-GÚ-A (= GÚL as in SAG-GÚL 'bolt'; <GÚ-UŠ ↑ III n. 31). For a similar phrase-word, cp. μαγύδαρις, part of Silphium (Thphr VI iii 4, Dsc III 80, etc.) ?<*GAG-Ù-DAR "bolt-and-socket"; cp. also BAram תקל ופרסין Dan 5:25 etc. ↓ VI pp. 45f.

For a biblical play on a Semitic form of *GÚ-TAL-Ù-DUN, cp. II Kgs 9:30 הֲרֹג אֲדֹנָיו, for "א קְטַל ? ? ↓ XVIII p. 185; and unintentionally, Pl XIII 129 of the parasite growing on thorn-bushes *Athenis in longis muris*, ?<כּוֹתָל אַתוּנָא 'wall of Athens', ↓ XIII pp. 110f.: and possibly in the description of *Aizoüm*, 'House-leek' (also called ἐριθαλές, ?<ערדילא ('mushroom' ERI4-TÌL-LA ↓ n. 18): ἐπὶ τῶν τειχῶν ἀνδηρόις ?<כותלא אדמתנא "earthy walls". For a NT play on קטל and איתון 'entrance' (of Temple), ↓ VI n. 42. For the forcible disruption of the joint as "crucifixion" ↓ XII p. 106.

9. ↓ XII pp. 103f.

10. BH אָטָד (= Sum ú GÍR = ATTU, giš ÁD Acc *iṭṭidu* 'buckthorn') ?<AD-AD "mighty father" (cp. il *Adad* = d ISKUR "big-penis" ↑ III n. 5), here = 'phallic mushroom' ↑ III n. 21. For other examples of confusion between the fungus and the thorn, cp. the 3-day Bacchic festival of Anthesterion, when the votaries were said to chew 'buckthorn'! (↓ XVII pp. 155ff.), and Pliny's "royal thorn" of Babylon ↑ n. 8. In the 'thorn' allusions in the sacred mushroom, *Amanita muscaria*, there is a reference to the bitter taste (↓ XVII pp. 156ff.), cp. Sum AL-UŠ-SA ("erect-piercer") *šikku* (BH & cogn. שֵׁךְ 'thorn'), 'alum? pickle?' (as sharp-tasting).

11. For "protective" significance of lordship, ↓ XV n. 4; XVIII p. 178.

12. BH קִיקָיוֹן <*GIG-IÀ-U5-NÁ "pod-of-fecundity" i.e. womb, comparable with Sum ŠE-GIG ("seed-pod") 'wheat'; GIG-GÍR *uṭṭetu* 'grain' (of wheat); cp. *ciccos*, κίκκος 'membrane' (around grains of a pomegranate); Lat *cicer* 'chick-pea' (see Pl *NH* XVIII 124 = "dove-pea" (*columbinum*, ↓ n. 13 for 'dove') or "Venus-pea" (*Venerium*, ↑ III n. 1 for 'Venus'), ". . . bright, white, round, smooth . . . used in watch night service rituals") <GIG "pod"; cp. NU-GIG (= NU-MAŠ, "seed-, sperm-pod" i.e. womb) *ištaritu* 'cult-prostitute' (<*ÙŠ-TAR "womb" > goddess *Ištar* (Sum UIA)); Sum GIG <GI6-GI6 and> GÍG *ṣalāmu* 'shade' i.e. make a covering or protection (>GEME, MÍ 'womb'; cp. μήτρα, *matrix*, ?<*MÉ-TAR/TÙR as in ŠÀ-TÙR *šaturru* 'womb; larva'; Aram קוּקְיָאנֵי 'parasite worms' is comparable in origin, <*GUG ("pod") – IÀ-U5-NÁ "womb" as larvae). Cp. ὤκιμον

'Basil', ?<*ú GIG; cp. Pl *NH* XIX 119: "seeds covered with a skin" (↓ VIII n. 16); from "pod" or "uterus" shape, NH Aram קיקין *Ricinus communis* Linn. (Löw *Pfl* i pp. 609ff.) = κίκι, κίκινον, Egyp. *k3k3*; cp. שֶׁמֶן קִיק M. Sabb 2:1; ↓ XI p. 96; = κρότωνος ῥίζα (Gal XIX 115; Thphr I x 1); cp. κροτών, *croton* 'tick', Syr ܩܸܪ̈ܛܵܢܵܐ 'Ricinus'; ܩܸܪ̈ܛܵܢܵܐ 'tick' (the *Ricinus* being so called "because of the resemblance of the seed pod to that insect" – the seed-pod being "like a slender grape of pale colour" (Pl *NH* XV 25); κροτών ?<*GÚR-TÙN "womb-pod" = Γόρτυν, Gortyn(a), the town in Crete where stood the famous plane tree (XII n. 40) in whose shade Zeus impregnated Europa (Pl *NH* XII 11) = μύρτον 'myrtle berry; vulva'.

With BH קיקין cp. Lat *ciconia* 'stork', as a "womb-bird" ↓ XI p. 96; and/or derived from the shape of the mushroom, cp. *ciconia* 'a 'T-' shaped implement used for measuring furrows'; and for shape factor, cp. Aram צלוליבא 'little cross' = mushroom and transferred to the Ricinus (see Löw *Pfl* p. 610) ↓ XII n. 72. For the mushroom as a 'volva' plant, ↓ XI pp. 91ff. and Pl *NH* XXII 93f.; similarly the Carob, Acc *šam ḫarûbu*, NH חרוב and cogn. <*ḪAR-UB "hollow-pod" > ḪARUB 'ant' (i.e. larva insect) and (via *GAR-UB ?) > MURUB 'vulva', cp. Arab خَرُب 'anus', خَرَبَة 'sieve; vulva'; cp. the goddess Καλυψώ (?<*GAR-UB-ŠÚ "fructified-womb") who gave Hermes Nectar and Ambrosia, *Od* 5.93; and χάρυβδις (?<*GAR-UB-TÌL/TÉŠ "womb-of-life/sex"), the vortex opposite Σκύλλα "Scylla" (?<*SI-GÙL-LA "knobbed-bolt" i.e. the phallus ↑ n. 8.

Of the Carob, the pods were "not longer than a man's finger, and occasionally curved like a sickle, with the thickness of a man's thumb" (Pl *NH* XV 95). For Carob as synonymous with the mushroom, cp. Sum ᵘERI₄-TÌL-LA ("semen-of-life") = Acc *ḫarûbu*, hardly the *Ceratonia siliqua*! Cp. the purposeful play on the name in Enoch 32:3ff. in describing the "tree of life" with "leaves like a carob" (↓ XVII p. 155).

For Lat *siliqua* 'pod': ?<*SILA-GU "groin/womb-pod"; by transposition, ?>Σεμέλη (i.e. *silagu>*simalu> Σεμέλη), mother of Dionysus.

For the "doves' dung" of II Kgs 6:25: ?<*ḪAR-IÀ-U₅-NÁ = *BÁR-IÀ-U₅-NÁ (= Παιωνία ↑ II n. 25) "container-of-fecundity" i.e. the womb, and thus = "Carob".

13. BH יוֹנָה 'dove' <*IÀ-U₅-NÁ "fecundity" as in *BÁR-IÀ-U₅-NÁ = βαριωνᾶ Matt 16:17 and Παιωνία ↑ II n. 25. Cp. Περιστερεών 'Holy Plant' and περιστερά 'dove' <*BÁR-ÙŠ-TAR "womb" (on "womb-birds" ↓ XI), hence the dove is the bird of Venus (↑ III n. 1), cp. Διώνη, Dione ?<*IÀ-U₅-NÍ

"fecundity", and *Dionaeus* (*columba*: Statius, P. Papinius, *Silvae* 3, 5, 80); as the bird of fertility, cp. Sum TU-MUŠEN = Acc *summatu* (?<ZUM 'womb'); cp. Pl *NH* X 107 of pigeons and turtle-doves, "the equal of sparrows in salaciousness": cp. BH צִפּוֹר and cogn. *ŠEN-BUR₅ "womb-bird" = στρουθίον <*ÙŠ-TAR-TU "fecund-womb" = τρυγών 'turtle-dove' ?<*ÙŠ-TAR-UGÙN "fecund, pregnant-womb".

Cp. also BH גּוֹזָל 'young of birds' ?<*GÚ-ZAL "white-pod" i.e. egg, and cp. Acc *pilû* 'egg' and = Mandrake (Sum NAM-TAR pp. 41f.).

14. ↓ XIII pp. 115ff.

15. In southern Mexico recent study of the religious use of hallucinogenic mushrooms has identified at least 20 species, belonging to *Conocybe, Panaeolus, Psilocybe, Stropharia,* and most important, *Psilocybe mexicana*; see R. Heim and R. G. Wasson, *Les Champignons Hallucinogenes du Mexique* (Editions, Museum d'Histoire Naturelle, Paris, 1958); for the drugs involved, see A. Hofmann in *Chemical Constitution and Pharmocodynamic Action*, ed. A. Burger, New York, 1968, p. 169.

16. There seems good reason to believe that the religious cult of the *soma* plant, subject of more than a hundred hymns in the Rig Veda, centred on the *Amanita muscaria* (↑ II n. 1; cp. the Pers *samārûḥ* 'mushroom' and the Magian name ζωμαρῖτις for "Hellebore": ?<*ŠÚ-MAR, of which perhaps the Rig Veda's *soma* is an abbreviation.

In Guatemala, "mushroom stones" may perhaps point to the existence of a sacred fungus cult some 3,500 years ago. In more recent times the use of the mushroom as an inebriant has centred in two main centres: extreme western Siberia, among the Finno-Ugrian peoples, the Ostyak and Vogul; and extreme northeastern Siberia, among the Chukchi, Koryak and Kamchadal. Among the Lapps of Inari in Europe and the Yakagir of northernmost Siberia, *Amanita muscaria* was used by the medicine-men. It has been suggested that it was this drug that gave the ancient Norsemen that maniacal fury on the battlefield called 'berserker' rage: see V.P. and R. G. Wasson, *Mushrooms, Russia and History*, New York, 1957; R. G. Wasson in *Ethnopharmalogic Search for Psychoactive Drugs* ed. D. Efron (USPHS Publication No. 1654) Washington DC (1967), p. 405; *Soma, Divine Mushroom of Immortality*, New York, 1969; R. E. Schultes "Hallucinogens of Plant Origin" in *Science* Vol. 163, No. 3864, 17 Jan. 1969, pp. 245–54.

17. BH כֹּתֶרֶת 'capital', כֶּתֶר 'crown' (Esther 1:11, 2:17, 6:8); Acc *katarru* 'mush-

room'; Neo-Syr ܟܘܡܐ 'umbrella' P-S 1860; Arab كَتَر 'higher camel's hump'; كَتَر 'dome-like structure'; Pers چتر *chatru* 'umbrella', – *mār* – of a snake = 'mushroom': <GÚ-TAR/TÁL *kutallu* 'back of the head' and so 'erect phallus' and phallic mushroom: > κίδαρις, var. κίτταρις 'a Persian headdress' = Lat *cidaris* (Vulg at Zech 3:5 BH צָנִיף 'turban' (? <SA 'tie, net' + NIGI(N) 'turn, encircle')); cp. Κυθέρια, *Cytheria*, a surname of Aphrodite, ?<GÚ-TAR i.e. "penis-raiser"; cp. Sum ŠE-IR-ZI ("grain – semen") *qutru* ('spelt' as aphrodisiac, cp. ZAG-ḪI-LI>Acc *siḫlu* 'tares' or 'cress' as sexually stimulative ↑ III n. 31) < GÚ-TAR.

18. μύκης 'mushroom' (generally), also 'any knobbed body shaped like a mush-room; fleshy excrescences, phallus' <MUL(U), MÚL ('star'), ?<MÙ 'grind' + LI 'cone' i.e. pestle head + UGU 'crown' > *MULUG>MUG (↑ III n. 26) > μύκης.

For MULU "knobbed pestle head" as 'star', cp. ἀστήρ <Sum AŠTAR 'bolt' (<*UŠ-TAR), and BH and cogn. כּוֹכָב, Acc *kakkabu* <GAG-GÀR-BA (*sikkat karri*) 'knobbed sword pommel' > ܪܹܫܡܐ 'head, summit of mountain, chief' = קַרְקְפָא 'skull head'; cp. the plant name Ἁλικακκάβα ?<*Á-RI-GAG-GÀR-BA "knobbed-bolt-plant" (= Στρύχνον ὑπνωτικόν Dsc IV 72, Pl *NH* XXI 177ff. = Δορύκνιον Dsc IV 74 = *Morion, Moly* (<Sum MULU) Pl *NH* XXI 180, etc.; cp. MUL *mulmullu* 'javelin' (as knobbed, cp. Sum GAG-KUD 'javelin' and 'key' (cp. Lat *pilum praepilatum*, a javelin with a blunt or rounded end, i.e. furnished with a *pila* ball, used in sieges; *pilum* II 'pestle') >BH קָדְקֹד, Acc *qaqqadu* 'skull').

βωλίτης, Lat *Boletus* ?<*ú BAL-TI "borer- phallus-plant" ↑ III n. 26; *Pezica* (Pl *NH* XIX 38) = Πέζις (Thphr I vi 5) = Ἀσχίον (Thphr I vi 9); Ἀγαρικόν Dsc III 1, etc. Lat *Agaricum* (Pl *NH* XX 103, etc.) ?<AGARGARÁ "purge" ↑ III n. 45; Ἀμανῖται Nic Fr. 79 ?<AGÁN (-TI) 'female breast' (from shape of cap; ↑ III n. 26; ↓ XIV n. 16; XVIII p. 179 n. 10); Ὕδνον Thphr I vi 5, 9: ?<*UD-NU₅-NU₅ > NUN "storm-seeded"; *Ceraunion* (Pl *NH* XIX 36) = Κεραύνιον 'thunder mushroom' Thphr I vi 5 = Γεράνειον Thphr I vi 5 acc. to Athenaeus 2.62a; Ἴτον, *Iton* Pl *NH* XIX 36; Μίσυ, *Misy* Pl *NH* XIX 36, Thphr *Fr* 167; *Spongiolus* Apicius Caelius 2, 1; 5, 1; 3, 20 = NH ספוֹג; Φόριγγες 'truffles' Hsch; Ἴσκαι Aëtius 7, 91, etc.; Οὔϊγγον (?) Thphr I vi 9, 11; Pl *NH* XXI 88 (*Oetum*).

For Semitic names for the mushroom in general, see Löw *Pfl* i pp. 26–44: NH Aram פּטְרָא פטריות, Arab فُطْر, ?<GÚ-TAR "glans penis" > Acc *katarru*, BH כּוֹתֶרֶת, ↑ n. 17; (by play upon פּיטְרָא ~ Πέτρος 'Peter' and perhaps

by transp. > Arab تَرْفَاس 'truffle' > French trufe, truffe, Eng "truffle");
NH כְּמֵהוּת־יִן, Arab كَمْأَة = خَدعُا, ?<*GIG-A "pod, womb" ↑ n. 12;
BH פַּקֻעֹת, Arab فِقْع, Acc piqqutu, ?<BALAG-GA/BULUG-GA "phallus"
↑ III n. 26; א/עֶרְדָּא, א/עֶרְדִּילָא, <ERI₄-TÌL-LA "semen-of-life" (Acc ḫarûbu
↑ n. 12); NH שמרקעים "that which is from heaven"; Arab قُرْحَان "scabby
one" ↓ XIV pp. 124ff.; Arab طُرْثُوث = θύρσος 'thursus' ↑ III n. 1; ↓ XVII
n. 21; <*TÙN-ŠÚS "womb-favourer"; Arab ذُوْنُوْن ?؟ Ύδνον; Arab جَبَأَة
'fungus' ?<*GÚG-A ↓ XIV p. 123 n. 23; Arab عُرْجُون; ذُعْلُوق; ذُبَح;
Pers سقراطيون saqrātiyûn ?<*UŠ-GÚ-RI (>ISKUR ↑ III n. 5) – UD "penis
of the storm" = Διόσκουροι, NT ᾽Ισκαριώθ ↓ XII p. 99 nn. 18–20; سماروخ
samārûḫ (زماروغ,سماروغ) ↑ n. 16; كشنه kašnah; كرنا karna; ا كارس akaris;
فوشنه fušina.

19. For a useful summary, see J. Ramsbottom, *Mushrooms and Toadstools*, London,
1953, ch. 3.

20. ↓ XV p. 134.

21. γίγαντες <*GÍG-AN-TI/TA "shade-of-heaven"> ᾽Αντίμιμον Ps-Dsc IV 75;
also = ᾽Ωκιμοειδές = ᾽Αμαρανθίς ↓ XV n. 14.

22. ↑ n. 18.

23. Sum UKÚŠ-TI-GIL-LA(-ŠAR) tigilû (= Aram תְּקָלָא 'stumbling-block'
↓ VI p. 45; ᵍⁱˢ GIL napraku 'bolt'; cp. SAG-GÚL(-NIM-MA) "bolt-head"
= Acc sikkûru <SI-GAR š/sigaru (BH and cogn. סגר, סכר), GAR = GÀR
as in GÀR-BA karru 'pommel' (↑ n. 18); cp. ᵍⁱˢ GAN(-NA) bukannu 'beater',
sikkûru 'bolt'; cp. BH בְּרִיחַ 'bar, bolt' <*BA-RI-GA> Acc parâku 'bar',
'make an obstacle', pirku 'bolt' (= Sum RI), Sum RI-RI-GA laqâtu 'seize'
maqâtu 'fall'; κλείς-ειδός, and κλεῖθρον 'key, bolt, bar' ?<*GIL 'bolt' +
É -TU(R)₅ "door-entrance".

For Sum UKÚŠ "gourd": <*Ú-KUŠ "skin-container plant", cp. KUŠ
zumru 'body', mašku 'skin' (? prop. "scrotum, testicle" <*MAŠ-GÚ "semen-
container" (for BH משכים in Jer 5:8?)); KUŠ-TAB-BA takâltu 'paunch,
container'; cp. κύσθος = κυσός 'vulva', κύστις 'bladder', etc., Arab كوساة 'small
gourd' <*KUŠ-TI "skin-container-organ".

UKÚŠ-TI-GIL-LA by metath. > Γλυκυσίδη = Παιωνία Dsc III 140, Pl

NH XXV 29, XXVII 84; so 'Peter' (~ פִּיטְרָא ↑ n. 18) βαριωνâ(ς) (<*BÁR-IÀ-U₅-NÁ) as the "key" (Matt 16: 18f.) ↓ VI p. 47.

24. Sum GÚL as in SAG–GÚL: ↑ n. 8; III n. 31.

25. Cp. 1QS x 4, where *Nun* "is the key of His eternal mercies", as a reference to the shape of the medial *Nun* in DSS palaeography, ∫ ; cp. W. H. Brownlee *The Dead Sea Manual of Discipline (Bulletin of the American Schools of Oriental Research,* Supp. St. 10–12) 1951, p. 39, n. 17.

26. Μανδραγόρα Thphr IX viii 8 = Belladonna, Thphr VI ii 9, etc. <Sum úNAM-TAR *namtaru, pilû* ("egg") 'Mandrake'; NAM-TAR = Acc *šimtu* 'fate'; ᵈNAM-TAR *namtaru* 'demon of death' (= Sum LÍL-LÁ-DARA, ↓ VI n. 23: cp. Νέμεσις, Nemesis ?<*NAM-ENSI (= PA-TE-SI) 'guardian-of-fate" ↓ VIII n. 63); + AGÁR 'field'. Cp. the famous Salamander, σαλαμάνδρα Lat *salamandra*: ?<SILA "womb" (>SAL-LA 'vulva') + NAM-TAR, i.e. originally the mushroom? Cp. Pl *NH* X 188ff.: "shaped like a lizard, covered with spots (↓ XIV), never appearing save in great rains and disappearing in fine weather. . . . It vomits from its mouth a milky slaver, one touch of which on any part of the human body causes all the hair to drop off, and the portion touched changes its colour and breaks out in a tetter . . . some creatures are born from parents that themselves were not born and were without any similar origin . . . some are infertile as, for instance, the salamander, and there is no male or female . . ." Cp. *NH* XXIX 74: "of all venomous creatures the salamander is the most wicked, for while others strike individuals and do not kill several together . . . the salamander can kill whole tribes unawares." Cp. Pliny on fungi, ". . . a third kind, hog fungi, have carried off whole households and all the guests at banquets", and XXII 96, "all these fungi spring up with showers". Cp. ↓ XI n. 21 for connection between the Salamander and the Phoenix bird.

27. ↑ IV p. 34.

28. On digging black Hellebore: Dsc IV 162.4: εὐχόμενοι 'Απόλλωνι καὶ 'Ασκληπιῷ (↓ XVII p. 165) Cp. Pl *NH* XXV 50: "First a circle is drawn round it with a sword; then the man who is going to cut it looks at the East with a prayer that the gods will grant him permission to do so." On gathering Anagallis: "Some instruct the diggers to say nothing until they have saluted it before sunrise, and then to gather it and extract the juice, for so they say its efficacy is at its greatest" (XXV 144f.; the real reference to the Essenes "praying to the sun as though entreating it to arise" (Jos *War* II 128) ?).

Cp. Pliny on gathering Parthenium: "the Magi recommend . . . gathering it with the left hand without looking back, while saying for whose sake it is being gathered (*NH* XXI 176). Cp. also the cutting of Cinnamon for which the god's permission was required: Thphr IX v 2; Pl *NH* XII 89f.; cp. Herodotus 3.111, and similarly of frankincense, 3. 107.

29. Cp. the similar precautions taken in ancient writings to preserve 'trade secrets'; e.g. in the seventeenth-century BC formula for glass in which all the rarest cuneiform signs were used (Gadd and Thompson *Iraq* III pp. 87–96).

30. See Allegro *The Dead Sea Scrolls*[2] (Penguin Books A 376), 1964, pp. 57ff.

31. ↓ XIX pp. 203ff.

CHAPTER VI

The Key of the Kingdom

1. ↑ V pp. 41f., n. 23.

2. ↓ VII p. 56.

3. Μώριος = Μανδραγόρα ἄρρεν Ps-Dsc IV 75; and = 'love potion' (Hsch). For relationship between 'mushroom' and 'fool', cp. Sum LIL, id. 𒇂 = Acc *lillu* 'fool' (?<LI-LI ↓ n. 16), cp. LÍL-LA-DA-RA *namtaru* 'plague demon' ↓ n. 23 (Sum NAM-TAR ↑ V p. 41 n. 26); cp. BH prop. name נָבָל 'Nabal' ?<*NÁ-BAL "boring-drill" (↑ III n. 26) and √ נבל 'be foolish'. For NT play between 'make foolish' and mushroom name *MAŠ-TAB-BA-RI(-TI), cp. I Cor 1:20: οὐχὶ ἐμώρανεν ὁ θεὸς τὴν σοφίαν τοῦ κόσμου (cp. Isa 29:14b), ܡܥܒ݂ܕ + ܒ݂ܪܝܬܐ 'Creation'.

4. Aram תְּקְלָא 'stumbling-block' תִּקְלָא 'weight' (esp. '(half-) shekel').

5. It was credited with having a womb (*volva*: Pl *NH* IX 166), spawned three times a year (66), had a "double beard on the lower lip (likened to pubic hair? 64); both sexes were "incautious in their wantonness" (59). Cp. χελών, χελών, 'kind of mullet', ?<Sum ḪAL *ḫallu* 'inner thighs' (= ḪAŠ 'thigh' and 'rub'); cp. χελών 'tortoise' and χελιδῶν 'swallow' = Sum ŠÈN-MUŠEN "womb-bird" ↓ XII n. 4.

6. *NH* XIX 35.

7. מְנִי (וַד Isa 65:11) ?<*ME-NÈ/NÍ "mighty-oracle, decision" ?>INIM *amatu*, *šiptu* 'incantation'.

8. Nic *Alex* 99–103; cp. Pausanius *Periegeta* 5.14.3; the derivation of the place name from μύκης goes back to Hecataeus (*Fr.* 360 M. cited Gow and Scholfield *Nicander* 1953, p. 192), ↓ XI n. 26.

9. ↑ V n. 8.

10. ↓ XII pp. 101ff.

11. ↑ II n. 25.

12. ↑ V n. 23.

13. For a possible misunderstanding of פִּטְרָא 'mushroom' as πέτρα 'rock', cp. Thphr IV vii 2: "when there is more rain than usual, mushrooms (μύκητες) grow in a certain place close to the sea, which are turned to stone by the sun."

14. ↑ V pp. 41f.

15. *Setanium, setania* (Pl *NH* XIX 101) = σητάνια, σητάνιον, also a kind of Medlar, Thphr II xii 5 (σατάνειος), cp. Pl *NH* XV 84; ?<*ŠE-TÙN "seed-container" (dist. fr. שָׂטָן Σατανᾶς ?<*ŠÈ-TÙN "abort-womb" ↑ III n. 45). Cp. name of Dionysus at Teos, Σητάνειος: *CGS* v p. 123.

   For Κηφᾶς (John 1:42 etc.), cp. *caepa, cepa* 'onion' ?<GÀR-BA 'pommel' ↑ V n. 18, and Aram כִּיפָא 'ball, stone' ↓XIV n. 34 (as πέτρα: ?<GÚ-TAR "phallus" > Aram פִּטְרָא 'mushroom' (↑ V n. 18); cp. βολβός, *bulbus* (= *volva*) ?<BULUG (<*BAL-UGU "crown of the borer" = glans penis ↑ III n. 26). For Lat *pallacana* 'kind of onion' (Pl *NH* XIX 105) ?<*BALAG-AN (-TA); cp. also another onion name, γήτειον, γήθυον, Thphr VII iv 8f. ?<GÚ-TAR, as above.

16. ↓ n. 23; *MAŠ-BALAG-ANTA-TAB-BA-RI, deduced from Sum ᵍᵃᵐ KUR-KUR = Acc *maštabbariru* = *šammu quddušu* 'Holy Plant' (*Maqlu* VI 85, IX 111), i.e. Sum *MAŠ-TAB-BA-RI-RI = 'Hellebore' *DAB* pp. 151ff.; Labat *Man* ※366; so Aram ܚܒ̈ܫܐ, ܢܣܘܕ̈ܚܒܐ (P-S 1366); Arab خَرِبَق, both ?<*KUR-BA(LA)G-AN(-TA) (for NT play on κορβάν, ↓ n. 41); for a parallel *MAŠ-BA(LA)G-AN(-TA), cp. NH מַסְבֵּךְ (M. Par III 3) 'cone', and ܡܨ̈ܪ:ܡܣ̈ܢܐ (P-S 4318), for *ܡܨ(ܪ):ܚܣ̈ܠܐ (*maš-ri-baḥantā*) 'spindle-whorl' (= ܦܠܟܐ P-S 3162, Arab فلك, BH פֶּלֶךְ, <BALAG (↑ III n. 26 and ↓ n. 38)); cp. also Aram ܡܨ̈ܦܚܐ 'Scammony' = Sum ᵘ LI-DUR ("navel" -plant; ↑ II n. 2), Acc *abukatu* (?<*Á-BULUG) (= Arab مَحْمُودَة as if < √ مصب 'praise': ↓ XIX n. 7) <*MAŠ-BA(LA)G (Scammony, like Agaric and Hellebore, is a purge and abortifacient: Dsc IV 170; Pl *NH* XXVI 59ff. ↑ III n. 45). For LI/RI "cone" as in ᵍⁱˢ LI 'pine' (= ŠEM-LI), LI(-'U/U₅-UM),

'tablet', etc. ↑ II n. 2. Cp. Sum UKÚŠ-LI-LI-GI *liligu* 'gourd; mushroom (?)', i.e. GI 'reed' and two 'cones' as in Sum KUR-KUR,?> Acc *kirkirânu* (= Sum ŠE-LI) 'pine-cone', and Κιρκαῖον, *Circaeon* 'Mandrake': Ps-Dsc IV75; Pl *NH* XXV 147; cp. Κίχορα, Κιχόριον (= ᾿Αναγαλλίς Dsc II 178, etc.), vars. Κόρχορον, Κορχόριον, (Pl *Acoron* = *Anagallis NH* XXV 144); cp. *Cichorium* 'Chicory' (?) (= *Chreston* Pl *NH* XX 74, ↓ p. 51; ↓ X n. 24, XIX p. 201); cp. Κρόκος, *Crocus* (Sum KUR-KUR, from 'glans-'shape).

17. *MAŠ-BA(LA)G-ANTA ∼ Aram שבק 'remit, pardon; release' (↓ n. 42) and אַנְתְּ(ה) (Heb אַתְּ(ה)), ܐܰܢ̱ܬ, 'thou'.

*TAB-BA-RI ∼ ܕܰܒ݂ܪ̈ܳܐ 'guiding, management'; ܕܘܽܒܳܪ̈ܐ 'order, rule, government'; *TAB-BA-RI(-GI, as in LI-LI-GI ↑n. 16) ∼ ܕ-ܒ݂-ܫܡܰܝܳܐ 'that which is in heaven (↓ XVI n. 16; XVII p. 159); and ܕ-ܒ݂-ܐܰܪܥܳܐ 'that which is on earth' (↓ n. 41). Cp. the Lord's Prayer: καὶ ἄφες ἡμῖν τὰ ὀφειλήματα ἡμῶν ὡς καὶ ἡμεῖς ἀφήκαμεν τοῖς ὀφειλέταις ἡμῶν ?<*LI-MAŠ-BA(LA)G-ANTA-TAB-BA-RI ܠܡܳܐ ܡܚܰܣܶܢ 'whatsoever we have remitted . . .' and ܬܶܫܒ݂ܽܘܩ thou remit'. Cp. Matt 18:21: ποσάκις ἁμαρτήσει εἰς ἐμὲ ὁ ἀδελφός μου καὶ ἀφήσω αὐτῷ ?<*LI-MAŠ-BA(LA)G-ANTA-TAB-BA-RI ܠܡܳܐ ܡܚܰܣ ܚܳܛܶܐ ܕܚܰܒ݂ܪܶܗ "how many times shall (one) forgive the sin of a companion?" (lit. 'a sinner who is a companion'); for ἕως ἑπτάκις; ?<*-BALAG-TAB-BA-RI-TI ܦܠܳܓ̈ܶܐ ܕ-ܒܪ̈ܝܳܬ݂ܐ read as 'divisions of Creation' i.e. seven: as 'days' (Gen 1:1–2:4) and 'periods' of Creation, the heavens, planets, etc. Cp. John 1:29: (the Lamb of God) ὁ αἴρων τὴν ἁμαρτίαν τοῦ κόσμου ?<*MAŠ-BA(LA)G-ANTA-TAB-BA-RI-TI ∼ ܡܚܰܣܶܐ 'remit', ܚܰܛܳܝ̈ܶܐ 'sinners' ('sins') and ܕ-ܒܪ̈ܝܳܐ, of Creation' (the world). √שבק also = 'send away (a wife), divorce', hence: Matt 19:3 Εἰ ἔξεστιν ἀπολῦσαι τὴν γυναῖκα αὐτοῦ κατὰ πᾶσαν αἰτίαν; ? < *LI-MAŠ-BA(LA)G-ANTA ∼ ܠܡܳܐ ܡܚܰܣ ܐܢ̱ܬ݁ܬ݂ܐ 'shall one divorce a wife?' (↓ XIX pp. 201ff.), and cp. Matt 22:25–28: ἀφῆκεν τὴν γυναῖκα αὐτοῦ τῷ ἀδελφῷ αὐτοῦ . . . τίνος τῶν ἑπτὰ ἔσται γυνή; ?<*LI-MAŠ-BA(LA)G-ANTA ∼ ܠܡܳܐ ܡܚܰܣ ܐܢ̱ܬ݁ܬ݂ܐ 'to whom has he left (his) wife?', and similarly underlying Gen 2:24 עַל-כֵּן יַעֲזָב-אִישׁ אֶת-אָבִיו וְאֶת-אִמּוֹ וְדָבַק בְּאִשְׁתּוֹ וְהָיוּ לְבָשָׂר אֶחָד: ?<*LI-MAŠ-BA(LA)G-ANTA ∼ שבק 'leave', מִשְׁפָּחָה 'family' (↓ n. 41), ספק 'cleave', and אנתתא 'wife'. For the probable play on the mushroom name and שבק 'send', see ↓ XV n. 24 on the pseudo-translation in John 9:7 on Σιλωάμ as ᾿Απεσταλμένος.

18. E.g. the "cotyledon" play on הרג (קטל) אדניו in II Kgs 9:30 ↑ V n. 8; cp. מס־עבד (פלח) in Gen 49:15 XVI p. 147.

19. NH Aram מַרְדְּל מְנִזְּלֹו, Arab خَرْدَل (Qur 21:4, 31:5: *For. Voc.* p. 122) ~ ע/אַרְדִּילָא 'mushroom'; for חרדל itself, cp. Sum ᵍⁱˢ ḤAR-ḤAR *ḫaldappânu* 'mustard' i.e. husked (κόκκον (σινάπεως Matt 17:20, etc.) <Sum GÚG-GÚG, KUK-KA *kukku* 'pod' (Sum GUG <GÚ-GÚ as in ᵘ' ˢᵉ GÚ *kakku* 'pea')); Acc *ḫaldappânu* <*ḤAR-TAB-BA, cp. KUŠ-TAB-BA 'sheath'; Sem חרדל ?<*ḤAR-DAL (= TAB-BA 'twin'). For σίναπι ?<Sum*AB-SÍN ('furrow, vulva')-È i.e. vulva-enveloped, cp. Sum GÚ-È *ḫalâpu* 'be enveloped', ᵗᵘᵍ GÚ-È *naḫlaptu* 'garment'.

20. ↑ n. 17.

21. ἔνθεος; cp. Plato *Phaedrus* 253 A.

22. *CGS* v p. 161.

23. ↑ n. 16; Sum *LI-MAŠ (= LI-LI as in (UKÚŠ-) LI-LI-GI) ?> *lamastu* 'demon' = Sum ᵈDÌM-ME (cp. ᵈ DÌM-ME-GÍG *lilitu* = BH לילית <*LI-LI-TI; cp. LÍL-LA-DA-RA *namtaru* 'plague-demon', ↑ n. 3; ↓ XVII pp. 173f.; where GÍG = 'night'; BH ליל(ה)? <Sum LI-LI as inverted cones "overshadowing" and thus casting "darkness" (Sum GI₆, GÍG), cp. DIM in GEDÍM *etemmu* 'spectre' (id. ⊢⊰ = MAŠ + ŠU₄=ŠÚ *katâmu* 'cover'), i.e. GE₆ + DIM *dimmu* 'column' – a canopy and stem, as figure of a mushroom or umbrella; so related to *lamassu* (= Sum ᵈLAMMA) properly a protective demon, fem. *lamaštu* 'demon of child-birth, nursing', etc.; ?> λοιμός 'plague' (*Il* 1.61; Hes. *WD* 243, etc.); λιμός (Hsch) 'hunger, famine' (see Zimmern *Fremdw.* 69 > סמל 'idol'). For play between *LI-MAŠ and לְמַס 'to the corpse' (decaying one) at Acts 9:40, ↓ XVI n. 1.

For the ending -ANTA/TI, 'top' (or 'raised'), note the misunderstanding involved in the name of the Mandrake in Ps-Dsc IV 75, ξηρὰ ἄνθη, probably <*GI-SUR-ANTA/TI "top of a spindle"=BH כִּישׁוֹר (Pr 31: 19) ↓ IX n.16), where Sum GI = 'reed' and SUR *ṭamû* 'weave', id. ⩙ (Lab *Man* ⁑101; ↓ XVI n. 10; cp. MUG 'ferula' (?<*MUL(U)-UGU ↑ III n. 26) and 'thread' id. ⟼ (Lab *Man* ⁑3). Thus BH כֹּשָׁרוֹת Ps 68:7 = Bacchantes (<*BALAG-ANTA/TI "phallus (-mushroom)-raisers/-raised" ↓ X pp. 86ff. n. 16) cp. Ugar *Ktr* (Aqht V 10, 31); see W. F. Albright *Arch. and Relig.*⁴, 1956, pp. 81f. For a more purposive play on *GI-SUR-ANTA/TI, cp. Jos *War* II 123 on the Essenes: "oil they consider defiling and anyone who is anointed with it scours his person; for they make a point of keeping a dry skin (αὐχμεῖν 'squalid, unwashed; dry, parched' ≃ ξηραίνω 'parch', ξηραντέον 'one must dry' (Dsc V 88, etc)" as a play on ξηρα-ανθη "Mandrake"? In NT note the use of ξηραίνω of plants (Matt 13:6, 21:19, 20 etc.), of a hand (Mark 3:1), even of an epileptic! (Mark 9:18). The use of the verb with 'blood' (Mark 5:29) is particularly significant in view of other mushroom word-plays in the passage, ↓ n. 42.

Derived from the 'whorl-'shape of the eye, ξῆρις 'heron' = Lat ardeola, ardea ≃? א/ערדילא 'mushroom'; cp. ἐρῳδιός 'heron' ?<Sum ERI₄ + *IÀ-U₅-DA (= ERI₄-TÌL-LA) "seed-of-fertility"; cp. Aram קוֹרָא Gen R s. 64 end; Yalk. ib. 111, 'heron' (cp. BH קוֹרֵי in Isa 59:5, 'spindle' (<*GÚ-RI "erect-head", i.e. the glans penis; (cp. Pers قور qûr 'top of a gourd'); thus עֵין־קוֹרֵא 'heron's eye', the "place name" as scene of Samson's exploit with the "jaw-bone of an ass' (לְחִי חֲמוֹר); cp. Lat name for Mandrake, mala canina 'dog's jawbone, cheek' Ps-Dsc IV 75; BH לְחִי 'cheek, jawbone' <Sum LI-GI "cone-reed"; ↓ n. 31; cp. BH פֶּלַח <Sum BALAG (↑ III n. 26); both עֵין־קורא and לְחִי חֲמוֹר folk-names for the mushroom?

For "heron's eye" as indicating specifically the red-topped Amanita muscaria, note the tradition cited by Pliny that "in mating cock herons shed blood from their eyes" (X 164), i.e. that they are red-eyed? For a similar comparison between the eye and the mushroom, cp. the folk-name for the fungus "gazelle" (↓ X p. 87 n. 20), and possibly, like עֵין־קורא, in a play upon a place-name, עֵין־גְּדִי "goat's eye", "goat's spring": Ct 1:14.

In NT, ἐρῳδιός 'heron; mushroom(?)' regularly represented by "Herod" ('Ηρῴδης) and "Herodians" ('Ηρῳδιανοί; Matt 22:16, etc.) and "Rhoda" ('Ρόδη; Acts 12:13 (↓ XVI p. 144; note connection between "Herod" and "doves", הרדסיאות M Shabb 24:3. Hull 12:1; cp. Danby Mish p. 121 n. 3, "domesticated, indoor doves". Herod is supposed to have bred them, Jos War V 181 (πελειάδων ἡμέρων); possibly a covert reference to Περιστερεών, 'Holy Plant'.

24. Sum KUR šadû 'mountain'; id. ▲▰▲ > ⚹ (Lab Man ✳366) (?<*KU-ÙR "base-roof": cp. KÚR-KÚR kapapu 'curve over'); cp. κύρβεις 'triangular tablets of law'; κυρβασία 'Persian bonnet, poultice on a woman's breast', ?<KUR+ BAR-SI(G) (Acc parsigu) 'turban', cp. Sum ᵗᵘᵍBAR(-SIG) 'poultice'; cp. κύρτος = κύρτη 'lobster-pot; bird-cage'; κυρτός 'bulging, swelling, convex', etc. ?<*KUR-TI.

25. NH XX 74.

26. χρηστός.

27. *Life of Claudius* XXV 4, cp. Justin *Apology* I 4, Tertullian *Apology* III 5, Lactantius *Divine Institutes* IV 7.5, for pronunciation *Christus* as *Chrestus*.

28. 'Αλικάκκαβος = 'Αναγαλλις ἡ κυανῆ, Κόρχορον, Ps-Dsc II 178 (Δάκοι-κερκέρ i.e. Sum KUR-KUR); also = Στρύχνον and Στρύχνον ὑπνωτικόν (also called κακκαλίαν) Dsc IV 71, 72 ("Αφροι-κακκαβούμ, PS-Dsc IV 72); ?<Sum * Á-RI-GAG-GÀR-BA, "bolt-knobbed-pommel plant" ↑ V n. 18.

29. *NH* XXI 180ff.

30. John 3:14; ↓ XVII p. 154.

31. For the conception, as applied to the star, cp. ULU, UL *kakkabu*, id. <⇒ (Lab *Man* ✳441); MÚL id. ✄—✄ (Lab *Man* ✳376; also = TE-UNU, UNÚ 'cheek', cp. BH לְחִי? ?<*LI-GI, ↑ n. 23).

32. ↓ X pp. 83ff.; for BALAG <*BAL-AGA ↑ III n. 26. For μαινάς as "womb-mad" (cp. ὑστερικός), ↓ XII n. 1.

33. ↓ XII n. 4.

34. φάλαγξ, φαλλάγγιον; cp. φάλαγγωμα, a Dionysiac procession.

35. ↑ n. 15.

36. Nic *Th* 715–24; Pl *NH* XXIV 62.

37. 'Ασφάραγος Dsc II 125: "like a round root, having a knob . . ." ?<*UŠ-BALAG "erect-phallus".

38. ↑ n. 16; III n. 26; Arab فلك 'having rounded breasts'; n. 'globe, sky, hillock'; فلْكَة = BH פֶּלֶךְ 'spindle-whorl' (= Sum ᵍⁱˢ BAL *pilakku* 'spindle'; BH פֶּלַח 'millstone' (properly the lower stone (Job 41:16), as 'cone-shaped'), "fig-cake" (I Sam 30:12); 'pomegranate slice' (Ct 4:3 = 6:7: simile of a human 'temple'); √ פלג, פֶּלַח 'divide', n. 'half' (-circle, globe).

39. BH פַּקֻּעֹת II Kgs 4:39 ↑ V n. 18; X p. 86; cp. פְּקָעִים of the Temple ornaments, I Kgs 6:18, 7:24; Arab فقْع 'mushroom'; Syr ܡܦܩܥܐ (P-S 3221) *Colocynthis agrestis*.

40. √פלח, primarily agricultural, but extended to other creative work, e.g. Aram ܦܠܚ 'make bricks, tanning, working stone, metals', etc.

41. BH שבח Pi. ‖ ברך (Ps 63:4), הלל (Ps 117:1); BAram מְשַׁבַּח Dan 2:23, etc., also Aph. (↓ XIX p. 200). Thus ܡܫܒܚܐ (pass. part.) 'glorious, precious', etc.; ܡܫܒܚܢܐ 'singer'; ܡܫܒܚܢܘܬܐ 'praiseworthiness'; for possible play on

*LI-MAŠ-BA(LA)G-ANTA-TAB-BA-RI in Gen 12:3 (of Abraham, ↓ XVII p. 158): ונברכו בך כל משפחת האדמה, as if = "for a praising art thou" and reading *MAŠ-BA(LA)G as משפחה 'family, tribe', and -ANTA as את(נ)א 'thou', and -TAB-BA-RI as די-ב-ארעא "that are in the earth" ↑ n. 17).

For further plays on משפחה 'family', cp. Mark 3:31–35, etc. on the theme ἂν ποιήσῃ τὸ θέλημα τοῦ θεοῦ, οὗτος ἀδελφός μου καὶ ἀδελφὴ καὶ μήτηρ ἐστιν (Matt 12:50 θέλημα τοῦ πατρός μου τοῦ ἐν οὐρανοῖς ∼ *ANBAR /AB-BA-TAB-BA-RI-GI; ↓ XVII p. 159); i.e. *LI-MAŠ-BA(LA)G-ANTA, read as "thou art to me a family"; ἂν ποιήσῃ τὸ θέλημα . . . ∼ *MAŠ-TAB-BA ∼ ܡܨܛܒܝܐ 'acceptable', ܨܒܐ 'be willing'; ܨܒܝܢܐ 'will', etc.; and for καὶ ἔξω στήκοντες (Mark 3:31) ?<*TAB-BA-RI-TI ∼ ܕ-ܒܪܝܬܐ "who are in the street", cp. Aram בְּרָא 'outside'. Similarly, at Matt 7:21: οὐ πᾶς ὁ λέγων μοι Κύριε, κύριε . . . ἀλλ' ὁ ποιῶν τὸ Θέλημα τοῦ π. μ. τοῦ ἐ. τ. οὐρ. with play on Sum KUR-KUR > Κιρκαῖον 'Mandrake' (↑ n. 16); cp. also the Lord's Prayer, Matt 6:10: γενηθήτω τὸ θέλημά σου, ὡς ἐν οὐρανῷ καὶ ἐπὶ γῆς ∼ *MAŠ-TAB-BA-LI-GI read as ܡܨܛܒܐ ܠܟ "(let it be) acceptable to thee", and *TAB-BA-RI(-GI) ∼ ܕ-ܒ-ܐܪܟܐ ܕ-ܒ-ܫܡܝܐ "that which is in heaven (as) that which is on earth."

√ שבח 'increase' (↓ n. 42 on Matt 23:5); Mark 7:9–11 (on Exod 20:12, etc.): Ἐὰν εἴπῃ ἄνθρωπος τῷ πατρὶ ἢ τῇ μητρί Κορβάν, ὅ ἐστιν Δῶρον, ὃ ἐὰν ἐξ ἐμοῦ ὠφεληθῇς ?<*LI-MAŠ-BA(LA)G-ANTA ∼ מה-שבחתם "what ye have profited"; Κορβάν ∼ ܣܡܘܕܟܢܐ <*KUR-BA(LA)G-AN(TA), ↑ n. 16; ↓ XIX p. 200 [cp. the Κορύβαντες, κύρβας-αντος: 'Corybant, a priest of Cybele in Phrygia, associated with Dionysus; cp. Euripides Bacchae 125, etc.; used of frenzied, drunken persons, drowsily nodding and suddenly starting up; cp. Pl NH XI 147 (of hares, sleeping with their eyes open; cp. the 'silence of the Bacchantes, ↓ X pp. 85).

Cp. Matt 5:33–37 on swearing (↓ XIX p. 200 n. 10), ending: τὸ δὲ περισσὸν τούτων ἐκ τοῦ πονηροῦ ἐστιν ∼ *MAŠ-BA(LA)G-ANTA as if ܡܐ ܡܚܣܒ "what is in excess" and ܒܝܫܐ "the evil-doer."

שבח 'gain' as = מָמוֹנָא 'Mammon' in Matt 6:24: Οὐδεὶς δύναται δυσὶ κυρίοις δουλεύειν (∼ Sum KUR-KUR (> Κιρκαῖον, Κόρχορον, etc. ↑ n. 16, as in κύριε κύριε Matt 7:21) and BALAG ∼ פלח 'serve'. Cp. also phrase μαμωνᾶ τῆς ἀδικίας (Luke 16:9) ∼ *MAŠ-BA(LA)G-ANTA read as ܡܐ ܡܚܣܒ ܒܝܫܐ "what is of profit (is) evil."

For *MAŠ-BA(LA)G ∼ √spḥ, ḥsp, etc. 'peeling, scab, veil', etc., ↓ XIII n. 12 (on Manna); XIV pp. 122ff.; for further exx. of מִשְׁפָּחָה 'family, tribe' and *TAB-BA-RI ∼ 'David', ↓ XVI n. 1.

42. ↑ n. 17. שׁבק 'release', also of 'blood' (cp. ܟܣܐ ܕܡ̈ܐ = φλεβοτομία Gal. qu. P-S sv), hence Mark 5:25–34 of woman with issue of blood, plays on *MAŠ-BA(LA)G-ANTA as if ܡܒܘܥܐ 'source' and ܐܢܬܬܐ 'woman', with ἐξηράνθη ἡ πηγὴ τοῦ αἵματος αὐτῆς (v. 29) including a play on the Mandrake name ξηρα-ανθη (↑ n. 23). For ἥψατο τοῦ (κρασπέδου τοῦ Matt 9:20) ἱματίου αὐτοῦ: MAŠ as if ܡܫ 'touch'; and TAB-BA-LI as if ταβλίον = latus clavus (cp. Matt 23:5), here a word-play but ταβλίον was actually so derived, ↓ VIII p. 65 n. 7; XIV p. 121.

[Hence probably the reference in I Cor 11:10: διὰ τοῦτο ὀφείλει ἡ γυνὴ ἐξουσίαν ἔχειν ἐπὶ τῆς κεφαλῆς διὰ τοὺς ἀγγέλους, where 'authority' = latus clavus, i.e. the "purple", and ἀγγέλους ∼ *MAŠ-BA(LA)G read as "one who is sent forth" (שׁבק), the whole passage being a play on *MAŠ-BA(LA)G-ANTA read as ܐܢܬܬܐ ܡܫܒܚ "the glory of a woman" (her hair) (v. 15: γυνὴ δὲ ἐὰν κομᾷ, δόξα αὐτῇ ἐστίν and as מִסְפֵּה (BH) 'veil' (Ezek 13:18), ↓ XVI n. 19.]

In Matt 23:5: μεγαλύνουσι τὰ κράσπεδα is derived by play on *MAŠ-BA(LA)G and TAB-BA-LI, as if שׁבה 'increase' and ταβλίον and πλατύνουσι γὰρ τὰ φυλακτήρια similarly with תְּפִלִּין 'phylacteries' ∼ *TAB-BA-LI.

Further on the "blood" word-play on *MAŠ-BA(LA)G, cp. Matt 23:35 ἀπὸ τοῦ αἵματος Ἄβελ, i.e. ܡܒܚ and *TAB-BA-LI as if ܕܣܝܒܠ? (↓ XII n. 2), and ἕως τοῦ αἵματος Ζαχαρίου υἱοῦ βαραχίου ∼ *TAB-BA-RI-GI, as if ܟܪܟ? "he of Barachiah" i.e. the son of B. (ct. OT: בֶּן־יְהוֹיָדָע II Chr 24:20); for choice of "Zachariah", reference may be to the plant-name Ἐσκάρια = Ἠρύγγιον Ps-Dsc III 21 (↓ XII p. 98) or as a play on Διόσκουροι as ܘܟܪܟ? For the following ὃν ἐφονεύσατε μεταξὺ τοῦ ναοῦ καὶ τοῦ θυσιαστηρίου, we may recognize the "Cotyledon" word-play *GÚ-TAL-Ù-DUN > Κοτυληδών (↑ V p. 38 n. 8) ∼ קטל 'kill' but with אִיתוֹן 'Entrance' (of the Temple, Ezek 40:15), i.e. "between the Temple and the altar."

Cp. also the "mixed blood" theme of John 19:34: ἀλλ' εἷς τῶν στρατιωτῶν λόγχῃ αὐτοῦ τὴν πλευρὰν ἔνυξεν (↓ XII pp. 107f.), καὶ ἐξῆλθεν εὐθὺς αἷμα καὶ ὕδωρ <*MAŠ-BA(LA)G ∼ שׁפק 'pour out' and *TAB-BA-LI ∼ (א)ד־בליל "that which is mixed" (√בלל, Acc bullulu 'mix' ?<Sum BA preform. + LÙ-LÙ 'mix').

CHAPTER VII

The Man-child Born of a Virgin

1. *NH* XXII 93f.

2. J. Ramsbottom *op. cit.* p. 39.

3. *NH* XIX 35.

4. *NH* XIX 33.

5. Caesalpinus in *De Plantis*, 1583; qu. Ramsbottom *op. cit.* p. 14.

6. ↑ V n. 15; ↓ XII n. 33.

7. ↑ III n. 1.

8. √ חלק <Sum ḪA-LAM = ZÁḪ (= ḪA-A) ḫalâqu 'go to waste'; abâtu 'destroy' (= אבד, ↑ III n. 41), ?>ḪAL 'run' (as in ˢᵉᵐ ḪAL 'galbanum' (↑ II n. 20; III n. 36)) = Ugar ḫlq 'perish' ‖ mt 'dead' (*UM* Gloss. 710), prop. "semen of coitus – run to waste"; cp. ZAḪ = nâḫu 'be calm' = BH etc. √ נוח ?<*NU-ḪA "seed-run-away" i.e. post-coital rest (by transp. > ḪUN nâḫu); Sum ZAḪ ?<IÀ (= ZA, as IA₄ = ZÁ 'stone') – ḪA "juice, semen – run-away", cp. Acc pašâḫu 'quieten, appease' (BH שבח, ↓ XIII p. 116 n. 23) and πάσχω 'feel, suffer', all ?<*PEŠ-ḪA "foetus-expelled" (but פֶּסַח, πάσχα 'Passover lamb' <Sum USBAḪA <*ÙŠ-BA-ḪÁ 'small cattle': ↓ X n. 28; XVII p. 170f).

For the 'smoothness' of the fungus, cp. the story of Jacob (Gen 27:11, ↓ XIV p. 120) and Thphr I v 3: "the stem of galingale and sedge has a certain smoothness beyond those just mentioned, and still more perhaps has that of the mushroom;" cp. μύκης > μύξα, mucus 'mucous discharge' > "flattery", cp. Sum KA-TAR (transl. < Acc katarru 'mushroom') dalîlu 'flattery'; BH חלקות 'flatteries', cp. Ps 55:22, etc.

From the same Sumerian source, ḪA-LAM is BH and cogn. √ חלם 'dream', prop. "emit semen" as in Arab حلم 'emit semen at puberty', cp. Sum MÁŠ-GE₆ "night spermal-emission" = Acc šuttu 'dream'; cp. ἰαύω 'sleep' and ἴαυος = κοίτη (Hsch) ?<*IÀ-U₅ "semen"; ὄναρ 'dream' = אוֹנָן 'Onan' (Gen 38:4) ?<*U₅-NÁ-NÁ "ejaculate semen" ↑III p. 25 n. 42.

9. Cp. Isa 57:6 (~ חלק 'portion'): חלקי-נחל as objects of adoration: שַׁחֲטֵי הַיְלָדִים בנחלים (for גם-להם שפכת נסך העלית מנחה (v. 5); are these the

דְּרְשֵׁי הַחֲלָקוֹת of the DSS ?); cp. the similar phrase in I Sam 17: 40: כלי הרעים = ילקוט which he puts into his וַיִּבְחַר לוֹ חֲמִשָּׁה חַלֻּקֵי־אֲבָנִים מִן־הַנַּחַל (↓ n. 24; ↑ III n. 31).

10. חַלָּמוּת ?<Sum *GALLA-MUD "womb" (MUD *alâdu* 'bear children'; ct. Aram גַּלְמוּדָא 'menstruous woman' ?<*GALLA-MÙD where MÙD = 'blood' (prop. menses ?), BH גַּלְמוּד Isa 49: 21, etc. as "barren, unproductive woman", i.e. as menstruating and thus not pregnant ?), = SÌL-MUD 'womb' > BH צַלְמָוֶת ↓ XV p. 137; also ס(י)רמת 'volva'; 'mushroom' (?), as subject of word-play in II Kgs 4:40: מָוֶת בַּסִּיר "death-in-the pot" and probably in I Cor 15:56: τὸ δὲ κέντρον τοῦ θανάτου ἡ ἁμαρτία ~ סיר מות read as' "thorn-of-death". Cp. also I Sam 15:32 (of אגג; XVII n. 107): סר(מר)־המות; and read הַסַּרְמוֹת for הַשָּׁרֵמוֹת in Jer 31: 40 ↓ XV n. 28.

   Cp. I Sam 21:14 of 'slavering' David: וַיּוֹרֶד רִירוֹ אֶל־זְקָנוֹ; BH רִיר, ?<Sum RI-RI as in A-RI-A *rehû* 'fecundate' that is, pass semen, cp. ERI₄ (<E₄-RI) 'semen', ERI₄-TÌL-LA 'mushroom'. For further illustrations of the relevance of spittle to the mushroom, cp. Pl *NH* XXII 96 on the *pituita* – "viscous gummy moisture from trees from which fungi are derived", and the tradition among the Koryaks (↑ V n. 12) that the mushroom was derived from the god who spat on the earth, and out of his saliva agaric appeared. Note also the Polish story that mushrooms appeared where the apostle Peter spat on the ground as he walked behind Jesus (qu. Ramsbottom *op. cit.* p. 45); so Aconite was said to have sprung from the foam of the dog Cerberus when Heracles dragged him from the underworld (Pl *NH* XXVII 4; note that one of the names of Aconite, κάμμαρον (*NH* XXVII 9; Dsc IV 76), was also a name of the Mandrake (Dsc IV 75).

11. Nidd. 16ᵇ; ↑ III n. 8.

12. *NH* XXVIII 52.

13. *NH* VII 15; XXVIII 35; cp. also Nic *Th* 86 "noxious creatures flee in terror from man's spittle." For the connection, cp. Sum ÚḪ *imtu* 'venom' and *ru'tu* 'spittle'. As a cure for epilepsy, cp. Pl *NH* XXVIII 36 "we spit on epileptics in a fit, that is, we throw back infection" – because the epileptic slavers ? Cp. *NH* X 69 on quails: "it is customary to spit at the sight of them as a charm against epilepsy to which they are the only living creatures that are liable besides man." Cp. σίαλον, σίελον, Lat *saliva* 'spittle' with BH שְׁלָיו, NH סְלָיו, Syr ܣܲܠܘܲܝ, Arab سَلْوَى 'quail', ?<*SÌ-E₄-LA₆ (= ILLU) "eject-spittle, semen," etc. The connection of the birds with the mushroom

(and hence the Manna story of Exod 16:13), was probably through their colour, a general reddish-brown above, marked with dark brown and buff, and pale buff below, passing into white on the belly, and their reputation for ejecting spittle. Cp. the names: Lat *Coturnix*, Ὄρτυξ-υγος, Hsch Γόρτυξ (Fόρτυξ Skt *vártikā, vartakas*; L & S s.v.) ?<BUR₅ 'bird' + *DUG₄-GÌŠ "ejaculate-semen" bird (Sum GÌŠ-DUG₄-GA *reḫû* 'copulate', ↑ III n. 6).

14. *NH* XXVIII 37.

15. ↑ III pp. 20f.

16. Pl *NH* XXV 106.

17. Clementine *Homilies* III 13.

18. *War* V 218.

19. The secret was in the hands of one family, of Abtinos, who had a room in the precincts of the Temple for their compounding: jYoma 3:9 bab Yoma 38a, etc.; see art. *EB* ii 2167.

20. As Proculus' healing of Severus (Tertullian *ad Scalp.* iv) and as late as the time of Bede (*in Marci* i c. 24). Anointing of the dying was a heretical practice of the Marcosians (Irenaeus, I 21.5) and of the Heracleonites (Epiphanius *adv. Haer.* XXXVI 2) and for exorcism. In the Roman Church by the twelfth century healing by unction was apparently obsolete, being restricted to the dying (Council of Florence, 1439), applied before the Viaticum (1st Council of Mainz, Can. XXVI).

21. So called by Hugo de St Victore (*Summa Sententiar* vi 15); ordained as one of the seven sacraments of the Roman Church at the Council of Trent (*histrionica hypocrisis*, acc. to Calvin, *Inst.* vi 19.18).

22. רְפָאִים preferred by Asa (אָסָא) to dependence on Yahweh, II Chr 16:12; cp. v. 14 for his mourners' recourse to the embalmer's art: מרקחת מעשה and fire (שרפה גדולה).

23. √ חנט ?<*ḪEN (ḪE-ÈN)-DA, ↑ III n. 41: the '40 days' being the period of gestation before which the foetus was not considered human, cp. M Nidd 3:7; Pl *NH* VII 41; XXVII 62.

24. √ קדש ?<*ÙŠ-KUD = *ÙŠ-TAR > *u* Ištar; *ištaritu* = *qadištu*, BH קְדֵשָׁה 'cult-prostitute'; ὑστέρα, Lat *uterus* 'womb'. Cp. יַלְקוּט (= כְּלִי הָרֹעִים) ?<*ÙŠ-KUD (↑ III n. 31); cp. Arab خِرْب 'shepherd's bag' and خَرُبَة

'vulva'; see on 'Carob' < Sum ḪARUB = MURUB 'womb' ↑ V n. 12.

25. ↓ XV pp. 137f.

26. ↑ I n.2; III nn. 24, 27; cp. also βασιλεύς ? <Sum BAR-SÌL 'groin, womb' + UŠ penis; as βασιλεία 'kingdom' = site of king's fecundity; βασίλειον 'palace' ↓ VIII n. 16. Cp. BH שַׂר 'prince', שָׂרַי 'Sara' (Σαρα), Acc šarru = Sum SARA, ?<SÌLA ("groin, womb") ?>SAL-LA 'vulva'; √ שלט 'be lord' ?<*SAL(-LA)-DA; Lat dux, ?<DÙG 'penis' + ŠÚ 'pour out' > ŠUDÚG pašišu 'anointed'; cp. Sum EN (Acc bêlu) 'lord' _?_ ÈN 'seed' ↑ III n. 35, as NUN (Acc rubû) 'prince' <NU₅-NU₅ "seeder". For the 'protective' aspects of lordship, ↓ XVI p. 141.

27. BH כֹּהֵן <ˡú GÚ-EN-NA "man (in charge) of the qadûtu, seed-store, granary" ↑ III n. 35.

28. ↑ III p. 25.

29. ↑ III n. 36.

30. Ant III 172–78.

31. PS-Dsc IV 60: σιδηρῖτις = Περιστερεὼν ὕπτιος, 'Holy Plant'.

32. Ecclus 45:12; Jos War V 235: τὴν δὲ κεφαλὴν βυσσίνη μὲν ἔσκεπεν τιάρα, κατέστεπτο δ᾽ὑακίνθῳ, περὶ ἣν χρυσσοῦς ἄλλος ἦν στέφανος ἔκτυπα φέρων τὰ ἱερὰ γράμματα·

33. צִיץ זהב טהור; cp. 39:30; Lev 8:9; Jos Ant III 178; elsewhere of 'blossom': Num 17:23 (of Aaron's rod; פְּטוּרֵי צִיצִים of Temple ornaments I Kgs 6:18ff.) BH צִיץ <Sum SI-SÁ (Acc ešêru 'be straight'; cp. GAG-SI-SÁ "tipped-straight-staff" i.e. 'javelin'; ᵘᶻᵘ SI-SÁ = išaru 'penis' (Iraq VI, 177; IV 6–9); cp. Arab صِيصَة 'cock's spur; horn'; cp. BH צִיצִת 'tassel' Num 15:38f.; 'lock of hair' (on forehead) Ezek 8:3; cp. Acc ṣiṣitu 'peg' (of a yoke); Syr ܨܨ 'nail'; BH verb Hiph. = 'peep through' (as of the glans penis appearing through the prepuce?), of blossoming flower > 'shine, sparkle' (cp. BH נצץ, נִצָּה 'blossom'); of נֵזֶר 'crown' (Ps 132:18) ?<*NA₄-SUR "stone of extension" hence נזר = (a) 'boundary stone' (cp. Sum BULUG "crowned borer" (↑ III n. 26); ZAG "crownstone" (↑ III 31) miṣru 'frontier'; cp. Sum KI-SUR(-RA) kissurû 'frontier' and thus "set apart, circumscribed", so BH √ נזר 'consecrate'; (b) 'crown'.

34. M Sabb 19:6, shreds of the foreskin over the עֲטָרָה, corona, glans.

35. M Midd 1:9; acc. to M Tam 1:1 he returned to his fellow priests after cleansing in the Chamber of Immersion: see Allegro *Treasure of the Copper Scroll²*, New York, 1964, pp. 135ff.

36. ↑ III n. 36; שַׁמְשָׁן = רְקָחוֹת 'perfumers' I Sam 8:13; see next n.

37. ↑ III n. 35. NH שַׁמֵּשׁ, e.g. מְשַׁמֵּשׁ of the High Priest, M Yoma 7:5; 'copulate' M Ned 2:1; שַׁמָּשׁ 'server of tables' (e.g. M Pes 7:13) 'penis' (Nidd 11ᵇ 41ᵇ, etc.); שַׁמָּשָׁא 'concubine, prostitute' (Targ Exod 23:20 BH פִּלֶגֶשׁ (= παλλακίς, *pellex*, ?<*BALAG-UŠ "erector of the penis" = Sum AN-ZÍB *télitu* 'courtesan')); 'angels, seraphim' (Targ Isa 6:2); שַׁמְשָׁן 'perfumers' (Targ I Sam 8:13, ↑ n. 36).

38. ↑ III n. 29.

39. Θεραπευτής: θεραπεύω 'be an attendant; serve gods; worship; treat medically; train animals; cultivate land'; θεραπεία 'service, attendance; medical treatment', etc. ?<DÀRA-BAR ("organ of generation") = Acc *aialu* BH אַיִל 'stag' ?<*Á-A-RI-A "fecundator"; cp. DÀRA-MAŠ-DÀ; DÀRA-ḪAL-ḪAL-LA *naialu* 'roebuck' (?<*NÁ-A-RI-A, ?> NAR 'eroticist' as in BALAG-NAR '(erotic) musical instrument'; BH נַעַר, נַעֲרָה 'lad', 'girl'; Sum ᵈDÀRA = ⁱˡ Ea (?<*E₄-Á "powerful in semen"); also = ᵈ NU-DIM-MUD "seed of procreation"; etc. Sum DÀRA ?<*DA-A-RI-A "strong in fecundity"; for 'healing' significance, cp. φαρμακός ?<*BAR-MAḪ-UŠ "bigpenis" and as a 'server' (of god, land, etc.); cp. שׁמשׁ ↑ n. 37, and cp. كلمس <BALAG 'phallus'.

40. *Contemplative Life* i 2 (cp. ii 10–11).

41. *Ecclesiastical History* II xvii 3–23.

42. Σαμψαῖοι, שַׁמְשִׁין 'servers, givers of life, healers' <ŠEM-MAŠ; as meaning "sun-worshippers" Epiphanius *Haer.* liii 1, 2: Σαμψαῖοι γὰρ ἑρμηνεύονται 'Ηλιακοί < שֶׁמֶשׁ 'sun'.

43. *Haer.* xix 2, xx 3: 'Οσσηνοὶ δὲ μετέστησαν ἀπὸ 'Ιουδαϊσμοῦ εἰς τὴν τῶν Σαμψαίων αἵρεσιν, cp. xxx 3.

CHAPTER VIII

Woman's part in the Creative Process

1. *NH* VII 66.

2. NH VII 67.

3. *NF* II 3.

4. *NH* XXVIII 77.

5. *NH* XXVIII 80.

6. *NH* VII 64; cp. XXVIII 82.

7. ↑ VI n. 42 for ταβλίον; ↓ XIV p. 121; Lat *purpura* 'the purple fish' ?<Sum GUR-GUR 'twist, turn' – of the shape of the shell?

8. *NH* IX 135.

9. ὕσγινον ?<*ÚŠ-GÌN "purple-blood"; cp. ZA-GÌN *uqnu* 'lapis lazuli' ↓ XIV pp. 128ff. – "tinged with purple" (Pl *NH* XXXVII 121); cp. ὕσγη, the shrub source, ?<*ÚŠ-GE₆ "dark-blood" (= MÚD-GE₆ *adamatu* = Sum ADAMA); cp. ὄστρεον = Lat *ostrum* 'purple dye' ?<*ÙŠ-TAR "womb".

10. ὑάκινθος ?<*ÙŠ (U-A)-GÌN-TI (see prev. n.), as a precious stone = BH לֶשֶׁם (cp. Rev 21:20) ?<Sum ŠEM-LI *burâšu* 'pine', i.e. the resin.

11. *NH* XXVIII 77.

12. *NH* VIII 78.

13. *NH* XXIX 66.

14. *NH* XXVIII 85.

15. βασιλίσκος <BAR-SÌL 'groin, womb' + *ÚŠ-GE₆ "dark-blood". Cp. Pliny's tale (*NH* VIII 78) of one which "was killed with a spear by a man on horseback and the infection rising through the spear killed not only the rider but also the horse." The story perhaps derives in part from the 'riding' imagery of copulation (↓ XII p. 105) and dangers of intercourse with a menstruant (*NH* XXVIII 77).

16. *Saturnus*, ?<Sum ŠÀ-TÙR *šaturru* 'womb' = NÁ 'fecundate'; cp. *satur* 'sated'; of a pregnant woman (Plautus *Amphitruo* 2, 2, 35); cf. *sator* 'sower'; 'begetter'; *caelestum sator* = Jupiter (Cicero *Tusculanae Disputationes* 2, 9, 21; etc.); cp. Σάτυρος 'Satyr', of Dionysus, and the lascivious wood-deities generally; cp. σατύριον, *satyrion*: Pl *NH* XXVI 99: "the Greeks indeed always when they wish to indicate the aphrodisiac nature of a plant use the name *satyrion*;" cp. Σιληνός, Silenus, father of the satyrs, ?<*SÌL-U₅-NÁ, "womb" (> צִיּוֹן 'Zion'; in full *BAR-SÌL-U₅-NÁ, > βασιλείον 'palace' ↑ VII n. 26; cp. 'Jerusalem' ↓ XII n. 36); cp. βασιλικόν Ocimum basilicum = ὤκιμον (Thphr I vi 6f.) ?<*ú GIG "pod-plant" ↑ V n. 12; Pl *NH* 119ff.:

"seeds covered with a skin . . . no seed more prolific . . . purges the womb . . . is an aphrodisiac (XX 123) . . . wild ocimum is good for abscesses of the womb (XX 124).

17. *NH* XXIX 67.

18. *War* IV 479f.

19. *Histories* V 6.

20. ἄσφαλτος ?<*ÚŠ-GALA "womb-blood"; Sum KUNIN 'bitumen' ?<*KU-NIN "woman's excretion", cp. ἄφεδρος 'menses'; cp. Acc *kupru*, Heb כּוֹפֶר, Aram כּוּפְרָא, etc. ?<*KU-BARÁ "excrement" (cp. BÚRU, BURU₈ 'defecate'; ŠÈ-BAR-RA *id.*) (dist. fr. BH כֹּפֶר *Lawsonia inermis*, "Henna", <GÚ-BAR 'glans penis', from colour, ↓ XIV pp. 130f). Cp. BH חֵמָר 'bitumen' (?<*ḤE-MAR "excretion of womb"), in the Vale of Siddim (שִׂדִּים Gen 14:10 ?<*ŠEN-DÀRA "fecund womb"; thus > *sendayya* > *שַׁדַּי (plural form by a false Hebraization), also שַׁדַּי 'Shaddai' the divine name "fecundator of the womb" and BH שִׁטִּים 'Acacia' ↓ n. 34; cp. Lat *betula* 'Birch' (≟ BH and cogn. בְּתוּלָה 'virgin' (<Sum TÙN-BAR 'womb')) from which the Gauls extracted bitumen, Pl *NH* XVI 74; (cp. *baetulos* 'thunderbolt' ↓ XII n. 33); = Arab سَنْدَرَة <*ŠEN-DÀRA; and σάνδαλον, NH סַנְדָּל 'foetus' ('footwear' significance secondary ?).

With BH חֵמָר 'bitumen' cp. Arab حُمْرَة 'reddish-brown', colour of menses? Cp. BH זֶפֶת, Aram זִיפְתָּא and cogn. ?<*ZI-BÌD "life-excretion", cp. μάσπετον = *semen ferulae* ?<*MAŠ-BÌD (cp. ˢᵉᵐ MAŠ 'styrax'); cp. BH and cogn. אֶרֶז 'cedar', ?<IR-ZI "juice-of-life" i.e. menses ? ↓ n. 60.

21. *War* IV 481.

22. I 73; cp. Pl *NH* XXXV 182; for the connection between Aloes and the Dead Sea bitumen, cp. *NH* XXVII 15, ↓ XII n. 11.

23. Jos *Ant* XVII 171f.

24. H. B. Tristram *The Land of Moab*, London, 1873, pp. 247f.

25. *War* VII 178.

26. Sum LUḤ-MAR-TU ("womb-cleanser") Acc *šibburratu*, Syr ܦܲܓܢܐ Talm Aram שְׁבָרָא 'Rue' (↓ XVII n. 78) <*ŠEN-BURU₈ "womb-excrete" (cp. ἔμβρυον 'embryo; young one', ?<*ÁM-BURU₈ "womb-excrete", cp. βρύω 'be full to bursting' < BURU₈ 'defecate'/BÚRU *pašāru* 'release'; cp. Syr

עֹלָל 'little children under five years'. (Comparable but not exactly similar Sum ŠÈ-BAR-RA ṣanâḫu 'have diarrhoea'; see on 'Satan' and 'widow' ↑ III n. 45. Cp. names of Mallow, said to assist in parturition Pl NH XX 226, called Πλειστολοχεία Plistolochia <*BAR-ÙS-TAR-LUḪ "womb-cleanser" (= LUḪ-MAR-TU, 'Rue') = 'Ἀρίστηλεχούσαις (expl. NH XXV 95 as ἀρίστη λεχούσαις) ?<*(B)AR-ÙS-TAR-LUḪ = 'Ἐφεσία, Ps-Dsc III 4 ?<*E₄-BI-ÙS (?>PEŠ₄) "juice of pregnancy" (". . . helps women in pregnancy").)

27. NH XX 132ff.; cp. Dsc III 45, etc.

28. War VII 185.

29. War VII 181.

30. NH XX 132f.

31. NH XXV 41; cp. XXXV 178.

32. NH XXV 180.

33. NH XXIV 109.

34. W. R. Smith, Religion of the Semites³, 1927, p. 133 n. 4. BH שִׁטִּים, Arab سَمُرة, Egyp. šnḏ.t, 'Acacia': ↑ n. 20.

35. ↑ II p. 13.

36. CGS v pp. 153, 196; cp. Euripides Ion 1125: πῦρ πηδᾷ θεοῦ βακχεῖον.

37. BH שָׁקֵד ?<UŠ-GÍD "stretched-penis" as in É-UŠ-GÍD-DA "house of the stretched penis" = 'granary' (↓ XV n. 22); cp. ἀμυγδάλη 'almond' ?<*Á-MUG-DAL "at the raising of the head" (for MUG <*MUL(L)-UGU prop. "crown of pestle", ↑ III n. 26; and cp. Sum ZAG-MUG 'New Year' ↑ III n. 31), cp. μύκηρος = ἀμυγδάλη (Laconian word) and cp. μύκης <*MUGU 'mushroom' ↑ III n. 26.

38. Pl NH XVI 103: "Of the trees we have spoken of as budding in winter at the rising of Aquila, the almond blossoms first of all, in the month of January, while in March it develops its fruit."

39. Sum Á-GÚ-ZI-GA "at the raising of the head".

40. πυρὸς δέσποινα (Id. Phaethon fr. 781, 1.55); cp. ἐσχάρα 'hearth' ?<*ÙŠ-ḪAR 'foetus-container' i.e. womb = Sum IŠḪARA, a mother goddess like Ištar (*ÙŠ-TAR "womb"), cp. Sum ARḪUŠ 'womb', ?<*ḪAR-ÙŠ; ἑστία,

vesta ?<*PEŠ₄-TE "womb" (↓ n. 56 for equivalent Sum *Á-TÙN "womb" > אָתוֹן 'she-ass' associated with Hestia/Vesta (Virgil *Copa* 26), and Aramaic אַתּוּנָא Acc *utûnu* 'fire-place, stove' (<UDUN, ?<*Á-TÙN)).

41. See *CGS* v pp. 347ff.; she is called Hestia Πρυτανεία in Syros, Lesbos, and Sinope (*ib.* p. 348). The word in derivation means 'womb' (Sum TÙN-BAR) of the same source as παρθένος; cp. Παρθενών 'young woman's chamber, Parthenon'; = βασιλεία, 'kingdom'; βασίλειον, 'treasury, palace' ↑ n. 16; VII n. 26 (cp. Hestia's title Ταμίας, 'stewardess'; reff. *CGS* v pp. 371f. n. 48).

42. *Hom. Hymns* V 21ff.

43. *Hom. Hymns* XXIX 4–6.

44. Hes *Th* 495–97.

45. *NH* XXVIII 79.

46. *NH* II 221.

47. *NH* II 78.

48. Cp. Ovid *Fasti* 6.297: *ignis inextinctus*; Cicero *Oratio de Domo sua* 144: *ignem illum sempiternum*; cp. the "deathless fire" (πῦρ ἀθάνατον) worshipped at Delphi in its own right, but associated with her in the Amphictyonic oath, qu. *CGS* v p. 369 n. 28.

49. Cp. Plutarchus *Numa* 10.

50. A. Gellius I. 12.

51. Dionysus Halicarnassensis *Antiquitates Romanae* I. 76. 3.

52. Plutarchus, *ib.*

53. *Hom. Hymns* IV 110ff.

54. ↓ XVII pp. 162f. nn. 64–66; מַצְרֵף = πειρασμός; cp. K. G. Kuhn, *ZTK* xlix (1952) pp. 200–22; "New Light on Temptation, Sin and Flesh in the NT" in *The Scrolls and the New Testament* ed. K. Stendahl, 1957, pp. 94–113. מַצְרֵף ‖ כּוּר Pr 27:21, in BH metaph. or as simile for human sufferings in punishment or discipline; of Egypt as a place of bondage: Deut 4:20; Jer 11:4; I Kgs 8:51, all כור הברזל 'iron smelting furnace' = כַּוֹּרָ; cp. כַּוֹּרָ 'beehive', all < Sum KUR "cone-shape"; cp. the worship of Sebadios (Sabazios) in a temple "of a round type, with an opening in the middle of the roof" (Macrobius, I. 18, 11:

eique deo in colle Zilmisso aedes dicata est specie rotunda, cuius medium interpatet tectum).

55. To Dardanus (Arctinus ap. Dion. Hal. I. 69); or to his descendant Ilus (Ovid *Fasti* 6.419–22).

56. παλλάς ?<Sum GALLA 'womb'; 'Aθήνη ?<*Á-TÙN, ↑ n. 40; cp. Sum ᶻᵃ PEŠ₄-ANŠE (= Acc *bişşur atâni* 'ass's vulva') 'a thunderbolt'.

57. See *HGM* p. 48; cp. Sum idd. for 'star' (MULU, prop. 'pestle-head' ↑ III n. 15); MÚL ✕—✕ stylized form of UL ⟨⟹⟩ ↑ VI n. 31; cp. the *baetulos* thunderbolt, ↓ XII n. 33.

58. See *CGS* ii pp. 612ff.

59. E.g. *Il* XI 270; Hes *Th* 922.

60. Εἰλείθυια (var. 'Ελείθυια, Εἰλήθυια, etc.), i.e. ἐλάτη (?<Sum E₄-LA₆ + TU "juice of conception") 'pine' and Θυία (?<*TU-IÀ *id.*); cp. Sum A-TU in A-TU-GAB-LIŠ *şarbatu* 'plane-tree' (↓ XII p. 103); cp. ERIN *erenu, erennu* 'cedar', ?<Sum ERI₄-AN-NA (= Acc ˢᵃᵐ*maštakal*) "semen of heaven" = 'tragacanthe', = Sum A-RI-A-NAM-LÚ-ULÙ ˡᵘ "semen of mankind"; Acc *maštakal* ?<*MAŠ-DÀ A-KAL(= E₄-LA₆) "semen of progeny"; cp. Lat *Abies* 'silver-fir', ?<*A-BI-ÙŠ (? > PEŠ₄) "juice of pregnancy" (= 'Εφεσία, ↑ n. 26); BH אֶרֶז 'cedar', ?<IR-ZI "resin of life" (↑ n. 20); cp. Sum IR(-SIM) "squeezed-juice" = 'resin' and ŠE-IR-ZI *qutru* ('spelt' ?), "seed of the resin of life".

61. V ix 8; ↓ IX p. 78.

62. 'Ελένη, Helena, Helene 'Helen': ἐλένη, ἐλάνη 'torch' all < Sum ERIN 'cedar', ↑ n. 60; ↓ XII nn. 14, 15: for Helen as a tree-goddess, see *HGM* p. 230.

63. ↑ V n. 26; Νέμεσις, prop., like νέμησις, "distribution of what is due" (νέμω 'deal out' : see *CGS* ii p. 496) <Sum NAM + ENSI "guardian of fate"; cp. νεμέτωρ 'avenger' (of Zeus) < Sum NAM-TAR ("fate-decider") 'plague demon' = Acc *šimtu* 'fate' and also *pilû* ("egg") 'Mandrake' (↑ V n. 26).

64. *Od* 4.219ff.

65. *NH* XXI 59.

66. *NH* XXI 159.

67. *NH* XXII 96.

68. *Maqlu* VI 37–40: [37]Šiptu. ⁿᵃKukru ⁿⁱᵃkukru [38]ʳⁱᵃkukru ina šadâni^meš ellûti^meš quddušuti [39]ṣiḫrûti^meš tirḫi ša eniti [40]ṣiḫrâti^meš iṣterinnâti^meš ša qašdâti; cp. *DAB* pp. 262f.

68a Pliny *NH* XVI 49; cp. Thphr II ii 6.

69. ↓ XI n. 25: κύκνος, Lat *cycnus* ?<*GÚG-NU "seed-pod"; cp. Sum ˢᵉᵐ GÚG-GÚG *kukru* 'turpentine' = ˢᵉᵐKU₇-KU₇, cp. KU₇-KU₇ *matqûti* 'lice'; cp. the pine called 'louse-tree', φθειροφόρος, φθειροποιός Thphr II ii 6; *Phthirophoron* Pl *NH* XVI 49.

70. ↓ XIV.

71. *War* VII 181; ↓ XIV pp. 124f.

CHAPTER IX

The Sacred Prostitute

1. Cp. Isa 57:3–7; ↑ VII n. 9.

2. Cp. κυών 'dog' ?<*KU-NÁ "buttocks-copulate".

3. ↑ III n. 31.

4. *War* VII 181.

5. *NH* XXVIII 78.

6. *NH* XXV 29, cp. Thphr IX viii 6; for *picus Martius,* red-headed Black Woodpecker, cp. Pl *NH* X 40; the beak was considered a prophylactic against stings (*NH* XXIX 92); note the strange plant "which, carried by the bird, forced out by its touch a wedge driven into the tree by shepherds" (*NH* XXV 14).

7. *NH* XXV 107.

8. ↑ V. p. 41 n. 23.

9. *CT* xvii 19, 32; see R. Campbell Thompson *Devils and Evil Spirits of Babylonia* ii, 1904, p. 67; *DAB* p. 84.

10. *War* II 148f.

11. The mystic quality of iron perhaps owed something to the magnetic characteristics of lode-stone (*sidérites*: Pl *NH* XXXVI 127, as amber had a prophylactic use in amulets (*NH* XXXVII 51f.). Note the name σιδηρῖτις for "Holy Plant" (Ps-Dsc IV 60), and the instructions for cutting Mandrake: "one should draw three circles round it with a sword, and cut it with one's face towards the west; and at the cutting of the second piece one should dance round the plant and say as many things as possible about the mysteries of love (περὶ ἀφροδισίων: Thphr IX viii 8). For the magical, deterrent qualities of iron, cp. also the Talmud Berakhoth 6ᵃ, and Tosephta vi.13; see *HDB* iv 603.

12. NH XXV 30 of Panaces, Πάνακες ("after which Asclepius called his daughter Panacia"); cp. Thphr IX viii 7 ("offering of all kinds of fruit and cake": παγκαρπίαν (καὶ) μελιττοῦταν); for derivation of Πάνακες ?<*GAN-n-b-s = Κάνναβις, Cannabis, ↓ XVIII p. 188 n. 44. Cp. also Ἀσκληπιάδα 'White Hellebore' (mushroom ?), Ps-Dsc IV 148; and note the invocation to Apollo and Asclepius required when cutting Black Hellebore, Dsc IV 162. The name Lat *Aesculapius*: ?<*UŠ-GUL (= BH אֶשְׁכֹּל, ὠσχός 'vine-cluster' = 'glans penis' ↓ XVII p. 155 n. 20) + BI-UŠ 'erect' (penis); i.e. the cone-shaped top of the mushroom; cp. ἀσκληπιάς 'haemorrhoids' (= BH עֹפֶל, also 'hill, tumulus' <*ú BAL 'mushroom' ↑ III n. 26).

For compensation (?) offerings of "handfuls of barley-flour and morsels of bread", of the female necromancers, ensnaring souls, Ezek 13:19.

13. ↑ VIII p. 73; Thphr V ix 8.

14. ↑ III p. 23.

15. *War* VII 181.

16. BH כסת <KI-ŠÚ *mesîru* (√ אסר) 'cord; magical imprisonment'; cp. KIŠI *kiššûtu* 'power'; ? = בתי הנפש of Isa 3:20, ↓ XIV n. 47; cp. Ezek 13:20: הנני אל־כסתותיכנה אשר אתנה מצדדות שם את־הנפשות (NH כסת 'cushion, bolster' ?<GÚ-SA (*dadânu*) 'nape of the neck', and hence play in Mark 4:38: ἐπὶ τὸ προσκεφάλαιον καθεύδων ? cp. LXX Ezek 13:18, 20) > κίστη 'basket' (for carrying mystery implements); cp. J. E. Sandys *Bacchae*⁴, 1900, pp. 107ff. and ref.

17. ↑ III n. 23.

18. *NH* XXII 95; cp. Nic *Alex* 521ff.

19. ↓ XVII pp. 155; cp. XVIII p. 178f.

20. Despite rejection of identity of the subject ("rightly or wrongly") as being a mushroom by R. G. Wasson: "for almost a half-century mycologists have been under a misapprehension on this matter" (qu. Ramsbottom *op. cit.* p. 48).

21. מֹשֶׁה 'Moses', < *MUŠ-È "emergent snake"; MUŠ 'serpent' ?<*GÚ-UŠ "erect head" > ḪUŠ 'red, fiery' (i.e. prop. of glans penis), and, + NÁ 'stretch', > BH נָחָשׁ 'serpent'; cp. נְחֹשֶׁת 'copper' < NA₄ 'stone' + ḪUŠ 'red'. Acc *ṣîru* 'serpent', ?<*ZI-RÁ "raise erect"; cp. *ṣîru* (Sum MAḪ) 'raised, eminent' (as sexually, Sum ᶻᵃ MAḪ *aban râmi* 'love stone talisman' (↑ III n. 31).

22. φάτνη (Luke 2:7; cp. Eurip. *Bacchae* 11.509ff. – of Dionysus (↓ XVI p. 149): καθείρξατ' αὐτὸν ἱππικαῖς πέλας φάτναισιν) ?<* PAD-NÁ "shaded-basket"; cp. φατνόω 'roof, ceil', φατνώμα 'coffered work of ceiling'; for an indication of the shape involved, cp. Sum id. for 'stretch out in the shade and sleep' (Ù-NÁ): 🏛 (Lab *Man* ✳455), also for 'brick mould', Sum Ù-ŠUB, Acc *nalbantu* (↓ XII n. 27); cp. BH אֵבוּס (Isa 1:3, etc.) 'cattle trough', ?<*É-BUR-ZI "house of food-of-life", cp. Sum ᵈᵘᵍ BUR-ZI *pursîtu* 'cooking-pot'.

23. *War* II 121.

24. By missing three consecutive periods? A curious test of a woman's fecundity is recorded by Pliny: ". . . a sure sign of fertility in women is, if when the eyes have been anointed with a certain drug, the saliva contains traces of menses blood" (*NH* VII 67).

25. *War* II 160f.

26. Hes *Melampodia* (Scholiast on *Od* 10.494), 3.

27. ↑ V n. 24.

28. Cp. Pl *NH* XXVIII 39.

29. ↑ V n. 24.

CHAPTER X

Religious Lamentation

1. *Poetics* 6.

2. BH קִינָה <GI-NA>GIN (↓ XII n. 1); cp. BH כִּנּוֹר 'harp' (κινύρα, Jos *Ant*

VII 306), ?<*GIN-URA "erect penis", and > κινύρομαι 'utter a plaintive lament', κινυρός 'wailing' = μινυρός 'whining'; cp. πενθέω, πένθος 'grief' (Lith *kenčiù* 'suffer', *pa-kantà* 'patience'; qu. L & S 1360ᵇ) ?<*GIN-DU; cp. BH גְּתִית 'musical instrument' ?<*GIN-TI "instrument to cause an erection"; and cp. BH √ זמר 'sing' ?<זְמוֹרָה 'penis', ↓ XVI p. 142; BH עוּגָב 'musical instrument', cp. שִׁיר עֲגָבִים Ezek 33:32, √ עגב 'lust after' < Sum ÁG-ÁG 'love', 'stretch' > ἀγάπη 'love' (= BH אַהֲבָה, <*Á-ÁG, ↓ XVII p. 173 n. 107) and ἄγω 'lead', etc. Cp. Sum ZAG-MÍN (= GIN 'erect') *tanittu* 'praise', ᵍⁱˢ ZAG-MÍN *sammû* 'harp', where ZAG (<*ZA-AGA "head-stone"; > SAG 'head', ↑ III n. 31) = 'phallus'.

3. Sum I-LU-BALAG-DI, I-LU-DU₁₁(-DU₁₁)/DI-DI *ṣāriḫu* ("screacher") 'lamentation-priest'; BH NH √ צרח, Arab صرخ (صُرَاخ) 'peacock') ?<*ZI-RI-ḪA "throat-howl"; cp. IM-RI-ḪA-MUN, (IM-GÁ =) RIḪA-MUN '(destructive) hurricane' (Sum RI-ḪA > BH and cogn. רוּחַ, רִיחַ 'wind, spirit').

4. See G. E. Post art. "Mandrake" in *HDB* iii 234ᵃ.

5. Κινύρας, ancestor of the Cinyrades, priests of the Aphrodite-Astarte cult at Paphos (Tacitus *Histories* 2.3); reputed founder of the cult of Aphrodite in Cyprus and introducer of the practice of sacred prostitution (Herodotus 1.199; Justinus *Epitome* (of Trogus) 18.5; ↓ XV p. 135); father of Adonis, famed as a musician and seer, favourite of Apollo.

6. Μοῦσα 'Muse', ?<Sum*MU-ŠÀ "raiser of the heart"; cp. ŠÀ-ZI-GA = Acc *niš libbi* 'raising of the heart' = 'sexual power'.

7. Διθύραμβος and Θρίαμβος, epithets of Dionysus: ?<Sum*DE/DI-DUL-AN-BI-UŠ "erector-chant", cp. DUL-DU = E₁₁ *elû* 'be high'; AN-DÙL, ANDUL "protection-from-above"; cp. ἀντλέω 'draw up, out' <AN-DÙL; by metath.> σφόνδυλος 'whorl of spindle' (Lat *spondulion* Pl NH XXIV 25f., a kind of fennel (*NH* XII 128); cp. Sum ᵍⁱˢ BAL *pilakku* 'spindle (-whorl)' and ˢᵉᵐ BAL 'Ferula' ↑ III n. 26), ?<*BI-UŠ-ANDUL, where ANDUL (as "cap"- or "umbrella"-shape) = the hemispherical whorl of the spindle.

8. Reff. *CGS* v p. 306, n. 95.

9. *CGS* v p. 144.

10. *NH* XXVIII 39; ↑ V. n. 24.

11. τραγῳδία 'tragedy', ?<*DÀRA-MU(=GÌŠ) + I-DU₁₁/DI "fecund-penis-erect"; DÀRA 'goat' etc.; I-LU-DU₁₁/DI 'lamentation-priest', ↑ n. 3; ↓ XIV p. 119.

12. Cf. *CGS* v p. 144.

13. ↑ III n. 26.

14. Sum BALAG-NAR = TIGI *tigû* 'musical instrument'; BALAG *balaggu* 'musical instrument' (and 'phallus' ↑ III n. 26); NAR ?<*NÁ-A-RI-A (BH נער, נערה, 'lad, girl'; > Acc *naialu* 'roe-buck' ↓ n. 20) 'eroticist'.

15. παλλακή, παλλακίς; BH פִּלֶגֶשׁ ?<*BALAG-UŠ "penis-erector".

16. i.e. Sum BALAG-ANTA/AN-TI "raised – or raiser of the phallus" or, as a the drug-plant, "top of the phallic mushroom"; thus Lat *Bacchante* is probably not a partic. of a dep. verb *bacchor* 'celebrate the Bacchic festival', but a noun in its own right. Of similar formation is Lat *pallacana* 'a kind of onion' (Pl *NH* XIX 105); and the Mandrake name ξηρα-ανθη <*GI-SUR-AN-TI 'top of a spindle' i.e. the whorl, likened to the cap of the mushroom (↑ VI n. 23).

17. Cp. Nic on the victims of drinking Coriander: "they are struck with madness and utter wild and vulgar words like lunatics, like crazy βάκχαι bawl shrill songs in frenzy of mind unabashed" (*Alex* 160f.).

18. Βάκχης τρόπον· ἐπὶ τῶν σιωπηλῶν, παρ' ὅσον αἱ βάκχαι σιγῶσιν Diogenianus Paroemiographus 3.43; for 'silence', ↓ n. 28. Cp. Eurip. *Bacchae* 11. 1084f.: σίγησε δ'αἰθήρ, σῖγα δ'ὕλιμος νάπη φύλλ' εἶχε . . .; so of the Korybantes, ↑ VI n. 41.

19. ↑ VI p. 49 n. 21.

20. Cp. ἐλαφινέ (var. ἐλαφυής), ?<*ERA-GIN "erect penis", a name of Hellebore, Ps-Dsc IV 162; cp. BH אַיָּל Acc *aialu* ?<*Á-A-RI-A "fecund organ" (Sum DÀRA(-BAR), ?<*DA-A-RI-A "strong in copulation"); MAŠ(-DÀ) "semen (progeny)" = Acc *ṣabítu* "gazelle" = BH צְבִי <SIPA "stretch-horn" i.e. phallus (↑ I n. 2); cp. BH אַיִל 'ram' and 'projecting pillar', so 'leader, chief' (for Acc *naialu* (= Sum DÀRA-MAŠ-DÀ, etc.) <*NÁ-A-RI-A> NAR 'eroticist', ↑ n. 14). Cp. BH אילת השחר 'hind of the dawn' (Ps 22:1) with הילל בן־שחר Isa 14:12 "Venus star", of the king of "Babylon" ~ βουβάλιον (or Sem vocal equivalent) ↓ XIII p. 110. Cp. βουβάλιον 'wild cucumber' (Ps-Dsc IV 150) = mushroom ?, with βούβαλος 'African

antelope', < Sum GÚ-BAR 'nape of the neck; penis' (> BH and cogn. גֶּבֶר 'man; penis'; cp. Sum GUBRU (= ŠU-KAL "big-hand").

For the gazelle as "shining-eyes", cp. Arab غَزَال (= Syr ܓܰܙܳܠܐ), Eng "gazelle" < Sum *IGI-ZAL "bright-eye(s)"; cp. Ἐριθαλές 'house-leek' (? < Sem ערדילא/א <Sum ERI₄-TÌL-LA, 'mushroom'), also called Oculum, Buphthalmos, Zoophthalmos (Pl NH XXV 160; see also XII n. 27); for similar play with real or mythical place-names, cp. עין־הקורא "eye of partridge/ heron", עין־גדי "goat's eye/spring", etc., ↑ VI n. 23, ↓ XIV n. 16.

21. BH עֹפֶר Arab غُفْر Sum UBUR 'breast' (= Acc tulû ?<Sum DU(L) 'hillock' (<Acc tillu, BH and cogn. תל 'hill, ruin')> Lat uber, οὖθαρ (Skt ūdhar) 'breast'; τύλος = τύλη 'callus, lump; anything rising like a lump, knob, penis'; cp. BH פלך, Arab فلك < BALAG, ↑ III n. 26.

For "twins" = "woman's breasts", cp. μαστός ?<*MAŠ-DU₆(L) "twin-hills"; ↓ XIV n. 16.

22. ↓ XIV. p. 125.

23. ↑ VII n. 9, cp. VIII p. 74.

24. II Kgs 23:10: להעביר איש את־בנו ואת־בתו באש למֹלֶךְ; cp. Jer 32:35: ומזַרְעֲךָ לא תתן להעביר למלך; butLev18:21: להעביר את־בניהם ואת־בנותיהם למלך interpretation of זרע as 'children' secondary and erroneous; cp. context of Lev 18 on sodomy (v. 22) and buggery (v. 23), and cp. Lev 20:2-5: לִזְנוֹת אחרי המֹלך 'harlotry after Molech' and v. 6 of witchcraft; cp. Isa 57:8-9 of ritual 'harlotry' (v. 8); i.e. the offence is sexual, זרע = 'semen' not 'off-spring'.

For מֹלֶךְ (μολοχ), cp. *MULUGU/MULAGA>MUG> 'mushroom' ↑ III n. 26; 'Mallow', Μαλάχη (Μολόχη) mucilaginous herbs of a large family (Post FP² I pp. 234ff.); = BH מַלּוּחַ, and cogn. Atriplex Halimus, but cp. 'Jew's Mallow' – Corchorus, Κόρχορον, Pl NH XXI 183; (Post FP² I p. 247 'Malta Jute'); Dsc II 178: Wellmann Κιχόριον varr. Κορχόριον, Κόρχορον ?<Sum KUR-KUR (= 'mushroom' ↑ VI n. 16: cp. Cichorium 'Chicory' (?), also called Chreston (Pl NH XX 74).

25. War II 133.

26. CGS v p. 162.

27. Waldemar I. Jochelson, qu. Ramsbottom op. cit. pp. 45ff.; cp. Jochelson,

Jesup N. Pacific Expedition Series vol. IX: The Yukaghir and Yukaghirized Tungus (American Museum of Natural History), N.Y., 1926.

28. BH שַׁבָּת ?<ŠÀ 'heart' + BAD petû 'open', pašâḫu 'appease, quieten' (= BH √ שבח 'quieten (of storms)', cp. Acc šapâḫu 'disperse': ↑ VII n. 8); cp. Sum ŠÀ-ḪUN nûḫ libbi 'peace': for derivation of √ נוח ↑ VII n. 8; and cp. σιγή 'silence' (↑ n. 18), ?<*IÀ-ḪA = ZÁḪ "seed-gone-to-waste" and ZAḪ nâḫu 'be at peace'.

CHAPTER XI

The Mushroom "Egg" and Birds of Mythology

1. ↑ VI pp. 51ff.

2. ↑ II n. 25; V n. 12; ↓ XII pp. 99f.

3. Ps-Dsc IV 59 περιστερεὼν ὀρθός (=ἱερὰ βοτάνη); 60:– ὕπτιος.

4. ↑ V n. 13.

5. BH NH and cogn. שָׁלוֹם 'be at peace, replete' etc., ?<*ŠÀ-LUM "fruitful womb/heart"; cp. εἰρήνη ?<*ERI₄-U₅-NÁ/NÍ "semen of fecundity" = ERI₄-TÌL-LA "semen of life" (= 'mushroom'); cp. the epithet of Hermes ἐριούνιος, ἐριούνης, e.g. σῶκος ἐ. Ἑρμῆς Il 20.72, and as abs. ἐριούνιος Il 24.360 etc., thus = "life-giving"?

6. ↑ VIII pp. 63f.

7. BH עוֹרֵב, Aram עוֹרְבָא, ܥܽܘܪܒܐ, Arab غُرَاب; Acc âribu, êribu; κόραξ, Lat corvus; all ?<*GÚR-UB "curved pod" (cp. γρυπός 'curved, hooked'; γρυπότης 'crookedness' and cp. γαμψότης (Sum GAM = GÚR), id.), "womb", like ḪARUB larva = חרוב & cogn. 'Carob', and קיקיון, ↑ V n. 12.

8. Cp. κυσθοκορώνη = νύμφη; cp. Pl NH X 32.

9. corvus = fellator Juvenalis II 63; cp. Martialis XIV 74.

10. NH II 116.

11. כַּפֹּרֶת ?<GE₆-PÀR gipâru 'frond, canopy' ("shade-spread"; cp. ᵍⁱˢ GE₆-PÀR 'Oleander').

12. γῆς κλεῖθρον Herodotus III 116; IV 13, 27; cp. Pl NH VII 10.

13. On the Aeginetan relief, cp. Furtwängler in 'Eros', Roscher's *Lexikon*, p. 1352; *CGS* ii p. 497.

14. ↓ XIV p. 132. "An hour after the ingestion of the mushrooms, twitching and trembling of the limbs is noticeable, with the onset of a period of good humour and light euphoria, characterised by macroscopia, visions of the supernatural and illusions of grandeur", R. E. Schultes 'Hallucinogens of Plant Origin' in *Science* 163, No. 3864 (17 Jan 1969), p. 246.

15. BH כְּרוּב 'cherub' = γρύψ 'griffin' ?<*GÚR-UB, ↑ n. 7.

16. Pl *NH* XV 95.

17. Sum ᵘ ERI₄-TÌL-LA ˢᵃᵐḫarûbu, ↑ V n. 12; ↓ XIV n. 24.

18. Gard. *EGr*³ F.45.

19. ↓ XV p. 134.

20. Herodotus II 73; Tacitus *Annals* VI 28; Pl *NH* X 3–5; cp. Türk in Roscher's *Lexikon* iii 3450ff.

21. ↓ XV p. 134 for the name and derivation; cp. ↓ XIV p. 121 for colour. Note the Arabic confusion between the Phoenix and the Salamander; ↑ V n. 26 for σαλαμάνδρα <*SILA-NAM-TAR "womb-of-fate", cp. Sum NAM-TAR 'fate; mushroom' ('Mandrake'). On the monuments the bird has the form of a heron, also connected with mushroom nomenclature, ↑ VI n. 23; ↓ XIV p. 124 n. 29.

22. Nic *Alex* 521, 525: ζύμωμα κακὸν χθονὸς . . . κεῖνο κακὸν ζύμωμα τὸ δή 'ρ' ὑδέουσι μύκητας παμπήδην . . .

23. ↓ XVII pp. 152ff.

24. ↑ V n. 12.

25. ↑ VIII p. 74 n. 69; κύκνος, Lat *cycnus* ?<*GÚG-NU "seed-pod"; cp. J. E. Sandys *Bacchae*⁴, 1900, p. 236 on 1.1365: "swans, as well as storks, were regarded by the ancients as notable for their affection towards their parents."

26. Ἑρμῆς ?<*ERUM-UŠ; cp. BH יַהֲלֹם ?<*IA₄-ERUM "penis-stone" = ἴασπις ?<*IA₄-SÍB/SIPA "penis-stone" (cp. LXX Exod 39:11) = BH and cogn. יָשְׁפֵה 'jasper'; ↓ XIV p. 130 (for play on similarly formed יוֹסֵף 'Joseph'; = Sum ZA-GUL *samtu* 'chalcedony' (GUL<*GÚ-UŠ "glans" > ḪUŠ 'fiery red')).

With ERUM (ÈRI, ÈR *ardu* 'slave', ?<*ÈRI-MU "erect penis", cp. id 𒂦 (Lab *Man* ⚹50); ÈRI ?<*E₄(= A)-RI-A "fecundate") cp. BH √ הלם 'strike' (cp. Sum BALAG/BULUG> πληγή, Lat *plaga* ↑III n. 26; X p. 86); and cp. Acc *elmešu* 'brass' (?); 'precious stone' (?: see Falkenstein *ZA* lii, pp. 304ff.) = BH חַלָּמִיש 'flint' as 'hard', ?<ERUM-UŠ "erect penis" as BH NH √ קשה 'hard', NH קֶשֶׁת 'penis' (Sum GÌŠ(-TI) *išâru*, *ušâru* 'penis'); cp. BH חֶרְמֵש 'sickle' (Deut 16:9, 23:26) as fitted with 'flints'; for BH place-name בֶּן־הִנֹּם 'Ben-Hinnom' ?<*BÁR-ERUM "penis-sheath, vagina", ↓ XV p. 137.

In NT, cp. Ἐλύμας (= "Hermes" (<*ERUM-UŠ)) = βαριησοῦς (Acts 13:6-8) ≃ βρηισεύς, βρησεύς, βρησσαῖος, titles of Dionysus, ?<*BAR-UŠ-SA "erect penis" (↓ XVIII p. 181 n. 21 = *בר־ישי (= BH בֶן־ישי, of David), and ישכר 'Issachar'); a "μάγος" ≃ "Persian" (Πέρσης) as a word-play on Περσεία, 'mushroom' (?) ↑ VI p. 46.

27. Ἀφροδίτη ?<*Á-BÚRU-DA-TI "organ of fertility", cp. Sum ú BÚRU-DA *urnu* 'mint' (as aphrodisiac, Dsc III 34), BÚRU *pašāru* 'release' > βρύω 'teem with, burst forth'; σπόρος 'sowing, seed'; Lat *spurium* 'womb'. Cp. Ἀβρότονον, Abrotonum 'Southernwood', "an aphrodisiac" (Pl *NH* XXI 162) ?<*Á-BÚRU-TÙN "womb-fructifier"; cp. μανδραγορῖτις as an epithet of Aphrodite (Hsch). Cp. Ἀπόλλων 'Apollo', ?<*Á-BÚRU-NÁ/NU "releaser of semen"; cp. Πλούτων 'Pluto' ↓ XVII p. 153. ?<*BÚRU-TÙN "deliverer, fructifer of the womb".

28. For Bacchus as a hermaphrodite and the ritualistic significance of transvestism, see *CGS* v p. 160, and the god's title βασσαρεύς, ?<βασσάρα 'woman's dress of fox skins', ?<*BAR(=TÚG)-SAL-LA (<SILA), "vulva/groin-garment" i.e. a loin-cloth.

CHAPTER XII

The Heavenly Twins

1. BH קִין Gen 4:1ff. (↑ II n. 24; ?<*GAR-ÈN "seed-container" = ENGAR 'peasant, cultivator' > Acc *ikkaru*, BH & cogn. √ אגר 'hire' (Sum ḪUN(-GÁ) ≃ GUN 'burden'), and BH NH √ אגר 'gather food', NH אֲגוֹרָה 'store-room'; Sum AGARIN (?<*Á-GAR-ÈN "seed-container") 'mother'; > ἀγείρω 'gather together; ἀγερμός 'collection (of money)', ἀγέλη 'herd' etc.; Sum

GARIN 'pond' = ἀγγεῖον 'vessel (for holding liquids); receptacle, capsule, afterbirth (cp. ἄγγος 'vessel, womb' ?<Sum ÁG 'womb; measure'); cp. Γεράνειον 'mushroom', Eustathius Comm. 1017.19 = Ὕδνον Thphr I vi 9 ap. Athenaeus 2.62ᵃ (om. codd. Thphr); cp. Pers كرنا karnā 'mushroom'; ?>μαινάς 'Maenad' i.e. womb-mad, cp. ὑστερικός.

(For Arab قَان 'fit together, fabricate, قَيْن 'worker in iron' etc., cp. Sum GÍN pâšu, pâltu 'axe' (↓ n. 4) <GI-NA (>GIN 'erect', > قَيْنَة 'singer' ↑ X n. 2).)

2. BH הֶבֶל LXX Ἀβελ, ?<*Á-BAL, ↑ III n. 26 for *ù BAL "mushroom" >ὀβελός, BH עֹפֶל, etc.; as רעה צאן (Gen 4:2) cp. SIPA, SÍB rê'u 'shepherd' ↑ I n. 2; for ἀπὸ τοῦ αἵματος Ἀβελ τοῦ δικαίου (Matt 23:35) ↑ VI n. 42, as a word-play on *TAB-BA-LI.

3. BH תּוּבַל־קַיִן ?<*TI-Ú-BAL + GAR-ÈN (cp. Sum UḪ-TI-BAL (AN-TI-BAL) > Acc bulṭitu, balṭitu 'wood-worm' ("borer") βωλίτης, Boletus 'mushroom' (and βαλλωτή, ballote 'leek' (Dsc III 103, Pl NH XXVII 54, etc., cp. NH בָּלוּט 'acorn, peg' (= βάλανος, Lat glans), בְּלוּטָא 'oak'), i.e. *u-ti-bal> *bal-u-ti> 'Tubal'.

4. *בַּר־צְלָה ~ בַּרְזֶל 'iron' = Acc parzillu = Sum AN-BAR ("stretched-out (= BÀR)-above" ↓ XVII p. 159f. n. 54); = ᵘᶻᵘ BAR-SÌL 'groin/womb' (cp. Lat dolabra 'mattock, pickaxe', ?<*DUL-ANBAR "shade-stretched-out-above", ↓ n. 38); cp. ἀξίνη 'axe-head' (= δίστομος πέλεκυς); Lat ascia (<*acsia) <AB-SÍN (= ŠEN) "opening of the womb" ('furrow' as "vulva" of the earth), as the central hole of the double-axe head (↑ III n. 9); BH גַּרְזֶן 'axe', ?<*MAR-SÍN/ŠEN; MAR marru 'mattock' (= μάρρον Hsch.) and MAR 'womb' (as in MAR-TE išpatu 'quiver' i.e. 'vagina' as φαρέτρα <TÙN-BAR = Acc šaptu šaplitu "lower-lips" = prepuce, vagina, also >παρθένος 'maiden' and BH & cogn. בתולה 'virgin'; išpatu = BH אַשְׁפָּה <*ÚŠ-BÀD "foetus-enclosure" i.e. womb, as in Ps 127:5: אשרי הגבר אשר מלא את־אשפתו מהם, of children under fig. of "arrows"; similarly BH מִשְׁפְּתַיִם 'sheep-fold' (Gen 49:14 ↓ XVI p. 147) <*MÁŠ-BÀD "livestock-enclosure"; i.e. two barriers set out in 'V'-formation) cp. BH etc. קַרְדֹּם 'axe' and NH גַּרְדֹּם, גַּרְדֹּן, 'gibbet' (<*MAR-DÙG "womb-favourer" i.e. penis (↓ n. 66; > ᵘ Marduk ↑ II n. 1) > νάρθηξ (<*mar-dug-giš) = ᵍⁱˢ BAL 'Ferula', ↑ III n. 26); > Κάρδαμον 'Cardamon' and Καρδαμίνη 'mint' (aphrodisiac, ↑ II n. 1; XI n. 27). Cp. Aram כּוּלְבָּא, Acc kalappatu 'axe', ?<*AB-GALA = AB-SÍN "opening of the womb" (> BH אֶשְׁנָב 'window'). Also from Sum

ŠEN "womb", cp. ŠEN-TAB-BA *pâštu, pâltu* (↑ n. 1; <*BAL-TI), prop. 'axe-handle' ("phallus") = πέλεκκος (<BALAG, ↑ VI p. 52); Syr ܦܳܣܳܩܳ 'woodman's axe', ?<*ŠEN-DÀ "womb" (↑ VIII n. 20), NH Aram √ שמט 'draw off shoes, unsheathe, pull out' (of slipping yoke), etc.; BH 'let drop' (II Kgs 9:33 of Jezebel from window), 'leave fallow', etc.; NH 'drawing embryo from womb; dislocation of joints, Arab سِنَة 'double-axe' (as well as Turkish-Arab *šanta* 'leather bag'). For characteristic 'V-'shape of Sum ŠEN, cp. ŠEN-MUŠEN *sinuntu* 'swallow' (from shape of wings?, cp. GÀM-GÀM-MUŠEN *'gamgammu*-bird', where GÀM = "crescent") = Syr ܣܘܣܝܳܐ (a) 'swallow', (b) 'tortoise' (= χελώνη < Sum ḪAL "interstice between the legs"), (c) 'arch', (d) 'bat'; cp. χελιδών (Lat *hirundu*) 'swallow; female genitals' (Suid. cp. Juvenal 6.365(6)); and with χελώνη 'tortoise' cp. χελλών, χελών 'a kind of mullet' (↑ VI n. 5).

Cp. πέλεκυς, prop. 'axe-shaft' (<BALAG 'penis' ↑ III n. 26), πελεκυνάριον, *id.* <BALAG-NAR 'eroticist' (↑ VI p. 52); πελεκύστερον (i.e. BALAG + *ÙŠ-TAR "penis-womb") = στελεόν 'haft of axe', but στελέα, στελειή = 'hole in the axe-head'; for "axe-head" as names for thunderbolts/mushrooms, ↓ n. 33. Note the word-play on a name for the axe-haft in II Kgs 6:5 where שָׁאוּל 'asked, borrowed' ~ שָׁאוּל (elsewhere the proper name 'Saul') < Sum UŠ-SA 'erect penis', i.e. the haft (√ שאל 'ask' <Sum ŠU-ÍL-LA *nîs qâti* ("raising of the hands") 'prayer' (cp. Ps 88:10) and > BH שֹׁעַל 'palm of hand'.)

5. Ἠρύγγιον, Dsc III 21 (also Ἠρύγειον Ps-Dsc; Wellm. varr. Ἔρμ(α)ιον (↑XI n. 26); κάρυον 'nut' <Sum * GAR-NU "seed container" = *GAR-ÈN (↑ n. 1); ἐρυγρίς; μῶλυ (↑ VI n. 23); λιβεννάτα, cp. BH and cogn. לְבֵנָה 'brick', (<Sum LI 'cone-, bun-shape' + BAN/GAN 'arch/bowl-lid', i.e. the primitive convex-topped clay brick).

6. *NH* XXII 20.

7. *NH* XXII 21.

8. ↑ VI n. 23.

9. Ἀλόη cp. Dsc III 22; Ps-Dsc Ἀμφίβιον, Ἠρύγγιον, ἔρμ(α)ιον.

10. Lucianus *de Astrologia* 11.

11. *NH* XXVII 14; Pl also notes a kind of "mineral aloes (*metallicam*) in Judaea beyond Jerusalem", inferior and darker, moister, apparently relating the bitumen of the Dead Sea with aloes, ↑ VIII p. 5.

12. Gen 4:15: כל־הֹרֵג קַיִן שִׁבְעָתַיִם יֻקָּם ?‿ ʿΗρύγγιον (or Sem equiv. of *ERUM-GAR-EN. For the "sign" (אוֹת) ?‿ תָּו (cp. Ezek 9:4, 6) <TUM ḫurdatu, ḫardatu 'cross-piece; yoke-peg' (as securing cross-piece of yoke); also 'loin-cloth, vulva' (?) (Gilgamesh VI 69: *CAD s.v.*), cp. Ezek 26:16, where חֲרָדוֹת יִלְבָּשׁוּ ?‿ "they shall wear loin-cloths" ("they shall put off their mantles") with a word-play on √ חרד 'tremble' in v. 16b. Cp. Syr ܓܝܳܪ̈ܐ 'mast, column, balk, timber, wooden frame, peg'; Arab عرَّادة 'ballista'; ?‿ א/ערדילא 'mushroom'; cp. Γεράνειον 'mushroom' (↑ n. 1) and γέρανος 'crane' (the bird, ↓ n. 28) and the lifting machine (OE *cran*; Lith *granỹs* 'stork'); cp. Lat *ciconia* 'stork' and a 'T'-shaped implement for measuring furrows (= קִיקָיוֹן 'mush-room' ↑ V n. 12). With Sum TUM 'cross-piece', cp. TÙM = TÚM *abâlu* 'carry', ?<*TI-UM "mother's organ" ?>BH תְּאוֹם 'twin', as ξύλον διδύμον "twin-wood" = 'gibbet, cross' (LXX Josh 8:29, ↓ n. 66), as 'yoke', ↓ pp. 105ff.; cp. BH תְּהוֹם 'the deep', i.e. the earth's womb, ↓ XV p. 133.

13. Gen 4:9: הֲשֹׁמֵר אָחִי אָנֹכִי ?‿ a mushroom name equiv. to Pers سماروخ *samarûḫ*, cp. Arab شِمْرَاخ 'cluster of grapes, mountain summit' (↑ IX n. 12): and Ζωμαρῖτις, the Magian name for "Hellebore", Ps-Dsc IV 162, ↑ II n. 1: <Sum *ŠÚ-MAR-UGU/AGA; cp. Aram שׁוּמָרָא 'Fennel'; that *šumārāʾ* was followed in a Sem form by *ʾaḥ*, and read as though *ḥayy* 'snake' (Arab), is indicated by the traditional linking of Fennel with snakes, as aids to sloughing skins and improving eye-sight, cp. Pl *NH* VIII 99, XX 254; (260 as an antidote to snake-bites). Cp. also Syr ܓܦܶܬܳܐ ܕܚܶܘܝܳܐ "snake's vine", 'Colocynth' (? a folkname for the mushroom; cp. similarly, "vine of the earth" = 'Mandrake' ↓ XVII p. 156 n. 30), and possibly as another indication of a Sem origin for the tradition, cp. Syr ܥܰܡܛܳܢܳܐ 'night-blindness'. Sum AGA/UGU 'crown' (<*Á-GÚ "top of the head") BH אָחוּ 'reed, rush' and cogn. Cp. ἄχυ (Dsc I 13, 'kind of Cassia') and cp. Sum MENBULUG "crowned Ferula" = Acc *pullukku* 'Oleander' = Sum ᵍⁱˢGE₆-PÀR ↑ XI n. 11.

14. Hom. Hymns XVII; the Twins and Helen from one egg: Servius Danielis *Aeneid* III 328- from two eggs: *Scriptores rerum mythicarum Latini tres* I 204 (G. H. Bode, 1834, p. 64); cp. Horace *Satirae* II l.26; etc. Leda visited by a swan: Euripides *Helena* 17ff.; is given the egg to hatch: Kratinos *ap.* Athenaios IX 373E. In general, L. Preller *Griechische Mythologie*⁴ ed. C. Robert, 1894-, III ii; *HGM* pp. 230ff.

15. *Il* III 238: for Helen's birth, cp. *Kypria* (ed. T. W. Allen, *Homeri Opera* V) fgt. 7.

16. ↑ VIII p. 73.

17. Hom. Hymns XVII: οἱ Ζηνὸς Ὀλυμπίου ἐξεγένοντο, XXXIII: Διὸς κούρους.

18. Διόσκοροι, Διόσκουροι; as dual, τώ Διοσκόρω, (<*UŠ-GÚ-RI-UD; cp. ᵈISKUR(=ⁱˡAdad); <*UŠ-GÚ-RI "erect penis", ↑ III n. 5; *GÚ-RI "knobbed bolt" > KUR₄ *kabâtu* 'be thick', *ba'âlu* 'be dominant'; > κύριος 'lord', ↑ III n. 24. Sum *GÚ-RI > BH קוּרִי 'spindle' (Isa 59:5: of "spiders" ‖ "asps' eggs" בֵּיצֵי צִפְעֹנִי, folk-names for the fungus ? note Κόρη the counterpart of Περσεφόνη <*BÁR-SÍB-U₅-NÍ "container-of-the-fecund-penis" i.e. the womb, thus being the two parts of the mushroom, ↓ XV n. 27; XVII p. 152 n. 5). Cp. Κυριάννος, 'Coriander' (↓ XIII n. 12) ?<*GÚ-RI-AN-NA "penis-raiser", i.e. an aphrodisiac; cp. Dsc III 63: Κόριον (Ps-Dsc Κορίαννος): σπέρματός ἐστι γεννητικόν, and cp. Sum ᵍⁱˢ KUR₄ 'Coriander' (?) = Acc *kiskibirru* <Sum ᵍⁱˢKIBIR *kibirru* 'fork; bolt' (cp. Acc *birku* 'penis' ↓ n. 65); BH גַּד 'Coriander' (Num 11:7) = NH Aram גִּדָּ(א) all <Sum GÍD 'stretch', ↓ XIII n. 12.

   With BH קוּרִי 'spindle' (cp. BH קוֹרָא 'beam'), note the name of Verbena, "Holy Plant", as Διὸς ἠλακάτη, also Κουρῖτις, Κουρί (Ps-Dsc IV 60), and the ref. by Pl to *Paeonia*, "Holy Plant", that "with this the table of Jupiter is swept" (*NH* 105), reading perhaps Διόσκουροι as Διος + κορέω (A) 'sweep;' κόρος 'besom' (Hsch).

19. Ισκαριώθ, Ισκαριώτης <*UŠ-GÚ-RI-UD; ↑ prev. n. For "betrayer" (מסור) ~ מצר/מזר 'stretch', ↓ XVII p. 171; for the drug as a purge, ↓ XVII p. 172.

20. سقراطيون *saqrātiyûn*: cp. I. A. Vullers *Lexicon Persico Latinum*. 2 vols, Bonn, 1855–64 (Suppl. 1867), *s.v.*

21. Κάστωρ ?<*MÁS-TÙN/TÙR "progeny-container" i.e. womb, > γαστήρ 'belly, womb'; cp. Sum ŠÀ-TÙR *šaturru* 'womb'; AMAŠ 'sheepfold'. For Lat *castor* = 'womb', cp. the women's oath, *Ecastor! Mecastor!* "by my womb!"

22. ↑ V n. 12; XI p. 91.

23. ↑ XI p. 91.

24. *NH* VIII 109.

25. *Th* 565.

26. For the mushroom as an "egg", cp. Acc *pilû*, 'egg'; 'Mandrake'; for "egg/testicle", cp. BH בֵּיצָה and cogn. ?<Sum *BÁR-ZI "sac of life" (the 'white' significance of Arab بيض is secondary, ref. being to the egg-shell), cp. Sum NUNUZ (*pilû* <*NU-NU-ZI "seed-bag(s) of life", cp. ᶻᵃ NUNUZ = ᶻᵃ PEŠ₄ ("pregnant") *aban arî* ("pregnant-stone"), 'geode'; cp. ᾠον (<ὤεον, ὤιον) Lat *ovum* (cp. Hsch ὤβεον) 'egg' <*Á-UIA-NU "seed-bag of fertility"; cp. the Service-tree, ὄα, ὄη (codd. Thphr II ii 10), οὖα III vi 5; the fruit ὄον var. ὠϊά, ὠά; οὖα, all <UIA (↑ III n. 1); cp. Syr כּוּזֿי 'Service-tree' ?<*KI-NU-ÚR "ground-testicle", cp. ⁽ᵍⁱˢ⁾ ŠENNUR (> Acc *šalluru*) 'Medlar' ?<*ŠEN-NU-ÚR "womb-seed bag"; cp. Sum NU-ÚR-MA > Acc *nurmu* 'pomegranate' (as "seed-bag"), and 'egg' connection gives Sem √ *nwr/nmr* 'be white, light'; cp. Sum (GIŠ-)ŠIR *išku* 'testicle' also *nûru* 'light'; ᵈGIŠ-ŠIR (-GAL) = ⁱˡ *Šamaš*.

Cp. the plant called Οὔϊγγον (var. Οὔϊτον, Pl *NH* XXI 88 *Oetum*) + Ὕδνον, Ἀσχίον ('fungi') as "underground plants", Thphr I vi 9, "called in Egypt Οὔϊγγον . . . an excellent thing, eaten, found when the river goes down by turning the clods"; ?<ᾠον, ὤιον 'egg' + γήϊνον 'of the earth'; cp. Syr ܥܢܒܐ ܕܐܪܥܐ 'grapes of the ground' and Lat *mala terrestris* = 'Mandrake' (Ps-Dsc IV 75; cp. *malum terrae* = Aristolochia, Pl *NH* XXV 95); ↓ XV n. 27.

27. *Pollux* <Sum ˡᵘ GEŠPÚ = Acc *amil ša umaše* ("man of fetters") 'jailer' = ŠU-DIM₄ "big-hand", cp. ŠU-KAL = GUBRU (>BH NH גבר 'man; penis' ↑ X n. 20), *umašu* 'violence' (cp. *umšu* 'storm'), cp. KIŠIB *upnu* 'fist', ?<Sum GIŠ-ŠUB> GEŠPU (= ILLURU) *tilpanu* 'bow, arch', id. ⟨⟩ (Lab *Man* ✳68); cp. ᵍⁱˢ Ù-ŠUB 'brick-mould', id. 🏛 (↑ IX n. 22).

Πολυδεύκες <ˡᵘ GEŠPU + DU₁₄ (= LÚ-NE) *ṣaltu* 'rivalry'; *muṣallu* 'adversary'; cp. ληνεύς = Bacchus, ληνίς 'Bacchante', ληναΐζειν 'rave'; and the Attic winter feast of Λήναια (*CGS* v pp. 208f.); cp. שמען and לוי as כלי חמס (Gen 49:5; ↓ XVI n. 24). Sum ˡᵘ GEŠPÚ > φύλαξ 'watcher, guard, sentinel' cp. epithet of Hermes, πυληδόκος "gate-watcher" (Hom. Hymns IV 15) ≃ Πολυδεύκες. For another possible transposition of consonants of GEŠPU, cp. the name of Ἐριθαλές ("House-leek" (?) ≙ Sem ערדילא/א 'mushroom' ↑ X n. 20), *Hypogeson* (Pl *NH* XXV 160, as if = ὑπογεῖσον "because it generally grows under eaves"; γεῖσ(ο)ον 'eaves, coping', etc. < Sum GISSU (= GIŠ-GÍG "shade") ?<GIŠ-ŠÚ "cover"), ?<*ú GEŠPÚ "arch (strong-man)-plant", i.e. *u-ges-pu> *upuges> hypogeson.

28. Cp. *Il* 3.237: πὺξ ἀγαθὸν Πολυδεύκεα, cp. NH אַמָּה 'forearm; penis' (Sabb 108ᵇ, etc.). For 'fist', BH אֶגְרֹף (Exod 21:18 Isa 58:4 (LXX πυγμή) ?<Sum

GÀR-BA *karru* 'pommel' (↑ V n. 18); πυγμή, *pugnus* <*BULUG-AN ("top of erect penis") Acc *bukannu* 'beater, stick'. Note the myth of the perpetual war between the pygmies and the cranes (↑ nn. 1, 12): *Il* 3.5ff.; Strabo 2.1.9, etc.; Pl *NH* IV 44, their home in Scythian territory on the East coast of Thrace, at *Gerania*, "their name in the local dialect *Catizos*", ?<Acc *qat ezzati, uzzi* 'strong hand' (Sum ŠU-DIM₄ = ˡú GEŠPÚ); *NH* VII 26: "in springtime the entire band of pygmies (of India), mounted on the backs of rams and she-goats and armed with arrows, goes in a body down to the sea and eats cranes' eggs and chickens for three months . . ." Is the origin of the myth the supposed antagonism between the two parts of the fungus, the stem (= Pollux) and the volva (= Castor)? cp. the story of Cain and Abel and Jacob and Esau.

29.   βοανηργές (Suid βοανεργεις as plural), Mark 3:17: <GEŠPÚ + *AN-ÚR "heavenly-roof" > οὐρανός.

30.   See G. Dalman, *Gramm.* p. 144; and rather differently, *Words* p. 42. Cp. the doubts of Jerome (*Comm. ad Dan.* I. 7) "emendatius legitur *benereem* (var. *baneraem, banarehem*), i.e. רעם, and so in his *Lib. de nomm. Heb.* under "John", ignored, however, in his commentary on Mark; cp. Drusius (*Ad voces NT Comm. prior* 39 (1616), Colassius (*Phil. Sacra* (1625), following Jerome, saw ργες as ργεμ (γ = ע), corrupted by Graecization of ending; Beza (*Adnotationes majores,* ad loc (1594), saw it as an error in a Semitic text, רעם as רעס; Kautzsch *Gramm.* thought ργες = רגז (רגיז) 'anger'; Dalman, following, cites as support, Job 37:2: רֹגֶז קֹלוֹ.

31.   ὅ ἐστιν Ὑιοὶ βροντῆς.

32.   Aram √ רגשׁ 'be agitated, in commotion'; ܪܓܫ 'feel, perceive; ܪܓܫܐ (a) up-roar, (b) sense, feeling'; ܪܓܫܬܐ 'rustling, sensation', etc. √רגז 'be angry'.

33.   ↑ VII p. 55; Κεραύνιον, Lat *Ceraunion*, Thphr I vi 5; Syr ܙܥܩܐ ܪܥܡ (P-S 2987ᵃ) = Arab بنات الرَّعْد; cp. Pl *NH* XIX 37: "cum fuerint imbres autumnales ac tonitrua crebra, tunc nasci, et maxime tonitribus . . ." For confusion between 'thunder-' mushrooms and thunderbolts, cp. Pl *NH* 134f.: "among the bright colourless stones there is also the one called *ceraunia*. . . . Sotacus distinguishes also two other varieties of the stone, a black and a red, resembling axe-heads (*securibus,* ↑ n. 4). According to him, those among them that are black and round are supernatural objects; and he states that thanks to them cities and fleets are attacked and overcome, their name being *baetulos*,

while the elongated stones are *ceraunias*. These writers distinguish yet another kind (of *ceraunias*) which is quite rare. According to them the Magi hunt for it zealously because it is found only in a place that has been struck by a thunderbolt (*fulmine*)." Cp. Pl on fungi, "they are of two kinds . . . red and black . . ." (XIX 34). For the *baetulos*, cp. BH and cogn. בתולה 'virgin' (<Sum TÙN-BAR 'womb') and βαίτυλος, a meteoric stone held sacred because it fell from heaven (Damascius *Vita Isiodori* 94. 203), of the stone swallowed by Kronos (Hsch); cp. the Palladium ('womb') preserved by the Vestals, ↑ VIII p. 72 n. 57; and the Περσεία (<Sum BAR-SÌL 'womb') that grew where Perseus dropped his scabbard-chape (μύκης; ↑ V n. 12 XVII n. 31). With this *baetulos*, cp. also *betula* (*betulla*) 'birch' (↑ VIII n. 20).

On prophetic thunderbolts, cp. Pl *NH* II 82; ". . . crackling fire is spit forth by the planet (Jupiter) as crackling charcoal flies from a burning log, bringing prophecies with it, as even the part of himself that he discards does not cease to function in its divine tasks." Of "earth" thunderbolts, cp. Pl *NH* II 138: "some also burst out of the ground, called "low" (bolts, *infera*) and these are rendered exceptionally direful and accursed by the season of winter, though all bolts that they (the Tuscans) believe of earthly origin are not the ordinary ones and do not come from the stars but from the nearer and more disordered element (air), a clear proof of this being that all those coming from the upper heaven deliver slanting blows, whereas these which they call earthly (*terrena*) strike straight. And those that fall from the nearer elements are supposed to come out of the earth because they leave no traces as a result of their rebound. . . ."

34. ↓ XIX pp. 193ff.

35. Lat *cunnus*: Martialis 1, 90, 7, etc.; as obscene already in Cicero *Orator ad Brutum* 45, 154; *Epistulae ad Familiares* 9, 22, 3; ?<Sum *GUN-TI "organ of burden"; GUN *biltu*, 'burden, tax', etc. <GÚ-UN "that which is placed on the nape of the neck (GÚ)"; cp. Sum UGÙN *alâdu* "give birth' (↓ n. 51), rel. to γυνή 'woman', γόνος, γονή 'offspring; womb;' cp. Κύνθος 'the mountain of Delos, birth place of Apollo and Diana; also the name Κύνθια 'Cynthia' = Diana; τέκνον 'child' <Sum * TI-GUN, as a 'burden' in the womb, cp. φορτίον 'child in the womb' (Xenophon *Memorabilia* 2.2.5).

36. חֶרְמוֹן <*ÁR-GUN; in full, חֶרְמוֹנִים (Ps 42:7), not plural, but orig. *ÁR-GUN + IM 'sky', "organ-bearing-the-sky", as יְרוּשָׁלַיִם 'Jerusalem' <*URU-SÌLA-IM (not dual), "city-of-the-groin-of-the-sky"; cp. אֶפְרַיִם

'Ephraim' (not dual) <*ANBAR-IM "heavenly-arch" (ANBAR = "stretch-out-above" ↓ XVII p. 159).

37. *Ὄλυμπος, Οὔλυμπος* ?<*URU-IM-BI-UŠ "city-of-the-support-of-heaven" ↓ XV p. 133.

38. Lat *Platanus*, *Πλάτανος* (<*πλατύς* "because of its broad crown" L & S 1413ᵃ) ?<TÙN-BAR 'groin, womb'; cp. Acc *ṣarbatu* <BAR-SÌL (*naglabu*) 'groin'; SÌLA id. ⛏ (Lab *Man* ※62); cp. Acc *ⁱˢdulbu*, Aram דְּלִיב, דּוּלְבָּא (= BH עַרְמֹן Gen 30:37, etc.); Pers-Arab دُلْب 'Plane-tree' ?<*DUL-BAR (cp. Lat *dolabra* 'pickaxe' ↑ n. 4; and BH אַפִּרְיֹן 'palanquin' Ct 3: 9 ?<*ANBAR (= AN-PÀR)-IÀ-U₅-NÁ "shaded nuptial couch").

Sum ᵍⁱˢA-TU-GAB-LIŠ 'Plane-tree' ref. in A-TU to the sap, "birth-juice" i.e. semen, cp. ᵘERI₄-AN-NA *mastakal* = A-RI-A-NAM-LÚ-ULUˡú ("semen of mankind") 'tragacanthe'; *Θυία* 'cedar' <*TU-IÀ "creation-juice" (↑ VIII n. 60); -GAB-LIŠ "flaking-skin" ref. to the annual shedding of its bark (*NHB* p. 346).

39. Cp. the epic poem qu. S. N. Kramer *History Begins at Sumer*, 1956, pp. 110ff.

40. Apollodorus III 2ff.; Ovid *Metamorphoses* II 843ff.; cp. Pl *NH* XII 11 (and for import of Plane-trees for the sake of their shade, XII 6). For the place in Crete, Gortyn = *μύρτον.*'vulva', ↑ V n. 12. Note the image of Dionysus in the hollow of a Plane-tree at Magnesia on the Meander, whence three Maenads were sent on instructions from the Delphic oracle to organize Bacchic thiasoi in Magnesia, called ὁ *Πλατανιστηνῶν* after the god of the Plane-tree, *CGS* v p. 152.

41. BH עַרְמֹן <*ÁR-GUN; cp. אַרְמֹנִי, a son of Saul, crucified by the Gibeonites, II Sam 21:8.

42. *ἁρμονία*; *ἁρμονή* 'joint'; *ἁρμόζω* 'effect a joint; give in marriage'; cp. related *ὄργανον* 'member, organ'; Sum AR-NIGIN ("turn") *bînâti* 'members' (*banû* 'create').

43. Phereclus, *Φέρεκλος*, ?<*ˡúBALAG, as "driller" (= Sum NAGAR *naggâru* 'carpenter', ?<NA + GUR as ˡúGUR-GUR *qurqurru* 'artisan' (GUR *târu* 'turn' ↑III n. 26) cp. *τέκτων* 'artificer, joiner', etc., ?<*TI-GI₄-DUN (*ḫerû* 'drill'), i.e. "borer-reed" (for *τεκ* <TI-G/KI -, cp. *τέκμαρ* 'fixed mark' < TI + KI-GAR *sikittu* 'place'); cp. כִּידֹן 'javelin', ?<*GI₄/KI-DUN as "driller". Cp. *Φέρεκλος: τέκτονος υἱὸν ʼΑρμονίδεω*, *Il* 5.59f.

44. Gard. *EG*³ U 24, in *ḥmt* 'craft' and related words.

45. Gard. *EG*³ U 26, in *wb3* 'open up' and derivatives.

46. = Sum NAGAR (↑ n. 43) > NH Aram נַגָּרָ(א) 'carpenter'.

47. ↑ III n. 26.

48. Sum ᵍⁱˢBAL *pilakku* 'spindle'; cp. ᶻᵃBAL *pilakku* 'thunderbolt'.

49. ↑ n. 4; cp. opp. √ שמט in 'slip the yoke, withdraw, let a foetus drop,' etc. For the sexual significance of drawing off the sandal, cp. Deut 25:9; W. R. Smith *Kinship and Marriage in Early Arabia,* Cambridge, 1895, p. 269, ↓ XV n. 34.

50. BH צֵלָע 'rib'; of buildings, ark; doorleaves; side-chambers, < Sum SÌLA, ↑ n. 38, as in BAR-SÌL 'groin, womb'.

51. ζυγόν Dor. δυγός Lat *jugum* (Skt *yuga*) <*IA₄/ZÁ-UGÙN "stone of bearing" (↑ n. 35; III n. 1), originally a fork-shaped birth stool and transferred to the yoke by shape-characteristic? Cp. *ZÁ-GUN > BH צָפֹון 'North' as the "fulcrum" of earth and sky (↓ XV p. 133); >διάκονος 'servant' as "load-bearer". Lat *jugum* 'cross-beam, door-panel'; cp. Sum GUN-GI 'part of a door'. Cp. also BH אֲגֻדָּה 'band', מֹוטָה "א 'bands, thongs of a yoke' (Isa 58:6), < Sum MUD as ᵍⁱˢMUD *uppu* 'strap, bridle', MUD-Á *uppi aḫi* 'clavicle'; cp. BH & cogn. עָמוּד 'pillar' < Á-MUD; cp. esp. Am 9:6; cp. also Sum MUD *uppu* 'tube' and *alâdu* 'bear children', thus BH צלמות "birth-canal" (↓ XV p. 137) as Sum SÌL-MUD 'groin' (?), and > BH & cogn. √ צמד 'yoke together'.

52. Hom. Hymns XXXIII: Κάστορά θ' ἱππόδαμον; cp. ζύγιος (sc. ἵππος) 'draught-horse'; δαμάω 'bring under yoke'; δαμάζω 'tame' (animals); 'subdue' (wives); <Sum DAM "copulate"; cp. δάμαρ-αρτος 'wife, spouse', ?<Sum DAM + AL-TI (= DUN₄ *níru* 'yoke'); cp. צמד, in prev. n.

53. ἅρμα, e.g. at Acts 8:28ff.; Rev 9:9, 'a two-wheeled war chariot', as Lat *jugum* 'pair of horses; chariot'. Sum MAR *marru* 'mattock', 'womb' (↑ n. 4), Acc *marratu* (?<* MAR-TI) 'rainbow', *narkabtu* 'chariot', cp. ᵍⁱˢ MAR-GÍD-DA ("long chariot') 'cart, waggon' (?> Acc *raqâdu* BH רקד 'hop, spring, dance' etc., orig. of the bouncing of chariots (Na 3:2)).

54. ↑ XI p. 94.

55. Ugar *rkb* '*rpt* 51: III: 11, 18; V: 122; 67: II: 7; 1Aqht: 43–44; 'nt: II: 40; as epithet of Baal; for *rkb* ≟ *brk*, ↓ n. 65.

56. ἐλατήρ, ?<Sum E₄-LA₆ + TÙN.

57. Ἐλατήριον Ecballium Elaterium, Ps-Dsc IV 150 = Σίκυς ἄγριος = Βουβάλιον
(↑ X n. 20 ↓ XIII p. 110, <Sum GÚ-BAR > BH NH גֶּבֶר 'man; penis'
↑ n. 27) Σίκυς, cp. Σικύα, Σικύη ('bottle-gourd, Κολοκυνθίς) <*SI-GÚ-A
"knobbed-horn" (GÚ-A = GÚL as in SAG-GÚL 'bolt' > NH Aram שְׂכְוִי,
שְׂכְוְיָא 'cock', and √ סכי 'look out for, hope' (cp. BH NH √ צפה <Sum
SIPA "erect penis" (↑ I n. 2)); > Aram √ סגי 'be great' (cp. √ גבר 'be
great').

58. قِثَّاء الحِمار. Cp. Post FP² i p. 481: "fruit oblong, echinate, watery, separated
at maturity from its peduncle, and contracting elastically at base, in such a
manner as to squirt out its juice and oblong seeds to a considerable distance . . . the inspissated juice is an exceedingly drastic and irritating
cathartic."

59. Cp. Lat Abiga, a plant causing abortion (= Chamaepitys, 'ground-pine',
Pl NH XXIV 29), abigeus 'cattle-driver, -stealer'; abigo 'drive away cattle;
abort'. Cp. Pl NH XIV 110: "in Thasos Hellebore is planted among vines, or
else the wild cucumber (= Σίκυος ἄγριος) or scammony; the wine thus
obtained is called phthorius (φθόρος ἐμβρύων, Dsc V 67).

60. Ἑλλέβορος <E₄-LA₆ + BURU₈ "strong-water of defecation" = Lat
Veratrum <*BÁRA-TÙN "empty-belly" (Pl NH XXV 52).

61. Ἀγαρικόν Dsc III 1 (καθαίρει δὲ καὶ κοιλίαν) <AGARGARA agargarû
'excrement' <*GAR-GAR a denom. from G/MAR "womb, belly" (cp.
Dsc ib: ἄγει δὲ καὶ ἔμμηνα καὶ ταῖς ἐμπνευματουμέναις ὑστέραν γυναιξὶν
ὠφελίμως τὸ ἴσον δίδοται; cp. AGARGARÁ agargarû 'spawn': ↓ XVII p. 172
on Iscariot.

62. so called ἐλατῆραβοῶν (cp. abigeus ↑ n. 59), Hom. Hymns IV 14, 22, 68ff.

63. Pindar Nemean Ode 10.60ff. Theocritus 22.137f.

64. crux ?<* ᵍⁱˢ GÚR (kanâšu 'bend over, submit').

65. furca; cp. Acc birku ('knee, penis') BH בֶּרֶךְ 'knee' < Sum KIBIR kibirru
'fork, bolt' (↑ n. 18; ? by metath. > √ rkb 'ride, copulate').

66. σταυρός (= palus) 'stake' ?<*UŠ-TAR "erect penis" > AŠTAR 'bolt'; Pesh
NT ܐܩܝܡ, ܐܩܡ 'erect (stakes, penis), crucify' (so in NT, elsewhere ܨܠܒ) =
Acc ziqpu 'point; stem, shoot', etc. < ZIG tebû 'rise' (cp. NH גַּרְדֹּם 'gallows'

= BH & cogn. קַרְדֹּם 'axe' (prop. 'haft = phallus, ↑ n. 4)); ξύλον = 'cross'
LXX Deut 21:22f.; Acts 5:30, 10:39, etc. <ᵍⁱˢÙR (Acc gišûru) prop. 'roof-
beam'; ~ διδύμον = 'gibbet' LXX Josh 8:29 (↑ n. 12; ↓ p. 106); NH Aram
etc. √ צלב <BAR-SÌL 'groin' i.e. forked place.

66a. πῆγμα Irenaeus *Heresies* II 24, 4; cp. Justin *Dialogue with Trypho* 91; Tertullian *Ag. Marcion* III 18.

67. *CGS* v pp. 32f.; i.e. ἑρμῆς <Sum *ERUM-UŠ "erect phallus" ↑ XI n. 26.
So also the κηρύκειον 'herald's wand'; κῆρυξ, κηρύσσω <Sum GURUŠ
("erect penis") 'hero' (↑ III n. 24), i.e. "bringer of good tidings (to the womb,
↑ III n. 6); BH & cogn. √ בשׂר 'give good news' ?<*BA-ŠUR (= Acc
ṣarâru 'spurt, let flow'; zanânu 'rain'; ṭerû 'spread out': cp. Sum BANŠUR >
Acc paššuru 'table'; pašâru 'deliver' (= Sum BÚRU, in the sense of fecundity,
↑ XI n. 27, in 'Aphrodite', etc.)

68. Plutarch. Περὶ φιλαδελφίας 478a–b; δόκανα cp. δοκάνη = στάλιξ 'forked pole
on which hunting nets are fixed'; δοκός 'beam' < Sum DÙG 'penis'.

69. ↑ n. 66.

70. As on the reverse of the oldest Roman denarius and sestertius coins, where
they are portrayed as the λευκόπωλοι 'riders on white steeds' (Pindar *Pythian
Ode* I.66; a further metath. of *Pollux* ?); cp. ταχέων ἐπιβήτορες ἵππων Hom.
Hymns XXXIII 19.

71. MÁŠ ṣibtu 'increase' (as MÁŠ (-DA-RI-A) irbu 'increase') also 'kid, lamb', etc.

72. צְלוּלְיבָא = קִיקִין, Sabb 21ᵃ; ↑ V n. 12.

73. אַרְמֹּי, ↓ n. 41.

74. רִצְפָּה cp. BH רִצְפָּה 'glowing coal'; for derivation and fungus connections,
↓ XIV p. 131 n. 65.

75. For the sacred mushroom as object and subject of atonement, ↑ IX pp. 78f.
↓ XVII pp. 129ff.

76. Hiph. √ יקע 'be separated, dislocated (of a joint); be severed, alienated',
Jer 6:8; Ezek 23:17, 18; Targ II Sam 21:6, Vulg *crucifigere, affigere*; Saadiah at
Num 25:4 صلب; cp. T. K. Cheyne *Expository Times* X, Aug. 1899, p. 522:
"a religious synonym of תלה".

77. Apollodorus *Bibliotheca* III 182–85; Ovid *Metamorphoses* X 298ff.; Hyginus
Fabellae 58; Bion *Bucolicus* (App: X, XI, in ed. U. von Wilamowitz-Möllen-

dorff[2], *Bucolici Graeci*, Bib. Class. Oxon.; Servius Danielis, *Bucolics* X 18; *Aeneid* V 72; Antoninus Liberalis 24; see Frazer *Golden Bough*[3] vols. V, VI; HGM pp. 124ff.

78. ↑ V n. 28; cp. BH פסח 'cripple', Arab فسخ 'disjoin' ?<Sum *BA-SUḪ 'snatch out' (as a bolt from its socket, hence Sum Á-SUḪ = AŠTAR 'bolt').

79. Aram √ נגד 'draw, drag out', Pa. 'scourge', נֶגְדָּא 'strap, lash'; נַגָּד 'one who draws; scourger'; for necromantic associations of 'drawing forth' (נְגִידָא Gitt 56[b] of Titus, 57[a] of Jesus (יֵשׁוּ), Sabb 152[b] of Samuel) ↓ XVII p. 171. Cp. the practice of "flogging" in necromantic (?) practices, as in the beating of the φαρμακοί at the Thargelion, on the genitals (CGS iv pp. 270ff.); φαρμακός = 'raised phallus' (<Sum<*BAR-MAḪ-UŠ ↓ XIV n. 47); cp. the Anthesteria festival as time of raising the dead, ↓ XVII pp. 172ff.

80. √ משׁה & cogn. "stretch, measure" cogn. with BH NH √ משׁך 'draw': < Sum SUḪ naš/sâḫu 'draw out, snatch' (BH נסח) = Sum ÁG-ÁG (madâdu, BH NH Arab 'measure') > ἀγαπάω 'love, draw forth, seduce' ↓ XVII p. 175; cp. of Jesus, ܡܫܚܝܢ ... and ... qu. P-S 2235, 2236; cp. זמורה/מסור (<Sum SUR 'stretch') ↓ XVI p. 143.

But √ משׁח 'anoint', מִשְׁחָא 'oil' <MAŠ "resin, seed" as in [sem] MAŠ 'styrax'; human semen in MAŠ-GE₆ 'dream' (↑ VII n. 8).

81. *Bacchae* 1125ff.

82. *Bacchae* 1139ff., calling it a 'lion's head' (κρᾶτα . . . λέοντος), to be nailed on the wall of the house. For the name Ἀγαυή = ἀγάπη <Sum ÁG-ÁG 'draw forth; love', ↓ XVI n. 20.

83. كَوْكَب الأَرْض.

CHAPTER XIII

Star of the Morning

1. ὁ ἀστὴρ ὁ λαμπρός, ὁ πρωινός; cp. 2:28 καὶ δώσω αὐτῷ τὸν ἀστέρα τὸν πρωινόν.

2. Περιστερεών (↑ XI p. 91 n. 3) ِ Aram בַּר + ἀστήρ-έως.

3. Referred to the Messiah in Targumim, Test. Levi XVIII 3; Test. Judah XXIV 1; by Rabbis of the second century, jTaan. iv 68d; of Bar Kozibah/Kochebah:

R. Akiba, jTaan, iv 2, 67d; Eusebius *Hist. Eccl.* iv 6; of Dositheus (Shahrastani i 170); in the Dead Sea Scrolls of דורש התורה, CD vii 19.

4. ↑ X n. 20; XII n. 57.

5. *NH* XIII 129.

6. ↑ V p. 38 n. 8.

7. *NH* II 36f.

8. ↑ VI n. 28.

9. *NH* II 38.

10. *NH* IX 107.

11. *NH* XI 37.

12. מָן Arab مَنّ, <MAN *šanû* 'double, do a second time', i.e. with reference to the reproductive qualities of "manna". The description in Num 11:7 is of the 'mixed-simile" type of Josephus' description of the High Priest's head-gear (↑ VII pp. 58ff. and Enoch 31:3f. on Eden's "tree of life" (↓ XVII p. 157, XVIII p. 178)): הַמָּן כְּזֶרַע גַּד הוּא וְעֵינוֹ כְּעֵין הַבְּדֹלַח. On גַּד = Κοριάννος, the aphrodisiac, ↑ XII n. 18, but ref. here to the "seed": ". . . one of the few umbelliferous plants producing fruits with a concave face" *Enc. Brit.*[23] vi p. 495[a], so NH Aram etc. כּוּסְבָּר(א) 'Coriander', ?<*GÚ-ZI-BAR "bowl-shaped surface" (cp. "Cotyledon" ↑ VIII n. 5), note the epithet of Περιστερεὼν ὕπτιος (Dsc IV 60). For בְּדֹלַח 'Bdellium', as 'speckled', ↓ XIV p. 126. For ref. to צפחת in Exod 16:31, comparison is with the idea of 'jar, flat-shaped jug' cp. Arab صَحْفَة 'hollow, large dish; wide bowl' and NH צפחת 'kind of waffle'; cp. BH ספחת 'scab' and cp. Exod 16:14: דק מחספס דק כלכפּר and Arab خشف 'have scabs' and the name of the mushroom, "scabby one" (قُرْحَان; ↓ XIV pp. 127f). The root *sph*, including BH מספחה 'veil', ?<*MAŠ-BA(LA)G (↑ VI n. 41), i.e. directly from the mushroom?.

On Exod 16:26: ששת ימים תלקטהו וביום השביעי שבת לא יהיה בו; cp. Pliny's tradition on the life of the mushrooms, as being no more than seven days (*NH* XXII 96). On the identification of Jesus with Manna, cp. John 6:31ff.: ἐγώ εἰμι ὁ ἄρτος τῆς ζωῆς (v. 35).

13. ↓ XVII pp. 173ff.

14. רְפָאִים, not plural (cp. חרמונים, אפרים, ירושלים, ↑XII n. 36), <*RI-GA-IM

"fallen from heaven" (Sum RI-GA = Acc *maqâtu* 'fall'; cp. NH שמרקעים,
'mushrooms' ↑ V n. 18) = נְפִילִים (i.e. the Sem equivalent, LXX Gen 6:4
Γίγαντες) = בְּנֵי־עֲנָק Num 13:33 (LXX *id*) = עֲנָקִים Josh 14:12, etc., בני ענקים
I Chr 1:28; <*GAN-NÁ-IM "heaven-stretched canopy" = 'Adonis gardens'
(↓ XVIII p. 186), and Ἄνακες = Διόσκουροι.

For older refs. on "fallen angels", see R. H. Charles on Enoch 6:2 (*APOT*
i p. 191), and of recent studies, F. Macler *Histoire de Saint Azazael* (Biblio-
theque de l'école des Hauts Études), 1902; L. Jung "Fallen Angels", *JQR*
XVI (1926) pp. 326ff.; B. Heller "La Chute des Anges", *REJ* LX pp. 202ff.;
B. J. Bamberger *Fallen Angels*, Philadelphia, 1952.

15. *NH* XXV 150.

16. Gen 3:5.

17. שמרקעים, ↑ V n. 18; Löw *Pfl* i p. 26.

18. *NH* II 101.

19. XXXIII 1–17.

20. ↑ VIII p. 73.

21. *NH* XXVIII 77.

22. ↑ n. 2.

23. ↑ VI n. 16: Sum *MAŠ-BA(LA)G > שבח; Ps 89:10, Acc *pašâḫu*, ↑ VII n. 8;
X n. 28 (שבח).

24. ↑ VI n. 16.

CHAPTER XIV

Colour and Consistency

1. ↑ V n. 15.

2. For the main outline of the story and refs., see *HGM* pp. 196–205.

3. Sum DÀRA (<*DA-A-RI-A "strong in fecundity" = *aialu* <*Á-A-RI-A
id.) *turaḫu* 'goat' = τράγος (↑ X n. 11): cp. SIG$_{14}$, ŠEG$_9$ *atûdu* (BH עַתּוּד)
'goat', and SÍG 'hair, fleece'; (sig)DARA$_4$ (*da'mu* 'dark red wool'); cp.
ADAMA (=MUD-GE$_6$) *adamatu* 'dark blood' (BH & cogn. √ אדם 'red')>

θρίξ 'hair'. Cp. αἴξ 'goat', αἰγίς 'the aegis' *Il* 5.738; 'a goat-skin coat' (*HGM* p. 48). ?<*ˢⁱᵍÁ-A-RI-A (>*aialu*, BH אֵיִל); for phallic significance of the אַיִל (and the αἰγίς ?) cp. BH אַיִל 'projecting pillar', I Kgs 6:31, etc., and 'leader, chief', Exod 15:15, etc., as 'tree-trunk', esp. אילה שלחה (Gen 49:21 (LXX στέλεχος)).

4. Θρᾷξ; Θρᾴκιος.

5. See *CGS* v pp. 85ff.; *HGM* p. 149.

6. *Ant* XIII 383.

6a. Thus, for the highly improbable θριδακίας 'lettuce'! (Ps-Dsc IV 75).

7. Note the "Thracian stone" (θρᾳκίας) said to catch fire by itself in water, is quenched with oil – ὅπερ καὶ ἐπὶ τῆς ἀσφάλτου γίνεται (Dsc V 129); cp. Pl *NH* XXXIII 94.

8. חלק, ↑ VII n. 8.

9. עָשָׂה ?<E₁₁ (= DUL-DU *elû* 'be high'; DUL *katâmu* 'cover') + ŠÚ-A *katâmu* (cp. ᵍⁱˢ ŠÚ-A 'stool' and GIŠ-ŠÚ> GISSU *ṣillu* 'shade' > קִשָּׁאָה "shady plant" i.e. mushroom (and then generally 'gourd, cucumber', etc.); cp. Arab عِشَاء 'nightfall', عَشْوَة 'dusk', عَشَاء 'blindness').

10. ↑ V n. 24; VII p. 58; ↓ XV p. 138.

11. אַדֶּרֶת (שער) ?<*EN-DARA₄ "possessor of hair" = בַּעַל־שֵׂעָר of Elijah (II Kgs 1: 8) and John the Baptist, ↓ p. 132.

12. ↓ XV p. 134; ↑ XI pp. 95ff. for the bird.

13. ↑ VI n. 42; VIII p. 72.

14. ˢⁱᵍGAN-NU = ˢⁱᵍGAN-ME-DA *tabarru* (?<*TAB-BA-R/LI ↑ VI n. 42, and √ טבל 'dip, dye', also *nabâsu* 'red wool'. The pigments of the *Amanita muscaria* have been extracted by Kögl and Erxleben, as a red crystalline glucoside, muscarufin, $C_{25}H_{16}O_9$; see N. M. Iwanoff 'The bio-chemistry of fungi', *Ann. Rev. Biochem.* I (1932) pp. 675–97.

15. ᵍⁱˢ GAN-NU(-UM) *kankannu* 'lid of a bowl' > κάνειον 'lid'; ⸗ ᵍⁱˢ BAN *qaštu* 'bow'; *tilpanu* (?<*DUL-BAN) 'arc' ↑ II n. 14.

16. AGÁN (*ṣertu* 'breast') <*Á-GAN (↑ III n. 26) BH אַגָּן 'bowl, basin', NH אוֹגֶן 'rim of vessel', Aram אוֹגָנָא 'disc'; אַגָּנָא 'bowl', etc., Arab إِجَّانَة 'urn,

tub' (cp. أَجِن 'beat cloth (dyer)'; مِسْجَنَة 'dyer's mallet'); cp. BH מָגֵן 'shield' (√ גנן 'cover, surround' (= GÁN 'field' > גַּן 'garden' ↓ XVIII p. 189), Lat *canthus* 'iron ring round a wheel'; = κάνθος, also 'eye; pot, pan'.

(For BH & cogn. √ גנז 'treasure', גְּנֶז 'treasury' <ZAG-GÁN 'sanctuary' = É-ZAG-GAR-RA, etc. ↑ III n. 31.)

*AGÁN(-TI)>'Αμανῖτα, Amanita 'mushroom'; Sum UBUR *tulû* 'breast', ↑ X n. 21.

AGÁN + DUL "breast-cover" > κάνδαυλος, κάνδυλος, 'Lydian dish' (cp. Κανδαύλης, a Lydian name for Hermes (Hipponax 1)); κανθύλη 'swelling, tumour'; κανθήλια 'panniers'; ≟ ܩܘܕܫܐ, ܩܘܕܫܐ = Arab كُنْدُس : P-S 3659, "Hellebore" i.e. mushroom (?); ≟ Arab قَدَس 'two-handled vessel', قُدَس 'cup', قُدَاس 'cistern cover' (?); Syr ܩܕܫܐ 'ear-, nose-ring'; with change of *n* to *r*: BH אֲגַרְטָל (Ezra 1:9), Aram קַרְטָלִיתָא, ܩܪܛܠܐ, Arab قَرْطَلَة, قَرْطَالَة, κάρταλος, κάρταλλος, 'basket with pointed bottom'; (LXX for BH דּוּדִים at II Kgs. 10:7); καρτάλωμα ≟ περίζωμα (Lydus *de Magistratibus populi Romani* 2.13) but properly a "breast-binder"?

In NT, Aram קרטליתא serves for word-play, indicating usage as a mushroom name like 'Αμανῖτα. Cp. Mark 5:41, ~ טליתא 'little girl' + ἔγειρε 'arise': καὶ κρατήσας τῆς χειρὸς τοῦ παιδίου λέγει αὐτῇ Ταλειθά κούμ, ὅ ἐστιν μεθερμηνευόμενον τὸ κοράσιον, σοὶ λέγω, ἔγειρε.

As תליתאה, 'three times' + קרא 'call', of the 'cock' (שָׂכְוִי) ~ σικύη 'gourd', as a generic determinative for the mushroom), Matt 26:34; as 'third time' + קרא 'pray' in Matt 26:44; etc.

The mushroom cap pictured as a woman's breast is probably the source of the figure in Ct 4:5, 7:4, coupled with the 'gazelle' reference (↑ X n. 21): שְׁנֵי שָׁדַיִךְ כִּשְׁנֵי עֳפָרִים תְּאוֹמֵי צְבִיָּה ||. The same significance may probably be sought for the strangely irrelevant passage in Jos *War* VIII 188f. on the "two breasts" (giving hot and cold water!) in the vicinity of the Baaras-Mandrake at Machaerus (note Acc *ṣertu* = Arab ضَرْع 'breast' < Sum ZAR > Acc *ṣarāru* 'spurt, flow' BH צְרִי 'resin').

17. NH חָנוּן, יַחֲנוּן Sabb 5⁴, jSabb 7ᶜ; <*(IÀ) -GAN-NU "(juice of) red dye"; not necessarily Henna (Jastrow, Ben Yehuda; see Löw *Pfl* ii p. 224; Arab حِنَّاء Sum INNA (*etqu*) 'fleece'; i.e. like DARA₄ *da'mu*, where ref. is primarily to the wool dyed red, and secondarily to the dye itself), but the red cap (or daub ?) placed on the ewe's head at conception or parturition (or after shearing? jSabb 7ᶜ). For the tradition that sheep are weak in the head and

thus needing special protective measures, see Pl *NH* VIII 199. Of the "two principal breeds" one was called *tectum*, "covered" according to the same authority (VIII 189), adding that *hoc in pascuo delicatius, quippe cum tectum rubis vescatur,* for which perhaps read *vesticula* 'little garment', or *vesica* 'bladder, purse' or 'cap' (?), and *rubra* 'red'. Pl adds: *operimenta eis ex Arabicis praecipue* 'the best coverings are of Arabian wool'. Cp Sum GANA₆ (*immertu*; Sum GANÀM *id*,?>Arab غَنَم 'small cattle'), related to GAN 'lid, cover'? cp. BH & cogn. כֶּבֶשׂ, כִּבְשָׂה, etc. 'sheep' and Acc *kubšu* 'cap' (Sum túg SAGŠU "head-cover"), *kabâšu* 'have a head-pad' (newly-born animals: CT 27, 42, 7, of *izbu* 'foetus') ?<*GÚG-ŠÚ "pod (head)-cover". Cp. Vergil *Eclogae* IV 45 (qu. Pl *NH* XXXV 40): *Sponte sua sandyx pascentis vestiet.*

For 'astral' reference of 'sheep' and 'red colour', cp. Sum mul UDU-IDIM ("wild sheep") *bibbu* 'planet', and Pl *NH* II 89, "the Greeks call them comets, in our language *erinitas*, because they have a blood-red shock of what looks like shaggy hair on their top."

18. For √ חנן 'be gracious', and connection with 'seed' ↑ III n. 41.

19. √ טבל BH NH Aram.

20. ↑ n. 11.

21. BH כִּרְכָּרָה ∼ κιρκαία (Dsc IV 75) < Sum KUR-KUR ↑ VI n. 24. For 'hump', cp. דַּבֶּשֶׁת Isa 30:6 <Sum *TAB-BA-LI, = דְּבֵלָה (& cogn.) 'lump of pressed figs, fig-cake' = παλάθη (LXX I Kgs 20:7), by metath. from *TAB-BA-LI.

22. Post *FP²* I p. 440.

23. BH גּוֹבַי Am 7:1 Na 3:17; Aram גּוֹבָא גּוֹבָאי; cp. Arab جَبٌ, جَبْأَة 'fungus' ?<Sum GÚG (*kukku*) 'pod, lentil' ↑ V n. 18.

24. ↑ XI p. 94; Sum ERI₄-TIL-LA (= Sem א/ערדילא), *šam*ḫarûbu cp. ḪARUB 'ant' (i.e. larva) etc. ↑ V n. 12.

25. *tabula* = τάβλα, ταβλίον 'tray', etc. = טַבְלָא, ܛܒܠܐ 'tray, plate'.

26. Sum *MAS-TAB-BA-R/LI ∼ מִשְׁתֶּה, ܡܫܬܠܐ 'feast' + בְּרוּרִים 'chosen' (cp. I Chr 7:40) and cp. Rev 19:17 (ref. Ezek 39:4, 17–20). So, behind Luke 14:7-11 "feast of the chosen" + ܕܒܪ̈ܐ, "those of the open places"; and "the marriage feast of the son" (Matt 22:2), ܕܒܪܐ, "of the son"; where "without a wedding garment" (vv. 11-14) is obtained from ܕܒܠܐ, "who (was) without . . ." and a combination of משתה 'feast' and preposition of

ܚܡܣܐ, BH כָּסוּי 'covering, clothing' (↓ XVI n. 19) ~ קִשָּׁאָה 'mushroom, gourd,' etc. ("shade-plant" < Sum GIŠ-ŠÚ-A > GISSU ↑ n. 9; XII n. 27).

27. *LI-MAŠ-BALAG-TAB-BA-RI ≗ ܫܠܡ 'half' and מַלְכוּ؟ 'kingdom, rule, government' (as in all the parables of the 'kingdom'); cp. also Arab لمس 'ask for a thing' (لَمَسَ 'touch, feel' = √משש, ܡܫ 'grope, feel, search out'), esp. interesting in view of the late Medinan Qur'anic Sura 5[112] "When the Apostle said, 'O Jesus, Son of Mary, is thy Lord able to send down to us a table (مائدة For. Vocab. pp. 255f.) from heaven . . .?" and v. 114: "Jesus, son of Mary, said, 'O Allah our Lord, send down to us a table from heaven, to be to us a festival (عيد) to the first and the last of us, and a sign (وآية), from Thee . . ." (for عيد as l.w. from הַוי؟, עידא (?< Sum UD 'time, day'), see For. Vocab. p. 218), the whole a word-play (or misunderstanding ↓ XVIII p. 195) of *LI-MAŠ-TAB-BA-L/RI, read as "he sought for a table" (cp. Arab طَبْلِية = טבלא, ܛܒܠܝܬܐ).

28. √ אסר ~ מסור (מצור) 'bind' ~ 'stretch out' ↓ XVI pp. 142ff.

29. 'Ηρώδης, 'Ηρωδίας, etc., ?<*ERI₄-IÁ-U₅-DA ≗ ERI₄-TÌL-LA 'mushroom', ↑ VI n. 23; ↓ XVI n. 25.

30. Koh. R. to 10[5] Tosef. Hull II 22, 24; jAb.Zar. II 40[d], jSabb XIV 14[d]; etc., פַּנְדֵּירָא, פַּנְטִירָא. Cp. G. Dalman Jesus Christ in the Talmud, Midrash, Zohar, etc. tr. A. W. Streane, Cambridge, 1893, pp. 19ff.; cp. Origen ad Celsum I: 28.

31. NH VIII 63.

32. "Amanita pantherina is very similar (to Am. muscaria) in its effects and its chemistry. It somewhat resembles the Fly-Agaric, but has a brownish grey or brown cap, darker in the centre, with white spots and striated margin. It grows principally in woods, in summer and autumn" (J. Ramsbottom, op. cit. p. 48. Cp. Pl NH XXII 93: ". . . there is a dry sort, similar to the genuine (mushroom) which shows as it were white spots on the top, standing out of its outer coat").

33. Cp. E. Schürer Geschichte d. jüd. Volkes[3], II, 1898, p. 218.

34. Καιάφας = קַיָּפָא (Par III[5]) = Acc qâpu 'entrust', qêpu 'overseer, governor', < Sum GÀR-BA (karru 'knob, phallus' (↑ V. 18; cp. SIPA, SÍB ("phallus") rê'û 'shepherd', and PA-TE-SI = ENSI iššakku 'governor', etc. (↑ I n. 2);

cp. BH פָּקִיד <*PA-GÍD "stretched-wing" i.e. 'guardian'); also > Lat *caepa* 'onion' and NT play on Καιάφας/Κηφᾶς (Peter) ↑ VI n. 15.

35. πάνθηρ; cp. Pl *NH* VIII 62: "It is said all four-footed animals are wonderfully attracted by their smell . . ." a mythical interpretation of πάνθηρ as παν-θηρ "all beasts"? Cp. also Hermes as 'lord of all beasts' in Hom. Hymns IV 568–71. Note also the panther symbolism of Bacchic imagery, J. E. Sandys *Bacchae*[4] pp. 208f. on 1.1017, who suggests that where the lion is referred to, panther is intended. Cp. Sum ÚG-BÀNDA "small lion" = leopard. Cp. ἄρκηλος 'young panther' <Sum *UR-GAL "big-dog", cp. U₄ (≟ UR)-GAL *ugallu* 'lion' = UR-MAH ("big-dog") *nešu* 'lion'.

36. πάνθηρ, Lat *panthera* (cp. πάρδαλις 'leopard') all ?<*BAR-DAR(A) "variegated skin" (Sum DARA > Acc *tarru* 'variegated'); cp. DAR-LUGAL-MUSEN> Acc. *tarlugallu*, Aram תרגולא, תרנגולת, תרנגולא‎, جُوذَلّ, etc., 'cock'. Cp. παρδάλειος (sc. λίθος) 'Jasper' (Pl *NH* XXXVII 190); >BH & cogn. √ ברד 'spotted, marked' (of small cattle Gen 31:10, 12; of horses Zech 6:3, 6); כָּמֻזְ‎ 'speckled, spotted; variegated'.

37. ↑ XIII n. 12; בְּדֹלַח & cogn. <*BAR-DAR(A) as prev. n.

38. *NH* XII 36.

39. παιδέρως, ?<*BAR-DAR(A); *Opalus* ?<*ú BAL "mushroom" ↑ III n. 26.

40. *NH* XXXVII 83f.

41. = Ἄκανθος Dsc III 177; = *Caerofolium* 'Chervil' Pl *NH* XIX 170.

42. L & S *sv.*

43. So Teleclides 49. Note use of παιδέρως of the Holm-oak (Pausanias 2.10.6) and spelt out as plural παιδὸς ἔρωτες Nic Fr 74.55 (Gow and Scholfield "acanthus").

44. "hanc gemmam propter eximiam gratiam plerique appellavere paederota" (XXXVII 84).

45. قرح : قَرْحَان‎ 'be covered with ulcers'; cp. BH קֶרַח 'frost, ice'; √ קרח 'be, make bald' ?<*GÚ-RI 'knobbed-bolt' ↑ X n. 20; for Κουρί = Περιστερεών ↑ XII n. 18.

46. בנות ציון : Hebraization of *BAR-SÌL(A)-U₅-NÁ (> βασίλειον 'palace, treasury' etc.: ↑ VII n. 26), "fecund womb". For 'Zion' and 'Jerusalem'

↑ XII n. 36; ↓ XV p. 134 n. 9. Cp. Περσεία < BAR-SÌL(A) 'womb, groin' (↑ V n. 12) and בָּצֵל BH & cogn. 'onion' (as a 'volva' plant' ↓ XV pp. 133f), like other 'onion' words applied to the mushroom (↑ n. 36; VI n. 15 on 'Peter'). For ברזל 'iron' ("axe-head") ↑ XII n. 4.

The phrase בתולת בת־ציון, perhaps then a mushroom title BAR-TÙN ('womb') + BAR-SÌL(A)-U₅-NÁ ('volva' plant). For connection between בצל and 'scabby, peeling', note Sum BAR-SÌL(A) = Acc naglabu 'groin', prop. the shaved place, pubes ? Cp. ψιλόω 'depilate' <BAR-SÌL(A).

47. Cp. v. 16: מַשְׁקִרוֹת עינים = 'fix the evil eye, fascinate' = סמם exactly reproducing βασκαίνω <*BA-SI-GAR-AN-NA "penis-raising": SI-GAR sigaru 'bolt' (↑ IX p. 81). Cp. Lat fascinus 'phallus', as an averter of the "evil eye", hung round children's necks, M. Terentius Varro De Lingua Latina 7.97; etc., and from a victorious general's chariot, Pl NH XXVIII 39; Sum SI-GAR > שׁ/סקר, סמם, 'cast evil eye'. Cp. γόης 'wizard', ?<*GÚ-UŠ "raised-head" i.e. phallus (↑ III n. 31), φαρμακεύς, φαρμακεία, etc. <*BAR-MAḪ-UŠ "big-penis" ↑ XII n. 79; cp. μαγγανεύω 'use charms, bewitch' and μάγγανον = βάλανος 'bolt-pin; glans penis', as well as μάγγανον = γάγγαμον 'hunting net', i.e. "trap" as σκάνδαλον 'stumbling-block' (↑ V n. 23) <SI-GAR 'bolt' + DAL 'door', i.e. the trap named after the bolt mechanism; μάγγανον ?<GAG-GÀR-BA 'knobbed pommel' and thus "bolt" (↑ VI n. 28), cp. ᵍⁱˢ GAG-KUD mupattitu 'key'. Cp. μάγος, Old Pers maguš <*MAḪ-UŠ "big-penis" > μαγεύω 'bewitch' (by philtres), and Acc šamaḫu 'sprout, be high'; šamḫu 'living luxuriously', šamḫâti 'courtesans' = BH שמח 'rejoice'.

The "finery" of Isa 3:18–23 must be understood now in terms of witches' and necromancers' equipment, cp. esp. בָּתֵּי הַנֶּפֶשׁ ? = the Bacchic cista, the כסתות of Ezekiel's witches (13:18), ↑ IX pp. 79 n. 16.

48. For the connection between "vines" and the sacred fungus, ↓ XVII p. 155.

49. ↑ III n. 1.

50. Λάζαρος, apparently an abbreviation of Ἐλεαζάρ, אֶלְעָזָר (Matt 1:15).

51. NH XXXVII 116.

52. Pers لاجورد lâjaward, لاژورد lâzhuward (Med. Lat lazulum Eng. 'lazuli'), Syr لازورد (~ "Λάζαρος"), all <*AR-ZAL-DAR "shining-specks-variegated", cp. Acc arzallu 'crystals of a geode' (= Sum ᶻᵃSIKIL); cp. Pl on lapis lazuli: "there the gold glistens as dots" (NH XXXVII 119).

53. Sum ZA-GÌN *uqnû* 'lapis lazuli'; cp. ^(zá) ZA-GÌN-DUR₅ *uqnu namru*, *zagindurû* 'sapphire'; cp. Pl *NH* XXXVII 120, where lapis lazuli is called *sappirus*, i.e. Sum Z-G-N > *s-p-r*, BH סַפִּיר, σάπφειρος.

54. Sum ZA-GÌN > ZIBÍN (*nappillu*) 'caterpillar' > Syr ܢܶܨܳܐ = ܘܙܡܣ 'centipede' P-S 1160 (lexx.) = *Sorbus domestica*, characterized by a "red, hairy caterpillar" that attacks and kills it, cp. Thphr III xii 8: "the tree itself also gets worm-eaten and so withers away as it ages, and the worm which infects it is a peculiar one, red and hairy" (καὶ ὁ σκώληξ ἴδιος ἐρυθρὸς δασύς); cp. Pl *NH* XVII 221: *vermiculis rufis ac pilosis*. The name of the tree, *Sorbus*, similarly from Sum ZA-GÌN > *z/s-r-b*; cp. Acc *arzallu* also = 'Medlar'; cp. also Acc *nabâsu* 'red wool' (= Sum ^{sig}GAN-NU, ↑ n. 17) <ZA-GÌN, i.e. metath. of Z-G-N> *n-g-z*>*n-b-s*.

55. *NH* VIII 69: "the Ethiopians give the name of *nabus* to . . ."; ναβοῦς = Syr ܐܢܡܦܐ = Arab زَرَافَة > French 'girafe' and Eng. "giraffe".

56. Suggestions for — ναβα(ς) include = נביא 'prophet', whose duties included παράκλησις (I Cor. 14:3; Acts 15:31f.); = נְוָתָא 'rest' (Klostermann *Probl. im Aposteltext*, 1883, pp. 8–14); = נַחֲמָא (נחמיה, נַחְמָן, etc.); cp. Dalman *Gramm.*² p. 178 following Deissmann (*Bibelstudien*, 1895, pp. 175–78; *Neue Bibelstudien*, 1897, pp. 15–17) who sought, as others, a heathen god's name in the title, "Son of Nebo" or the like: cp. *EB* i 485.

57. Ὑιὸς Παρακλήσεως: חָנוּן 'gracious' ∼ חָנוּן 'red-cap' ↑ n. 17.

58. Κύπριος ∼ Κύπρος, *Lawsonia inermis* (Dsc I 95; Jos *War* IV 469; LXX Cant 1:14 = BH כֹּפֶר, Aram כּוּפְרָא, etc. (Löw *Pfl* ii pp. 218ff.)).

59. ↑ X n. 20.

60. Sum ZA-GUL 'Chalcedony'; Sum GUL<*GÚ-UŠ "erect-head" i.e. glans > ḪUŠ 'be fiery red' = Sum RUŠ *ruššu id*.<*RÁ-UŠ "erect-head" > BH and cogn. רֹאשׁ 'head' and BH רֹאשׁ, רוֹשׁ 'bitter' (i.e. 'hot'-tasting).

61. ↑ III p. n. 22. Note also that Barnabas is a "Levite", Λευείτης (v. 36), i.e. the 'upper half' (לִוִּי) <Sum LI-U₅-UM, *li'u* 'tablet' ↑ II n. 2; ↓ XVI n. 24) of the mushroom volva.

62. ἴασπις, יָשְׁפֵה, ܝܫܦܐ, ܝܫܦ, <*IA₄-SIPA = BH יַהֲלֹם (LXX Exod 36:18 etc). <IA₄-ERUM ("Hermes"); ↑ XI n. 26.

63. ↓ XVII p. 172.

64. כְּתֹנֶת פַּסִּים, LXX χιτῶνα ποικίλον, Vulg *polymitam* (but at II Sam 13:18 LXX χιτὼν καρπωτός understanding פסים as plural of פַּס, NH Aram 'palm').

65. פַּסִּים was a Hebraized plural of an original * פסין (<ZA-GÌN, ZIBIN nn. 53, 54) = Syr ܦܣܐ *maculae cutis, lentigines* = Arab الكلف النمش (نمش? <ZA-GÌN n-b-s etc.) P-S 3183, qu. Bar-Bahlul *Lex. Syro-Arab*, cogn. with Syr ܙܘܦܐ 'sprinkling; freckles' (P-S 3876f.) = ἐφήλεις 'spots', etc.; ܙܘܦܐ ? ܦܣܐ = ἡ λεύκη 'leprosy' (ἔφηλες ἀργινόεσσα); and with צָרֶבֶת 'scab, scar' (Lev 13:23, 28); and with רִצְפָּה 'glowing coal' (with incandescent, glowing spots against the red) ↑ XV p. 131; and with σπινθήρ = *scintilla* 'spark', σπιλάς = σπίλος 'spot, fleck' (at the Agape, Jude v. 12; II Pet 2:13 (?); ↓ XVII p. 174); and with words for 'frog; toad': BH צְפַרְדֵּעַ & cogn. <ZIBIN/ZA-GÌN + DE ('torch, flame') = Sum NE-ZA-ZA ("stones of a furnace"); Acc *muṣa'irânu* 'frog'; cp. Lat *rana*<*NA4-NE furnace-stone(s); βάτραχος, βότραχος, βρόταχος, βρούχετος, βύρθακος, βρύτικος, ?<Sum GÚ-TAR "top of the head" i.e. glans + ḪUŠ 'fiery red' (↑ n. 60), "red-head"; so Lat *rubeta*, not directly related to "brambles" (*rubus, rubeus*) as their natural habitat (*ranae rubetae*, Pl *NH* VIII 10: "because it lives only in brambles") but with *rubeus* 'red'; hence the antidote to toad poison is *Neuras* (and *Phrynion*: Pl *NH* XXV 123; XXVII 122; *Neuras* = *Erythron* 'red' XXI 179) ?<*NE-URA "glowing-topped penis" i.e. the glans (cp. the phallic words for tadpole and frog: φρῦνος (Pl *NH* XXXII 50) = γυρῖνος, γύρινος 'tadpole', cp. Γρυνόν Sicus agrios Dsc IV 150, and related to κορύνη 'penis, club'; γρόνθος (= πυγμή) 'fist' ↑ XII n. 28; all <Sum GUR (<*GÚ-RI "knobbed-bolt") *kapâru* 'rub' + NA4 'stone', i.e. pestle, = Arab جُرْن.

CHAPTER XV

Mushroom Cosmography

1. *Enuma Elish* iv 135ff.

2. ↑ XII n. 37.

3. צָפוֹן <*ZÁ (=IA4)-GUN "stone-of-bearing" i.e. the fulcrum of heaven, cp. Ps 48:3 הַר־צִיּוֹן יַרְכְּתֵי צָפוֹן, where צִיּוֹן <*SÌL(A)-U5-NÁ "fecund-womb" (↑XIV n. 46), = יְרוּשָׁלַיִם <*URU-SILA-IM "city of the groin of

the sky") ↑ XII n. 36; ↓ n. 7. Cp. the Hittite myth of Ullikummu, the child born of a rock, who is carried on the shoulder of Ubelluri, a giant who bears heaven and earth. The stone child grows in the sea, which comes only to his waist, his head reaching the sky (see H. G. Güterbock in *Mythologies of the Ancient World* ed. S. N. Kramer, N.Y., 1961, p. 167). Cp. Sum ᶦᵐ SI-SÁ "erect-horn" (↑ VI n. 33) 'North', as the phallus holding up the groin of the sky; cp. ἄρκτος 'North' ?<*ÁR-GÍD-UŠ "organ of the stretched penis"; Acc *iltanu* 'North', ?<*AL-TI (= DUN₄)-AN-NA "yoke-of-heaven".

4. Ἄτλας (-αντος) (<*ANDUL-AN "protection, shade of heaven"): guardian of the pillars of heaven (*Od* 1.53), but later he himself holds up the sky (Hes *Theog* 517); Mount Atlas in Mauretania, on which heaven rested; *atlantion* 'the lowest vertebra of the neck on which the neck and head rests'; cp. BH תֹּרֶן 'mast', τύραννος 'tyrant', both <*DUL-AN-NA = ANDUL (cp.*AN-SUR "heaven-stretch" (as 'protection') > BH סֶרֶן Philistine 'tyrant', and > Acc *Aššur*, BH אַשּׁוּר, etc. 'Assyria') > אֲדֹנִי 'Adonis; lord' (↓ XVIII pp. 177f.).

5. ↑ V p. 40 n. 21.

6. BH חַרְמוֹן <*ÁR-GUN; in full, חַרְמוֹנִים <*ÁR-GUN-IM "organ bearing the sky" ↑ XII n. 36.

7. ↑ XII n. 36; ↑ n.3: יְרוּשָׁלַיִם (not dual) <*URU-SILA-IM.

8. ↑ XII p. 98 n. 4.

9. ↑ XIV n. 46.

10. ↑ XII pp. 99ff.

11. Φοῖνιξ <*GEŠPU (= ILLURU 'arch')-IMI> *pu-imi-geš > φοῖνιξ cp. Lat *foeniculum* 'fennel' as a small "palm-tree".

12. ↑ XI p. 95; with φοῖνιξ = "sky-arch", cp. *ciconia* 'stork' and a 'T'-shaped instrument, ↑ V n. 12.

13. GIŠIMMAR <*GIŠ-IM-MAR "heavenly-arch-tree"; MAR *marru* 'mattock', cp. Acc *marratu* 'rainbow' (↑ XII n. 4).

14. BH תָּמָר & cogn <*TI-MAR cp. MAR-TE 'quiver' (= vagina, ↑XII n. 4) cp. Lat *tamarix* 'Tamarisk' (< *ᵍⁱˢ TI-MAR > *tamar-giš > *tamarix*) > BH תִּימָרָה 'column of smoke' Job 3:2; Ct 3:6 (cp. עַמּוּד עָשָׁן Judg 20:4), תַּמְרוּרִים ‖ צִיֻּנִים Jer 31:21, cp. צִיּוֹן 'Zion' ↑ XIV n. 46; תִּימֹרָה 'palm-tree'

I Kgs 6:29, etc. (as a dim. of ?<*TI-MAR>*mōr*), cp. LXX at Jer 31 (38):21: τιμωρίαν (?<*τιμωριν — K-B *sv*), perhaps the origin of the name Ἀλοῖτις (≟ ἀλείτης 'avenger') = 'Mandrake', Dsc IV 75, through misunderstanding the transliterated תימרה "small palm-tree; mushroom (?)" as τιμωρός 'avenger': cp. τιμωρόν = Κώνειον 'Hemlock', Ps-Dsc IV 78. Cp. Μάραθ(ρ)ον, Marathron (= *Foeniculum*, ↑ n. 11) 'Fennel' ?<*MAR-AN-TA "heavenly-arch". Cp. Ἀμαρανθίς = Ἀντίμιμον (as names of Ὠκιμοειδές, Ps-Dsc IV 28), which is also a name for the Mandrake (Ps-Dsc IV 75 = γίγαντες ↑ p. 182, V p. 40 n. 21).

In OT, תמר דבורה (Judg 4:5) possibly a folk-name for the mushroom, read as "bee's palm-tree".

15. *NH* V 73; <σικύη + φοῖνιξ i.e. "palm-gourd" = mushroom? For a similar misunderstanding of σικύη as part of names for the mushroom, cp. *NH* XXII 99: "mushrooms are the only kind of food that exquisites (*deliciae* ≟ σικχός 'fastidious person') prepare with their own hands . . . handling them with amber knives (*sucinis novaculis*) and equipment of silver" (*argenteo apparatu* ≟ σκεῦος plural σκεύη + ἀργυρικός 'of silver' as if σικύη and ἀγαρικόν 'Agaric').

16. Cp. Sum ᵗᵘˡˢMAR-TU "womb-entrance" i.e. the West; ↑ III n. 29.

17. BH כְּנָעַן <*KI-NÁ-AN-NA "heavenly-couch" (KI-NÁ *maialu* "place of copulation", √ *na'alu*, i.e. nuptial couch; cp. Acc *nannaru* 'moon sickle', ?<*NÁ-AN-NA-RI "nuptial-couch of heaven"?; cp. the goddess of the new moon NANNA, NANNAR, and ᵈINNANA, *Ištar* ('womb').

Acc *kinaḫḫu* 'red purple wool' (Speiser, *AASOR* XVI, pp. 121f.) at Nuzi, implies that, like φοῖνιξ, כנעני or some related term was a title of the *Amanita muscaria* and similarly gave its name to the distinctive colour of the cap – the ref. of the epithet Συροφοινίκισσα (≟ כנענית), Mark 7:26?

18. ↑ XIV p. 130; cp. X n. 20 for Sum GÚ-BAR> GUBRU, etc.

19. ↑ X p. 85 n. 5. For a similar piece of fertility geography in myth, cp. Σκύλλα and Χάρυβδις, *Od* 12.85, 104, etc.: Σκύλλα <Sum*SI-GUL "knobbed-horn" (= SAG-GÚL 'bolt') > Aram סְגוּלָא = BH אֶשְׁכּוֹל 'grape-cluster' = glans penis (↓ XVII p. 155 n. 19), and thus, despite the personification as female, = the penis, and Χάρυβδις <Sum ḪARUB 'pod' (↑ V n. 12) + TÌL 'life' i.e. the womb, the "whirlpool" of the story.

20. βασίλειον, βασίλεια < Sum BAR-SÌL(A), ↑ III p. 25; VII n. 26; XIV n. 46.

21. I Chr 22:1; II Chr 3:1 (where אֲרַוְנָה = אָרְנָן); BH ארונה ?<*ARÀ-U₅-NÁ

"grinder of the womb" i.e. pestle; "phallus"; BH אֶרֶן <*UR₅-NA₄(-NA₄) = ᶻᵃ UR₅ (-UR₅) > Acc *uršu* 'mortar' (and > BH & cogn. צוּר 'rock', prop. "mill-stone; pestle", thus of God as procreator, Deut 32:18, cp. Isa 51:1 of Abraham as 'father of Israel'; BH סֶלַע, on the other hand, < Sum SILA 'groin' i.e. a 'V-' shape, thus a "cleft rock", a "cliff").

22. BH גֹּרֶן <*GUR₇-EN "seed-depository" > Sum GURIN, GURUN *inbu* 'fruit' and abbrev. to Sum GÚ-EN-NA *qadûtu* 'seed-depot', ˡᵘ GÚ-EN-NA 'man of the depot'>BH כֹּהֵן 'priest', ↑ III n. 35; VII n. 27; and > Sum ENGUR *apsu* 'ocean', etc., and > BH קַיִן 'Cain', ↑ XII n. 1.

23. See J. H. Middleton *JHS* XIX (1899) pp. 225–44; J. G. Frazer, *Pausanias*, 1913, pp. 314–20; W. H. Roscher 'Omphalos', *Sächsische Gesellschaft der Wissenschaften, Abh. Phil.-Hist. Kl.* (1913), no. 9; 'Neue Omphalosstudien' *ib.* (1915), no. 1; L. B. Holland *AJArch* XXXVII (1933) pp. 201–14; H. W. Parke, *History of the Delphic Oracle*, 1939, pp. 9f. The oldest cult-object of Delphi? cp. O. Kern, *Die Religion der Griechen*, 1928–38, I pp. 5ff.

24. BH שֶׁלַח (Σ(ε)ιλωαμ) <ŠU-LAḤ(-ḤA) *šuluḫḫu* 'lustration'; unrelated, of course, to √שׁלח 'send' (ὁ ἑρμηνεύεται Ἀπεσταλμένος, John 9:7; the occasion for this pseudo-translation being probably a word-play on MAŠ-BA(LA)G and √שׁבק 'release, send away' (↑ VI n. 17)).

25. The waters of Siloam ("sweet and abundant", Jos *War* V 140), were regarded as the most suitable for ritual purposes, indeed, as good as that of creation: G. Dalman, *Jerusalem und sein Gelände* (*Schriften des deutschen Palästina-Vereins*, bd. 4), Gütersloh, 1930, blz. 172 for refs. For archaeology, see J. Simons, *Jerusalem in the OT*, Leiden, 1952, pp. 157ff. The waters ran from the spring גִּיחוֹן (?<*GI₄-ḪUN "return-in-peace"; cp. Isa 8:5: מֵי הַשִּׁלֹחַ הַהֹלְכִים לְאַט).

26. ↑ X pp. 87f.

27. בֶּן־(בְּנֵי־)הִנֹּם; Hebraization of an original Sum *BÁR-ERUM "penis-sheath" (↑ XI n. 26; the med. daghesh a compensation for ê). Cp. ᵘʳᵘ BÁR-SÍB 'Borsippa' and Περσεφόνη ?<BÁR-SÍB + U₅-NÍ "fecundity"; cp. Περσεφόνη = Περιστερεών 'Holy Plant' Ps-Dsc IV 60; cp. μάρσιππος 'bag, pouch' ?<*MAR-SIPA/SÍB "penis-container"; and cp. the Sum phrase for 'granary', É-UŠ-GÍD-DA "house of the stretched penis" ↑ III n. 35.

　　　In the NT, υἱὸς γεέννης, 'son of Gehenna' (Matt 23:15), possibly a word-play on Οὔιγγον ?<ᾠὸν-γήινον "egg-of-the-earth", Mandrake ? ↑ XII n. 26.

28. ↑ XII n. 51. For a possible variant of צלמות as שׂ/סרמות cp. Jer 31:4;

צלמות ? שרמות i.e. ‏וכל־עמק הפגרים והדשן וכל־השרמות עד־נחל הקדרון,
<SÌL-MUD "birth-canal" as the name of the Hinnom Valley (↑ VII n. 10;
↓ XVII n. 28).

29. ‏وَاد النَّار.

30. ↑ III pp. 21f.

31. ↑ V n. 24; XIV p. 120.

32. ↑ VII p. 56.

33. BH ‏סִינַי ?<ZÁ/A-NE "furnace-stone" as in NE-ZA-ZA 'toad' ↑XIV n. 65.
Cp Judg 5:5; Ps 68:9 ‏זֶה סִינַי, where ‏זֶה is not a demonstrative or relative part,
but part of the name, = ZÁ, i.e. ZÁ-ZÁ (pl.)- NE i.e. the glowing coals of
the furnace or stove (Acc kinûnu).

34. The donning and removal of the veil (vv. 29–34) has a triple mushroom-
serpent-phallic significance. As the mushroom disrupts its sheath on the
spreading of the cap, the serpent sloughs its skin, and the penis retracts its
foreskin on erection. Moses (<*MUŠ-È "emergent serpent" ↑ IX n. 21,
the 'red-faced' one (*GÚ-UŠ > ḪUŠ 'fiery-red' ↑ XIV n. 60), i.e. the glans,
in phallic terms, retracts the "veil". The removal of the covering is a sacrificial and preparative act (Jer 4:4; 6:10), as in the practice of circumcision:
one 'sheath' is renounced for another (note Sum TÙN-BAR, Acc šaptu
šaplîtu "lower lips" i.e. the vulva and also the prepuce; cp. BH ‏חתן 'bridegroom, father-in-law', Arab ‏ختن 'circumcise' (?<*GÚ-TÙN "head (glans)-
sheath", i.e. prepuce). Hence the idea of circumcision and the foreskin as
constituting a bride-price (cp. Gen 34:17ff.; I Sam 18:25), BH ‏מֹהַר (?<MU
'gift' + A-RI-A 'copulation'), and as an atoning sacrifice (Exod 4:24ff.), like
the redemptive Mandrake-mushroom (cp. Gen 30:14–18 of Leah's purchase
of copulation with Jacob; and the sacred fungus itself as its own redemption,
↓ XVII pp. 169ff.). A similar idea underlies the circumcision of fruits as holy
to the god (Lev 19:23–25), of the circumcision of the Israelites before entry
into the Promised Land (Josh 5:2f.), of the removal of shoes on holy ground
(Exod 3:5; Josh 5:15), and the sexual symbolism of removing the sandal
(Deut 25:9): see W. R. Smith Kinship, p. 269, ↑ XII n. 49. Note the id. for
'life' in Egyp. hieroglyphs, ☥ = "sandal-strap" (Gard. EG³ S 34, 'nḫ), and
cp. Sum id. for ŠUDÚG pašîšu 'anointed priest', ☥.

35. ↑ II p. 12 n. 2.

36. For the number, "ten" represents a play on *MAŠ-TAB-BA-RI read as חמש 'five' and דבריא 'words'; i.e. five on each tablet; cp. NH Aram דִּיבּוּרַיָּא 'Ten Words'. For a similar play on MAŠ as חמש 'five', cp. the "five loaves" of Mark 6:44; etc., + *TAB-BA-RI ∼ פטירא 'unleavened bread'; and I Sam 21:4 חמשה־לחם. Cp. also the "five sparrows" that are "sold" for two pennies, Luke 12:6, i.e. חמש 'five' and צפרין 'sparrows' ∼ *MAŠ-TAB-BA-RI, and πωλοῦνται 'sold' Pesh ܡܶܙܕܰܒܢܺܝܢ similarly ∼ *MAŠ-TAB-BA-RI. Cp. also the name Πεντόροβον = Παιωνία ἄρρην (= Γλυκυσίδη ↑ V n. 23: Ps-Dsc III 140); a Graeco-Sem misunderstanding of a form of *MAŠ-TAB-BA-RI and Aram ܣܰܡܠܐ + ܟܽܙܐ = Ὄροβος 'vetch, chick-pea', P-S 2981.

CHAPTER XVI

David, Egypt, and the Census

1. ↑ III n. 17; BH דָּוִ(י)ד, Δαυ(ε)ίδ, NT Δαυείδ (Δαβίδ); <Sum DÙ-DÙ banu 'create' (dist. fr. BH √ דדה 'move slowly' Aram ܕܘܕ Pa. 'disturb', Arab دَأدَ 'run quickly' <Sum DU-DU (aláku) 'go').

    In the NT, the pronunciation wāw = β is used in word-play, as in Rev 22:16: ἡ ῥίζα καὶ τὸ γένος Δαυείδ, where ῥίζα ∼ *MAŠ-BA(LA)G, as ܡܰܚܣܰܡ 'shoot' (cp. צמח Isa 11:1) and מִשְׁפָּחָה 'family' (↑ VI n. 41) and *TAB-BA-RI-TI as Δαβίδ/Δανειδ (for phonetic development, cp. *TAB-BA-RI-TI > ταβαίτας 'wooden bowl', and in the word-play of the name Ταβειθά (Ταβιθά) Acts 9:36, 40 (where Δορκάς 'gazelle' (טביא) has a different mushroom ref. ↑ XIV n. 16); cp. play in ἐπιστρέψας πρὸς τὸ σῶμα εἶπεν ταβειθά . . . ∼ *LI-MAS-TAB-BA-RI-TI (↑ VI n. 23) as if לְמַס ? (√מסס, מסי 'melt away, decompose' as in ܡܟܰܙܒܳ ܘܡܰܪܝܳ 'a putrid corpse', cp. Pesh at Acts: ܡܟ as שְׁלְדָא 'decayed corpse'; for the 'washing, laying out' of the corpse, ~ *MAŠ-TAB-BA-RI-TI as if ܡܟܰܙܒܳ 'adorned one', as frequently, ↓ XVIII p. 185 n. 35.

    For further play with Δαβίδ, cp. Mark 12:37: πόθεν αὐτοῦ ἐστὶν υἱός; 'whence is he (David's) son?' ~ *AN-BAR-TAB-BA-RI-TI (↓ XVII p. 159) as if أَيْ ܟܙ ? يَسم, and so in Matt 12:23: μήτι οὗτός ἐστιν ὁ υἱὸς Δανείδ;

2. ↑ XV n. 4.

3. BH prop. name נַעֲמָן (Ναιμαν, Νοεμ(μ)αν); Isa 17:10 נַעֲמָנִים; Arab نُعْمَان

↓ XVII p. 159; XVIII pp. 178f. < NÁ 'stretch out' + IM(-A-AN) 'sky' and 'rain'. Cp. Arab شقائق النُّعْمَان "wounds of Adonis", the Anemone, Ἀνεμώνη, understood as "wind-flower" (Pl *NH* XXIV 165) as if from ἄνεμος, Lat *anima* 'wind, spirit', der. by metath. fr. Sum IM-A-AN, i.e. "rain-" wind; ↑ III n. 4.

4.   ↓ XVIII pp. 1ff.

5.   ↑ XI n. 26.

6.   ↓ XVIII p. 178.

7.   ↑ X n. 2.

8.   BH זִמְרָה (Isa 17:10; Ezek 8:17 = 'penis' as NH (as עונם מכשול Ezek 14:3, 4, 7; for "stumbling-block/phallus" ↑ V n. 23; VI n. 1; XIV n. 47); = 'vine-shoot' Num 13:23, etc.; NH: 'officer's rod' (cp. φάκελος, *fascis* <g¹ˢ BAL 'Ferula'; BALAG > πληγή, *plaga* ↑ III n. 26). In Isa 59:5 read זמרה 'fungus' for הזורה; for mushroom significance of the "spider's spindle" and "adder's eggs", ↓ XVII pp. 152f).

9.   φαλλοφορία; for refs. see *CGS* v p. 197. For the phallic name and nature of the thyrsus, ↑ III n. 1; ↓ XVII n. 21.

10.   BH זמר <MU 'high' + SUR 'stretch out' > מָזור Ob v. 7, Targ תקלא 'stumbling-block' (↑ n. 8); cp. Syr ܡܲܙܪ 'stretched out', Ethpe. 'stretch oneself' (on awakening, yawning); ܡܲܙܪܘܢܳ 'fuller's mallet' (= ܐܶܩܡܰܕ(ܠ)ܝ 'erected' (phallus); (Sum SUR also = 'weave', BH כִּישׁור <*GI-SUR: ↑ VI n. 23).
        Cp BH & cogn. √ אזר 'gird, encompass' < Á-SUR, ?> Acc *aṣâru*, *muṣṣuru* 'limit, define', and √ אסר 'bind, imprison'; cp. Sum SUR *eṭēru* 'hand over, pay'; and cp. Heb מַסוֹרֶת 'tradition', מוֹסֵר 'band, bond'; Syr ܡܳܣܳܪܢܳ 'girdle'; NH מָסוֹר 'informer, traitor' (esp. of Jews to Gentiles).

11.   Ἄφροι (i.e. Punic) Κουσ(σ)ι μεζαρ Ps-Dsc IV 150 = Σίκυς ἄγριος, Ἐλατήριον, Γρυνόν, etc., "Egyptian" cucumber (Löw *Pfl* i p. 545; DAB p. 85); as if = מָצור מִצְרַים, مِصر; cp. Acc *muṣṣuru* (↑ n. 10) 'define boundary' <Sum SUR 'stretch'; thus "Egypt" = "the two territories", Upper and Lower Egypt.

12.   ↑ III pp. 27f.; VIII pp. 70f.

13.   פִּיטְרָא, Arab فُطْر 'mushroom' (↑ V n. 18); cp. √ פטר 'split, break forth '(see Lane *Lex* s.v. on فُطْر: "such as has broken forth"); BH פֶּטֶר (רחם) 'first-born' Ezek 20:26; Exod 13:12; etc.; cp. Sum DU₈ *petû* 'open', *paṭâru* 'le, free', *taḫâdu* 'be abundant'; Sum GI-DU₈ *paṭiru* 'table of offerings' (as a token

or compensation for 'release' to secular use; ↓ XVII pp. 154ff. on the Πιθοιγία).
Aram פטירא 'unleavened bread' <*TAB-BA-RI 'mushroom' from the
'bun-'shaped loaf; BH & cogn. לֶחֶם similarly from Sum LI-' U/U₅-UM *li'u*
'tablet'; ↑ II n. 2.

14. ↑ XII p. 99.

15. ὃς . . . προδότης Luke 6:16.

16. As if ܡܛܠ 'that which is pleasing, acceptable', part. ܠܐ Ethpe, + TAB-
BA-RI, read as ܕܥܒ̈ܪܝܐ 'of the Hebrews'. So in the Lord's Prayer: γενηθήτω
τὸ θέλημά σου ∽ *MAŠ-TAB-BA-LI-GI as ܟܡܐ ܡܛܠ '(let it be) acceptable
to thee', and *TAB-BA-RI-GI read as ܕܒܫܡܝܐ 'that which is in heaven';
ܘܒܐܪܥܐ 'that which is on earth' (↑ VI n. 17; ↓XVII p. 160; for ܡܛܠ
'willing, submissive', similarly derived in the texts by word-play, ↓ XVIII
p. 187.

17. ↑ XIV n. 29.

18. BH קִשֻּׁאִים Num 11:5 < Sum GISSU <GIŠ-ŠÚ (cp. ᵍⁱˢ ŠÚ (-A) prop.
"something giving shade, covering" (↑ XIV n. 9) = Acc *littu* 'stool' as
'mushroom-'shaped?) = ᵍⁱˢ GÍG (<GI₆-GI₆ 'dark').

19. BH כָּסוּי (of skins) Num 4:6, 14 (not pass. part. but <Sum KI-ŠÚ>KIŠI>
Acc *kiššatu* 'totality' = BH כָּסוּת 'covering' (Sum ŠÚ = Acc *katāmu*
'cover' and *kiššatu* (for similarly derived BH כסתות = κίστη, ↑ IX p. 79));
Syr ܟܣܝܐ 'covering'.

Word-play in the NT indicates that קשאה was found as common determinative for the mushroom in folk-names: e.g. + *MAŠ-BA(LA)G-
ANTA (or derived equiv.) as ܫܒܚ 'glory' + ܐܢܬܬܐ woman' + ܟܣܝܬܐ
'covering' giving the theme "a woman's hair is her glory" in I Cor 11:2-15,
with the added play on *TAB-BA-LI and ταβλίον (= ἐξουσία, "the purple");
↑ VI n. 42.

Combined with "*mezorah*" as מָסֹרֶת 'tradition' (↑ n. 10), and Aram קַשָּׁא,
קַשִּׁישָׁא 'elder', in τὴν παράδοσιν τῶν πρεσβυτέρων, Matt 15:2 (should we seek
in a similar word-play, or popular misunderstanding, references to the
longevity of the Essenes? Cp. Jos *War* II 151; Philo *Apol.* 3).

As play on ܡܓܫܐ 'spy' in Luke 20:20: ἀπέστειλαν ἐνκαθέτους
ὑποκρινομένους ἑαυτοὺς δικαίους εἶναι, and on *MAŠ-TAB-BA-RI as if
ܡܬܚܫܒ, ܣܒܪ Ethpe., Ethpa. part., 'considered, supposed'; and on
*MAŠ-BA(LA)G as if ܣܒ 'send'.

As play on ܩܝܣܐ 'wood, cross; tree' and followed by fungus name Sum KUR-KUR in the colloquial equiv., ~ Aram كنّب 'walk up and down' in the incident of the blind man restored to sight, Mark 8:24: βλέπω τοὺς ἀνθρώπους ὅτι ὡς δένδρα ὁρῶ περιπατοῦντας.

20. ~ ἀγάπη, used as a name for the fungus in the Agape feast? ↓ XVII p. 173 n. 107; cp. ↑ XII n. 80; XIV n. 65. Note the name of Pentheus' mother who tore her son asunder in the Bacchic orgy, Ἀγαύη; ἀγανός 'illustrious, noble' (of kings, heroes); = ἀγάπη < Sum ÁG-ÁG 'draw out, love'; cp. Agag, אֲגַג, king of the Amalekites, I Sam 15:8, etc.; ↓ XVIII n. 28.

21. BH יִשָּׂשכָר Qre perpet. <Sum UŠ-SA 'erect penis' + KUR₄ 'large'; expl. in OT as יֵשׁ שָׂכָר Gen 30:18, LXX: Ἰσσαχαρ, ὅ ἐστιν μισθός.

22. BH רְאוּבֵן: Gen 29:32: כִּי רָאָה ײ בְּעָנְיִי.

23. BH שִׁמְעוֹן: Gen 29:33: כִּי־שָׁמַע ײ; ?<*SIG₄-U₅-NÁ "favourer, fructifier of the womb" = phallus (dist. from √ שמע 'hear, obey': ?<*SĔ-MU "favourable, acceptable word").

24. BH לֵוִי: Gen 29:34 יִלָּוֶה אִישִׁי אֵלַי; <LI-'U/U₅-UM (li'u 'tablet' II n. 2); in mushroom terms, the upper half of the fungus, the 'canopy' to Simeon's (phallic) 'stem' (cp. Gen 49:5: כְלֵי חמס 'instruments of violence', like the Dioscouroi, the Boanerges (↑ XII p. 100 nn. 27, 28), Cain and Abel, Jacob and Esau, etc. BH √לוה 'join' is of the same Sum origin, which gave לֶחֶם 'bread' and √לחם NH Aram 'suit well, fit together' (BH Niph. 'be joined in battle') as the 'fitting' of the two halves of the sphere.

25. BH יְהוּדָה: Gen 29:35: אוֹדֶה אֶת־ײ; <*IÀ-U₅-DA "giver, controller of fertility" (as daiwa 'demon' ↑ IV p. 34 n. 15); BH יָד 'hand, phallus' (Isa 57:8) = ἰῶτα; cp. prop. name 'Herod' Ἡρῴδης and 'heron' ἐρῳδιός, ?<*ERI₄-IÀ-U₅-DA; ↑ XIV n. 29.

26. שבח 'be still'; ↑ XIII p. 116 n. 23; and BH דְּבֵר, Aram דַּבְרָא 'pasture'.

27. On derivation of √n'm 'sweet, delightful' <*NA-IM(-A-AN), 'Na'iman, Adonis, mushroom', ↓ XVIII pp. 178f.

28. ↑ VI p. 48 n. 18.

29. מס־פלח ~ *MAŠ-BALAG; BH פלח 'cleave', cp. פלג 'divide', both <BALAG 'phallus'; Aram פלחא, ܦܠܚܐ Arab فَلَّاح 'labourer, husband-man'; cp. Exod 20:2 where בית עבדים perhaps for an original מס־פלח

(פּוּלְחָנָא) = "servitude", in a play involving √ שבק 'let loose, send away' (הוֹצֵאתִיךָ מֵאֶרֶץ מִצְרַיִם, ↓ XIX p. 201).

30. P. Sulpicius Quirinius (Κυρήνιος, Luke 2:2): Tacitus *Annals* 3.48: "mox expugnatis per Ciliciam Homonadensium castellis insignia triumphi adeptus . . ." Cilicia belonged to Syria, so that the victories would have been won by him during his tenure of that province in AD 6; see Jos *Ant* XVII 355; XVIII 1ff. The famous Lapis Tiburtinus (*CIL* XIV 3613, Henzen 5366) doubtfully witnesses to an earlier proconsulate of Syria in 3–2 BC (Mommsen *Mon.Anc.App.* pp. 161–78). Herod died 4 BC. For discussion, see A. R. C. Leaney, *The Gospel According to St. Luke*, N.Y., 1958, pp. 44–48.

31. Γρυνόν = Σίκυς ἄγριος, ↑ n. 11; Γεράνειον 'mushroom', ↑ V n. 18.

32. ↑ XII n. 4.

33. ↑ XII pp. 105f.

34. פִּטְרָא ~ פֶּטֶר; for ἐσπαργάνωσεν, cp. כֻּבְדָא 'swaddling-bands' ̰ KUR-KUR 'mushroom".

35. *Bacchae* ll.519ff. For φάτνη as a "covered basket", ↑ IX p. 80 n. 22.

CHAPTER XVII

Death and Resurrection

1. ↑ X pp. 83ff.

2. *War* II 154f.

3. *War* II 136.

4. Hes *Th* 913; Hom. Hymns II; Ovid *Metamorphoses* V 359ff.; *Fasti* IV 419ff.; Apollodorus I 29ff.; Hyginus *Fabellae* 146, 147; Claudian *de raptu Proserpinae* (XXXIII, XXXV, XXXVI); see *CGS* iii ch. II, pp. 29ff.; *HGM* pp. 91ff.

5. קוּרֵי עַכָּבִישׁ 'spider's spindle(s)' ‖ בֵּיצֵי צִפְעֹנִי 'asp's eggs', Isa 59:5, i.e. Κόρη and Περσεφόνη <*BÁR-SÍB-U₅-NÍ (XV n. 27), i.e. both parts of the mushroom, stem and volva.

6. Ps-Dsc IV 60: Περιστερεὼν ὕπτιος = ἱερὰν βοτάνην = Δημητριάς, Φερσεφόνιον, Κουρί (Κουρῖτις).

7. Θαυμαστὸν γανόωντα Hom. Hymns II 10.

8. ῥοιῆς κόκκον, with ῥοιά 'pomegranate', cp. Sum ᵍⁱˢ NU-UR-MA (Acc *nurmu*) "seed-pod of fertility", as 'egg', etc. ↑ XII n. 26. Virgil (*Georgica* I 38–39) implies that Persephone ate the fruits willingly.

9. Ἄιδης, ᾄδης, Ep. Ἀΐδης, etc. ?<*Á-ÌD-ÚŠ "place of the river of the dead" i.e. = Ἀχέρων *Od* 10.513, etc.; cp. Sum É-KUR-ÚŠ (= ARALI, *arallu*) "house of the land of the dead"; cp. BH שְׁאוֹל ?<*ÈŠ-ÚŠ "house of the dead"; ct. Enoch XXII where Sheol is in the far West, not in the underworld (for transpos. of elements, cp. BH שָׁאוּל 'Saul' <UŠ-SA 'penis').

10. ↑ VIII p. 68; XV p. 137.

11. ↑ III p. 21.

12. ↑ XI n. 27; hence πλοῦτος 'riches' and the god Pluto as god of riches; Phaedrus IV 12.5.

13. *NH* XXI 162.

14. *Od* XI 301–04.

15. ↑ VI p. 51.

16. ↑ VIII p. 69.

17. Πιθοίγια, Χόες, Χύτροι: *CGS* v pp. 214ff., and pp. 317ff. for refs.

18. πίθος: *CGS* v p. 214; φανόδημος πρὸς τῷ ἱερῷ φησι τοῦ ἐν Λίμναις Διονύσου τὸ γλεῦκος φέροντας τοὺς Ἀθηναίους ἐκ τῶν πίθων τῷ Θεῷ κιρνάναι, εἶτ' αὐτοὺς προσφέρεσθαι; Athenaeus 465A; etc.

19. GEŠTIN *karânu*; cp. id. ▽ TIN *balâṭu* 'live' = TÌL.

20. βότρυς, botrys ? <*GÚ-TAR-UŠ "top of the erect penis" (cp. כֹּתֶרת, Acc *katarru*; פִּיטְרָא, فُطْر all <Sum GÚ-TAR 'erect head; phallus': ↑ V nn. 17, 18); BH אֶשְׁכּוֹל <*UŠ-GÚL "top of the head" (of phallus, i.e. glans), cp. Sum SAG-GÚL(-NIM-MA) 'knobbed-bolt'; ZA-GUL *samtu* 'Chalcedony', as colour of the glans penis (↑ XIV n. 60); Aram סְגוֹל 'cluster' *<SI-GÚL 'knobbed-bolt' (↑ XV n. 19); cp. Lat *aesculus* 'an oak with edible acorns" i.e. = glans βάλανος, ↑ III n. 26; σκῶλος 'pointed stake' <*SI-GÚL, and + BI-UŠ 'erect' > σκόλοψ id. σκολοπισμός 'impaling', etc.; σκωλόομαι, 'be offended' = Aph ܣܟܠ 'give offence'; ↑ XIV n. 47.

    Ἀσκληπιός, Lat *Aesculapius*, similarly <*UŠ-GÚL-BI-UŠ "glans of the erect penis", cp. Ἀσκληπιάς = Κισσίον ("small ivy cluster": Dsc III 92) = "Hellebore" (Wellm. Ἀσκληπιάδα, Ps-Dsc IV 148; cp. Dsc IV 162: "on cutting it they stand εὐχόμενοι Ἀπόλλωνι καὶ Ἀσκληπιῷ"; cp. ἀσκληπιάς = 'haemorrhoids' (L & S Add. & Corr. 2054ᵇ; cp. BH עֹפֶל *ib*<*ᵘ BAL "mushroom" ↑ III n. 26. IX n. 12.

21. ↑ V n. 18; Θύρσος <*ŠUŠ-TÙN "womb-favourer" ↑ III n. 1; wreathed with ivy and vine-leaves, symbolic of the 'cluster/glans penis' (↑ n. 20), with a pine-cone at the end, a ref. not only to the 'cone-'shape of the glans but to the source of the *Amanita muscaria* in the conifer forests. Cp. Arab طُرْثُوث = Θύρσος 'mushroom'; see Lane *Lex sv*: "a fungus, used for medicinal purposes, a stomachic; plant of the sands, long and slender, inclining to redness . . . of two kinds, sweet and red, bitter and white . . . length of about a cubit, no leaves, as though it were a kind of truffle . . . red, with a round head, like a glans penis . . ."

22. ὀσχός, ὀσχοφόρια; ὠσχός, ὠσχοφόρια = BH אֶשְׁכּוֹל 'cluster' (↓ n. 35) ↑ n. 20; see *CGS* v pp. 201f., and refs., p. 322 n. 128.

23. Cant 7:9 אֶשְׁכֹּל הַכֹּפֶר דּוֹדִי לִי. cp. 1:14: שָׁדַיִךְ כְּאֶשְׁכְּלוֹת הַגֶּפֶן.

24. ↑ VII pp. 58f.

25. Enoch XXXII 4.

26. ↑ VIII p. 73.

27. ↑ V n. 12.

28. I Kgs 4:40 מָוֶת בַּסִּיר, ? for בסיר־מות ⇄ שׂ/סרמות <SÌL(A)-MUD "birth-canal" (= BH צלמות; ↑ XII n. 51) ⇄ שרמות in Jer 31:4, ↑ XV n. 28. As a word-play in סר(מר־)המות of Agag (XVI n. 20), I Sam 15:32?

29. פַּקֻּעֹת שָׂדֶה (v. 39), cp. Arab فُقَّع 'fungus', <BALAG; ↑V n. 18; VI p. 52 n. 39.

30. גֶּפֶן שָׂדֶה (v. 39); cp. Syr ܢܘܒܐ P-S 4129; ↑ XII n. 13 for "snake's vine" = Colocynth.

31. πέμψον σου τὸ δρέπανον τὸ ὀξὺ καὶ τρύγησον τοὺς βότρυας τῆς ἀμπέλου τῆς γῆς;

cp. Joel 4:13 : שָׁלְחוּ מַגָּל. For the significance of the sickle in mushroom mythology and imagery, cp. the story of Perseus losing the chape of his sickle
scabbard (ἅρπη, Nic *Alex* 103) and founding Mycenae, ↑ VI p. 46 n. 8; XII
n. 33; and the play on a mushroom name and the *Sicarii*, "Zealots", ↓ XVIII
p. 183; and possibly in the combined reference to Machaerus (the "sword"
fortress), Rue, and the Mandrake by Josephus *War* VII 178ff. ↓ n. 79.

32.   Cp. the Bacchic title "Dionysus the Vine-cluster", οἱ περὶ ᾽Ροῦφον ζείπα μύστε
βότρυος Διονύσου on an inscription from Philippi in Thrace of the Roman
period: *BCH* (1900) p. 317; cp. Clemens Alexandrinus *Protrepticus* 22:
Διόνυσον τὴν ἄμπελον, ὡς Θηβαῖοι προσηγόρευσαν.

33.   So already R. Graves, *op. cit.* pp. 319–43; *Greek Myths*[4] 1965, p. 3.

34.   *CGS* v p. 198.

35.   ὁ χοῦς, cp. ὀσχός, although χοῦς < *GÚ-UŠ "top of the head" (>GÚL as
> גלגלת 'skull'; cp. Sum GÚ-ZI "erect head" > BH & cogn. כּוֹס 'cup,
bowl'), as also the last element of ὀσχός, <*UŠ-GUŠ/L = BH אֶשְׁכּוֹל (↑ n. 20).

36.   Cp. ποτήριον 'cup', also < Sum GÚ-TAR "head of the penis" > Acc *katarru*
and cogn. 'mushroom', ↑ V n. 17.

37.   Sum AŠTAR 'knobbed bolt'; ↑ V n. 18; VI p. 51 n. 28. Cp. "Bacchantes"
?<*BA(LA)G-AN-TA/TI (↑ X p. 86).

38.   *CGS* v p. 217; p. 284 for refs.

39.   Cp. Aristotle ᾽Αθηναίων πολιτεία 3: ἔτι καὶ νῦν γὰρ τῆς τοῦ βασιλέως γυναικὸς
ἡ σύμμιξις ἐνταῦθα γίνεται τῷ Διονύσῳ καὶ ὁ γάμος.

40.   ↑ IX.

41.   μιαρά: *CGS* v p. 221.

42.   Photius *sv.* μιαρὰ ἡμέρα· ἐν τοῖς χουσὶν ᾽Ανθεστηριῶνος μηνός, ἐν ᾧ δοκοῦσιν
αἱ ψυχαὶ τῶν τελευτησάντων ἀνιέναι ῥάμνων ἔωθεν ἐμασῶντο καὶ πίττῃ τὰς θύρας
ἔχριον ↓ pp. 172f. and n. 102.

43.   ↑ VIII p. 65f.

44.   ἐλελεῦ, and as a surname of Bacchus Eleleus, ᾽Ελελεύς, cp. Ovid *Metamorphoses* 4.15; and a cultic cry at the ὠσχοφόρια, Plutarch *Theseus* 22; an epithet
of Apollo, Macrobius *Saturnalia* 1.17, 46; and as a war-cry, Aristophanes
Aves 364, cp. Schol. ad loc.

45. <Sum E₄-LA₆ + UIA (<*IÀ-U₅)> הַלְלוּ־יָהּ ‖ הַלְלוּ יָהּ‏ זמרו לשְׁמוֹ Ps 135:3, הַלְלוּיָהּ
Ps 106:1, NT ἀλληλουιά Rev 19:1, 3, 4, 6.

46. *Eleleides,* Ovid *Heroides* 4, 47.

47. *Il* 22.391, sung by the Achaeans after the death of Hector; in thanksgiving for
deliverance (*Il* I.472–74); traditionally explained as an invocation to Apollo:
'Ἀπόλλωνι Παιᾶν *BCH* 11.94; for other refs. see *CGS* iv p. 378, n. 98.

48. Παιωνία <Sum *BÁR-IÀ-U₅-NÁ > βαριωνᾶ(ς) ↑ II p. 18 n. 25; Pl *NH*
XXV 29: 'Vetustissima inventu paeonia est, nomenque auctoris retinet."

49. Dsc IV 162; ↑ n. 20.

50. אֵלִיָּהוּ, אֵלִיָּה < Sum E₄-LA₆ (= ILLU) + *IÀ-U₅, ↑ III n. 1; = יוֹאֵל <*IÀ-
U₅-E₄-LA₆.

51. 'Ελωί, ἐλωί λεμὰ σαβαχθανεί; Matt 27:46; Mark 15:34. The number of variants
exhibited in the MSS testify to early doubts about the phrase (see Tischen-
dorf *Nov. Test. Gr.* ll. cc.), and in particular the supposed Heb 'Ελωί, vars.
ηλι, ηλει, ελωει (Ps 22:1 אֵלִי?), suggested to Epiphanius (*Haer.* LXIX 68 on
Matt 27:46) that the words ηλι ηλι were spoken by Jesus in Hebrew and the
rest in Aramaic (the Gospel of Peter 5:19 read it as = Aram חילא 'power':
ἡ δύναμίς μου, ἡ δύναμίς (μου) . . . The language mixture continues in
λαμα (Mark), λεμα (Matt), which is better Hebrew (לָמָּה? 'why?') than Aram
(cp. Pesh ܠܡܢܐ), and σαβαχθανεί (var. σαβαχθανι) requires the hard third
radical of Aram שבק (= Heb עזב) to be rendered as χ (cp. σαβακτανει Vati-
canus); for which the example of 'Αχελδαμάχ (Acts 1:19) can now offer no
support, ↓ p. 172; cp. Dalman *Gramm.* p. 304.

52. ↑ VI n. 17 ∼ שבק 'forsake', as in John 18:23 ∼ ספק 'slap': τί με δέρεις 'why
did you slap me?'

53. ↑ XVI n. 3; ↓ XVIII p. 178; here ∼ ܢܐܡ 'sleep', part. ܢܐܡܐ 'sleeper' =
ὁ καθεύδων. For "Ἔγειρε καὶ ἀνάστα ∼ Aph. ܢܒܗ 'awaken from sleep' (cp.
Hiph. קיץ, Dan 12:2). For ἐκ τῶν νεκρῶν ∼ Sum (or derived equiv.) *MAŠ-
BA(LA)G, read as Aram שְׁוָחְתָא(מִן־) = BH שַׁחַת 'the pit' (of Sheol, Job 33:24,
etc.), cp. BH √ שׁוּח Pr 2:18 (+ אֱלִי־מֽוֹת).
    For similar word-play on *MAŠ-BA(LA)G, reading the B of the original
as Sem *w* and producing Heb מָשׁוּחַ 'anointed', cp. Peter's confession Σὺ εἶ
ὁ χριστός . . . (Matt 17:16) ∼ *MAŠ-BA(LA)G-ANTA (∼ אנתא, אַתָּה
'thou'), and John 11:27 (Martha's confession): ἐγὼ πεπίστευκα ὅτι σὺ εἶ ὁ

χριστὸς ὁ υἱὸς τοῦ Θεοῦ ὁ εἰς τὸν κόσμον ἐρχόμενος ∼ *TAB-BA-RI-TI as
﬙﮻ ﬙ "coming to the Creation" (= κόσμος). As "anointed" in the sense
of 'king', cp. the phrase βασιλεὺς τὼν Ιουδαίων and β. τοῦ 'Ισραήλ Matt
2:2; Mark 15:32; etc. ∼ *MAŠ-BA(LA)G-TAB-BA-RI read as Aram
ד־עבריא "of the Hebrews". Similarly, מָשׁוֹחַ as 'anointed' = High Priest, in
the phrase "High Priest of the Jews" ∼ *MAŠ-BA(LA)G-TAB-BA-RI,
especially at Acts 19:14: Σκευᾶ 'Ιουδαίου ἀρχιερέως, where there is an additional play on Σικύη 'gourd, cucumber' as a common determinative for the
mushroom, like קשָׁאה, ↑ XVI n. 19. In Acts 23:4: τὸν ἀρχιερέα τοῦ Θεοῦ
λοιδορεῖς; the additional word-play is on Aram סֹﬥ Aph. 'mock, deride' =
λοιδορέω and Sum *E₄-LA₆-UIA (IÀ-U₅). So, here in Ephes 5:14, καὶ ἐπιφαύσει
σοι ∼ הלל Hiph. (cp. LXX Job 31:26, 41:9 (10), 'shine forth'.

54. ↑ XII n. 36 for אֶפְרַיִם 'Ephraim', ?<*ANBAR-IM "heaven-stretched arch";
↑ III n. 35 for Sum AGRIG 'steward' = Acc abaraqqu ?<*ANBAR-AG
"protector of the womb" = אַבְרָ(הָ)ם 'Abraham' <*ANBAR-ÁM (= ÁG);
thus as "father" (Gen 15:5 (Rom 4:18); Isa 51:2; etc.; for the blessing of Gen
12:3, ↑ VI n. 41). ANBAR (AN-BAR (= BÀR(A) 'stretch out') = Acc
parzillu 'iron' prop. 'axe-head' (< BAR-SÌL(A) 'groin', ↑ XII n. 4) ?> AB-BA
(= Acc abu, BH אָב, Aram אַבָּא, etc. 'father' as "protector" (cp. אדני 'lord;
Adonis' < AN-DUL 'shade' ↑ XV n. 4).

55. 'Αββά ὁ πατήρ Mark 14:36; Rom 8:15; Gal 4:6.

56. As in Aram פַּטִּירָא 'unleavened bread', ↑ XVI n. 13.

57. ↑ VI n. 17; XVI n. 16; <*AB-BA-TAB-BA-RI-GI.

58. Apart from the Patristic material, three codices were known prior to the Nag
Hammadi finds of 1945: the fourth-century Codex Askewianus, containing
the *Pistis Sophia* and a treatise on penitence; the fifth-century Codex Bero-
linensis, containing the two *Books of Yeu* and an untitled work; and the
Codex Brucianus, containing the *Apocryphon of John*, the *Wisdom of Jesus*,
and part of the *Gospel of Mary*. There were also two papyrus fragments, one
from the fourth century in the British Museum, and the other, Rylands Pap.
463, from the third century. The 1945 discoveries yielded 13 papyrus codices
of Gnostic works, representing 44 separate works written in Coptic of the
Sahidic dialect, most, if not all, being Coptic translations of Greek works.

For the *Gospel of Truth*, see *Evangelium Veritatis* ed. M. Malinine, H. C.
Puech, G. Quispel, Zurich, 1956; cp. *The Jung Codex: A Newly Discovered
Gnostic Papyrus. Three Studies by H. C. Puech, G. Quispel, and W. C. van*

Unnik; tr. and ed. F. L. Cross, London, 1955. The earliest ref. to the "Gospel" is in Irenaeus, *c.* AD 185, *Ad. Haer.* III, 2.9: "Those who are from Valentinus, being . . . entirely reckless, while they issue their own compositions, boast that they possess more Gospels than there really are. Indeed, they have reached the ultimate in daring in calling their comparatively recent composition "the Gospel of Truth", though it agrees nowhere with the Gospels of the Apostles, so that they have no Gospel which is not replete with blasphemy."

59. It puzzled Origen in the third century, who sought in vain for an example in other Greek writers: *De Oriatione* 27.7.

60. ? $< \epsilon\pi\lambda$ τὴν ἰοῦσαν (sc. ἡμέραν): cp. *quotidianus* of the Old Latin (Itala); from a supposed Aramaic original, M. Black maintains the interpretation "give us our bread day by day" (*An Aramaic Approach to the Gospels and Acts*[2], Oxford, 1954, p. 153).

61. ? $< \epsilon\pi\lambda$ + εἶναι 'to come' i.e. bread for the future, as ἡ ἐπιοῦσα (ἡμέρα); cp. Jerome: "In evangelio, quod appellatur secundum Hebraeos, pro *super-substantiali pane* reperi *mahar* (מחר), quod dicitur crastinum ut sit sensus: panem nostrum crastinum, id est futurum, da nobis hodie (*Comm. in Matth.* 6:11; VII 34 Vallarsi). Cp. Bohairic, Sahidic, and Marcion, and the Cure-tonian Syriac: "continual" (? "daily": E. Lohmeyer, *Das Vater-unser*[2], Gött., 1947, p. 99); with some Armenian support (D. Y. Hadidan, *NTS* V (1958), pp. 75–81).

62. $< \epsilon\pi\lambda$ + οὐσία 'for subsistence, needful'; Pesh: ܠܚܡܐ ܣܘܢܩܢܢ; so Jerome's *superstantialis*, i.e. *super* = ἐπί, *substantia* = οὐσία; note Luke's placing of the prayer after 10:42: ὀλίγων δέ ἐστιν χρεία ἡ ἑνός . . .

63. ~ BH Aram √ שׂ/ספק 'suffice'; Aph. 'give what is needful; grant'; and ~ *TAB-BA-RI read as פַּטִּירָא 'unleavened bread' ↑ n. 56; XVI n. 13.

64. πειρασμός = מַצְרֵף ↑ VIII p. 72 n. 54.

65. עת המצרף הבאה *DJD* V; 4Q 171 ii 18; 174 ii 1; 177 3 (?).

66. ܟܘܢܫܢܐ، ܣܘܢܩܢܐ ~ ܟܘܕ ܟܘܢܫܢܐ Arab خَرَبَتَ ↑ VI n. 16.

67. See Andrija Puharich *The Sacred Mushroom*, N.Y., 1959, pp. 113ff.

68. Cp. Pl *NH* XXV 52: "Both Hellebores when ground to powder, either by themselves or combined with *radicula* . . . cause sneezing, and both cause sleep . . ." Note the name of Hellebore, Ἐλαφινέ (var. Ἐλαφνής) 'fawn' (?) given by Ps-Dsc (IV 162), and the story of "the wild animal of Egypt called

the gazelle (*oryx*) that . . . stands facing the lesser dog-star at its rise, and gazing at it as if in worship, after first giving a sneeze . . . (Pl *NH* II 107), and the story recounted by Josephus of the magic root which had the ability of drawing forth the evil spirit from an afflicted person through the nose (*Ant* VIII 46f.).

For present-day practice of narcotic snuff-taking, see particularly the reports of S. Henry Wassén of the Gothenburg Ethnographical Museum, to whom the present writer is indebted for drawing his attention to the practice, and the following works by that author: *The Use of Some Specific Kinds of South American Indian Snuff and Related Paraphernalia* (Etnologiska Studier 28), Göteborg, 1965, with bibliography; "Om Några Indianska Droger och specielt om snus samt tillbehör" (Särtryck ur Etnografiska Museet, Goteborg, Årstryck 1963–66), 1967, pp. 97–140; "An Anthropological Survey of the Use of South American Snuffs", in *Ethnopharmalogic Search for Psychoactive Drugs,* Proceedings of a Symposium held in San Francisco, Cal., Jan. 28–30, 1967, *Workshop Series of Pharmacology, NIMH No. 2,* Public Health Service Publ. No. 1645, US Gov.Pr.Off. Wash. DC, 1967, pp. 233–89.

69. *NH* XXV 56–61.

70. J. Ramsbottom, *op. cit.* p. 44.

71. *NH* XXV 49.

72. IX x 4.

73. IX x 1.

74. Pl *NH* X 75; ἥρως μυίαγρος in Arcadia, Pausanias 8.26.7.

75. Pl *NH* XXIX 106.

76. Dsc IV 162.

77. *NH* XXV 51.

78. BH סַנְוֵרִים, Aram שַׁבְרִירֵי: Yom 28ᵇ; cp. Gitt 69ᵃ, Ab Zar 12ᵇ; Pes 112ᵃ; cp. J. A. Montgomery *Aramaic Incantation Texts from Nippur,* 1913, p. 93. BH סנורים usu. assumed to be a causative form of √ נור (*šunwuru:* Montgomery *Kings* (ICC) 1951, p. 383) in the sense of 'dazzle' (B. Landsberger *MAOG* IV p. 320 n. 3), but perhaps <Sum *ŠEN-BURU₈ (>Acc šib-burratu,* Aram ܣܰܒܪܳܐ, שִׁבְרָא 'Rue', the abortifacient ↑ VIII n. 26; ↓ p. 163; i.e. the temporary blindness earned its name from the drug.

79. If פֻּטְרָא = *Amanita muscaria*, as well as 'Rue', this could account for the latter's being famed as an antidote to fungi, and for Josephus' ref. to the giant Rue at Machaerus, *War* VII 178ff.; ↑ n. 31; VIII p. 67.

80. ↑ XI p. 78 n. 14.

81. *NH* XXII 96.

82. Gen 1:1–2:3.

83. Exod 25:31–40 = 37:17–24; Jos *Ant* III 146; *War* VII 149: ἑπτὰ δ' ἦσαν οὗτοι τῆς παρὰ τοῖς Ἰουδαίοις ἑβδομάδος τὴν τιμὴν ἐμφανίζοντες.

84. Ps 90:10.

85. אַסְיָא = 'Ασία ~ אַסְיָא 'physician', √ אסי 'heal'.

86. Cp. Jos *War* II 136: ἔνθεν αὐτοῖς πρὸς Θεραπείαν παθῶν ῥίζαι τε ἀλεξητήριοι καὶ λίθων ἰδιότητες ἀνερευνῶνται. For older exponents of this identification of the name Ἐσσηνός, Ἐσσαῖος, Ὀσσαῖος, Ἰεσσαῖος, see J. B. Lightfoot, *Colossians*[3], 1879, p. 350, and for a more recent exposition, cp. G. Vermes *Rev. de Qum.* VII (June 1960) pp. 427–43. A better understanding of the origin and meaning of the name Θεραπευταί, relating both to service of the god and healing of the body, makes the old objections to the identification largely irrelevant (cp. Schürer *Geschichte*[3] III ii, 1898, pp. 559–60; and recently, F. M. Cross *The Ancient Library of Qumran*, N.Y., 1961, p. 52 n. 1); to 'heal' was to 'serve' the deity (↑ VII pp. 6of). See Allegro *The Treasure of the Copper Scroll*, 1960, pp. 145f., n. 97, for a possible confusion between the name "Essenes" given to a gate in the south wall of Jerusalem (Jos *War* V 145), and Aram אַסְיָא 'myrtles' = Heb הֲדַסִּים, and חרסות of Jer 19:2; cp. Zech 1:8 where LXX read בין ההדסים of MT as if it were בֵּין הֶהָרִים (ἀνὰ μέσον τῶν (δύο) ὀρέων), and cp. MT Zech 14:5 גֵּי הָרִים, for גֵּי־הֲדַס 'Valley of the Myrtles'?

87. 4Q 171 iv 23–24: שבע מחלקות שבי ישׂ[ראל]; *DJD* V p. 45; cp. the seven divisions of the Promised Land at the conquest, Josh 18:5, etc.

88. 4Q 177 Catena (A) 10–11, ll.1–4: *DJD* V p. 70.

89. See the recent work of S. Laeuchli *Mithraism in Ostia: Mystery Religion and Christianity in the Seaport of Rome*, 1967, and his interesting essay on 'Urban Mithraism' in *Biblical Archaeologist*, XXXI Sept. 1968, pp. 74–99.

90. ↑ III pp. 27f; IX pp. 78f.

91. *War* VII 181; ↑ IX p. 81.

92. 'nt III 10–14: tḥm aliyn.b'l.hwt ¹¹aliy.qrdm.qryy.barṣ mlḥmt.št.b'pr(t/m!).
ddym ¹³ sk.šlm.lkbd.arṣ ¹⁴ arbdd.lkbd.šdm. (*UM* II p. 88); cp. IV 54, 69, 74;
(*UM* Gloss. ※235) "the message of the Mighty Borer, the word of the
Womb-favourer: 'Put bread in the ground, set Mandrakes in the dust, pour a
compensatory offering in the midst of the earth, a peace offering in the midst
of the fields!' "

    For *b'l* 'borer', <*BA-AL = "penis", ↑ III n. 26; for *qrdm* <*MAR-DUG
"womb-favourer" i.e. penis, ↑ II n. 1; XII n. 4; *arbdd* <*ÙR-BAD(-BAD)
"furrow-appeaser", ?>Ὀροβάδιον = Γλυκυσίδη = Παιωνία, Ps-Dsc III 140;
↑ V n. 23.

93. Πιθοίγια <Sum GI-DU₈ (Acc *paṭíru* "liberated, free") 'offerings-table' +
IGI 'face, presence' = BH לֶחֶם הַפָּנִים.

94. BH √ מצץ, מצה, and cogn. ?<Sum ZUM *mašâdu* 'squeeze out', *ḫâlu* 'make
sweat' (denom. fr. *ḫîlu* 'sweat, resin, etc'. < E₄-LA₆ "strong-water"), cp.
μᾶζα 'barley-cake', and the μαζῶνες of Phigaleia in Arcadia: Athenaeus
149B from Hardmodios I: περὶ τῶν κατὰ φιγάλειαν νομίμων ἐν ἅπασι τοῖς
δείπνοις μάλιστα δὲ ἐν τοῖς λεγομένοις μαζῶσι, τοῦτο γὰρ ἔτι καὶ νῦν ἡ διονυσιακὴ
ἔχει τοὔνομα, cp. *IG* V ii *Inscriptiones Arcadiae*, ed. F. Hiller von Gaertringen,
1913, 178 (Tegea); cp. *CGS* v pp. 123; 238 n. 27.

    Cp. Pl *NH* XXII 98: 'Hog fungi are hung up to dry, skewered on a rush'';
Ramsbottom *op. cit.* pp. 45f.: "Fly Agaric is dried in the sun or over the hearth
after it has been gathered". Cp. II Kgs 23:9 for the cultic eating of מצות at
high places; here a misunderstanding or interpretation of an original פטריות
'mushrooms'?

95. For derivation of פסח, ↑ VII n. 8.

96. ? related to BH & cogn. √ פסח 'limp' (i.e. hop?), cp. Arab فسخ 'be dislocated', < Sum *BA-SUḪ 'withdraw' (as a bolt from a socket, hence
Á-SUḪ = AŠTAR 'bolt' ↑ V n. 23).

97. ↑ VII n. 8; X n. 28.

98. ↑ XII n. 80.

99. ↑ XII p. 106.

100. Ἀγαρικόν < Sum AGARGARA *agargarû* 'excrement' ↑ XII n. 61; cp. also
↑ n. 78 on Rue, the abortifacient.

101. ↑ XIV p. 130, on Barnabas and the sale of his field. Ἀκελδαμά(χ) < Aram אֲכַל־דָּמֵי "food of compensation, price" (Targ Aram = BH מחיר). Aram & cogn. אכל 'food; eat', ?<Sum A-KAL "strong-water" (= E₄—LA₆), primarily the life-giving semen of man and animals, and the 'sap' of plants (cp. Ἀκαλήφη, Ἀκαλύφη, Thphr VII vii 2 codd. 'stinging-nettle', <? A-KAL + ú GÍR 'thorn' i.e. the poisonous juice of the nettle). For דָּמֵי, √דמה 'be equivalent, resemble, compare', ?<Sum DAM "set side by side; copulate", so = 'spouse'; cp. Aram √דמך 'sleep' ?<*KI-DAM "copulate" as KI-ÁG râmu 'love'.

102. ↑ n. 42 for Photius; cp. Hsch. sv: μιαραὶ ἡμέραι τοῦ Ἀνθεστηριῶνος μηνός, ἐν αἷς τὰς ψυχὰς τῶν κατοιχομένων ἀνιέναι ἐδόκουν.

103. ↑ III p. 21 n. 11.

104. MT יָקֶן, LXX ὄρθιον = יְקֶן (S. R. Driver Notes on the Hebrew Text of Samuel², 1913, p. 215), cp. OLat (ed. Vercellone Var. lect. Vulgatae, 1860, p. 64). Cp. Syr ܩܘܡ of 'erection' of phallus, P-S 1148.

105. ↑ VI n. 23.

106. Pesh ܒܚܘܒܝܟܘܢ = ἐν ταῖς ἀγάπαις ὑμῶν (and Pesh at II Pet 2:13); agape pro mortuorum quiete habita, cp. ܘܟܢܘܫܝܐ ܘܚܘܒܐ ܕܡܝܬܐ 'memorials and love-feasts for the departed', Bar Hebraeus Ethica 31v; P-S 2317.

107. Cp. L & S sv ἀγαπάω; LXX = BH √אהב, <Sum ÁG-ÁG (râmu 'love'; madâdu 'draw, measure') > ἄγω 'lead, draw forth' and > BH √עגב 'lust after', עוּגָב 'musical instrument' ‖ כּוּר, ↑ X n. 2. Cp. the proper names Ἀγαύη daughter of Cadmus and Harmonia, Ἄγαβος Ac 11:28, 21:10, (↑ XVI n. 20) and אֲגַג king of the Amalekites (↑ VII n. 10).

108. = הֵסִית II Chr 18:2; cp. √נגד 'draw forth' of necromancy, ↑ XII n. 79.

109. ↑ XIII pp. 112–16.

CHAPTER XVIII

The Garden of Adonis, Eden and Delight; Zealots and Muslims

1. "et ecce ibi mulieres sedebant plangentes Adonidem".

2. "Bethlehem nunc nostram . . . lucus inumbrabat Thamus, id est Adonidas"

(ed Vallarsi P 321); cp. Plato *Phaedo* 276 b; Theocritus Scholia. Pl. l.c.; 15.113. For the origin of the phrase 'Αδώνιδος κῆποι (Thphr VI vii 3) from Sum *GAN-NA-IM-A-AN = mushroom, ↓ pp. 178ff.

3. Thphr (VI vii 3) compares the propagation of 'Αβρότονον (↑ XI n. 27) by layering in pots to the "gardens of Adonis"; Arab associates the Anemone with the god (↑ XVI n. 3).

4. Andrija Puharich, *op. cit.* p. 111.

5. Ramsbottom, *op. cit.* p. 180.

5. ↑ XVII p. 163.

7. Sum ᵈ DUMU-ZI *il Tammuz*.

8. ↑ XV n. 4; cp. the function of kingship in Jotham's parable, ↑ V p. 38 (of the אטד).

9. ↑ XVI n. 3.

10. Sum GÁN(A) *eqlu* 'field' BH & cogn. גַּן 'garden', as an enclosed area; cp. Sum ᵍⁱˢ GAN-NU(-UM) 'bowl-lid' and related BAN 'arch'; ↑ XIV n. 16.

11. BH נַעֲם, Arab نَعِمَ 'be plentiful, easy, pleasant'; BH = NH נָעִים 'pleasing, lovely'; cp. Arab تَرْفَاس 'fungus' (↑ V n. 18) and ترف 'lead a delicate life' (cp. τρυφή 'softness' and Θιβρός (Θιμβρός) II 'delicate, luxurious'); BH & cogn. √ פנק 'indulge, pamper' ? < *GAN-nabas (> Πάνακες the plant-name, ↑ IX n. 12.

12. BH עֵדֶן 'luxury'; hithp. (denom.) 'luxuriate' Neh 9:25; NH Pi. = لي Pa.; עֵדֶן בַּן עֵדֶן ‖ גַּן־יהוה Isa 51:3, עדן גַּן־אלהים, גַּן־אלהים Ezek 28:13, 31:9 (LXX Ezek ἡ τρυφή; Isa παράδεισος).

13. جَنَّات النَّعِيم, ↓ p. 182.

14. ↑ XIV p. 121.

15. ↑ II n. 17; √ קנא & cogn. = Arab قَنَأ 'be intensely red; dyed red (beard)'; קִנְאָה 'ardour, zeal, jealousy', adj. קַנָּא, of God; as a divine name, Exod 34:14; cp. אֵל קַנּוֹא Josh 24:19; Nah 1:2 ‖ נָקַם.

16. *Ant* XII 271: "εἴ τις ζηλωτής ἐστιν τῶν παρίων ἐθῶν καὶ τῆς τοῦ Θεοῦ Θρησκείας . . ." (Mattathias).

17. *War* IV 160f.: . . . τοῖς ζηλωταῖς . . . ἀλλ' οὐχὶ ζηλώσαντες τὰ κάκιστα τῶν

ἔργων . . .; cp. VII 268ff. . . . διὰ πάντων ἀνομίαν, ἐν ᾗ τὸ τῶν ζηλωτῶν κληθέντων γένος ἤκμασεν, οἳ τὴν προσηγορίαν τοῖς ἔργοις ἐπηλήθευσαν . . . καίτοι τὴν προσηγορίαν αὐτοῖς ἀπὸ τῶν ἐπ' ἀγαθῷ ζηλουμένων ἐπέθεσαν . . .

18. *War* VII 275–401.

19. See Yadin's magnificent volume, *Masada, Herod's fortress and the Zealots' Last Stand,* London, 1966.

20. *War* VII 332.

21. *War* VII 343–49.

22. *War* II 154

23. קַנָּאִים ?< *GAN-NA-IM(-A-AN).

24. ↑ XIII n. 14.

25. Deut 9:2; עַם גָּדוֹל וָרָם בְּנֵי עֲנָקִים; LXX at Deut 1:28: υἱοὺς γιγάντων.

26. ↑ V p. 40 n. 21.

27. Ἄνακες, σωτήροιν Ἀνάκοιν τε Διοσκούροιν *IG* 3.195, etc.; as an old plural of ἄναξ 'lord' (L & S *sv*), but properly <*GAN-NA-IM(-A-AN)>*annagim> Ἄνακες.

28. *War* II 254–62.

28a *Ant* XX viii 186.

29. Cp. the accusation against Paul of being ὁ Αἰγύπτιος ὁ πρὸ τούτων τῶν ἡμερῶν ἀναστατώσας καὶ ἐξαγαγὼν εἰς τὴν ἔρημον τοὺς τετρακισχιλίους ἄνδρας τῶν σικαρίων. Acts 21:38. Cp. Jos *War* II 261: περὶ τρισμυρίου. In NT ",δ σικαρίοι" ("4000 sicarii") ᷉ Διόσκουροι and ὁ Αἰγύπτιος ᷉ מצור/מסור ↑ XVI p. 143.

30. ↑ XVII pp. 156, 167 nn. 31, 79; Acc *usqaru, askaru, asqaru,* etc. 'sickle', and cp. σκίρον 'large white sunshade' carried at the Σκιροφόρια, the festival of Athena Σκίρα, Schol. Aristophanes *Ecclesiazusae* 18: ἐν ᾗ ὁ ἱερεὺς τοῦ Ἐρεχθέως φέρει σκιάδειον λευκὸν ὃ λέγεται σκίρον.

31. Avestic *pairidaēza,* in the plural, 'circular enclosure' (*AIW* 865) > παράδεισος (Xenophon *Anabasis* I ii 7, etc.), Acc *pardîsu,* BH פַּרְדֵּס, etc. (Syr ܦܪܕܝܣܐ appends the Pahlavic *pānak* 'protector, keeper'; Pers. بان 'gardener', P-S 3240; cp. P. Horn, *Grundriss der neupersischen Etymologie,* Strassbourg, 1893,

para. 176); into Arab from Christian sources? (*For. Vocab.* p. 224); ?<Sum BÁRA 'sanctuary' + TÉŠ *bâltu, bâštu, bûltu* 'sexual force'.

32. See *For. Vocab.* Introduction; W. Rudolph *Die Abhängigkeit des Qorans von Judenthum und Christenthum*, Stuttgart, 1922; K. Ahrens 'Christliches im Qoran' *ZDMG* LXXXIV (1930) pp. 15–68, 148–90; cp. Jefferey: ". . . the conviction that not only the greater part of the religious vocabulary, but also most of the cultural vocabulary of the Qur'ān is of non-Arab origin." (*For. Vocab.* p. 2.)

33. See Wright *Early Christianity in Arabia*, 1885; L. Cheikho النَصْرَانِيَّة وادآبهـا عرب الجاهليّة بيـن, Beirut, 1912–23; Tor Andrae *Der Ursprung des Islams und das Christentum*, Upsala, 1926. The oldest Christian community in South Arabia was thought to have been at Najran (Andrae, pp. 7–24); cp. Qur. Sur. 85:4ff.; Muhammad is said to have listened to a sermon there preached by the Bishop (Jāḥiẓ *Bayān* i 119; *Khizāna* i 268). Muhammad's contact with the Syrian Church is confirmed by the Traditions, and he is said to have gone in his youth on trading journeys to Syria, aṭ-Ṭabarī *Annales* (ed. De Geoje and others, 15 vols. Leiden, 1879–1901) i 1124; etc., and perhaps even passed by the Dead Sea (Sur 37:137; see A. Sprenger *Muhammed und der Koran*, p. 6). On the legends of Nestor and Baḥīra (aṭ-Ṭabarī *loc. cit.*) and their evidence of the Prophet's contact with Christians of the Syrian Church, see H. Hirschfeld *New Researches into the Composition and Exegesis of the Qoran*, London, 1902, p. 22ff.; Gottheil *ZA* XIII, pp. 189ff.; A. Sprenger *Das Leben und die Lehre des Mohammad*[2], 1861–69, i, pp. 178ff.; ii, pp. 381ff.; L. Caetani *Annali dell'Islam*, Milan, i, 1905, pp. 136, 169; Th. Nöldeke 'Hatte Muḥammed christliche Lehrer?' *ZDMG* XII (1858), pp. 699ff.

34. حُورعِين Qur. 44:54, 52:20, 55:72, 56:22; حَوَرٌ 'contrasting the black and white of the eye' (esp. of gazelles, cows). For exx. of use in pre-Islamic poetry, see *For. Vocab.* p. 118.

35. مَنْزَكْئَا Ethpa. part. √ܨܒ, Pa. denom. fr. ܨܒ, ܨܒ 'ornament, etc.' = 'improve, embellish'; Targ Aram צִבְתָא (= BH מרוק Esther 2:12 of harem preparations) <Sum BI-ZI-DA (>*ZI-BI-DA) as in ŠEM-BI-ZI(-DA) *egû* 'stibium') στίβι, Lat *stibium*; στιβίζομαι 'paint eyelids' LXX Ezek 23:40 = BH √ כחל; etc., Sum ZI-DA = Acc *kênu* 'be right, normal' (BH √ כון), as in Á-ZI-DA (*imnu* 'right' (direction)) > BH חָסִיד 'faithful'; NÍG-ZID (<ZI-DA) *kettu* 'justice'.

36. ↑ XVI n. 1.

37. ↑ V n. 8.

38. √ ܪܨ, Ethpe. partic. ܐܬܪܨܝ̈ܘ 'willing'; ܐܬܪܨܝ̈ܘ 'acceptable', ↑ XVI n. 16; for play on Ταβειθά ↑ XVI n. 1.

39. √ סבר Ithpa. 'hope, look for' (Syr ܣܒܪ Pa.) = BH חכה Ps 106:13.

40. مُسْلِمُون.

41. *Kitāb al-Aghāni* VII 174.

41a. *al-Bukhāri* 67. 83.

41b. Cp. R. Levy *The Social Structure of Islam,* Cambridge, 1957, pp. 385ff.

41c. *Kitāb al-Aghāni* X 54.

41d. Cp. Sur. 24:30ff., 33:59f. and comm.

41e. Cp. Levy, *op. cit.* pp. 127f.; see also on the question of the veiling and seclusion of women in Islam; S. Hurgronje *Verspreide Geschriften,* Bonn, I, 1923, pp. 305ff.; A von Kremer, *Culturgeschichte des Orients,* Vienna, XXX 1875–77, II, ch. 3.

42. فِدَاوِىّ.

43. حشيش 'dry herbage', esp. *Cannabis sativa* L., Post *FP²* p. 513.

44. حشيشة الحَمْراء.

44a. Cp. B. Lewis (*The Assassins,* London, 1967) who thinks the name merely "a derisive comment on their conduct rather than a description of their practices" (p. 12).

45. ↑ XIV pp. 121f.

46. ↑ n. 11; IX n. 12.

47. *NH* XXV 30.

CHAPTER XIX

The Bible as a Book of Morals

1. E.g., P. Humbert: "La désert est la patrique classique du yahvisme" in 'Osée,

le prophète bedouin', *RHPR* i (1921) p. 106; cp. the same author's 'La logique de la perspective nomade chez Osée et l'unité d'Osée 2:4–22', in *Festschrift für Karl Marti* ed. K. Budde (*Beih. z. ZAW* XLI (1925)) pp. 158–66, and, even further along the same lines, E. Meyer, *Die Israeliten und ihre Nachbarstämme*, with supplements by B. Luther, Halle, 1906, pp. 129–41, to the ultimate idealization of the desert idea in J. W. Flight, 'The Nomadic Idea and Ideal' *JBL* LXII (1923), pp. 158–226, and, somewhat less extremely, M. Soloweitschik 'המדבר בתולדותיו והשקפת עולמו של עם ישראל' *Debir* II (1923) pp. 16–45. For an objective review of the extremes of "desert ideology", with a study of the textual data, see esp. S. Talmon in *Studies and Texts: Vol. III: Biblical Motifs* (Philip W. Lown Institute of Advanced Judaic Studies, Brandeis University, ed. A. Altmann), Harvard Univ. Press, 1966, pp. 31–63.

2. ↑ XV p. 139 n. 36.

3. ↑ XVI pp. 142ff.

4. ↑ III n. 1.

5. ↑ XVI p. 147 n. 29.

6. Aram √ דבר 'lead, guide'.

7. אֱלָה 'l' 'no god' + 'l'ן 'l' 'except' + אלהי 'god' <*E$_4$-LA$_6$-UIA. Cp. the Islamic witness: لا إِلَهَ الأَ اللهُ followed by ومُحَمَّد رَسُول الله ? *MAŠ-BA(LA)G-ANTA as if Aram ܡܫܒܚܐ "glorious, praised" + ܐܢܬ (אנתא) 'thou'; cp. مُحَمَّد "praised one" and note the plant name ܡܫܒܚܝܐ 'Scammony' (<*MAŠ-BA(LA)G, ↑ VI n. 16) taken into Arab as if of the root ܫܒܚ 'praise' and so rendered مَحْمُودَة "praised" (!); رَسُول 'messenger' ? *MAŠ-BA(LA)G as if √ שבק 'send forth' as in ܡܠܟܐ ܡܫܕܪ ܩܪܘܙܐ (ὁ βασιλεὺς κήρυκας ἀπέστειλε) *praecones a rege circummissi* Apocr. Acts of the Apostles, ed. W. Wright, 1871, ܩܪ 19, qu. P-S 4040.

8. BH √ אלה vb. and noun; Arab آ لَى 'swear, take on oath', أَلْوَة 'oath'; + ܚܣܡ 'remit' + ܚܛܝܐ 'wicked' (עַנְתָּא), cp. ܚܛܐ 'deceit, villainy'.

9. ναὶ ναί, οὖ οὖ for Aram ܐܝܢ 'l', ܐܝܢ 'l', pronounced as *ēllā'ēllā* ~ *E$_4$-LA$_6$-UIA (indicating a western Syr *zeqāfā* (Wright *CGSL* p. 85) as *â* or *ō*).

10. τὸ δὲ περισσὸν τούτων ἐκ τοῦ πονηροῦ i.e. ~ *MAŠ-BA(LA)G-ANTA read as NH Aram שְׁבַח, שְׁבָחָא, 'gain, increase' + ܒܝܫܐ 'the evil one'; ↑ VI n. 41.

11. *MAŠ-BA(LA)G giving √ שבח 'be still' (↑ XIII p. 116 n. 23) and √ שבח 'praise honour'; פלח, פולחנא 'work' (↑ XVI p. 147 n. 29); and *TAB-BA-RI-TI ∼ ?ܒܪܝܬܐ 'of Creation'.

12. i.e. √ שבח 'praise' + *TAB-BA-RI-GI as ד־ברייך cp. Targ Aram בָּרְיָא = בּוֹרְיָיא = BH בּוֹרְא 'Creator, God', as 'father' Mal 2:10; and for the general tenor of the passage, cp. Eccles 12:1–7 . . . וכר את־בוראיך בימי בחורתיך.

13. ↑ n. 10; VI n. 41 (on 'Mammon').

14. √ ספק; ↑ XVII n. 63.

15. ↑ VI nn. 16, 41.

16. i.e. KUR ∼ Aram √ גּר 'commit adultery', n. ܓܘܪܐ; and-BALAG-∼ √ פלח 'use', and -ANTA ∼ אנתתא 'woman' ↑ VI n. 17.

17. The theme of the whole passage being a play on *MAŠ-BA(LA)G-ANTA-TAB-BA-RI read as √ שבק 'divorce', אנתתא 'woman', and דיבוריא "The Words" i.e. the Law, ↑ VI n. 17.

18. ↑ VI n. 17; in Gen 2:24 (Heb דבק), ∼ NH ספק 'cleave together', and -BALAG ∼ √ פלג 'divide'.

19. *TAB-BA-RI(-A) ∼ (BH רַע) ד־ב־רַעֲוָתָא 'that which is in the will'.

20. *MAŠ-BA(LA)G-ANTA-TAB-BA-RI-TI ∼ ܣܟ ܡܢ ܩܕܡܝܐ 'from the origin' (↑ XVII n. 53) + ?ܕܒܪܝܬܐ 'of Creation', ↑ n. 11.

21. i.e. מְשַׁבְּקָא 'divorcer' Pa. part. + אנתתא 'woman, wife', and לגּר 'for adultery', פלח אנתתא "serves a woman" (?).

22. ↑ VII pp. 60f.

23. *per flagita;* cp. para. 4: *cuncta . . . atrocia aut pudenda,* as both hideous cruelties and immoralities; cp. *flagitia cohaerentia nomini* in Pliny's letter to Trajan (*Epp.* X 96.2).

24. Only here mentioned by a Roman historian, Jos (*Ant* XVIII 89) gives his procuratorship from AD 27–37, and mentions his recall by order of Vitellius, legate of Syria. Cp. also Philo *Legatio ad Gaium* 38, and Eusebius (*H.E.* 2, 7) who gives the story of his suicide in exile.

25. *exitiabilis superstitio:* the epithet used of disease (*morbo exitiabili correptos* XVI 5.2); cp. Pliny's letter to Trajan, *superstitio prava immodica* (para. 8).

26. *Annals* XV 44. 2–8.

27. Cp. Sulpicius Severus *Chronica* 2, 29, who has verbally transcribed much of Tacitus: "neque ulla re Nero efficiebat, quin ab eo iussum incendium putaretur. Igitur vertit invidiam in Christianos . . ."

28. Cp. the similar charge made by Tacitus against the Jews: "adversus omnis alios hostile odium" (*Historia* V 5.2). The Medicean *coniuncti* for *convicti* stands alone; cp. *correpti* earlier.

29. *Life of Claudius* XXV 4.

30. ↑ VI pp. 51f for the drug *Chreston*, the juice of which, smeared on the body, gave health and granted wishes (Pl. *NH* XX 74).

31. *Life of Nero* XVI 2: *malefica*, possibly a specific charge of witchcraft frequently brought against the Christians.

32. Θυέστεια δεῖπνα and Οἰδιπόδειοι μίξεις; cp. Minuncius Felix *Octavius* 9.1; Tertullian *Apologeticum* 7ff., etc.

33. Cp. 1QS i 9–11.

General Index

Biblical Index

OLD TESTAMENT

NEW TESTAMENT

Word Index

The references are to chapters and notes.

Sumerian

A > U	II 22	AGÁN (-TI)	V 18; XIV 16
*A-U₅	III 11	AGÀN	III 26
*A-BI-ÙŠ	VIII 60	AGÁR	V 26
A-KAL	XVII 101	AGARGARÁ	III 45; V 18; XII
A-RI-A	I 2; II 6; III 15, 41;		61; XVII 100
	VII 10; XV 34	AGARIN	II 24; XII 1
A-RI-A-NAM-LÚ-	III 35; VIII 60;	AGRIG	III 35; XVII 54
ULÙˡᵘ	XII 38	AL	III 26
A-TU	VIII 60; XII 38	ᵍⁱˢAL(-LA)	III 26
⁽ᵍⁱˢ⁾A-TU-GAB-LIŠ	VIII 60; XII 38	ALLA-nu	III 26
A-ZU (Ì-ZU)	IV 2, 14	ᵍⁱˢAL-LA-AN	III 26
*Á-A-RI-A	II 25; VII 39; X 20;	ᵈALÁD	III 41
	XIV 3	AL-DÙ	III 26
*Á-AG	X 2	AL-KAD₍₅₎	III 31
*Á-BAL	XII 2	AL-TI	XII 52
*Á-BIR-UŠ₁₂	III 7	*AL-TI (= DUN₄)-	XV 3
*Á-BULUG	VI 16	AN-NA	
*Á-BÚRU-DA-TI	II 1; XI 27	AL-UŠ-SA	V 10
*Á-BÚRU-NÁ/NU	XI 27	*ÁM-BURU₈	VIII 26
*Á-BÚRU-TÙN	XI 27	AMA	II 22
*Á-GAN	III 26; XIV 16	AMAŠ	XII 21
*Á-GAR-ÈN	XII 1	AN	I 1ᵃ; II 16
*Á-GIN	III 43	AN-NA	III 11
*Á-GÚ	XII 13	AN-BAR	III 35; XII 4, 36;
Á-GÚ-ZI-GA	VIII 39		XVII 54
*Á-ÍD-ÚŠ	XVII 9	*ANBAR-ÁG	XVII 54
Á-MUD/MUD-Á	II 13; XII 51	*ANBAR-ÁM/G	XVII 54
*Á-MUG-DAL	VIII 37	*ANBAR-IÀ-U₅-NÁ	XII 38
Á-RAG-GA	III 35	*ANBAR-IM	XII 36; XVII 54
*Á-RI-GAG-GÀR-BA	V 18; VI 28	*ANBAR (AB-BA)-	VI 41
Á-SUḪ	XII 78; XVII 96	TAB-BA-RI-GI	
*Á-SUR	III 31; XVI 10	*ANBAR-TAB-BA-RI-	XVI 1
*Á-TÙN	VIII 40, 56	TI	
*Á-U₅ (-A)	II 22	AN-DUL (ANDUL)	XV 4; XVII 54
*Á-UIA-NU	XII 26	*AN-DUL-AN	XV 4
*Á-ZAG	III 31	AN-DÙL	II 16; X 7
Á-ZÀG	III 31	*AN-IM-A(= IM-A-AN)	III 7
Á-ZI-DA	III 14, 44; XVIII 35	AN-PÀR	XII 38
AB-BA	III 35; XVII 54	*AN-SUR	XV 4
*AB-BA-TAB-BA-RI-GI	XVII 57	-ANTA/TI	VI 23; XIX 16
*AB-GALA	XII 4	AN-TI-BAL	III 26; XII 3
*AB-ḪA-ŠEN/SÍN	III 41	*AN-ÚR	XII 29
AB-SÍN	II 15; III 9, 41; VI	AN-ZÍB	III 31; VII 37
	19; XII 4	*AR-ZAL-DAR	XIV 52
AB-ZU(= ZU-AB)	III 11	ÁR	III 41
AD(-AD)	III 2, 21; V 10	*ÁR-GALA	III 45
ᵍⁱˢÁD	III 21; V 10	*ÁR-GÍD-UŠ	XV 3
ADAMA	VIII 9; XIV 3	*ÁR-GUN	XII 36, 41; XV 6
ÁG(-ÁG)	II 11, 15; III 35;	*ÁR-GUN-IM	XV 6
	X 2; XII 1, 80, 82;	ÁR-NIGIN	XII 42
	XVI 20; XVII 107	*ÁR-ÙŠ-TAR	III 46
AGA/UGU	XII 13	ARÀ-U₅-NÁ	XV 21

316

DU-DU — XVI 1
DÙ-DÙ — III 17; XVI 1
*DU$_6$-AMA — X 21
DU$_8$ — XVI 13
DU$_{14}$ — XII 27
DÙG — III 27, 43; VII 26; XII 68
DÙG-GAN — II 9
DUG$_4$-GÌŠ (see also GÌŠ-DUG$_4$-GA) — VII 13
DUGGAN — III 31
DU(L) — X 21; XIV 9, 16
*DUL-AN-NA — XV 4
*DUL-ANBAR — XII 4
*DUL-BAN — XIV 15
*DUL-BAR — XII 38
DUL-DU — X 7; XIV 9
^{d}DUMU-ZI — XVIII 7
DÙN(= TÚL) — II 16
DUN$_4$ — XII 52

É-AZAG — III 31
*É-BUR-ZI — IX 22
*É-DÙG — III 31
É-GAL — III 33
É-KUR-ÚS — XVII 9
*É-LAM — III 29
*É-LAM-TUR$_5$ — III 29
É-TU(R)$_5$ — V 23
É-UŠ-GÍD-DA — III 31, 35; VIII 37; XV 27
É-ZAG-GAR-RA — III 31; XIV 16
*E$_4$-Á — VII 39
*E$_4$-BI-ÙŠ — VIII 26
E$_4$-LA$_6$(= ILLU) — III 1, 31; VIII 60; XII 56, 58; XVII 45, 50, 53, 94, 101
*E$_4$-LA$_6$-IÀ-U$_5$ — III 1
*E$_4$-LA$_6$-UIA — XIX 7, 9
*E$_4$-RI(-A) — II 6; VII 10; XI 26
E$_{11}$ — X 7; XIV 9
EN — VII 26
*EN-DARA$_4$ — XIV 11
ÈN — VII 26
ENGAR — II 24; XII 1
$^{(d)}$ENGUR — III 11; XV 22
ENSI(PA-TE-SI) — VIII 63; XIV 34
ÈR (ÈRI, ERUM) — II 6
*ERA-GIN — X 20
ÈRI — XI 26
*ÈRI-MU — XI 26
ERI$_4$ — VI 23; VII 10
ERI$_4$-AN-NA — III 35; VIII 60
*ERI$_4$-IÀ-U$_5$-DA — XIV 29; XVI 25
^{ù}ERI$_4$-TÌL-LA — V 8, 12, 18; VI 23; VII 10; X 20; XI 5, 17; XII 38; XIV 24, 29
*ERI$_4$-U$_5$-NÁ/NÍ — XI 5
ERIN — VIII 60, 62

ERUM (ÈR, ÈRI) — XI 26
*ERUM-GAR-EN — XII 12
*ERUM-UŠ — XI 26; XII 67
*ÈŠ-ÚŠ — II 17; XVII 9

G = π — II 15
GA — III 31
GA-MÁ-SIG$_7$-MAḪ — III 31
GA-ZUM — III 31
GAB-LIŠ — XII 38
*GAG-Ù-DAR — V 8
GAG-GÀR (-BA) — II 13; V 18; XIV 47
$^{(giš)}$GAG-KUD — V 18; XIV 47
GAG-SI-SÁ — VII 33
*GAL-AG — III 12
GALA (GALLA) — III 31; VIII 56
GAL(L)A(-DA/À) — II 23
*GALLA-MUD — VII 10
*GALLA-MÙD — VII 10
GAM (= GÚR) — XI 7
GÀM — XII 4
GÀM-GÀM-MUŠEN — XII 4
GAN/BAN — XII 4; XIV 17
^{giš}GAN(-NA) — V 23
*GAN-n-b-s — IX 12; XVIII 11
^{šig}GAN-ME-DA — XIV 14
*GAN-NÁ-IM — XIII 14; XVIII 2, 23, 27
$^{(giš)}$GAN-NU — II 14, 17, 18; XIV 15; XVIII 10
^{šig}GAN-NU — XIV 14, 54
*GAN-ZU-ZU — III 31
GÁN(A) — XIV 16; XVIII 10
GANA$_6$ — XIV 17
GANÀM — XIV 17
GAR/MAR — II 12; III 45; XII 61
*GAR-GAR — XII 61
*GAR-ÈN — II 24; XII 1, 3, 5
*GAR-NU — XII 5
*GAR-UB — V 12
*GAR-UB-ŠU/Ú — V 12
*GAR-UB-TÌL(TÉŠ) — V 12
GÀR(= GAR) — V 23
GÀR-BA — V 23; VI 15; XII 28; XIV 34
GARIN — II 24; XII 1
GEDÍM — VI 23
GEME (MÍ) — V 12
GEMÉ — II 5
GEŠPU — XII 27
*GEŠPU-IMI — XV 11
^{lú}GEŠPÚ — XII 27, 28, 29
*^{ú}GEŠPÚ — XII 27
GEŠTIN — XVII 19
GI — VI 16, 23
*GI-BAL — II 21
GI-DU$_8$ — XVI 13; XVII 93
GI-NA(GIN) — II 17; III 43; X 2; XII 1
*GI-SUR-ANTA/TI — VI 23; XVI 10

*GI$_4$(KI)-DUN	XII 43	GUBRU	X 20; XII 27; XV 18
*GI$_4$-ḪUN	XV 25	GUG(GÚ-GÚ)	VI 19
GI$_6$/GE$_6$-GI$_6$/GE$_6$(GÍG)	V 12; XVI 18	GUG-A	V 18
(giš)GE$_6$-PÀR	XI 11; XII 13	*GUG-IÀ-U$_5$-NÁ	V 12
*GIB-TUR$_5$	III 31	GÚG	XIV 23
GIBIL	II 21	GÚG-GÚG/KUK-KA	VI 19
GÍD	XII 18	šemGÚG-GÚG	VIII 69
GIG	V 12	*GÚG-NU	VIII 69; XI 25
*úGIG	V 12	*GÚG-ŠÚ	XIV 17
*GIG-A	V 18	GUL	II 17; III 31, 41; XI 26; XIV 60
GIG-GÍR	V 12		
*GIG-IÀ-U$_5$-NÁ	V 12	*GUL-IA$_4$(= ZA)-TI	II 17; III 31
gišGÍG(GI$_6$)	V 12; VI 23; XVI 18	GÚL	V 8, 24; XII 57; XVII 35
*GÍG-AN-TI/TA	V 21		
(giš)GIL	III 41; V 23	GUM	II 18
GIN	III 31; X 2; XII 1	*GUM-ÚR-RA	II 19; III 43
*GIN-DU	X 2	GÚM	II 18
*GIN-TI	X 2	GUN	XII 1, 35
*GIN-URA	II 13; X 2	GUN-GI	XII 51
GÍN	XII 1	*GUN-TI	XII 35
GÍR	II 12	GUR	III 26; XII 43; XIV 65
úGÍR(= ATTU)	V 10; XVII 101		
GISSU	XII 27; XIV 9, 26; XVI 18	lúGUR-GUR	XII 43
		*GÚR-TÙN	V 12
GIŠ-GÍG	XII 27	*gišGÚR	XII 64
*GIŠ-IM-MAR	XV 13	*GÚR-UB	XI 7, 15
(d)(GIŠ-)ŠIR(-GAL)	XII 26	GUR$_4$	III 24
GIŠ-ŠÚ(-A)	XII 27; XIV 9, 26; XVI 18	*GUR$_4$-EN	XV 22
		*GUR$_7$ÈN (-NA)	III 11, 35
GIŠ-ŠUB	XII 27	GURIN, GURUN	XV 22
GÌŠ/UŠ	II 4	GURUŠ	III 6, 24; XII 67
GIŠ-DUG$_4$-GA	III 6, 41; VII 13	GUŠ(= ḪUŠ)	II 17, 18
*GÌŠ(-TI)	XI 26	GUŠKIN	II 17
GIŠIMMAR	XV 13		
GIŠIMMAR-U$_4$-ḪI-IN	III 41		
GÚ(= GUN)	II 22; XII 35		
ú’šeSÚ	VI 19		
GÚ-A	XII 57	Ḫ = $\mathbf{y}$ = Ċ (γ)	II 19
GÚ-BA(R)	II 17; VIII 20; X 20; XII 57; XV 18	ḪA	VII 8
		ḪA-A	VII 8
(túg)GÚ-È	VI 19	ḪA-LAM	III 41; VII 8
lúGÚ-EN-NA	III 11, 35; VII 27; XV 22	giš ḪA-LU-UB	II 20
		ḪAL	III 36; VI 5; VII 8; XII 4
*GÚ-TAL-Ù-DUN	V 8; VI 42	ḪAL-ḪAL-LA	II 20
*GÚ-RI	I 2; III 24; VI 23; XII 18; XIV 45, 65	šemḪAL (see also ŠEM-ḪAL)	VII 8
*GÚ-RI-AN-NA	XII 18		
*GÚ-RI-UŠ	III 27	ḪAR	III 31
GÚ-TAR/TÁL	III 1; V 17, 18; VI 15; XIV 65; XVII 20, 36	gišḪAR-ḪAR	VI 19
		*ḪAR-ḪAR-ZANGA	III 31
		*ḪAR-DAL(= TAB-BA)	VI 19
*GÚ-TAR-UŠ	XVII 20	*ḪAR-IÀ-U$_5$-NÁ	V 12
*GÚ-TÙN	XV 34	*ḪAR-UB (> ḪARUB)	V 12
GÚ-UN(= GUN)	XII 35	*ḪAR-ÙŠ	VIII 40
*GÚ-UŠ	II 17, 31; V 8; IX 21, 26; XIV 47, 60; XV 34; XVII 35	ḪARUB	V 12; VII 24; XIV 24; XV 19
		ḪAŠ	VI 3
*GÚ-ZAL	V 13	*ḪE-ÈN(> ḪEN)	III 41
GÚ-ZI	XVII 35	*ḪE-MAR	VIII 20
*GÚ-ZI-BAR	XIII 12	ḪENBÚR	III 41
GÙB	II 18	ḪEN-DA/DÙ	III 41; VII 23

*ḪEN-DÚR	III 41	KA-TAR	VII 8
ḪENDUR	III 41	KI-A	III 11
ḪI-LI	III 31, 41	KI-ÁG	XVII 101
ḪUB(-ḪUB)	II 18	*KI-DAM	XVII 101
ḪUB-ŠÚ	II 18	*KI-DUR	III 31
ḪUM	II 18	KI-EN/IN-KI	II 1
ḪUN(-GÁ)	VII 8; XII 1	KI-GAR	XII 43
ḪUŠ(= GUŠ)	II 17, 18; IX 12; XI 26; XIV 60, 65; XV 34	KI-NÁ	XV 17
		*KI-NÁ-AN-NA	XV 17
		*KI-NU-ÚR	XII 26
		KI-SUR(-RA)	III 31; VII 33
I	III 31	KI-ŠÚ	IX 12; XVI 19
I-BÍ(= IGI)	II 14	giš KIBIR	XII 18, 65
I-DU₁₁/DI	X 11	(giš)KIN	II 17
I-LU-BALAG-DI	X 3	ú KIN-TUR	III 21
I-LU-DU₁₁(-DU₁₁)/DI-DI	X 3, 11	KIŠI	IX 12; XVI 19
I-ZAG	III 31	KIŠIB	XII 27
Ì(-BA)-ŠÉŠ	III 36	*KU-BARÁ	VIII 20
Ì-ZU see A-ZU		*KU-MAR	III 31
IÀ	III 1; VII 8	*KU-NÁ	IX 2
*IÀ-AMA	III 11	*KU-NIN	VIII 20
*(IÀ-)GAN-NU	XIV 17	*KU-ÙR	VI 24
*IÀ-ḪA	X 28	(šem)KU₇-KU₇	VIII 69
*IÀ-U₅(-A)	III 1, 22; VII 8; XVII 45, 50, 53	KUK-KA see GÚG-GÚG	
		KUNIN	VIII 20
*IÀ-U₅-DA	IV 15; VI 23; XVI 25	KUR	II 4; VIII 54; XIX 16
*IÀ-U₅-E₄-LA₆	XVII 50	KUR-KUR	VI 16, 24, 28, 41; XIV 21; XVI 19, 34
*IÀ-U₅-NÁ	II 25; V 13		
*IÀ-U₅-NÍ	V 13	ú KUR-KUR	II 2; VI 16
*Ì-A-U₅-NU(-ŠU/ÚŠ)	III 1; IV 18	*KUR-BA(LA)G-AN(-TA)	VI 16, 41
*IÀ-U₅-ŠÚ-A(ŠU/ÚŠ)	III 1, 51		
*IÀ-ZAG	III 31	*KUR-TI	VI 24
IA₄ = ZA/Á	VII 8	KÚR-KÚR	VI 24
*IA₄-Á-GUB	III 31	(giš)KUR₄	III 5, 24, 27; XII 18; XVI 20
*IA₄-ERUM	XI 26; XIV 62		
*IA₄-GUN	III 1	KUŠ-TAB-BA	V 23
*IA₄-GUŠ	III 31	*KUŠ-TI	V 23
*IA₄-UGÙN	III 1; XII 51		
*IA₄-SÍB/SIPA	XI 26; XIV 62		
IGI(= I-BÍ)	II 14; XVII 93		
*IGI-ZAL	X 20	L = sem n	II 16
ÌL	II 16	LÁ(= LAL)	II 10
ÍL-MÁ-SIG₇SIG₇	III 31	LAG	III 31
ILLU(= E₄-LA₆)	XVII 50	LAL see LÁ	
ILLURU	XII 27; XV 11	LAM	III 21
IM	III 1; XII 36	ú LAM-MA	III 21
IM-A-AN (see also *AN-IM-A)	III 7; XVI 3	d LAMMA	VI 23
		LI = ÈN	III 31
IM-RI-ḪA-MUN	X 3	(giš)LI	II 2; III 26; V 18; VI 3, 16; XII 4
IM-GÁ	X 3		
IN-KI see KI-EN		LI-LI	VI 23
INIM	VI 7	LI-LI-EZ(= LILIZ)	II 2
INNA	XIV 17	LI-LI-GI	VI 17
d INNANA	XV 17	*LI-LI-TI	VI 23
IR(-SIM)	VIII 60	ú LI-DUR	VI 16
IR-ZI	VIII 20, 60	uzu LI-DUR	II 2; III 26
d ISKUR	I 2; III 5; V 10, 18; XII 18	LI-GI	VI 23, 31
		*LI-MAŠ	VI 23
ISÍŠ/ÉR-ŠÈM-MA	III 36	*LI-MAŠ-BA(LA)G-ANTA(-TAB-BA-RI)	VI 17, 41
IŠḪARA	VIII 40		

*LI-MAŠ-BA(LA)G-TAB-BA-RI	XIV 27	MIR	II 12
*LI-MAŠ-TAB-BA-RI-TI	XVI 1	MU	XV 34; XVI 10
LI-'U/U₆-UM	II 2; VI 16; XIV 61; XVI 13, 24	*MU-ŠÀ	X 6
		MÙ	III 26; V 18
LIL	VI 3	(giš)MUD	II 13; VII 10; XII 51
LÍL-LÁ-DARA	V 26; VI 3, 23	MUD-Á (see also Á-MUD)	XII 51
LÙ-LÙ	VI 42	MÚD-GE₆	VIII 9; XIV 3
LÚ-NE	XII 27	MÙD	VII 10
LUḪ-MAR-TU	VIII 26	(lú)MUG	III 26; VI 23; VIII 37; X 24
		šemMUG	III 26
M = U(w)	II 22	*MUGU	VIII 37
MAḪ	II 19; III 27; IX 21	MUL(U) (MÚL)	III 26; V 18; VI 31; VIII 57
zá MAḪ	IX 21		
MAḪ-DI	II 19	*MUL-UGU	III6 2; VI 23; VIII 37; X24
*MAḪ-UŠ	XIV 47		
MAN	XIII 12	*MULUG(> MUG)	V 18
MAR (see also GAR)	II 12; XII 4, 53; XV 13	MÙL	II 17
		MURUB	V 12; VII 24
*MAR-AN-TA	XV 14	MUŠ	II 17, 22; IX 21
*MAR-DU₁₀(= DÙG)	II 1; III 31; XII 4; XVII 92	*MUŠ-È	IX 21; XV 34
		MUŠ₄	II 17
giš MAR-GÍD-DA	XII 53		
*MAR-SÍN/ŠEN	XII 4		
*MAR-SIPA/SÍB	III 31; XV 27	NA	XII 43
MAR-TE	XII 4; XV 14	*NA/Á-BAL	III 26; VI 3
*MAR-TI	XII 53	*NA(= ZA, IA₄)-ḪUŠ	II 17
tu₁₅MAR-TU	XV 16	*NA-IM (-A-AN)	XVI 27
MAŠ	II 22; III 36; VI 23, 42	zá NA-ZAG-ḪI-LI(-SAR)	III 31
		NÁ	VIII 16; XVI 3
šem d MAŠ	III 35; VIII 20	*NÁ-A-RI-A	II 25; VII 39; X 14, 20
lú MAŠ-MAŠ	III 36		
*MAŠ-BÌD	VIII 20	*NÁ-AN-NA-RI	XV 17
MAŠ(-DÀ)	III 19	NA₄	III 26; XIV 65
*MAŠ-IÀ	III 36	*NA₄-NE	XIV 65
*MA/ÁŠ-BÀD	XII 4	*NA₄-SUR	VII 33
*MAŠ-BALAG(-ANTA-TAB-BA-RI)	VI 16, 17, 41, 42; XIII 12, 23; XV 24; XVI 1, 19, 29; XVII 53; XIX 7, 10, 11, 17, 20	NAGAR	III 26; XII 43, 46
		NAM	VIII 63
		*NAM-ENSI(= PA-TE-SI)	V 26
		(d)NAM-TAR	V 26; VI 3; VIII 63
MAŠ(-DÀ)	X 20	ú NAM-TAR	V 13, 26; XI 21
*MAŠ-DA-A-KAL	III 35; VIII 60	ú NAM-TÌL-LA	IV 18
*MAŠ-DU₆(L)	X 21	NANNA, NANNAR	XV 17
*MAŠ-GÚ	V 23	NAR	II 25; VII 39; X 14, 20
*MAŠ-TAB-BA-LI-GI	VI 41		
*MAŠ-TAB-BA-RI-RI/LI-LI(-TI)	II 2; VI 3; 16; XIV 26; XV 36; XVI 19	*NE-URA	XIV 65
		NE-ZA-ZA	XIV 65; XV 33
		NÍ-RI-A	I 2
MÁŠ	XII 71	NÍG-ZID	III 14; XVIII 35
MÁŠ(-DA-RI-A)	XII 71	NIGI(N)	V 17
MÁŠ-GE₆	VII 8	NITLÁM	III 21
*MÁŠ-TÙN/TÙR	XII 21	*NU-NU-ZI	XII 26
*ME-NÈ/NÍ	VI 7	d NU-DIM-MUD	VII 39
MÉ see also MÍ		NU-GIG	III 1; V 12
*MÉ-TAR/TÙR	V 12	NU-ḪA	VII 8
MENBULUG	XII 13	NU-MAŠ	III 1; V 12
MÉR (see also IM)	III 1	*NU-MA/ÁŠ-DA	II 22
MÍ/É see GEME		mul NU-*MUŠ-DA	II 22
MIN	III 46	(giš)NU-ÚR-MA	XII 26; XVII 8

NU₅(-NU₅)	III 27; VII 26
ᵍⁱˢNUMUN-GISAL	III 26
NUN	III 27; VII 26
⁽ᶻᵃ⁾NUNUZ	XII 26
PA	I 2
*PA-GÍD	XIV 34
PA-TE-SI(= ENSI)	I 2; XIV 34
*PAD-NÁ	IX 22
*PEŠ-ḪA	VII 8
⁽ᶻᵃ⁾PEŠ₄	VIII 26, 60; XII 26
PEŠ₄ANŠE	VIII 56
*PEŠ₄-TE	VIII 40
*PEŠ₍₄₎TU	III 29
PIRIG	II 21
*RÁ-UŠ	XIV 60
RI	V 23
RI-RI	VII 10
RI-RI-GA	V 23
RI-A	I 2
RI-GA	I 2; XIII 14
*RI-GA-IM	XIII 14
RI-ḪA	III 3; X 3
RIG₇	I 2
RIḪAMUN	X 3
RUŠ	XIV 60
SA	V 17
*SA-UŠ sec UŠ-SA	
SAG	III 31; X 2
SAG-GÚL	II 17; V 8, 24; XII 57; XV 19
SAG-GÚL(-NIM-MA)	V 23; XVII 20
SAG-ÍL-LA	II 16
ᵗᵘᵍSAGŠU	XIV 17
SAL-LA	V 26; VII 26
*SAL(-LA)-DA	VII 26
SANGA	III 31
SAG-ÍL-LA	II 16
SANGÁ	III 31
SARA	VII 26
SI	I 2; II 10
*SI-DÙG	II 19
SI-GAR	II 46; V 23; XIV 47
*SI-GÚ-A	V 8; XII 57
*SI-GÚL(-LA)	V 12; XV 19; XVII 20
*SI-GÚ-TAL	V 8
ⁱᵐSI-SÁ	XV 3
⁽ᵘᶻᵘ⁾SI-SÁ	VII 33
SÌ	III 7, 43
*SÌ-E₄-LA₆	VII 13
SIG	III 46
*SIG-ÙŠ-TAR	III 46
SÍG	XIV 3
*SIG₄-U₅-NÁ	XVI 24
SIG₁₄	XIV 3
ᶻᵃSIKIL	XIV 52
SILA	V 26; XI 28; XV 21
*SILA-GU	V 12
*SILA-NAM-TAR	XI 21
SÌLA(=SILA)	II 10; VII 26; XII 38, 50
SÌL-MUD	II 10; VII 10; XII 51; XV 28; XVII 28
*SÌL(A)-U₅-NÁ	VIII 16; XV 3
SIPA(SÍB)	I 2; II 1; III 18, 19, 22; X 20; XII 2, 57; XIV 34
*SIPA-UD	III 5, 19
SIPA-ZI	III 23
ᵐᵘˡSIPA-ZI-AN-NA	III 23
*SIPA-ZI(-UŠ)	III 21
SUG(-KU)	III 31
SÚG	II 18
SUḪ	III 31; XII 80
ᵘᶻᵘSUḪ-BAR-SÌL	III 31
*SUḪ-ZÍB	III 31
SUH₆	II 18
SUḪUŠ (SUḪ-UŠ)	II 18
SUR	III 26; VI 23; XVI 10, 11
SUSBU see ŠUZBU	
ŠÀ	X 28
ŠÀ-ḪUN	X 28
*ŠÀ-LUM	XI 5
ŠÀ-SUR	III 31
ŠÀ-TÙR	V 12; VIII 16; XII 21
ŠÀ-ZI-GA	X 6
ŠÈ-BAR-RA	III 45; VIII 20, 26
ŠE-BID-DA	III 41
ŠE-DÙ-A	III 41
ŠE-GIG	V 12
ŠE-IR-ZI	V 17; VIII 60
ŠE-LI	VI 16
*ŠE-MU	XVI 23
ŠE-MUŠ₅	II 12
*ŠE-TÙN	VI 15
*ŠÈ-TUN	III 45; VI 15
ŠE₈(-ŠE₈)	III 36
ŠEG₉	XIV 3
ŠEM-BI-ZI(-DA)	XVIII 35
⁽ᵍⁱˢ⁾ŠEM-ḪAL	II 20; III 36
ŠEM-LI	VI 16; VIII 10
ŠEM-MAŠ	III 35; VII 42
ˡᵘŠEM(-MÚ)	III 36
ŠÈM (ŠEM₄)	III 36
ŠEN	III 9; XII 4
*ŠEN-BUR₅	V 13
*ŠEN-BURU₈	VIII 26; XVII 78
*ŠEN-DÀ	XII 4
*ŠEN-DÀ-BALAG	III 35
*ŠEN-DÀRA	VIII 20
*ŠEN-NU-ÚR	XII 26
ŠEN-TAB-BA	III 9; XII 4
ŠÈN-MUŠEN	VI 5; XII 4

Accadian

^{il}*Ea*, III 11; VII 39
abu, III 2, 21; XVII 57
abubu, III 15
abaḥšinnu, III 41
abukatu, VI 16
abâlu, XII 12
aban arî, XII 26
aban râmi, III 31; IX 21
abunnatu, III 26
abaraqqu, III 35; XVII 54
abšinnu, III 9
abâtu, III 41; VII 8
egû, XVIII 35
aggu, III 3
uggu, III 3
ugallu, XIV 35
agargarû, XII 61; XVII 100
edu, III 35
idu, III 31
^{il}*Adad*, I 2; III 2, 5, 21; V 10; XII 18
adamatu, VIII 9; XIV 3
azamillu, III 31
izbu, XIV 17
aḫu, III 31
uḫênu, III 41
iṭṭidu, V 10
eṭêru, XVI 10
eṭittu, III 21
uṭṭetu, V 12
aialu, 11 25; VII 39; X 20; XIV 3
ûmu, III 1, 2, 3
êkallu, III 33
ikkaru, II 24; XII 1
elû, I 1^ᵃ; II 16; X 7; XIV 9
elîtu urṣi, III 31
têlitu, VII 37
ilu, III 1
alâdu, III 17; VII 10; XII 35, 51
alâku, XVI 1
allânu, III 26
allu, III 26
ellu, III 36
elmešu, XI 26
almattu, III 45
emêdu, II 7
amil ša umaše, XII 27
imnu, III 14, 44; XVIII 35
ummu, II 22
immertu, XIV 17
emûqu, III 1
umâšu, XII 27
umšu, III 1, 2, 3, 19; XII 27
âmatu, VI 7
amtu, II 5
imtu, VII 13
inbu, XV 22
^{il}*Engur*, III 11
andunânu, II 16

enêšu, III 46
asû, IV 2, 14
asakku, III 31
usukku, III 31
usqaru (askaru, asqaru), XVIII 30
upnu, XII 27
apsû, III 11; XV 22
uppu, II 13; XII 51
uppi aḫi, II 13; XII 51
epêšu, III 17
epitatu, II 21
aṣaru, XVI 10
eqlu, XVIII 10
uqnû, XIV 53
uqnû namru, XIV 53
âru, I 2
âribu (êribu), XI 7
irbu, XII 71
ardu, II 6; XI 26
arzallu, XIV 52, 54
araḫḫu, III 35
arallu, XVII 9
urnu, II 1; XI 27
urṣu, XV 21
arâru, III 41
erêšu, III 15
išdu, II 18
išku, XII 26
iššakku, I 2; XIV 34
^{il}*Išum*, III 41
âšipu, III 36
išpatu, XII 4
^{il}*Aššur*, III 35; XV 4
ešêru, VII 33
išâru (ušâru), II 7; VII 33; XI 26
ašertu, III 31
aštabelu, III 35
ištarîtu, V 12; VII 24
Ištar, III 1, 44; V 12; VII 24; VIII 40; XV 17
atûdu, XIV 3
etqu, XIV 17

ba'âlu, XII 18
bêlu, III 27; VII 26
bibbu, XIV 17
bakû, III 36
bukannu, III 26; V 23; XII 28
balaggu, X 14
baluḫḫu, II 20
balâṭu, II 16; XVII 19
bâltu (baštu, bûltu), XVIII 31
bulṭittu (balṭîtu), III 26; XII 3
bullulu, VI 42
biltu, II 22; XII 35
banû, III 2, 17; XII 42; XVI 1
bînâti, XII 42
biṣṣur atâni, VIII 56

324

bârû, IV 14
birku, XII 18
barasigû, III 31
burâšu, VIII 10
bît asakki, III 31

da'mu, XIV 3, 17
dînu, III 14
[is]*dulbu*, XII 38
dalîlu, VII 8
dimmu, VI 23
dumqu, III 43

[il]*Gibil*, II 21
naglabu, II 10; XII 38; XIV 47
gamâlu, III 1, 50
gipâru, XI 11
giṣṣu, III 21
garâru, II 20
gišûru, XII 66

zagindurû, XIV 53
zumru, V 23
zanânu, III 6; XII 67
ziqpu, XII 66

ḫâlu, III 31; XVII 94
ḫîlu, III 31; XVII 94
ḫaldappânu, VI 19
ḫalḫallatu, III 36
ḫallu, VI 5
ḫalâpu, VI 19
ḫaluppu, II 20
ḫalâqu, III 41; VII 8
ḫamâšu, II 18
ḫerû, III 26
ḫarâbu, III 41
[šam]*ḫarûbu*, V 12, 18; XI 17; XIV 24
ḫardatu (*ḫurdatu*), XII 12
ḫarḫazinnu, III 31
ḫašâlu, II 18

tebû, I 1[a]; XII 66
ṭamû, VI 23
ṭerû, XII 67

kabru, III 24
kibru, III 11
kibirru, XII 18, 65
kabâšu, XIV 17
kubšu, XIV 17
kabâtu, XII 18
kudurru, III 31
kuzbu, III 31, 41
kakku, VI 19
kukku, VI 19; XIV 23
kakkabu, II 13; V 18
kukru, VIII 68, 69
kalû, III 31
kalappatu, XII 4
kamâru, II 18
kimtu, I 2
kânu, III 43
kênu, III 14, 44; XVIII 35
kettu, III 14; XVIII 35
kanzuzu, III 31
kinaḫḫu, XV 17
kankannu, II 14; XIV 15
kinûnu, XV 33
kanâšu, XII 64
kiskibirru, XII 18
kisurrû, III 31; VII 33
kapâpu, VI 24
kappu, I 2
kapâru, XIV 65
kupru, VIII 20
kaṣâṣu, II 18
kirkirânu, VI 16
karmu, III 41
karânu, XVII 19
karru, V 23; XII 28; XIV 34
kaṣâdu, II 4
kiškanu, II 17
kiššatu, XVI 19
kiššûtu, IX 12
katâmu, VI 23; XIV 9; XVI 19
katarru, V 17, 18; VII 8; XVII 20, 36

li'u, II 2; XIV 61; XVI 13, 24
labbu, III 3
lillu, VI 3
liligu, VI 16
lilitu, VI 23
lamassu, VI 23
lamastu, VI 23
leqû, I 2
laqâtu, V 23
lâšu, III 31
littu, XVI 18

madâdu, II 11; XII 80; XVII 107
maialu, XV 17
mullilu, III 31
mesîru, IX 12
mupattitu, XIV 47
muṣallu, XII 27
muṣa'iranu, XIV 65
miṣru, III 31; VII 33
muṣṣuru (see also *aṣâru*), XVI 10, 11
maqâtu, V 23; XIII 14
[il]*Marduk*, II 1; III 1, 17; XII 4
marru, XII 4, 53; XV 13

marratu, XII 53; XV 13
muraqqu, III 36
mašâdu, III 31; XVII 94
mašku, V 23
maštabbariru, II 2; VI 16
ˢᵃᵐmaštakal, III 35; VIII 60; XII 38
matqûti, VIII 69
mâtu, II 4

na'âlu, III 34; XV 17
nabâsu, XIV 54
nagâru, III 26
naggaru, XII 43
nadû, III 7
nâḫu, VII 8; X 28
nûḫ libbi, X 28
nûru, II 21; XII 26
nazâzu, II 18
naḫlaptu (see also *ḫalâpu*), VI 19
naialu, II 25; VII 39; X 14, 20
nikiptu, III 35
nalbantu, IX 22
namaššu ša ⁱˡAdad, II 22
namtaru, V 26; VI 3
nannaru, XV 17
nas/šâḫu, XII 80
nappillu, XIV 54
napraku, V 23
nîru, II 16; XII 52
nurmu, XII 26; XVII 8
našû, II 16
nîš libbi, X 36
nîš qâti, XII 4
nêšu, XIV 35

s/šigaru, V 23; XIV 47
sûqu, II 10
siḫlu, III 31; V 17
s/šuḫar šêpi, II 18
sikkûru, V 23
sikkat karri, II 13; V 18
sikittu, XII 43
sammû, X 2
summatu, V 13
sâmtu, II 17; XI 26; XVII 20
šangu, III 31
sangamaḫḫu, III 31
sinuntu, XII 4
sapâḫu, III 7
sapânu, III 43
sippu, III 31

paṭâru, XVI 13
paṭîru, XVI 13; XVII 93
pilû, V 13, 23; VIII 63; XII 26
palukku, II 1; III 26
pilakku, III 26; VI 38; X 7; XII 48
pulukku, III 31

pullukku, XII 13
palâšu, III 26
pâltu, XII 1, 4
piqqutu, V 18
parzillu, XII 4; XVII 54
parâku, V 23
parakku, III 31
pirku, V 23
parsigu, VI 24
pursîtu, IX 22
pašâḫu, VII 8; X 28; XIII 23
pašâru, VIII 26; XI 27; XII 67
paššuru, XII 67
pašâšu, III 35, 36
pašîšu, III 27, 36; VII 26; XV 34
piššatu, III 36
pâš(t)u (pâltu), XII 1, 4
petû (see also *mupattitu*), X 28; XVI 13

ṣabîtu, III 19; X 20
ṣibûtu, III 41
ṣibtu, XII 71
ṣaḫâtu, III 31
ṣalâmu, V 12
ṣaltu, XII 27
ṣanâhu, III 45; VIII 26
ṣiṣitu, VII 33
ṣîru, IX 21
ṣarbatu, VIII 60; XII 38
ṣâriḫu, X 3
ṣarâru, III 6; XII 67; XIV 16
ṣertu, XIV 16

qâpu, XIV 34
qêpu, XIV 34
qadištu, VII 24
qadûtu, VII 27; XV 22
qilutu, II 21
qaqqadu, V 18
qarâdu, II 1
qarnu, I 2
qurqurru, XII 43
qaštu, XIV 15
qutru, V 17

rê'û, I 2; XII 2; XIV 34
ru'utu, VII 13
râmu, II 11; III 35; XVII 101, 107
rabû, III 27
rubû, VII 26
redû, II 8
reḫû, I 2; II 6; III 6, 15, 27, 41; VII 10, 13
rakâbu, III 2
rikibtu, III 2
narkabtu, XII 53
ramku, III 31
raqâdu, XII 53
ruššu, XIV 60

Ugaritic

Semitic

Sanskrit

Hebrew/Aramaic

328

חרף XII 12
מחפפט XIII 12
חרדות XII 12
חרדל VI 19
חרוב V 12; XI 7
חרבון(ים) XII 36; XIII 14; XV 6
חרמש XI 26
חרסות XVII 86
חרצנים III 31
חתן XV 34
טביא XVI 1
שבל(א) XIV 14, 19, 25, 27
טלית XIV 16

יד IV 15; XVI 25
יהודה IV 15; XVI 25
יהו(ה) III 1, 23
יהושע III 1, 51
יהלם XI 26; XIV 62
יואל XVII 50
יונה II 25; V 13
יוסף III 22; XI 26
יהנון XIV 17
יין IV 18
ילקוט VII 9, 24
ים III 11
ימים III 44
יצף III 31
יקוש III 31
יקע XII 76
ירה III 15
ירושלים XII 36; XIII 14; XV 3, 7
יש(ץ)חק III 31
ישבר II 7; XI 26; XVI 21
ישו XII 79
ישי XI 26
ישע II 50
ישפה XI 26; XIV 62
ישר II 7
בבש(ה) XIV 17

הלם XI 26
הנם XV 27
הרוסיאות VI 23
הרג אדונין V 8; VI 18
הרג קין XII 12

ואר I 2

וג III 31
זה (סיני) XV 33
הזורה XVI 8
זמר X 2; XVI 10
זמורה X 2; XVI 8
זפת VIII 20
זקף XVII 104
זקף XVII 104
זרע X 24

חדר III 34
חגה II 22
חטא III 41
חטה III 41
חילא XVII 51
חצה XVIII 39
חלם VII 8
חלמות VII 10
חלמיש XI 26
חלק VII 8, 9; XIV 8
חלקות VII 8
חלקד-נחל VII 9
בחלקות XVII 87
חמר VIII 20
חמש II 18
חמש(ה) XV 36
חנט III 41; VII 23
חנן III 41; XIV 18
חנן II 18; XIV 17, 57
חסיא III 36
חסיר III 44; XVIII 35

<table>
<tr><td>XVII 93 לחם הפנים</td><td>III 35; VII 27; XV 22 בזן</td></tr>
<tr><td>VI 23 ליל(ה)</td><td>II 17 גובע</td></tr>
<tr><td>VI 23 לילית</td><td>II 13; V 18 גובב</td></tr>
<tr><td>XVII 51 למה</td><td>XII 4 גזלבא</td></tr>
<tr><td>I 2 לקח</td><td>III 31 גומר</td></tr>
<tr><td>VIII 10 לשם</td><td>III 44; XVIII 35 גון</td></tr>
<tr><td></td><td>XVII 35 גוס</td></tr>
<tr><td></td><td>XIII 12 גוסבר(א)</td></tr>
<tr><td>II 19 מגד</td><td>VIII 20; XIV 58; XVII 23 גופר(א)</td></tr>
<tr><td>II 19 מגדיאל</td><td>VIII 54 גור</td></tr>
<tr><td>XVII 31 מגל</td><td>I 2 גורש</td></tr>
<tr><td>XIV 16 מגן</td><td>VI 23 גושרות</td></tr>
<tr><td>XV 34 מהר</td><td>V 8 גותלא</td></tr>
<tr><td>XVI 10 מוסר</td><td>V 8 גותל אזוטא</td></tr>
<tr><td>XII 51 מוטה</td><td>XVIII 35 גאל</td></tr>
<tr><td>VII 10 מות בסיר</td><td>XII 43 גידון</td></tr>
<tr><td>XII 19 מזר</td><td>VI 15 גיפא</td></tr>
<tr><td>XVI 10 מזור</td><td>VI 23; XVI 10 גישור</td></tr>
<tr><td>XVII 101 מחיר</td><td>XII 27; XVI 24 גלי חמס</td></tr>
<tr><td>XVII 61 מחר</td><td>VII 9, 24 גלי הרעים</td></tr>
<tr><td>III 12 מלאך</td><td>V 18 גמהות</td></tr>
<tr><td>X 24 מלוח</td><td>X 2; XVII 107 גנור</td></tr>
<tr><td>X 24 מלקה</td><td>XV 17 גנן</td></tr>
<tr><td>VI 41 ממונא</td><td>XIV 26; XVI 19 גסי.</td></tr>
<tr><td>XIII 12 מן</td><td>XVI 19 גסגת</td></tr>
<tr><td>VI 7 מני</td><td>IX 12; XIV 47; XVI 19 גסת</td></tr>
<tr><td>VI 23; XVI 1 מס, מסי</td><td>XI 11 גברת</td></tr>
<tr><td>VI 18; XVI 29 מס־עבד</td><td>XI 15 גרגב</td></tr>
<tr><td>VI 16 מסבך</td><td>XIV 21 גרברך</td></tr>
<tr><td>XII 19 מסר</td><td>XVI 8 גבשול עונה</td></tr>
<tr><td>XII 19; XIV 28; XVI 10; XVIII 29 מסור</td><td>V 17 גתר</td></tr>
<tr><td>XVI 10, 19 מסורת</td><td>V 17, 18; XVII 20 גתרת</td></tr>
<tr><td>III 31 מפתן</td><td>XIV 64 בתנת</td></tr>
<tr><td>XVII 94 מצה</td><td></td></tr>
<tr><td>XIV 28; XVI 11, 29; XVIII 29 מצור</td><td>XII 5 לבנה</td></tr>
<tr><td>XVII 94 מצץ</td><td>XVI 24 לוה</td></tr>
<tr><td>XVII 94 מצות</td><td>II 2 לוח</td></tr>
<tr><td>III 34 מקור</td><td>XII 27; XIV 61; XVI 24 לוי</td></tr>
<tr><td>II 19 מרח</td><td>VI 23, 31 לחי</td></tr>
<tr><td>II 19 מרק</td><td>XVI 24 לחם</td></tr>
<tr><td></td><td>XV 36; XVI 13, 24 לחם</td></tr>
</table>

מִדָּם II 19; III 43
פִּינֵי. XV 33
סִיר XVII 28
סִיר מוּת VII 10
הֵסִית XVII 108
סֵבִי XII 57
סבר see סבגר
סלע XV 21
סלק VII 13
ספל VI 23
סגריל VIII 20
סגורים XVII 78
סף III 31
ספחת XIII 12
ספיח III 7
מספח VI 42
ספחת XIII 12
ספיר XIV 53
ספק VI 17; XVII 52; XIX 18
ספרת VII 10
סרן XV 4

ע = ץ XII 30
ע • ﻉ (غ) II 19
עבריא XVII 53
עגב X 2; XVII 107
עדן XVIII 12
עורב XI 7
עזב XVII 51
עזקא III 31
עטרת VII 34
עירא. XIV 27
עין־גורי VI 23; X 20
עין־קורא VI 23; X 20
עליה· III 34
עמי II 7
עמור II 13; XII 51; XV 14
עמ'רה II 19; III 43
עוקים XIII 14; XVIII 25
עותא XIX 8
עפל. III 26; IX 12; XII 2; XVII 20

ברוק XVIII 35
משה IX 21
משח XII 80
משיח III 27, 36
משוח XVII 53
משן XII 80
משבים V 23
משפתים XII 4
משש XIV 27
משתה XIV 26

נביא XIV 56
נבל III 26; VI 3
נגד XII 79; XVII 108
נגד א. XII 79
נגידא XII 79
נגר(א) III 26; XII 46
נוח VII 8; X 28
נוחא XIV 56
נור XVII 78
נזר VII 33
נחמא XIV 56
נחש IX 21
נחשת II 17; IX 21
נחשן III 21
נסח XII 80
נעים XVIII 11
נעם XVIII 11
נעמן(ים) XVI 3
נער(ה) II 25; VII 39; X 14
נפילים XIII 14
נצץ VII 33
נצה. VII 33
נקם XVIII 15

סבר XVIII 39
סגול XVII 20
סגולא XV 19
סגי XII 57
סב/גר III 46; V 23

Syriac

 XIX 9
 XIX 7
 VI 17; XIX 7
 / VI 17, 42; XVI 19
؛ III 45
؛ / VI 17, 41; XVI 16
 XII 33
 XIV 26
 XIV 36
 XVIII 31
 VI 3, 17; XIV 26; XVII
    57; XIX 11, 20
 VI 41
 VI 42
 XIX 16
 XVI 19

 VI 17
 VI 17; XIV 27
؛ XVI 1
 XVI 1
 IV 15
؛ VI 42

 VI 42
 XVII 53

 III 14
 VI 42
 XII 66; XVI 10
 XII 66; XVII 104
 XIV 54
 XIV 55

 VI 17

 XVII 66
 VI 16, 41
 XV 36
 VI 19

 XIV 25, 27

 XIV 62

 XIV 26
 XVI 19
 XVII 66
 VIII 54
 VIII 54
 V 18
 XII 26
 XVI 19
 XIX 7
 XVI 19
 XVI 34
 XII 13
 V 17

 / XIX 7
 XIV 52
 XVII 62
 XVII 51

 XVI 10
 XV 36
 XVI 10
 XVI 10
 VI 41; XVI 16
 XVI 1; XVIII 35

 XVI 19
 VI 42; XIV 27
 VI 41; XIX 7
 VI 41
 VI 41
 VI 16; XIX 7
 VI 3
 VI 16
 XIV 26

 XVII 53
 XVII 53
 XIV 54
 XII 79
 XVII 53
 XVII 106

 XVI 19; XVIII 39
 XVII 20
 VII 13
 XII 4

 XIV 27
 XVI 16
 XVIII 12
 X 20
 XI 7
 XII 26; XVII 30
 VI 17, 41; XIX 8, 10
 XV 36
 XII 12
 XIX 8

 VI 17
 XIV 27
 VI 17
 VI 40; VII 39; XVI 29
 VI 16

 III 26
 XIV 65

 VI 39
 III 31

 VI 41; XVI 16
 XVIII 35
 XVIII 35
 VI 41
 XII 66
 XVIII 35
(VII 33

. XIV 16
 XIV 16
see XIV 16
 XVI 19
 XIV 16
 V 12
 II 1
 XIV 16
 V 18

 XII 32
 XII 32
 XII 32
 XIV 65
 VI 17, 41; XVI 16

 XVI 1
('glory') VI 42; XVI 19; XIX 7
 VI 16, 41, 42
 VI 17, 42; XVI 19; XIX 8

 VI 42

337

338

Arabic/Persian

إجابة	XIV 16		خَرْبة	V 12; VII 24
أُجْنة	III 26		خَرْدَل	VI 19
أجِن	XIV 16		خَرْبَق	VI 16; XVII 66
أكارِس	V 18		خشف	XIII 12
ألوة آلى	XIX 8			
	XIX 8			
			دَأدأ	XVI 1
			ذُلُب	XII 38
بان	XVIII 31		دَوَاء	IV 15
مثر	III 6		دوى	IV 15
بنات الرعد	XII 33		ديو، ديوان	IV 15
بيض	XII 26			
			ذَبّج	V 18
ترف	XVIII 11		ذَنَلوى	V 18
تِرْفاس	V 18; XVIII 11		ذؤنون	V 18
جِبْأة، جبء	V 18; XIV 23		رسول الله	XIX 7
جرن	XIV 65			
جنات التعيم	XVIII 13		زرافة	XIV 55
			زكى	III 14
چتر	V 17		زكاة	III 14
حشيش	XVIII 43		سقراطيون	V 18; XII 20
حشيشة الجمراء	XVIII 44		سلوى	VII 13
حكيم	IV 2		سماروخ	II 1; V 16, 18; XII 13
حلم	VII 8		سندرة	VIII 20
خمرة	VIII 20		سنطة	VIII 34
جِناء	XIV 17		سِتّة	XII 4
حنط	III 41		شقائق النعمان	XVI 3
جِنطة	III 41		شمار	II 1
حوى	XVIII 34		شمراح	II 1; XII 13
حور عين	XVIII 34		شيطان	III 45
ختن	XV 34		صاعقة	III 31
خَرْب	V 12		مخففة	XIII 12
خِرْب	VII 24		صرخ	X 3

Greek

Ἀββά ὁ πατήρ	XVII 55	Ἀρά	III 41
Ἀβελ	XII 2	ἀρά	III 41
Ἀβρότονον	XI 27; XVIII 3	ἀργυρικός	XV 15
Ἄγαβος	XVII 107	ἀριστερός	III 46
ἀγαπάω	II 11, 15; XII 80; XVII 107	ἀρίστη λεχούσαις	VIII 26
		ἄρκηλος	XIV 35
ἀγάπη	X 2; XII 82; XVI 20	ἄρκτος	XV 3
ἀγαρικόν	XV 15	ἄρμα	XII 53
Ἀγαρικόν	III 45; V 18; XII 61; XVII 100	ἁρμόζω	XII 42
		ἁρμονή	XII 42
Ἀγαυή	XII 82; XVI 20; XVII 107	ἁρμονία	XII 42
		ἅρπη	XVII 31
ἀγανός	XVI 20	Ἀσία	XVII 86
ἀγγεῖον	XII 1	Ἀσκληπίαδα	IX 12
ἄγγελος	III 12	ἀσκληπιάς	IX 12; XVII 20
ἀγγέλους	VI 42	Ἀσκληπιός	XVII 20
ἄγγος	XII 1	ἀστήρ	III 26; V 18; XIII 1
ἀγείρω	XII 1	ἀστήρ - ἕως	XIII 2
ἀγέλη	XII 1	ἄσφαλτος	VIII 20
ἀγερμός	XII 1	Ἀσφάραγος	VI 37
ἄγω	XVII 107	Ἀσχίον	V 18
ᾅδης	XVII 9	Ἄτλας	XV 4
Ἀδώνιδος κῆποι	XVIII 2	ἄφεδρος	VIII 20
Ἀθήνη	VIII 56	Ἀφροδίτη	II 1; XI 27
αἴγις	XIV 3	Ἄφροι	XVI 11
Αἴγυπτος	XVIII 29	Ἄφροι-κακκαβούμ	VI 28
Ἀΐδης	XVII 9	ἀφρός	III 7
Ἄιδης	XVII 9	Ἀχελδαμάχ	XVII 51
αἵματος	III 7	Ἀχέρων	XVII 9
αἴξ	XIV 3		
ἀκαλήφη	XVII 101		
ἀκαλύφη	XVII 101	βαίτυλος	II 24
ἄκανθος	XIV 41	βάκχαι	X 17
Ἀκελδαμα(χ)	XVII 101	βακχεῖον	III 31
ἀλείτης	XV 14	βάλανος	II 13, 15; III 26; XII 3; XVII 20
Ἀλικακκάβα	V 18		
ἀλικάκκαβος	VI 28	βαλλωτή	XII 3
ἀλληλουιά	XVII 45	βαριησοῦς	XI 26
ἀλόη	XII 9	βαριωνᾶ	II 25; V 13, 23
ἀλοῖτις	XIV 14	βαριωνᾶ(ς)	XVII 48
Ἀμανῖτα	XIV 16	βασίλεια	XV 20
Ἀμανῖται	V 18	βασιλεία	VII 26; VIII 41
Ἀμαρανθίς	XV 14	βασίλειον	VIII 41; XIV 46; XV 20
ἀμαρανθίς	V 21	βυυιλειυν	VII 26; VIII 16
ἀμυγδάλη	III 26; VIII 37	βασιλεύς	VII 26
ἀμφίβιον	XII 9	βασιλικόν	VIII 16
Ἀναγαλλίς	VI 16	βασιλίσκος	VIII 15
Ἄνακες	XIII 14; XVIII 27	βασκαίνο	XIV 47
ἄναξ	XVIII 27	βασσάρα	XI 28
ἄνεμος	XVI 3	βασσαρεύς	XI 28
Ἀνεμώνη	XVI 3	βάτραγος	XIV 65
ἀντίμιμον	V 21	βλήχων	II 15
Ἀντίμιμον	XV 14	βοανεργει	XII 29
ἀντλέω	X 7	βοανηργές	XII 29
ἀξίνη	II 15; III 9; XII 4	βολβός	VI 15
Ἀπεσταλμένος	VI 17	βόσκω	II 15
Ἀπόλλων	XI 27	βότραχος	XIV 65
Ἀπόλλωνι παιᾶν	XVII 47	βότρυς	XVII 20

341

βουβάλιον	XII 57	διδύμον	XII 66
βούβαλος	X 20	Διθύραμβος	X 7
βούνιον	III 26	δίκη	III 14
βρηισεύς	XI 26	Διόνυσος	III 1; IV 18
βρησεύς	XI 26	διός	III 1
βρησσαῖος	XI 26	Διὸς ἠλακάτη	III 26; XII 18
βρότακος	XIV 65	Διος + κορέω	XII 18
βρούχετος	XIV 65	Διόσκοροι	XII 18
βρύτικος	XIV 65	Διοσκόρω	XII 18
βρύω	VIII 26; XI 27	Διόσκουροι	V 18; XII 18; XIII 14;
βύρθακος	XIV 65		XVIII 29
βωλίτης	III 26; V 18; XII 3	Διὸς κούρους	XII 17
		δίστομος πέλεκυς	XII 4
		Διώνη	V 13
γάγγαμον	II 13	δόκανα	XII 68
γαῖα	II 23	δοκάνη	XII 68
γαιάδας	II 23	δοκός	XII 68
γαμψότης	XI 7	Δορκάς	XVI 1
γαστήρ	XII 21	Δορύκνιον	V 18
γεῖσ(σ)ον	XII 27	δυγός	XII 51
γεράνειον	XII 1, 12; XVI 31		
Γεράνειον	V 18		
γέρανος	XII 12	Εἰλείθυια	VIII 60
γῆ	II 23	Εἰλήθυια	VIII 60
γήθυον	VI 15	εἶναι	XVII 61
γήϊνον	XII 26	εἰρήνη	XI 5
γῆς κλεῖθρον	XI 12	ἐλάνη	VIII 62
γήτειον	VI 15	ἐλάτη	VIII 60
γίγαντες	V 21; XIII 14; XV 14	ἐλατήρ	XII 56
Γλήχων	II 15	’Ελατήριον	XII 57; XVI 11
Γλυκυσίδη	I 2; V 23; XV 36; XVII	ἐλαφινέ	X 20; XVII 68
	92	ἐλαφυής	X 20; XVII 68
γόης	XIV 47	’Ελεία	III 1
γονή	XII 35	’Ελείθυια	VIII 60
γόνος	XII 35	ἐλελεῦ	III 1; XVII 44
γόνος ἥρωός	III 24	’Ελελεύς	XVII 44
Γόρτυν	V 12	‘Ελένη	VIII 62
γόρτυξ	III 6; VII 13	ἐλένη	VIII 62
γρόνθος	XIV 65	’Ελιεύς	III 1
γρυνόν	XIV 65; XVI 11, 31	‘Ελλέβορος	XII 60
γρυπός	XI 7	’Ελύμας	XI 26
γρυπότης	XI 7	ελωει	XVII 51
γρυψ	XI 15	’Ελωί	XVII 51
γυνή	XII 35	’Ελωί ἐλωί	III 1
γύρινος	XIV 65	ἔμβρυον	VIII 26
γυρῖνος	XIV 65	ἔνθεος	VI 21
		ἐξουσία	XVI 19
		ἐπὶ τὴν ἰοῦσαν	XVII 60
Δαβιδ	XVI 1	ἐρῆμος	III 41
δαίμων	IV 15	’Εριθαλές	X 20
Δάκοι-κερκέρ	VI 28	ἐριθαλές	V 8; XII 27
δαμάζω	XII 52	ἐριούνης	XI 5
δάμαρ-αρτος	XII 52	ἐριούνιος	XI 5
δαμάω	XII 52	ἔρμ(α)ιον	XII 5, 9
Δανείδ	XVI 1	ἑρμῆς	XII 67
Δαυ(ε)ίδ	XVI 1	‘Ερμῆς	XI 26
δεξιός	III 46	ἐρυγρίς	XII 5
Δημητριάς	XVII 6	ἐρῳδιός	VI 23; XVI 25
δῆμος	II 23	ἐσκάρια	VI 42
διάβολος	III 45	ἐσπαργάνωσεν	XVI 34
διάκονος	III 1; XII 51	’Εσσηνός	IV 14; XVII 86

342

Ἐσσαῖος	IV 14; XVII 86	ἵππος	XII 52
ἐστία	VIII 40	Ἴσκαι	V 18
ἐσχάρα	VIII 40	Ἰσκαριώθ	XII 19
Ἐφεσία	VIII 26, 60	Ἰσκαριώτης	XII 19
ἐφήλεις	XIV 65	ἴασπις	XI 26; XIV 62
ἔφηλες ἀργινόεσσα	XIV 65	Ἰασώ	III 1
		ἴανος	VII 8
		ἰαύω	VII 8
Ζαγρεύς	III 31	Ἰησοῦς	III 1, 51
Ζεύς	III 1	Ἰσσαχαρ	XVI 21
Ζεύς πατήρ	III 1	Ἴτον	V 18
ζύγιος	XII 52	ἰῶτα	IV 15; XVI 25
ζυγόν	III 1; XII 51		
ζωμαρῖτις	II 1; XII 13		
ζώνη	III 1	καθεύδων	XVII 53
ζωμαρῖτις	V 16	Καιάφας	XIV 34
ζῷον	III 1	κακκαλίαν	VI 28
ζωός	III 1	Καλυψώ	V 12
ζωσώ	III 1	κάμμαρον	VII 10
		Κανδαύλης	XIV 16
		κάνδαυλος	XIV 16
ηλει	XVII 51	κάνδυλος	XIV 16
ἠλέκτωρ	III 29	κάνειον	II 14
ηλι	XVII 51	κανθήλια	XIV 16
Ἡρακλέης	III 24	κάνθος	XIV 16
Ἡρακλεία	III 24	κανθύλη	XIV 16
Ἠρύγγιον	XII 12	Κάνναβις	IX 12
ἠρύγγιον	XII 5, 9	κάρδα	II 1
ἠρύγγειον	XII 5	κάρδακες	II 1
Ἡρώδης	VI 23; XIV 29; XVI 25	Καρδαμίνη	XII 4
Ἡρῳδιανοί	VI 23	Κάρδαμον	II 1; XII 4
Ἡρῳδίας	XIV 29	κάρταλλος	XIV 16
ἥρως	III 24	κάρταλος	XIV 16
ἥρως μνίαγρος	XVII 74	καρτάλωμα	XIV 16
		κάρυον	XII 5
		Κάστωρ	XII 21
Θαυμαστὸν γανόωντα	XVII 7	κέντρον	III 21
θεραπεία	VII 39	Κεραύνιον	III 31; V 18; XII 33
Θεραπευταί	XVII 86	κηρύκειον	XII 67
Θεραπευτής	VII 33	κῆρυξ	III 6; XII 67
θεραπεύω	VII 39	κηρύσσω	III 6; XII 67
Θιβρός	XVIII 11	Κηφᾶς	VI 15; XIV 34
θιμβρός	XVIII 11	κίδαρις	V 17
Θρακίας	XIV 7	κίκι	V 12
Θράκιος	XIV 4	κίκινον	V 12
Θρῆξ	XIV 4	κίκκος	V 12
Θρίαμβος	X 7	κινύρα	X 2
θριδακίας	XIV 6ᵃ	Κινύρας	X 5
θρίξ	XIV 3	κινύρομαι	X 2
θυέστεια δεῖπνα	XIX 32	κινυρός	II 13; X 2
Θυία	VIII 60; XII 38	κιρκαία	XIV 21
Θύρσος	III 1; V 18; XVII 21	Κιρκαῖον	VI 16, 41
θφειροφόρος	VIII 69	Κισσίον	XVII 20
		κίστη	IX 16; XVI 19
		κίτταρις	V 17
ἰάομαι	III 1	Κίχορα	VI 16
ἴασις	III 1	Κιχόριον	VI 16; X 24
Ἴαχος	III 31	κλεῖθρον	V 23
ἱερὰν βοτάνην	XVII 6	κλείς - εἰδός	V 23
Ἰεσσαῖος	XVII 86	κοίτη	VII 8
		κόκκον	VI 19

343

344

ὄη	XII 26	πενθέω	X 2
Οἰδοπόδειοι μίξεις	XIX 32	πένθος	X 2
οἶνος	IV 18	Πεντοροβον	XV 36
Ὄλυμπος	XII 37	περίζωμα	XIV 16
ὀμφαλός	III 26	περιστερά	V 13
ὄναρ	III 42; VII 8	Περιστέρεων	II 25; XIII 2, 12; XIV
ὄον	XII 26		45
ὄργανον	XII 42	περιστερεών	V 13; VI 23; XV 27
Ὄροβος	XV 36	Περιστερεών ὀρθός	III 26
ὄρθιον	XVII 104	Περιστερεών ὕπτιος	III 26; VII 31; XIII 12;
Ὀσσαῖος	XVII 86		XVII 6
Ὄρτυξ-υγος	III 6; VII 13	Περσεία	XI 26; XII 33; XIV 46
ὄστρεον	VIII 9	Περσεφόνη	XII 18; XV 27; XVII 5
ὀσχός	XVII 22, 35	Πέρσης	XI 26
ὀσχοφόρια	III 1; XVII 22	πέτρα	VI 13, 15
ὀύ	XIX 9	πέτρος	V 18
οὖα	XII 26	πῆγμα	XII 66^{a}
οὖα	XII 26	Πιθοιγία	XVI 13; XVII 17
οὖθαρ	X 21	Πιθοίγια	XVII 93
Οὒϊγγον	V 18	πίθος	XVII 18
οὒϊγγον	XII 26; XV 27	Πλατανιστηνῶν	XII 40
οὒϊτον	XII 26	πλάτανος	XII 38
Οὔλυμπος	XII 37	πλατύς	XII 38
οὐρανός	XII 29	Πλειστολοχεία	VIII 26
οὐσία	XVII 62	πληγή	III 26; XI 26; XVI 8
		Πληϊόνη	II 25
		πλοῦτος	XVII 12
Παιάν	II 25	Πλούτων	XI 27
παιδέρως	II 24; XIV 39, 43	Πολυγονον ἄρρεν	III 24
παιδὸς ἔρωτες	XIV 43	Πολυδεύκες	XII 27
Παιήων	II 25	ποτήριον	XVII 36
Παιών	II 25	Πρυτανεία	VIII 41
Παιωνία	I 2; II 25; V 12, 13, 23;	πυγμή	XII 28; XIV 65
	XVII 48, 92	πυληδόκος	XII 27
Παιωνία ἄρρην	XV 36	πῦρ ἀθάνατον	VIII 48
παλάθη	XIV 21	πυρὸς δέσποινα	VIII 40
παλλακή	X 15		
παλλακίς	VII 37; X 15		
παλλάς	VIII 56	ργεμ	XII 30
Πανακες	IX 12; XVIII 11	ργες	XII 30
πάνθηρ	XIV 35, 36	Ροβάδιον	XVII 92
παν-θηρ	XIV 35	Ῥόδη	VI 23
παράδεισος	XVIII 12, 31	ῥοιά	XVII 8
παράκλησις	XIV 56	ῥοιῆς κόκκον	XVII 8
παρδάλειος	XIV 36		
πάρδαλις	XIV 36		
παρθένος	II 24; VIII 41; XII 4	Σαβάδιον	III 23
Παρθενών	VIII 41	Σαβάζιος	III 23, 31
Πασιθέη	I 2	σαβακτανει	XVII 51
παστάς	III 29	σαβαρίχη	III 31
παστός	III 29	σαβαρίχις	III 31
πάσχα	VII 8	σαβχθανεί	XVII 51
πάσχω	VII 8	σαβαχθανι	XVII 51
πατήρ	III 1	σακός	III 31
Πάων	II 25	σαλαμάνδρα	V 26; XI 21
Πέξις	V 18	σάμφειρος	XIV 53
πειρασμός	VIII 54; XVII 64	Σαμψαῖοι	VII 42
πέλεκκος	XII 4	σάνδαλον	VIII 20
πελεκυνάριον	XII 4	Σατανᾶς	III 45; VI 15
πέλεκυς	XII 4	σατάνειος	VI 15
πελεκύστερον	XII 4	σατύριον	VIII 16

Σάτυρος	VIII 16	Ταμίας	VIII 41
Σεμέλη	V 12	τέκμαρ	XII 43
σηκός	III 31	τέκνον	XII 35
σητάνια	VI 15	τέκτων	XII 43
σητάνιον	VI 15	τελεστήριον	III 31
σίαλον	VII 13	τιμωρίαν	XV 14
σιδηρῖτις	VII 31; IX 11	*τιμωριν	XV 14
σίελον	VII 13	τιμωρόν	XV 14
σικύα	XII 57	τιμωρός	XV 14
σικύη	XII 57; XIV 16; XV 15	τράγος	XIV 3
σίκυος	V 8	τραγῳδία	X 11
σίκυος ἄγριος	XII 59	τρυγών	V 13
σίκυς	XII 57	τρυφή	XVIII 11, 12
σίκυς ἄγριος	XII 57; XVI 11, 31	τύλη	X 21
σικχός	XV 15	τύλος	X 21
Σιληνός	VIII 16	τύρανος	XV 4
Σιλωάμ	VI 17		
σίναπι	VI 19		
σκαιός	III 46	ὑάκυνθος	VIII 10
σκεύη	XV 15	ὕδνον	V 18; XII 1
σκεῦος	XV 15	Ὕδνον	XII 26
Σκίρα	XVIII 30	υἱὸς γεέννης	XV 27
Σκιροφόρια	XVIII 30	υἱὸς γιγάντων	XVIII 25
σκολοπισμός	XVII 20	Ὑιὸς Παρακλήσεως	XIV 57
σκόλοψ	XVII 20	Ὑπερίων	II 25
Σκύλλα	V 12; XV 19	ὑπερίων	III 29
σκυταλή	V 8	ὑπνωτικόν	VI 28
σκυταλίας	V 8	ὑπογεῖσον	XII 27
σκυτάλιον	V 8	ὕπτιος	XI 3
σκωλόομαι	XVII 20	ὕσγη	VIII 9
σκῶλος	XVII 20	ὕσγινον	VIII 9
σπέρμα	III 7	ὑστέρα	VII 24
σπιλάς	XIV 65	ὑστερικός	VI 32
σπίλος	XIV 65		
σπινθήρ	XIV 65		
σπόρος	XI 27	φάκελος	XVI 8
στάλιξ	XII 68	φάλαγγωμα	VI 34
σταυρός	XII 66	φάλαγξ	VI 34
στελέα	XII 4	φαλλάγγιον	VI 34
στελειή	XII 4	φαλλός	III 26
στελεόν	XII 4	φαλλοφορία	XVI 9
στέλεχος	XIV 3	φαρέτρα	XII 4
στίβι	XVIII 35	φαρμακεία	XIV 47
στιβίζομαι	XVIII 35	φαρμακεύς	XIV 47
στρουθίον	V 13	φαρμακός	VII 39; XII 79
στρύχνον	VI 28	φάρξις	III 31
Στρύχνον ὑπνωτικόν	V 18	φατνη	IX 22; XVI 35
Συροφοινίκισσα	XV 17	φατνόω	IX 22
σφόνδυλος	X 7	φατνώμα	IX 22
σῴζω	III 50	Φέρεκλος	XII 43
σῶκος	XI 5	Φερσεφόνιον	XVII 6
σωτήρ	III 1	φθειροποιός	VIII 69
		φθόρος ἐμβρύων	XII 59
		φλεβοτομία	VI 42
ταβαίτας	XVI 1	φλεγέσθω	II 21
Ταβειθί	XVI 1; XVIII 38	φλέγω	II 21
ταβέλλα	II 2	φλόξ	II 21
Ταβιθά	XVI 1	Φοῖνιξ	XV 11
τάβλα	XIV 25	φοῖνιξ	XV 11, 12, 15, 17
ταβλίον	VI 42; VIII 7; XIV 25; XVI 19	Φόριγγες	V 18
		φορτίον	XII 35

φράξις	III 31	Χύτροι	XVII 17
φρῦνος	XIV 65		
φύλαξ	XII 27	Ψιλός	II 10
		ψιλόω	XIV 46
		ψυχή	III 7
χαλβάνη	II 20		
Χάρυβδις	V 12; XV 19	ᾦα	XII 26
χελιδών	XII 4	ᾦβεον	XII 26
χελιδῶν	VI 5	ᾦεον	XII 26
χελλών	VI 5; XII 4	ᾠϊά	XII 26
χελών	VI 5; XII 4	ᾦιον	XII 26
χελώνη	XII 4	Ὠκεανός	III 11
χιτῶνα ποικίλον	XIV 64	Ὠκιμοειδές	XV 14
χιτὼν καρπωτός	XIV 64	ὠκιμοειδές	V 21
Χόες	XVII 17	ᾦκιμον	V 12; VIII 16
χοῦς	XVII 35	ᾦον	XII 26
χρηστός	VI 26	ᾠὸν γήινον	XV 27
χρῖσμα	II 20; III 36	ὠσχός	IX 12; XVII 22
χυλός	III 36	ὠσχοφόρια	XVII 22, 44

Latin

Juno, III 1
Jupiter, III 1

latus clavus, VI 42
Lawsonia inermis, VIII 20; XIV 58

magester, III 27
magister, III 27
mala canina, VI 23
mala terrestris, XII 26
malefica, XIX 31
malum terrae, XII 26
matrix, V 12
Misy, V 18
Moly, V 18
Morion, V 18
mucus, VII 8

Nemesis, V 26
Neuras, XIV 65

Oceanus, III 11
Ocimum basilicum, VIII 16
Oculum, X 20
oetum, XII 26
Oetum, V 18
Opalus, III 26; XIV 39
ostrum, VIII 9

Paeanis, II 25
Paeonia, XII 18
pallacana, VI 15; X 16
palus, XII 66
Panaeolus, V 15
panthera, XIV 36
pellex, VII 37
Phrynion, XIV 65
picus Martius, IX 6
pila, V 18
pilum, V 18
pilum praepilatum, V 18
pituita, VII 10
plaga, XI 26; XVI 8
platanus, XII 38
Plistolochia, VIII 26
Pollux, XII 27, 70
polymitam, XIV 64
Porrum nigrum, III 26
Psilocybe, V 15
Psilocybe mexicana, V 15
pugnus, XII 28
purpura, VIII 7

quotidianus, XVII 60

rana, XIV 65
ranae rubetae, XIV 65

Ricinus, V 12
Ricinus communis, V 12
rubeta, XIV 65
rubeus, XIV 65
rubra, XIV 17
rubus, XIV 65

salamandra, V 26
saliva, VII 13
sanctus, III 31
sappirus, XIV 53
sator, VIII 16
satur, VIII 16
Saturnus, VIII 16
satyrion, VIII 16
scintilla, XIV 65
semen ferulae, VIII 20
Seminalis, III 24
setania, VI 15
Setanium, VI 15
Sicarii, XVII 31
Sicus agrios, XIV 65
siderites, IX 11
Silenus, VIII 16
siliqua, V 12
sinistrum, III 46
Sorbus, XIV 54
Sorbus domestica, XIV 54
spiritus, III 7
spondulion, X 7
Spongiolus, V 18
Spurium, XI 27
stibium, XVIII 35
Stropharia, V 15
substantia, XVII 62
subula, III 26
sucinis novaculis, XV 15
super, XVII 62
superstantialis, XVII 62

tabella, II 2
tabula, II 2; XIV 25
tamarix, XV 14
tectum, XIV 17

uber, X 21
uterus, VII 24

Venerium, V 12
Venus, III 1
Veratrum, XII 60
vesica, XIV 17
vesticula, XIV 17
vinum, IV 18
volva, VI 5, 15

Zoophthalmos, X 20

Fungus Redivivus:

New Light on the Mushroom Controversy

Carl A.P. Ruck

Toadstools

It was a story that eventually acquired the status of myth, the quest of Persephone for the narcotic flower that opened the vision to another world. "I will draw an account of our mushroom quest," R. Gordon Wasson wrote, in his final book, *Persephone's Quest*, which appeared just before his death in 1986, "Valentina Pavlovna my late Russian wife's and mine."[1] In August of 1927, they were celebrating a delayed honeymoon in a friend's lent chalet in the Catskills. After lunch, they took a walk down a path that led eventually upwards to a slope toward a forested mountain.

> Suddenly, before I knew it, my bride threw down my hand roughly and ran up into the forest, with cries of ecstasy. She had seen toadstools growing, many kinds of toadstools. She had not seen the like since Russia, since 1917. She was in a delirium of excitement and began gathering them right and left in her skirt.

Gordon was aghast: "They are toadstools, I said, they are poisonous." It was, as he said, their "first marital crisis." In five years of courtship, they had never discussed anything as fundamental as mushrooms, and "here she was possessed by the mushrooms!" She insisted on incorporating them into the dinner she prepared, while hanging others out to dry in the sun for future use. "I was beside myself. I acted the perfect Anglo-Saxon oaf confronting a wood nymph." He would eat nothing with mushrooms in it. Later she claimed that he had predicted that he would wake up the next day a widower, which would have fit the myth, but he always denied this allegation.

---

[1] R. Gordon Wasson, Stella Kramrisch, Jonathan Ott, and Carl A.P. Ruck, *Persephone's Quest: Entheogens and the Origins of Religion* (New Haven; Yale University Press, 1986), 17. Translated as *La busqueda de Persefone. Los enteógenos y los orígenes de la religion* (México, DF: Fondo de Cultura Económico, 1996).

Irrational Loathing

But they did begin to wonder why they had such different attitudes to a common plant, and they discovered among their respective friends the same dichotomy, the irrational fear of all mushrooms among the Anglo-Saxons, contrasting with the special fondness of Tina's Slavs. While they each pursued their individual careers, his eventually as banker, and hers as pediatrician, they found themselves drawn as an avocation to this weird innate difference in their attitude toward mushrooms. They spent years gathering instances of mushrooms in literature and art, noting the most strange fact that English had only three words for this remarkable plant, the folkloric metaphor of "toadstool",[2] a Latin quasi-scientific term "fungus", which is also metaphoric and cognate with sponge, and the borrowed French "mushroom", from *mousseron*, of uncertain derivation,[3] while the Russian vocabulary was endless. The fact that English has no real word for the plant, since fungus and mushroom distance the English speaker from it via foreign importations, speaks volumes, as does the loathsomeness of the toad's stool.

As amateurs in ethnography, botany, and languages, the Wassons always sought out experts in the various fields in the thirty years they devoted to the subject together, and they came to suspect that the differing attitudes to the humble mushroom, which they termed *mycophobia* and *mycophilia*, testified to some deep-seated religious phenomenon. As Gordon, looking back on his long and wide-ranging investigations, summed it up:

> I suggest that when such traits betoken the attitudes of whole tribes or peoples, and when those traits have remained unaltered throughout recorded history, and especially when they differ from one people to another neighboring people, then you are face to face with a phenomenon of profound cultural importance, whose primal cause is to be discovered only in the well-springs of cultural history.[4]

---

2   Literally, a toad's stool or chair, going back to Middle English *tadestool*.
3   On the probable derivation, see below.
4   Wasson, *Persephone's Quest*, 19.

María Sabina

Gordon and Valentina Pavlovna published their findings, shortly before her death, in the seminal ethnographic compilation, *Mushrooms, Russia and History.*[5] Not everything that they had discovered, as the subject evolved and broadened—the two-volume book had begun originally as just a cookbook(!)—found its way into the publication. Because of the political situation, field research among the Siberian shamans was an impossibility at the time,[6] but in 1952, the poet, novelist, and Classical scholar Robert Graves alerted them to an article that Richard Evans Schultes of Harvard Botanical Museum had published some twenty years earlier about the ritual use of a psychoactive mushroom among the monolingual Mazatec people of central Mexico. This gave them an opportunity to check their intuition about the sanctity of the mushrooms. Starting in 1953, Gordon and Tina organized yearly field expeditions to the Mexican highlands, and in 1955, they were the first outsiders in modern times to participate with the shaman María Sabina in her nightlong ceremony, the *velada*, with the sacred mushroom.[7] As Gordon later described that night of wonders:

> Your body lies in the darkness, heavy as lead, but your spirit seems to soar and leave the hut, and with the speed of thought to travel where it listeth, in time and space, accompanied by the shaman's singing and by the ejaculations of her percussive chant.... As your body lies there in its sleeping bag, your soul is free, loses all sense of time, alert as it never was before, living an eternity in a night, seeing infinity in a grain of sand.[8]

---

5   Valentina Pavlovna Wasson and R. Gordon Wasson, *Mushrooms, Russia and History* (New York: Pantheon, 1957).

6   The Communist regime made a concerted effort to suppress Siberian shamanism in order to assimilate the tribesmen into the state.

7   Eventually published as R. Gordon Wasson, G. Cowan, and W. Rhodes, *María Sabina and her Mazatec Mushroom Velada*, Ethnomycological Studies No. 3 (New York: Harcourt Brace Jovanovich, 1974).

8   R. Gordon Wasson, Albert Hofmann, and Carl A.P. Ruck, *The Road to Eleusis: Unveiling the Secret of the Mysteries* (New York and London: Harcourt Brace Jovanovich, 1978), 20-21, reprinted and enlarged, 20th anniversary edition, Los Angeles: Hermes Press, 1998; 30th anniversary edition, Berkley: North Atlantic Books, 2008). Translated as *El camino a Eleusis: Una solución al enigma de los misterios* (Fondo de Cultura Económico: México, DF, 1980). German and Modern Greek translations are now also available.

Christian Heresies

Although they had looked in vain for explicit mention of mushrooms in the scriptures of Judeo-Christianity, they nevertheless thought it likely that the mushroom that is so prevalent in the folktales and art of Europe was at the heart of various secret societies and heretical sects persecuted by the Church of Rome. Such were the Manicheans, with their special fondness for red mushrooms, a sect that Saint Augustine had embraced for a time.[9] They also knew that a version of this same dualistic Zoroastrian heresy was later persecuted as the religion of the Cathars in the Albigensian Crusade, begun in 1209 under Pope Innocent III.[10] The Wassons were also already intrigued with the pagan Greco-Roman possibilities, again because of Robert Graves, who had called their attention to the Etruscan mirror in the British Museum, showing the immolation of Ixion, with a double annotation of what he thought might be a mushroom.[11] The Wassons included it in *Mushrooms, Russia and History*. Too late for inclusion was another object that Graves discovered. Friends had sent him a postcard with the now famous Pharsalos bas-relief from northern Greece, now in the Musée de Louvre,[12] depicting the goddesses Demeter and Persephone, each holding a large fungal specimen, erroneously identified as flowers. In a letter dated September 15, 1958, Gordon wrote back: "[it] does not represent a flower: everybody now agrees to that." Graves used it, without comment, for the cover of the revised 1960 edition of his immensely successful *The Greek Myths*,[13] which has gone through numerous re-printings and, although ignored by Classicists, as is Graves' work in general, despite nearly fifty books, it inevitably sparked

9   See Carl A.P. Ruck, Blaise Daniel Staples, and Clark Heinrich, *The Apples of Apollo: Pagan and Christian Mysteries of the Eucharist* (Durham, NC: Carolina Academic Press, 2001), 174 *et seq.*

10   See Carl A.P. Ruck, Blaise Daniel Staples, José Alfredo González Celdrán, and Mark Alwin Hoffman, *The Hidden World: Survival of Pagan Shamanic Themes in European Fairytales* (Durham, NC: Carolina Academic Press, 2006), chap. XII, "Melusina of Plaincourault," 309 *et seq.*

11   Printed as plate xvii in Arthur B. Cook, *Zeus: A Study in Ancient Religion* (Cambridge University Press, 1914-1940; republished New York: Biblo and Tannen, 1964). The flower is probably not a mushroom, but the Datura, a plant equally significant for the role of psychoactive sacraments in ancient religion: see Ruck and Staples, "Mistletoe, Centaurs, and Datura": 15-40, in Ruck *et al.*, *Apples of Apollo*.

12   N° 701, the so-called "Elevation of the Flower."

13   Robert Graves, *The Greek Myths* (Hamondsworth, UK: Penguin, first published 1955, revised edition 1960).

speculation about the ancient Eleusinian Mystery. Graves himself made the case for a mushroom as the psychoactive ingredient in the potion for the initiation in his *Food for Centaurs: Stories, Talk, Critical Studies*.[14] Mushrooms were clearly in the air as the decade of the psychedelic 60s dawned.

The Wassons had undeniably uncovered psychoactive sacraments in the shamanism of Mesoamerica, traceable back to the pre-Conquest indigenous religions, well documented by the many mushroom-stones and mushroom idols, and they suspected a similar situation existed behind the European folklore they had amassed about the mushroom, and, in particular, the *Amanita muscaria*, commonly depicted as the fairytale mushroom. With that in mind, they had visited the little 12th-century chapel of Saint-Éligie de Plaincourault as early as 1952. The fresco in the apse depicts the Tree of Genesis as a decidedly fungal design, unmistakable even as to its species, the red-capped Amanita, with its distinctive white scabby remnants of the universal veil shattered as the mushroom quickly expands with growth. The fresco supposedly dates from 1291, although there is evidence that it was already there as early as 1184[15] and was built by returning Crusaders of the Order of Malta. The fresco was first officially noticed at a meeting of the Mycological Society of France in 1910, and then published in their *Bulletin*.[16] Other European mycologists confirmed the resemblance of the Tree to the psychoactive mushroom.[17]

The chapel is located in the Indre district of southwestern France, near Orleans, the region of Aquitaine, where the Cathar heresy once had flourished. But the Wassons quickly dropped their inquiry because of the opinion of art historians, including Erwin Panofsky, that the mushroom-tree was simply another example, common in medieval art, of the stylized Italian "umbrella pine" (*Pinus pinea*). Although Wasson himself publicly dismissed the fresco, he did so with reluctance and included it as a plate for his readers' consideration in his 1968 *Soma: The Divine Mushroom of Immortality*, in which he advanced the theory

---

14   Robert Graves, *Food for Centaurs: Stories, Talks, Critical Studies* (Garden City, NY: Doubleday, 1960). The collection includes a chapter written at the instigation of Gordon and Tina on the death of the Emperor Claudius by mushroom poisoning.

15   Berry, in Giorgio Samorini, "The Mushroom-tree of Plaincourault": 29-37, in *Eleusis*, 4 (1997).

16   Vol. xxvii, p. 31-33.

17   Wasson cites five English publications in his *Soma: Divine Mushroom of Immortality* (New York: Harcourt Brace Jovanovich, 1968), 179.

that the ancient sacred plant-god of the Sanskrit *RgVeda* was originally this same fascinating and empowering mushroom. Two years later the fresco would appear in John Allegro's *The Sacred Mushroom and the Cross*, doing much to popularize both the fresco and Allegro's theory that early Christians knew and used the psychoactive mushroom as a sacrament, and adding to the interest in the magic mushroom already sparked by Andrija Puharich's documentation of the psychic Harry Stone's Ra Ho Tep persona, a decade earlier.[18] Allegro, the linguist and scholar of the Dead Sea Scrolls, an academic with impeccable credentials in ancient Classical and Near and Middle Eastern languages, had read Wasson's writings and appropriately acknowledged them, knew of his Mexican discoveries, accepted his identification of Soma as the fly-agaric, and obviously had drawn the conclusion that Wasson was still reluctant to make, although it was mentioned in his *Soma*.[19]

Allegro ill-advisedly presented his investigation of the mushroom in the Holy Land with the express purpose of debunking the validity of the Judeo-Christian tradition.[20] He made the error of arguing that such a visionary Eucharist rendered Christianity a sham,[21] although he was well aware that Wasson and others were documenting the valid and still thriving vitality of such sacraments in other religions. The outraged and unconsidered rejection was immediate and vituperative; he was essentially stripped of his academic credentials: there was no proof of any of this, and as far as his critics were concerned, the mushroom didn't even grow in the Near East. Allegro was personally devastated by the scornful rejection of his scholarship. Allegro, who never experienced a psychoactive substance, was responding with distaste to the temper of the times with its widespread random and irresponsible abuse of psychedelic substances, amidst the turmoil of generational and political transition.[22] The notoriety of drug abuse in

---

18   Andrija Puharich, *The Sacred Mushroom: Key to the Door to Eternity* (Garden City, NY: Doubleday, 1959).

19   Wasson, *Soma*, 178-180, 214-215, 220-222.

20   The Dead Sea Scrolls call into question the historicity of Jesus, whose story seems to be modeled on the Essene "Teacher of Righteousness," whose persecution and crucifixion, along with 800 other members of the sect, by the Jewish "Wicked Priest" Alexander Jannaeus about a century earlier is better documented. Without a divinely incarnated historical Jesus, Christianity lacks its foundation.

21   John Marco Allegro, *The End of the Road* (New London: MacGibbon and Kee, 1971).

22   A recent biography of Allegro by his daughter documents the evolution of

the 1960s led even Mircea Eliade, the renowned authority on religion, mysticism, and shamanism, to disavow his own considerable evidence about shamanism in Siberia and elsewhere and declare that drugs were characteristic only of the decadent last stages of a cult, affording only inauthentic hallucinatory communion with the divine.[23] Inevitably, anyone who thought differently was assumed to have ruined his mind on drugs.

Psychoactive Sacraments

Since then the wider cultural context in antiquity has been established; and the judgment must be reversed.[24] Drugs of all kinds were always involved in ancient Middle and Near Eastern and Egyptian religions as a mode for achieving ecstasy and shamanic contact with the otherworld.[25] Further east, there was the *haoma* cult of the Persians and the similar Soma cult of the Brahmans of India, traditions that the migrating Indo-Europeans carried with them into Europe as the basis of Druidism and other Celtic cults. In the Greco-Roman world, furthermore, there was frequent contact across the deserts, most notably through the Persian conquest of Egypt, the Babylonian captivity of the Jews, and the two invasions of Greece, followed a century later in the opposite direction by Alexander's conquest of India, where he reportedly conversed with the gymnosophists, the "naked sages." Hellenic philosophers shared ideas with visiting eastern magicians or shamans, called "magi," like the three who supposedly showed up to confirm the birth of Jesus. And Apollonius of Tyana, a contemporary of Christ and similarly deified, was even initiated into the Brahman cult

---

the controversy and the final period of her father's life. Judith Anne Brown, *John Marco Allegro: The Maverick of the Dead Sea Scrolls* (Grand Rapids, MI and Cambridge, UK: William B. Eerdmans Publishing Co.: 2005).

23   Mircea Eliade, *Shamanism: Archaic Techniques of Ecstasy* (New York: Pantheon, 1964).

24   Weston La Barre, "Hallucinogens and the Shamanic Origins of Religion": 261-278, in *Flesh of the Gods: The Ritual Use of Hallucinogens*, Peter T. Furst, editor (New York: Praeger, 1972).

25   Chris Bennett and Neil McQueen, *Sex, Drugs, Violence, and the Bible* (Gibsons, BC: Forbidden Fruit Publishing Company, 2000); Mark Hoffman and Carl A.P. Ruck, "Entheogens (Psychedelic Drugs) and Shamanism": 111-117, in *Shamanism: An Encyclopedia of World Beliefs, Practices, and Culture*, Mariko Namba Walter and Eva Jane Neumann Fridman, editors, (Santa Barbara, CA: ABC-Clio, 2004).

upon his visit to India.[26]

The earliest Indo-European immigrants, moreover, who are termed the "battle-axe people" from their burials with small symbolic battle-axes, encountered an earlier culture already resident in Europe, originating probably from Spain and Africa, similarly designated generically as the "beaker-people" from their burials in which the corpse was laid to rest in fetal position, holding an unglazed ceramic beaker, suggesting that some psychoactive potion was involved in their contact with the otherworld. Persistent folkloric traditions make it likely that the two cultures had similar rites centering not only upon visionary botanical sacraments, but ones in which the mushroom had a primary role.[27] This is not surprising, in view of the culturally unrelated Mesoamerican rites,[28] since shamans testify that the plant itself plays a determinative role in communicating with psychically sensitive persons like shamans.[29]

Rupestrian art in northern Africa and southern and northern Europe from as early as the Paleolithic period document, moreover, the antiquity of the use of psychoactive plants in shamanism, sometimes quite explicitly mushrooms,[30] such as a drawing from the Tassili plateau in the southern Algerian desert, depicting a shamanic figure with the face of a bee and mushrooms sprouting from his body, indicating his consubstantiality with the spirit of the fungal entheogen.[31] With the

---

26   See Ruck *et al., Apples of Apollo*, 148 *et seq.* According to an eye witness, Apollonius bathed in a sacred spring and was anointed by the Brahman priests with an amber drug, which caused a profuse sweating, as if they were washing themselves with fire, after which he had the sensation of levitation, followed by the singing of songs and philosophical discussions about the nature of the soul and reminiscences of previous incarnations, all of which he termed an initiation into Mysteries. See also Carl A.P. Ruck, "Classical World Shamanism": 478-484, in *Shamanism.*

27   See Carl A.P. Ruck and Mark Alwin Hoffman, "Overture: Remnants of a Forgotten World," chapter 1, in Ruck *et al., Hidden World.*

28   See the parallel mythology of Hercules and Quetzalcóatl, in José Alfredo González Celdrán, *Hombres, dioses y hongos: Hacia una visión etnobotánica del mito* (Madrid; EDAF, 2002), 122-131.

29   Jeremy Narby, *The Cosmic Serpent: DNA and the Origins of Knowledge* (New York: Tarcher Putnam, 1999).

30   Terrence McKenna, *Food of the Gods: The Search for the Original Tree of Knowledge* (New York: Bantam, 1992).

31   Giorgio Samorini, "Prehistoric Psychoactive Mushroom Artifacts": 69-78, in *Integration*, n° 2, 3, 1992. On the rock art and shamanism, see David S. Whitley, "Rock Art and Shamanism": 219-223, in *Shamanism.*

Entheogen is a neologism, now widely accepted, to designate a sacramen-

subsequent climate change and ensuing desertification of northern Africa and southern Spain, even when the mushroom became difficult to find, the folkloric traditions about it were often perpetuated in the myths and botanical substitutes employed, as in the magical food called manna that nourished the Israelites in the desert and allowed them to see God.[32] The mushroom, moreover, has a remarkable persistence and can be found wherever the higher elevations provide a suitable environment, and it has been observed growing with a wider variety of host trees than the usual conifers and birch, such as the cedars of Lebanon and the Greek olive.[33] It has been sighted on the sacred inspirational mountains like Mount Olympus, home of the gods, and Helicon, where the Muses congregate and dance. Other psychoactive mushrooms of the Psilocybe species grow commonly upon animal dung and can even be cultivated upon appropriate growing mixtures of composted vegetative matter. Nor was it impossible to import specimens from suitable distant habitats, as was the case with the annual arrival of a special Hyperborean offering from Scythia to the

---

tal plant that was considered to be animate (from the Greek *entheos*, inspired with "god within"), a food consubstantial with the "spirit" of deity; hence entheobotany is a branch of ethnobotany and ethnopharmacology, studying the role of sacred psychoactive plants within a culture. In the Eucharistic sacrament of all religions, the celebrant-shaman came to share an identity with the deity through the medium of the sacred plant. Combining the ancient Greek adjective *entheos* ("inspired, animate with deity") and the verbal root in *genesis* ("becoming"), it signifies "something that causes the divine to reside within one." Entheogens are sacramental foods whose ingestion makes the celebrant consubstantial with the deity, providing a communion and shared existence mediating between the human and the divine. This new word replaces words such as hallucinogen, psychedelic, psychomimetic, psychotropic, narcotic, drug, etc., all of which are pejorative and inappropriate for the unbiased discussion of authentic religious experience, and all of which imply that the resultant visionary religious experience is illusory or otherwise inauthentic.

For a reprint of the original proposal published as Carl A.P Ruck *et al.,* "Entheogens," *Journal of Psychedelic Drugs* 11(1-2) (1979): 145-146, see the *Entheos* website at: http://www.entheomedia.com

32   Dan Merkur, *The Mystery of Manna: The Psychedelic Sacrament of the Bible* (Rochester, NY: Park Street Press/Inner Traditions, 2000).

33   Mark Hoffman, Carl A.P. Ruck, and Blaise Daniel Staples, "Conjuring Eden: Art and the Entheogenic Vision of Paradise": 13-50, in Entheos, vol. 1, n° 1 (summer), 2001, 42, footnote 30, citing an article in the Greek press. Robert Graves, "What Food the Centaurs Ate": 319-43, in Steps (London: Cassell, 1959) reprinted as: 257-282, in Food for Centaurs, noted that the fly-agaric grows in Palestine, and suggested its possible use similar to that of the Berserkers by the Israeli liberation forces, who took the name of "Samson's Foxes," from the fox-grape metaphor in the Song of Songs.

sanctuary of Apollo on the island of Delos.[34] The Modern Greek *manitari* for "mushroom" and the botanical Latin Amanita probably derive from the Amanus Mountains of Lebanon, where the mushroom could be found conveniently in the Holy Land.

Within the Hellenic context, the cult of Dionysus, the god who as patron of the Theater was perhaps most responsible for the enduring cultural heritage of the Classical World, quite simply involved drugs as additives, used in the widespread and customary manner to fortify and modify the psychoactive effects of the wine. In this way, the fungal growth that is the basis for the manufacture of alcohol through the controlled process of fermentation was employed as the medium for assimilating the wide array of other psychoactive agents, including cannabis, opium, henbane, mandrake, lotus, and datura, that were available and commonly used, both medicinally and for recreation, in the Greco-Roman world.[35] The primacy of the fungal medium in the vinous mixture, however, was commemorated in Greek art by the typical depiction of the clustered bunch of grapes as mushroom-shaped.

A recognizably fungal toxin derived from the ergot parasitic on grains was similarly assimilated as the basis for the psychoactive potion of the great Eleusinian mystery initiation, displacing the opium and other substances earlier employed in the worship of the Goddess.[36] The Eleusinian rite was also practiced in lesser regional sanctuaries; and it was apparently the one at Pharsalos in northern Greece that is the provenance for the bas-relief that attracted Robert Grave's attention: such a work of art that so blatantly reveals the secret, we must assume, was never intended for profane viewing.[37]

---

34   Carl A.P. Ruck, "The Offerings from the Hyperboreans": 225-256, in Wasson *et al., Persephone's Quest*; González Celdrán, "Los hijos del frío," 185-222, in *Hombres, dioses y hongos.*

35   David C.A. Hillman, *The Chemical Muse: Drug Use and the Roots of Western Civilization* (New York: St Martin's Press, 2008).

36   Wasson *et al., The Road to Eleusis.* Hofmann proposed ergonovine as the supposedly water soluble alkaloid; for a refinement of the chemical procedure through the use of an alkaline solvent, see Peter Webster, Daniel M. Perrine, and Carl A.P. Ruck, "Mixing the Kykeon": 55-86, in *Eleusis* n.s. vol.1, n° 4, 2000; the active principles are achieved by partial hydrolysis yielding ergine and isoergine, which easily convert to their water-soluble salts, the same chemicals that are responsible for the visionary effects of *Ololiuhqui*, the morning glory Ipomenea. See Carl AP. Ruck, *Sacred Mushrooms of the Goddess: Secrets of Eleusis* (Berkeley, CA: Ronin Publishing, 2006).

37   Ruck, *Sacred Mushrooms*, 48 et seq.

And the mythical traditions about the Eleusinian sanctuary above Sparta on Mount Taygetus with its dense forests of conifers seem to have involved the mushrooms commonly to be found there.[38] The mushroom itself was probably not always available in sufficient supply to meet the needs for the initiation of large numbers of persons, as in the major Eleusinian rite, but was substituted by other psychoactive substances, as was also the case with the Soma ceremony, for which archaeological evidence demonstrates the use of cannabis and ephedra or "Syrian rue," the latter having the same chemical properties as one of the ingredients of the South American *ayahuasca* potion, and like it, requiring the addition of another plant to access its visionary properties, in this case probably supplied by the acacia tree, explaining its connotations of sanctity in ancient Judaism.[39]

The Eleusinian rites were only one version of other mystery initiations, such as that of the Orphics and the Kabeiroi, including what the early Christians claimed as their own mystery. These all involved visionary sacraments, although secret and strenuously denied. The 2nd-century bishop Clement of Alexandria, a professed authority on the ancient mysteries, expressly told a neophyte that he should lie if asked about the contents of the secret gospel of Mark in his possession.[40]

Psycholinguistics

Officially, Wasson distanced himself from the Allegro controversy.[41]

---

38   González Celdrán, "La montaña de Deméter," 147-154, in *Hombres, dioses y hongos.*

39   Benny Shanaon, "Biblical Entheogens: A Speculative Hypothesis": 51-74, in *Time and Mind: The Journal of Archaeology, Consciousness, and Culture*, vol. 1, issue 1 (March 2008).

40   Morton Smith, *Clement of Alexandria and a Secret Gospel of Mark* (Cambridge, MA: Harvard University Press, 1973).

41   In a letter to the editor of the *Times Literary Supplement*, dated 16 September 1970, Wasson wrote: "I think Allegro must have got his idea of the fly-agaric from us, yet his book does not show any influence of us, apart from the fly-agaric." (Wasson Collection, Harvard Botanical Library.) This overlooks the full acknowledgement of Wasson's work made in notes 15 and 16 to Chapter V of *The Sacred Mushroom and the Cross*. Wasson was aghast at the financial profit Allegro stood to gain from the serialized rights by the publication of his book in the *Sunday Mirror* (London), although simultaneously boasting of the success of his *Soma*. (Letter dated 25 February 1970 to Donald Webster of Helix Investments Limited, prior to the publication of *The Sacred Mushroom and the Cross*, Wasson Collection, Harvard Botanical Library: "The mushroom is the fly-agaric, which I hope he can find in the texts, but I have my fingers

Although Wasson inadvertently launched what came to be known as the Psychedelic Revolution by his *Life* magazine article, he was frightened by many of the leaders who took up the cause, such as Timothy Leary and Carlos Castaneda. Like Puharich, Allegro presented his findings to the popular press, instead of inserting it piecemeal in scholarly journals; the argument is, however, all of one piece, and peer-reviewed journals would never have accepted so revolutionary a theory in any form under any circumstances. The argument rests almost totally on linguistic analysis, and his critics are of one voice in deferring to others on the basis of incompetence.[42] Generally, the procedure has been to assume that someone else, more competent than oneself in the many languages that Allegro mastered,[43] must be correct in dismissing the linguistic evidence.[44]

The basic objection is that Sumerian is apparently *sui generis*, a language unrelated to any other, and hence similar-sounding words in Hebrew, Greek, and other ancient languages had no bearing on the case for Christianity's Sumerian origin. Linguists also complained that Allegro often hypothesized words not actually extant in Sumerian, although standard linguistic procedure involves doing exactly that, to recreate the necessary missing bridges.

The first objection fails to recognize that geographically proximate peoples borrow, assimilate, and pun on foreign words, especially when the words are part of a sacred vocabulary that pertains to imported religious rituals. Cults, moreover, are apt to spread by importing foreign leaders, priests, or even priesthoods, *en masse*, and these people continue to conduct their rites, at least at first, by reciting magical-religious formulae of their native tongues. For example, when the Romans imported the practice of worshipping Cybele from Anatolia in 205 BCE, the related rituals continued to be performed exclusively

crossed.")

42   Jonathan Ott, *Pharmacotheon: Entheogenic Drugs, their Plant Sources and History* (Kennewick, WA: Natural Products Co., 1996), 334: "Since I am not an expert in Biblical philology, I will not attempt to evaluate his arguments. It should be noted, however, that specialists in the study of Biblical languages have unanimously rejected Allegro's thesis, and the fundamental assumptions that underlie it."

43   Namely: Sumerian, Akkadian, Ugaritic, Semitic, Sanskrit, Hebrew, Aramaic, Syriac, Arabic, Persian, Greek, and Latin.

44   Thorkild Jacobsen and C.C. Richardson, "Mr. Allegro among the Mushrooms," in *Union Seminary Quarterly Review*, vol. 26 n° 3 (1971). The disdainful title of the review indicates immediately the authors' attitude.

by an Oriental priesthood up until the Emperor Claudius assumed the throne in 41 CE. One need merely cite *hocus pocus dominocus* from the Latin consecration of the Host (*hoc est corpus Domini*) to see how easily foreign rituals are assimilated and given new, but complementary, significance, namely bogus magic or pure charlatanry, probably first employed in Satanic parodies of the Mass.

In addition, the new discipline of psycholinguistics, going back to Freud and early experiments in word association under conditions of fatigue and stress, demonstrates what Jung called an autonomous group of archetypal associations exerting an extraordinary influence in the formation of dreams, symptoms, and linguistic associations. This phenomenon, in which the semantic meanings of words are displaced to some extent by sound similarities or phonetic components,[45] would have been activated during rituals involving drugs and the induced stress and fatigue of traditional initiations.

A simple example of using phonetic components over semantic elements can be sensed in the associative word cluster, apt to surface in dreams or altered consciousness, either chemically or otherwise induced, that combines sexual "violation" (derived from the Latin *violare* for "harm by violence") with the totally unrelated name of a flower, the violet (Latin *viola*, from Greek *wíon* and the mythical sexually abducted maiden *Wióle* or *Ióle*) and the metaphor of virginal "defloration;" in fact, the mythical defloration of *Ióle* implies a psychoactive role for the viola in a shamanic context, similar to the rape of Persephone via the narcotic *narkissos* flower.[46]

Similar clusters occur across language barriers, as, for example the German *Blut* for (menstrual) "blood" has a plural *Bluten*, which suggests *Blümen* or "flowers." We might compare the English "carnal" knowledge, which suggests both the violation of "carnage" and the "carnation," named for its "fleshy" blood red color. Hungarian is not an Indo-European language, but the same phonetic cluster occurs: *ver*

---

45 Paul Kugler, *The Alchemy of Discourse: An Archetypal Approach to Language* (Lewisburg, PA: Bucknell University Press, 1982, republished as *The Alchemy of Discourse: Image, Sound and Psyche* (Einsiedeln: Daimon Verlag, 2002).

46 On *Ióle* and toxins, see Ruck and Staples, "The Shaman of Lake Stymphalos": 46-49, in Ruck *et al.*, *Apples of Apollo*; Carl A.P. Ruck and (Blaise) Danny Staples, *The World of Classical Myth: Gods and Goddess, Heroines and Heroes* (Durham, NC: Carolina Academic Press, 1994), 86-186; Carl A.P. Ruck, "On the Sacred Names of Iamos and Ion: Ethnobotanical Referents in the Hero's Parentage": 235-252, in *Classical Journal*, vol. 71 n° 3 (1976).

means "blood", *veres* is "bloody," and *verag* denotes "bloom, flower."[47] The root is homophonous with Latin *ver* (from Greek *wéar*) for "spring" (whence "vernal" in English), which is the season of flowering.

The truth of the matter is simply that the world's language tree is a hybrid formed by intermixing different language families; and the criticism of Allegro's linguistics is based upon outmoded and simplistic assumptions about a still evolving discipline. A strict application of Grimm's laws of sound shifts, in fact, sometimes isolates words that are obviously cognate.[48] Nevertheless, critics, who hastened to silence him forever for having proposed unseemly pharmacological and overly sexual origins for the Judeo-Christian religion, dismissed the erudition seen in Allegro's notes and references to ancient sources. According to Allegro, Judeo-Christianity had been scandalously embedded in the Anatolian fertility traditions of drug-induced ecstatic communion with the deity, something not only prevalent in the area, but also expectable in view of the shamanic origins of all ancient religions. Judaism, like many of the cultures of the region, underwent a patriarchal revision, which strenuously strove to obliterate the formerly dominant goddess. As a brilliant demonstration of mythopoeia and mythical analysis, Allegro's work never would have been acceptable to his critics—most if not all of whom were in no position to analyze the breadth of ethnobotanical material and ancient Classical sources that Allegro cited.

A Mushroom Goddess

The deposed goddess had names like Ishtar, Astarte, Cybele, Asherah, Isis, Demeter, Persephone, and ultimately Eve in the Judaic tradition. An inscription from a 7th-century BCE cultic divinatory temple at Ekron (Accaron), just 35 kilometers southwest of Jerusalem, bears the name of a hitherto unknown goddess whose identity testifies to a Canaanite mushroom cult still practiced in this region.[49] One letter of the name

---

47   Kugler, *Alchemy of Discourse*, 26.

48   Jacques Rosenman, *Primitive Speech and English,* vols.1 & 2 (Austin, TX: San Felipe Press, 1969 & 1972); *The Onomatopoetic Origins of Language I and II* (Austin, TX: Morgan Press, 1991, originally self-published and distributed in 1982).

49   Stephen R. Berlant, "The Mysterious Ekron Goddess Revisited," *Journal of Ancient and Near Eastern Studies*, pdf format on the website. The city was founded somewhere between the 15th and 14th centuries by indigenous Canaanites, and changed hands many times, belonging to the Philistines in the 12th century, Israel's United Monarchy under King David in the 10th century, passing under Egyptian control and then

is damaged and questionable, but is probably best read as a *resh*. The name is Ptryh (pronounced pet-ree-yah), with the final syllable a suffix indicating divinity, as in the name of Yahweh. It is a personified form of an anciently widespread Afro-Asiatic word, for, among other things, "seeing, beholding, explaining and interpreting," appearing in Egyptian, Nabataean, Jewish Aramaic, Phoenician, Punic, Neo-Punic, and Hebrew. The cultic use of the temple as an oracle reinforces this interpretation of the goddess as a seer. Ptryh is a form of Pidray, a Ugaritic goddess of illumination and lightning, who was the daughter of Baal Zeebub, the so-called Lord of the Flies.[50] The inscription was found near a figurine, probably of this goddess, squeezing the milk from her breast as the divine potion; and the temple contained a number of drinking vessels, suggesting that the potion was drunk there. We should expect that the sacrament, therefore, was visionary. And indeed, the design of the vessels is mycological, and the goddess's name also means "mushroom," not incompatible with her role in affording access to vision.

This goddess was an anthropomorphized *A. muscaria* whose ingestion endowed her priests with the power to prophesize by rendering them consubstantial with her and the sacrament. The Hebrew word for mushroom PTR (*ptr*) resulted from de-personifying Ptryah, and the Hebrew injunction against worshipping her and other Canaanite goddesses in sacred groves was actually an injunction against ingesting the sacred mushroom.

---

the control of Aram-Damascus between the 10th and 8th centuries; by the mid-8th century, it was again under Hebrew control, but later in the same century it was conquered by the Assyrians under Sennacherib, who subsequently converted it into a Neo-Assyrian city-state. Eventually, it was destroyed by the Babylonian king Nebuchadnezzar *ca.* 66 BCE.

50   Variously explained essentially as driving flies away from the sacrificial offerings and compared to Apollo as *Muiagros* or "fly-hunter." The epithet is inextricable from the folk motif of the fly-agaric.

The Tree in Eden

Wasson, himself, however, was in the process of changing his opinion. From his letters, we know that he was intrigued with the work of Allegro and frustrated by his unanswered attempt to initiate correspondence.[51] Ruck independently was similarly unsuccessful, except for having received a polite reply from a man who had withdrawn from the world.

Subsequently, Wasson went on to uncover the presumably similar mushroom cults of Mesoamerica, identifying *Kakuljá Hurakan*, the Mayan "Lightning-bolt One-leg," one of a trinity whose other members were *Chipi*, the "dwarf lightning-bolt" and *Raxa*, the "green lightning-bolt," as the ordinary name in Quiche for the *Amanita muscaria*.[52] In *Persephone's Quest*, Wasson finally identified the Fruit of the Tree in Eden as *Amanita muscaria*:

> I once said that there was no mushroom in the Bible. I was wrong. It plays a hidden role (that is to say, hidden from us until now) and a major one, in what is the best known episode of the Old Testament, the Garden of Eden story and what happened to Adam and Eve. ... To propose a novel reading of this celebrated story is a daring thing: it is exhilarating and intimidating. I am confident, ready for the storm.[53]

---

51   In a letter to Allegro from his Danbury home dated 14 September, 1970, Wasson wrote: "Though we are utterly opposed to each other on the role played by the fly-agaric, we agree that it was important. I think we can correspond with each other on friendly terms, like opposing counsel after hammering each other all day in court, who meet for a drink together in a bar before going home. I wish you would tell me one thing: when did the idea of the fly-agaric first come to you and from where?" (Wasson Collection, Harvard Botanical Library.) Wasson is responding to a letter by Allegro in *The Times Literary Supplement* (11.9.70) concerning the footnote IX. 20 in *The Sacred Mushroom and the Cross* mentioned above, where it is not clear whether Allegro is referring to Wasson or to Ramsbottom, author of *Mushrooms and Toadstools*, on the subject of the Plaincourault fresco. Wasson had corrected Ramsbottom on the subject of the fresco, who had added the "rightly or wrongly," etc. to a second edition of his book.

52   Wasson, *Persephone's Quest*, 47-54, citing Bernard Lowry, "*Amanita muscaria* and the Thunderbird Legend in Guatemala and Mexico," in *Mycologia* vol. 66 n° 1, Jan.-Feb. (1974).

53   Wasson, "The Tree of the Knowledge of Good and Evil": 74-77, in Wasson *et al., Persephone's Quest*.

There was no storm, and Wasson got off scot-free.

Similarly, in his earlier collaboration with Albert Hofmann and Ruck on the Eleusinian Mystery, he proposed what should have been an equally controversial theme: the involvement of a visionary fungal sacrament at the center of the Hellenic initiation rite. This religion dated back to the mid 2nd millennium BCE and lasted until it was desecrated in the conversion of the Roman Empire to Christianity in the 3rd century.[54] The greatest minds of Classical antiquity, the philosophers, poets, and politicians, all testified to the sublime importance of what was a drug-induced religious experience. Cicero called it a divine institution, the most essential gift of the city of Athens to the world. But an even more effective method of silencing a theory than attempting to refute it is simply to ignore it.

The Mushroom as Universal Mediator

Actually, Wasson had in his hands a paper by the brilliant Russian linguist, Vladimir Nikolaevic Toporov, which should have laid the basis for a reexamination of Allegro's etymologies. Wasson's long-time friend and intellectual supporter, the great linguist and semiotician Roman Jakobson[55] had called his attention to it and Wasson afterward commissioned an English translation, "On the Semiotics of Mythological Conceptions about Mushrooms," that the well-respected journal *Semiotica* published.[56] The paper combined the structural anthropologist Claude Lévi-Strauss's[57] discovery that mushrooms played an important

---

54   Wasson *et al*, *The Road to Eleusis*.

55   Wasson in *Persephone's Quest* (19-20) described his meeting with Jakobson as the second event in his and Tina's investigations: "The next event, momentous for the success of our fungal enterprise, was our encounter with Roman Jakobson, Russian refugee lately arrived on our shores, prodigious scholar, breath-taking lecturer, bon vivant. We met him in the early '40s and disclosed to him our feeling about the religious role played by mushrooms in the prehistoric background of the European peoples. His response bowled us over. The thought had never occurred to him, but his instinct told him we were right. He could not contain his enthusiasm for our idea. We became fast friends: he and his wife often dined with us and we with them. ... He fed us ideas about mushrooms continually, citations in books, proper names in Russian with their etymologies." Roman died in 1982.

56   Vladimir Nikolaevic Toporov, "On the Semiotics of Mythological Conceptions about Mushrooms": 295-357, in *Semiotica*, vol 53 n° 4 (1985), translated from the Russian by Stephen Rudy.

57   Wasson knew Levi-Strauss, who wrote a review of Soma: "Les Champignons dans la culture: A propos d'un livre de M. R.G. Wasson": 5-16, in *L'Homme* vol. 10 (1970).

part in the culinary and dietary regimes of different cultures with the discoveries of Wasson and of the French mycologist Roger Heim,[58] showing the important role that mushrooms played in mythopoeia and mythological systems.

More specifically, Toporov demonstrated that (1) cultures tend to create similar oppositional symbol systems (such as sacred vs. profane, feminine vs. masculine, raw vs. cooked, food vs. poison, celestial vs. chthonic, decent vs. indecent, accepted vs. tabooed, etc., as Allegro had claimed); and (2) within these dichotomies, mushrooms are archetypal, universal classifiers mediating these oppositions. As such, similar semiotic clusters occur in unrelated languages that were later extended by multi-lingual puns.

The mushroom, for example, is widely identified with death as the mold that grows upon the corpse. Hence, the French word *mousseron* for a type of edible fungus, (perhaps related to *mousse* or "moss," itself traceable back to Sanskrit for "urine"), which yielded English "mushroom" (via Middle English *muscheron*), can be traced back to Late Latin *mussirio*. *Mussirio* is perhaps related to (1) Post-Classical Latin *mussatio*, "suppression of the voice, silence"; (2) Classical Latin *mussito*, "keep silent"; and (3) *musso*, "be silent about something." These words are cognate (4) with ancient Greek *mysterion* or "mystery"; and (5) with English "mute." This all suggests that whatever the plant was actually called in English was a word that has been lost, perhaps because it was too sacred for profane utterance. *Mushroom*, like *toadstool*, is then only a metaphor and hints at the word's involvement in secret visionary initiatory rites like the ancient pagan and Christian "Mysteries."

The Greek verb *myao* appears to be the ultimate origin of the whole series, meaning "to moo," or to make the "moo sound," the labial with lips pursed, which can imply minimal sound (as in English "mum's the word"); hence the mushroom lent itself to cow and bull metaphors of mooing and bellowing, as well as the taurine rumbling of thunder.[59] Such metaphors coincidentally reinforced similar clusters for the Vedic sacrament.

---

58   Heim collaborated with the Wassons in the 50s and contributed watercolors to the 1957 *Life* magazine article.

59   See Ruck *et al., Apples,* 80. See Wasson's exhaustive compilation of traditions linking the sudden appearance of mushrooms in the forest to the fall of the thunderbolt, rather than the rainfall which actually precipitates their growth through the absorption of the water: "Lightningbolt and Mushrooms": 83-94, in Wasson et al., *Persephone's Quest.*

In the Greek, *myops* (from which English has myopic for "squint-eye," i.e., the eyelids similarly pursed), designated the gadfly, also called *oistros* ("estrus" in English), who as the ghost of the cowherd Argos goaded the mooing estrous cow-maiden Io,[60] implicating ecstatic sexual rapture in the verbal complex of the mystical secret.[61] Alongside this mystery metaphor, an Old French version of *mousseron* occurs as *moisseron* and is closer actually to meaning "mushroom," persisting in modern French as *moisi* and *moisissure* meaning "mold," and *moisir* "to cover with mold," derived ultimately from Latin *mucere* "to grow moldy" and Greek *mykes* for "mushroom" as something "slimy." In English, the latter occurs in both "moist" and "mucus," the point being simply that the true etymology as in the scientific designation "mycologist" is displaced by "mushroom," which is the item that is distanced as a foreign import and placed under the prohibition of silence. Lurking in the metaphoric "toadstool," however, is the hidden knowledge that the toad secretes the toxin bufotenine, named after it as *Bufo vulgaris*, and that frequently is an ingredient in psychoactive brews.[62]

> In the poisoned entrails throw.
> Toad that under cold stone
> Days and nights hast thirty-one
> Swelter'd venom sleeping got,
> Boil thou first i' the charmed pot.[63]

---

60   The names of Ío, Ióle, the Athenian founding hero Íon, the shaman Íamos, the mother of Oedipus Io-káste (Jocasta), are all similarly involved in the ethnobotanical cluster of the violet, that extends to the homophony of the words for toxins and arrows, *íos*, and hence the metaphor of intoxication as "struck with a poisoned arrow." See Ruck, "On the Sacred Names"; also "The Shaman of Lake Stymphalos:" 46-49, in Ruck *et al., Apples of Apollo*. Ultimately, the violet as a fairy flower, as in Shakespeare's *A Midsummer Night's Dream*, derived from the clearly discerned face suggested by its blossom. See Ruck *et al., Hidden World*, 206-207.

61   This tradition of estrous rapture caused by the insect's goad persists in Pulgia, the "heel" of the Italian peninsula, which was originally a Greek colonization as Magna Graecia, in the medieval dancing madness of the Tarentella, which still celebrated or experienced in that region today. The dancers, primarily women or girls, fall unconscious into a trance. As practiced today, the dancing lasts through the night, with liberal drinking of alcohol and certain prohibited substances. The songs that are sung have assimilated the Virgin as their patroness.

62   Ott, "The Riddle of the Toad and Other Secrets Entheogenic," 177-179, in *Pharmacotheon*.

63   Shakespeare, *Macbeth*, act IV, scene I, vv. 5-9.

The Wassons' original distinction of mycophobic and mycophilic cultures, however, is more complex than they at first had suspected. Within the same culture, the same dichotomous attitude can be seen, sometimes with the taboo observed only officially, but relaxed in secret within certain restricted groups, like boys alone in the woods or maidens in private. Such taboos often work to obscure the true knowledge of the role of mushrooms among a people, unless one is aware of the diversity of metaphors under which they hide. Hence absence of words is as significant as a plethora.

French *champignon*, on the other hand, which has also been assimilated into English, is derived from Latin *campus* "field" and is merely a mistranslation of the Late Latin *agaricus* for "mushroom" (assuming its relationship to *ager* for "field," as in "agriculture," although mushrooms are not common in fields). *Agaricus* was assimilated from Classical Greek *agarikon* (the "dark" variety *mélan* designating the fly-agaric[64]), whereas the *agarikon* itself is so called by relationship to Agaria, a town in Sarmatia, roughly in the same region as the ancient Scythians, a people strongly associated in their rituals and traditions with the *Amanita muscaria* that finds a suitable habitat there.[65]

When dealing with an item so rich in archetypal sacred and sexual symbolism, the normal linguistic rules of dialectal vowel and consonant phonetic shift are not totally applicable, yielding to importations, verbal puns, and obfuscations. Toporov traces the widespread occurrence of typical metaphors. To choose just one, the convex-concave dichotomy of the appearance of different mushrooms, or of the same mushroom at different stages of its growth, associates them with (1) male versus female genitalia, and with (2) male, female, or animal names, and with (3) sexually divided coded allusions governing how to gather and eat mushrooms. In some cases, these allusions relate to intercourse, as in French *consommer*, which means both "consume" and "consummate," a metaphor of particular significance for ingesting psychoactive mushrooms because the resulting ecstatic rapture suggests mystical

---

64   Dioscorides 3.1.

65   On the Scythians and fly-agaric, i.e., the myth of Herakles and the nymph of Scythia, see Ruck and González Celdrán, "Melusina of Plaincourault": chapter 12, in Ruck *et al., Hidden World*: the Scythians commemorated their descent from this mythical encounter by wearing golden fungal-shaped drinking disks or salvers on their belts. On Scythia as the origin of the annual fungal offering from the Hyperboreans to the sanctuary of Apollo on the island of Delos, see Ruck, "The Offerings from the Hyperboreans": 225-256, in Wasson *et al., Persephone's Quest*.

union with the deity resident in the plant.

The upward versus downward thrust implied in the opposition convex-concave is simply depicted as a right-side-up umbrella or parasol versus one upside down, or directional arrows pointing to opposite destinations, stylized as a star of David. In other terms, the mushroom is designated as the world tree, affording a gateway to the upper and lower worlds, often with birds signifying the flight of the spirit along this cosmic axis.[66] The sexual opposition is often preserved as archaisms embedded in children's jocular verses and warring games or game broads and in fairytales whose origins are no longer understood.

Toporov, moreover, accepted the Wassons' discoveries of mushrooms and mushroom themes in European and Oriental art—particularly in the paintings of Hieronymous Bosch (e.g., *The Haywain, The Last Judgment, The Garden of Delights*) and in alchemical symbolism, making it clear that mushrooms occurred as "classified" knowledge in Christian and mystical-chemical contexts. To these, Toporov added a few examples of his own (e.g., from Etruscan tombs) indicating that the religious role of mushrooms could probably be traced back to pre-Christian cults. His conclusion was that the identification of Soma as the fly-agaric was correct and neatly fit the overall structural archetype of the mushroom, including the unique function that urine and semen played as analogues in such cults.

Mary Jane

An analogous argument about multilingual etymologies can be made for the many names for *Cannabis sativa*, arising from the need for secrecy surrounding the use of a banned controversial substance and the special shared awareness of private groups of aficionados.[67] These names include ones celebrating its spirituality, such as the Sanskrit *Indracana*, "the food of Indra," and Turkic *esrar,* "secrets." Medieval Muslim commentators referred to it as "the shrub of understanding."

One of the commonest names, as marihuana, has a storied past

---

66   Toporov cites depictions of a doubled image of the world tree in the presence of mushrooms, in particular a 1st century BCE to 1st century CE textile from a Mongolian tomb, which is similar, purely from an archetypal source, to a common Hopi pattern. See page 303 and note 19.

67   Alan Piper, "The Mysterious Origins of the Word 'Marihuana,'" *Sino-Platonic Papers*, n° 153 (July, 2005).

through many languages. The earliest occurrence of the word as "*mariguan*" is noted by an amateur American ethnographer in 1894 as a hexing herb found along the Texas-Mexican border "used by discarded women for the purpose of wreaking terrible revenge upon recreant lovers." There are subsequently numerous variant spellings of the word (*marihuma, mariahuana, marihuano, marahuana, maraguango*). Since Cannabis was apparently not native to the New World, its name, like the plant, which was widely cultivated as early as the 16th century for its hempen fibers, must be an importation. Possible sources include: (1) Chinese immigrant workers, as *ma hua* or *hua ma* or *ma ren hua* (hence *orégano chino* or Chinese oregano in Mexican slang, although oregano or *oreganum* appears to have been confused with Cannabis in ancient Rome as well); (2) a Semitic loan word in Spanish arriving with Moorish servants of the conquistadores, from Arabic as the consonantal group *mrj*; this root yields marjoram (Spanish *majorana*), which goes back to Medieval Latin *majorana* by confusion with *mayor* or "larger," although it actually derives from Greek *amarachos*, as the "bitter herb," Latin *amarus*, with parallels in Semitic as **murr-* ("bitterness of myrrh") and Sanskrit *maruvakah*; (3) an African word such as Bantu *ma'kaña* (Portuguese *maran guango* "intoxication") that arrived in Brazil with the slaves imported to cultivate the hemp. Folk etymology associating it in Mexico with the Virgin Mary probably influenced the shift to marijuana, equating it with other plants used in indigenous sacred contexts, such as *Maria Pastora* ("herb of Mary the Shepherdess") for *Salvia divinorum* and *semillas de la Virgen* ("seeds of the Virgin") for *Ololiuhqui*.

However, Cannabis residue has been detected in tissues of naturally mummified cadavers from coastal Peru from the pre-Conquest period, some dating back as early as 115 CE. A Chilean word *mariguanza* designates a superstitious ritual hand gesture of a *curandero* or healer, a cursing gesture, and a vigorous leaping, suggesting the use of marijuana in indigenous shamanism, and the possibility even of pre-Conquest contact with China. Hence the word may have been a South American loan into Spanish; it has phonetic similarities in Nahuatl and Quechua. Equally astonishing is the discovery of New World drugs, specifically cocaine and nicotine residues, in Egyptian mummies.[68]

The botanical name as Cannabis became current only after Herodotus reported on the Scythian fumigation rite. It cannot be traced back to Indo-European. Instead it appears to be assimilated from a near or Middle Eastern language: *kanna* in Greek means "reed," derived from Babylonian kanû and Hebrew *kaneh* for "reed." It occurs in Hebrew as *kaneh bosem*, which is usually translated as "fragrant cane." It is now recognized as actually Cannabis, involved in the anointing rituals of the Jewish priesthood and the censing of the Tabernacle, rituals which inevitably were a visionary experience.[69] Hemp and its psychoactive properties were known however to the Greeks as early as the Homeric tradition under other names, such as the "smoke," and Aristophanes presented a parody of the Scythian rite in his *Clouds* comedy.[70]

Plaincourault

Even if we were to persist in rejecting Allegro's mythopoeia and linguistics, we would still have the evidence offered by European Christian art.[71] The tree in the Plaincourault fresco is, in fact, exactly what it looks like: a giant specimen of the *Amanita muscaria*, and it should have given Allegro's critics pause to consider whether a heretical Christian mushroom cult having ancient precedents and later ramifications could have existed in 12th century France and persisting well beyond the Renaissance among certain of the ecclesiastical elite.

The many other depictions of mushroom-trees in early Christian and later Renaissance churches and manuscripts constitute a huge body of proof, but they were all dismissed as evidence. Without irrefutable proof of a mushroom cult, such trees—even the most blatantly fungal examples and those in the most explicit narratives—could only be, in the opinion of notable art historians, just the ordinary manner of

68   Svetla F. Balababova, S.F. Parsche, and W. Prisig, "First Identification of Drugs in Egyptian Mummies": 358, in *Naturwissenschaften*, vol. 79, 1992; favorable review on the web by Samuel A. Wells, "American Drugs in Egyptian Mummies: A Review of the Evidence." It is assumed, however, by those opposed that the samples have been contaminated by the drug use of the examiners.

69   Bennett and McQueen, *Sex, Drugs, Violence, and the Bible*; Ruck *et al., Apples of Apollo*, 147, footnote 18.

70   Ruck *et al., Hidden World*, chap. V: "Conniving Wolves."

71   Fulvio Gosso and Gilberto Camilla, *Allucinogeni e Christianesimo: Evidenze nell'arte sacra* (Milan: ORISS SISSC Colibri. 2007).

portraying the common Mediterranean umbrella pine. Nor did it make any difference to these people that these mushroom-trees had dome-shaped downward curving caps and fringed annulus rings strongly suggesting that the trees' hanging fruits were mushrooms, whereas the umbrella pine is fruitless and characterized quite differently in nature by its uplifted branches.

Samorini has gathered other representations of these mushroom-trees,[72] and further research has confirmed their identification as depictions, not of the pine tree, but of the mushroom symbolizing the magical tree.[73] Gilberto Camilla and Fulvio Gosso offer a comprehensive presentation of the evidence, both architectural, ranging from France, Italy, Germany, Scandinavia, to Eastern Europe, and in manuscript illuminations.

One example alone should suffice to silence the argument of the art historians: a painting from a 14th-century alchemical manuscript, now in the Bodleian library in Oxford.[74] It is a treatise discussing the "salamander." A drawing in the manuscript depicts a man apparently intoxicated, dancing or perhaps staggering, with one hand to his forehead, suggesting he is dizzy or that he has just had an intense revelation. In the other hand, he holds a mushroom, which he evidently picked from a typical mushroom-tree beside him. The mushroom has a red cap spotted with white, and similar mushrooms branch from its stipe-like trunk, smaller, the size of the one that the man has apparently eaten.

The Plaincourault mushroom-tree is similar in displaying smaller mushrooms branching from its trunk. Adam and Eve have attempted to cover their nakedness naively with the nearest objects at hand—which look like large dried *Amanita muscaria* caps—rather than the top of this "umbrella pine," which, in any case, would not likely have been within their reach, nor has it been plucked off. Instead, a serpent winds its way

---

72   Giorgio Samorini, "The Mushroom-tree of Plaincourault" ("L'albero-fungo di Plaincourault"): 29-37, in *Eleusis*, 8 (1997): 29-37, available on the web. Giorgio Samorini, "Mushroom-Trees" in Christian Art" ("Gli 'alberi-fungo' nell'arte cristiana"): 87-108, in *Eleusis* new series n° 1 (1998). Giorgio Samorini, *Los Árboles-Hongo en el Arte Cristiano* (Barcelona: Cáñamo, Especial, 2001), 150-156.

73   Hoffman *et al.*, "Conjuring Eden."

74   Chris Bennett, Lynn Osburn, and Judy Osburn, *Green Gold, the Tree of Life: Marijuana in Magic and Religion* (Frazier Park, CA: Access Unlimited, 1995), 240-243. Available on the web: "Cannabis: The Philosopher's Stone, part 4: Medieval Alchemists and Cannabis."

upwards twined around the trunk, offering the red "apple" in its mouth. The trunk branches below the cap, left and right, as an indication of the annulus ring. The mushroom in both cases is obviously specifically the *Amanita muscaria*.

A salamander (like frogs and newts, equally a source of the toad-venom) in the manuscript illumination rises up parallel to the trunk, indicating that it is equivalent to the symbolism of the toxic tree, while another roasts upon a fire above a grid upon the ground. "Roasting the salamander" is the alchemical enigma, for the alchemists delighted in hiding whatever they openly revealed. It is a cryptic reference to the Amanita.

The reptile, like the toad, stands in as metaphoric for the mushroom, probably because like the fly-agaric its skin is maculate: Pliny called it *animal stellatum*, the "animal set with stars,"[75] or perhaps with the visionary "eyes,"[76] as in the tail of the peacock,[77] whose brilliant tail display was emblematic of the completion of the changes of color in the retort;[78] the "eyes" in the peacock's tail were formerly the multiple disembodied eyes of Argos, who goads the estrous mooing cow-maiden Io. The salamander's association with visionary psychoactive consubstantial monster-plants can be traced back to the Gorgon Medusa, whose fungal head the Greek hero Perseus harvested in the form of a mushroom.[79]

75   Pliny, *Natural History* 10, 67, 86. 188. Samorini, "Mushroom-Trees in Christian Art," 100-102. *Stellatus* could also mean "with many eyes," as an epithet of Argos *Panoptes*, the "all-seeing" myopic goader of the estrous cow-maiden Io. On the association of Argos with fly-agaric, see Ruck *et al., Apples of Apollo*, 53-54. Argos was traditionally depicted with a multiplicity of "disembodied eyes;" such eyes are metaphoric for the visionary experience.

76   The *stella* or "star" is another word for the pupil of the eye. On the visionary symbolism of the "disembodied eye," see Jonathan Ott, "Carved 'Disembodied Eyes' of Teotihuacán": 141-148, in Wasson *et al., Persephone's Quest*. On the "eye" as the gateway for the visionary journey, see Ruck, Staples, and González Celdrán, "Into the Eye of the Beholder": chapter VIII, in Ruck *et al,, Hidden World*.

77   "*gemmis caudam (pavonis) stellantibus implet.*" Ovid, *Metamorphoses* 1.723.

78   For example S. Trismoisin, *Splendor solis*, (British Library, 16th century) illumination of genesis in the retort, depicting the splendid display of the peacock's tail, with the arrival of Venus in the sky. See Alexander Roob, *The Hermetic Museum, Alchemy and Mysticism* (Köln: Taschen, 1997), 151: "The arrival of Venus in the sky brings sensual pleasure; a magnificent play of colors called the 'peacock's tail' appears. Basil Valentine said that this phenomenon, like a rainbow, indicates 'that in future the matter will come from the moist to the dry.'" (*Philosophischer Hauptschlüssel*, Leipzig, 1718).

79   An archaic bronze urn from Boeotia, depicting the decapitation, with the partially equine Medusa annotated by a juxtaposed salamander. Ruck *et al,, Apples of*

The salamander had the reputation in antiquity for being impervious to flames and able to extinguish fires,[80] and hence similar in symbolism to the phoenix as emblematic of rebirth and immortality. It is frequently depicted in alchemical treatises in the midst of flames, with other indications of the work that will yield the final Elixir, refined by the fire.[81] And the salamander's association with intoxication survived in the phrase *"einem einen salamander reiben"* ("to rub someone a salamander"), a drinking toast used by 19th-century German students.

The Heavenly Banquet

But if no tree of any sort, mushroom or not, will satisfy the skeptical reader, we should turn our eyes to the great west portal of the 13th-century Basilica of San Vicente in the city of Ávila. There, above its central pillar is a blatant display of a mushroom as the food of the heavenly banquet.[82] Here there is no question of a stylized tree; it is just a mushroom, complete with annulus ring. The figure on the pillar or mullion is the evangelist Luke, as indicated by the two ox heads in the capital above him, and the scene in the tympanum above him illustrates Luke's story of the leprous beggar Lazarus at the gate of the banqueting rich man (*Luke* 16.19-31). The scene on the left depicts dogs licking the beggar's sores, while he waits for the scraps from the rich man's table. On the right, Lazarus has died and is in heaven; while the rich man has gone to hell, as angels on either side point up and downward. These scenes on the two hemi-tympana on either side of the mushroom identify it—namely, a mushroom—as the food of the celestial banquet, the sacrament that opens the pathways.

Mithraism

Apollo, 41-85.

80   Aristotle, *Historia animalium* 552b 16, etc.

81   On the alchemical salamander, see C.G. Jung, *Alchemical Studies*, (New York: Princeton University Press, 1967), 138.

82   We owe its identification to José Alfredo González Celdrán, who asked a friend, a Franciscan friar, to confirm what it was. "It looks just like a mushroom, although I don't know why it's there!" Ruck and Staples noted it at least twenty years ago; and independently, Vincent Wattiaux of Belgium just recently made the same observation. It is a mushroom, not even a mushroom-tree, just a mushroom! See Ruck and González Celdrán, "Melusina of Plaincourault": chapter 12, in Ruck *et al.*, *Hidden World*. See also Ruck, *Sacred Mushrooms*, 26-27.

This was the Zoroastrian religion of the Persian god-messiah Mithras, going back to the ancient warrior cult of the Persian Kings of the Achaemenid dynasty, contemporary with Classical Greek antiquity. They still celebrated the *haoma* sacrament, including the drinking of urine for intoxication.[83] The religion was assimilated in the West as Mithraism, an initiatory brotherhood that united the emperors, bureaucrats, and soldiers that were the cohesive foundation that maintained the Empire. Its philosophy was Stoicism, the dominant belief of the Romans, and it programmed the initiate through seven stages in order to experience the final shamanic journey to the edge of the cosmos.[84] Nero was the first Emperor documented to have been initiated in the year 66 CE with what was termed a "magical dinner."[85] Can there be any doubt about what was eaten?

As a perpetuation of the Indo-European Soma rites, the Persian mushroom cult as Mithraism spread throughout the Roman Empire, firmly establishing it as the very foundation of European civilization

---

83   Zoroaster, Yasna 32.10; the haoma priests are condemned as literally "drunk on urine." Later scholars and translators did not understand the significance of this urine-drunkenness and explained it as simply "filthy drunkenness."

From the Wasson Archives, Persian file, Harvard Botanical Libraries: Idnde Shah, an Arabic scholar and authority on Eastern and Western orgiastic religions provided the following information on Amanita urine drinking among the Hazaras (with copy sent to R. Graves), dated 8-1-61: "The Haza'ras (from *haza'r*, a 'thousand') are members of the military communities settled in Central Asia by the Mongol conquerors. There are Hazars in the USSR, Iran, Afghanistan, and what is now Pakistan. They are Moslems, but preserve certain early practices. *Amanita muscaria* is eaten by Hazars (and by no other Afghan, Iranian, or Pakistani community known to me, for orgiastic purposes. No religious ritual is involved. It is said that the urine of participants is drunk. I have heard that the Hazars call Amanita QIZILAK ("red-white"). Unheeding of the possible scientific importance of such practices, the generality of present-day Central Asians conceal, deny, or play down activities that they consider to be opposed to civilization. Hence information is hard to come by. In general, the fear of fungi is strong indeed, assuming curiously intense proportions among non-Hazars. This does not encourage the Hazars to be communicative about the subject."

84   Mark Hoffman, Carl A.P. Ruck, and Blaise D. Staples, "The Entheogenic Eucharist of Mithras": 13-50, in *Entheos*, vol. 2, n° 2 (summer) 2002; Carl A.P. Ruck, Mark Alwin Hoffman, and Blaise D. Staples, "The Brotherhood of the Warriors of Mithras": 225-262, in *New England Classical Journal*, 2004, August; Carl A.P. Ruck, Mark Alwin Hoffman, and José Alfredo González Celdrán, *Mushrooms, Myth, and Mithras: The Drug Cult that Civilized Europe* (San Francisco, CA: City Lights Press, 2010).

85   *Cenis magicis*, Pliny, *Natural History* 30.1.6. Alternatively, the phrase might be translated as a "dinners of the Magi," although that would hardly diminish the significance.

and the military and political forces that administered it. Its theology and sacraments were so similar to early Christianity that it took merely the "nominal" conversion of the warrior Emperor Constantine to transfer the urban centers, at least, to the new religion, although the rural people or *pagani* tended to persist in the old way, pejoratively termed "Paganism."

The Christians were well aware of the similarity of their rites to those of Mithraism and persecuted its adherents. They also assimilated it. They made the confraternity of warriors one of their sacraments as Confirmation; and moved the Nativity from Epiphany closer to the solstice and transposed the Jewish Sabbath to Sunday, the day that the followers of Mithras celebrated in honor of the Unconquered Sun or *sol invictus*.

Basilica of Aquilegia, Italy

Not only, however, was the Roman Empire administered by initiates into a mushroom cult, and similarly such a cult in the Eleusinian rites was the basis for the humanistic vision of the Classical World, but the early Christians had similar psychoactive sacraments at the origin of what would later become their symbolic Eucharist. The mosaic uncovered beneath the 4th-century Basilica of Aquilegia in northern Italy preserves the decoration of the earlier Christian agape hall: it depicts baskets of mushrooms and snails in a Gnostic context. The fondness of Romans for eating mushrooms and snails is irrelevant in this context, since this was a religious sanctuary—not a restaurant— and whatever was eaten there had sacred connotations. It was the original Eucharist. The mushrooms appear to be fly-agarics; and snails, like all other animals, that feed upon psychoactive substances become in themselves psychoactive delicacies.[86] Their spiral shape, curving inward to infinity and hence the gateway to another world, would have added to their magical-religious symbolism.

Return of the Mushroom

The concerted and biased attempts to destroy Allegro's discoveries

---

86   Franco Fabbro, "Mushrooms and Snails in Religious Rituals of Early Christians at Aquileia": 69-80, in *Eleusis*, new series 3, 1999; Ruck *et al., Apples of Apollo*, 207.

have failed. The confirmatory evidence is mounting in his favor. The critics can now raise their voices again. Let us hope that they do, since the matter is not settled, but they should be advised to do so with more careful consideration. This book that many have prized in secret is now available again. It demands the serious consideration of theologians, mythologists, and students of religion. No account of the history of the Church, both West and East, can afford to leave the poor despicable fungus unconsidered, nor the role that entheogens in general have played in the evolution of European civilization.